Child Development

Take a global tour of childhood that spans 50 countries and explore everyday questions such as 'Why does love matter?', 'How do children learn right from wrong'? and 'Why do adolescent relationships feel like a matter of life and death?' Combining psychology, anthropology, and evolution, you will learn about topics such as language, morality, empathy, creativity, learning and cooperation. Discover how children's skills develop, how they adapt to solve challenges, and what makes you, you. Divided into three chronological sections – early years, middle childhood, and adolescence – this book is enriched with a full set of pedagogical features, including key points to help you retain the main takeaway of each section, space for recap, a glossary of key terms, learning outcomes and chapter summaries. Embedded videos and animations throughout bring ideas to life and explain the methods researchers use to reveal the secrets of child development.

Paul Ibbotson is Senior Lecturer in Child Development at The Open University. He teaches, researches, and writes about how children think and behave, with a particular interest in language and cognitive development. He is the author of numerous scientific papers, popular articles, and books.

Child Development
Birth to Adolescence

PAUL IBBOTSON
The Open University

Shaftesbury Road, Cambridge CB2 8EA, United Kingdom

One Liberty Plaza, 20th Floor, New York, NY 10006, USA

477 Williamstown Road, Port Melbourne, VIC 3207, Australia

314–321, 3rd Floor, Plot 3, Splendor Forum, Jasola District Centre, New Delhi – 110025, India

103 Penang Road, #05-06/07, Visioncrest Commercial, Singapore 238467

Cambridge University Press is part of Cambridge University Press & Assessment, a department of the University of Cambridge.

We share the University's mission to contribute to society through the pursuit of education, learning and research at the highest international levels of excellence.

www.cambridge.org
Information on this title: www.cambridge.org/highereducation/isbn/9781009591263

DOI: 10.1017/9781009591287

© Paul Ibbotson 2025

This publication is in copyright. Subject to statutory exception and to the provisions of relevant collective licensing agreements, no reproduction of any part may take place without the written permission of Cambridge University Press & Assessment.

When citing this work, please include a reference to the DOI 10.1017/9781009591287

First published 2025

Printed in the United Kingdom by CPI Group Ltd, Croydon CR0 4YY

A catalogue record for this publication is available from the British Library

A Cataloging-in-Publication data record for this book is available from the Library of Congress

ISBN 978-1-009-59126-3 Hardback
ISBN 978-1-009-59127-0 Paperback

Cambridge University Press & Assessment has no responsibility for the persistence or accuracy of URLs for external or third-party internet websites referred to in this publication and does not guarantee that any content on such websites is, or will remain, accurate or appropriate.

CONTENTS

Content Overview		*page* vi
Preface		ix
Acknowledgements		xii
1	Perspectives on Child Development	1

SECTION I THE EARLY YEARS

2	Why Does Love Matter?	19
3	Are Children Mind Readers?	36
4	How Do Children Learn Language?	51
5	How Do Children Learn So Much So Quickly?	67
6	Growing Up Globally: The Early Years	86

SECTION II MIDDLE CHILDHOOD

7	How Do Children Learn Right from Wrong?	105
8	How Do Children Think About Groups?	122
9	How Does Imagination Develop?	137
10	How Does Children's Memory Work?	150
11	Growing Up Globally: Middle Childhood	166

SECTION III ADOLESCENCE

12	Who Do Teenagers Think They Are?	179
13	How Do Adolescents Think About Risk and Reward?	194
14	Are Young People Happy?	213
15	Growing Up Globally: Adolescence	231
16	The Many Paths of Development	239
17	Reflections on Child Development	259

Glossary	264
One-Minute Methods	266
Video Summary	274
Index	278

CONTENT OVERVIEW

Preface ix
Aims and scope; the chapters; structure of the book.

1 Perspectives on Child Development 1
Identify different perspectives on child development; describe important features about how children grow, adapt, and change; illustrate what is unique about human childhood.

SECTION I THE EARLY YEARS

This section explores the early years of children's lives, following their development from birth to 5 years old. It is a period that sees huge change in how children behave, think, and learn. We will explore the significance of early experiences, how children begin to read other people's minds and learn language, and the importance of play, imitation, and discovery. We also look at the role that cultural differences and caregivers have on shaping children's experiences, as well as how children begin to shape the world around them.

2 Why Does Love Matter? 19
Describe some important features of infant–caregiver relationships; evaluate the role of early life experiences on later development; understand what emotions are for and how they develop.

3 Are Children Mind Readers? 36
Describe what theory of mind is and how it develops; understand the importance of theory of mind for children's later development; consider the implications of theory of mind for collaboration and human uniqueness.

4 How Do Children Learn Language? 51
Describe the challenges children face in learning language; understand key features of child language development; explain the strategies children use to learn sounds, words, and grammar.

5 How Do Children Learn So Much So Quickly? 67
Understand how children direct their own learning and learn from others; describe the importance of imitation, play, and instruction; explain how children transfer what they know across different contexts.

6 Growing Up Globally: The Early Years 86
Understand why the cross-cultural perspective is important for understanding children's development; consolidate what you learned in Chapters 1–5; revisit the ideas you came across in Chapters 1–5 in a cross-cultural context.

SECTION II MIDDLE CHILDHOOD

This section explores middle childhood, covering the period between 6 and 12 years of age. During this time, children consolidate and expand upon what they have learned in the early years, building on their understanding of the physical world around them, relationships, play, and language. Middle childhood also sees children develop a new repertoire of increasingly sophisticated social, cognitive, and cultural skills. In this section we explore children's growing sense of right and wrong and the norms that regulate their moral thinking and behaviour, how their sense of self is tied to the group they belong to, and the roles of intergroup contact, cooperation, and empathy in bringing groups together. We will also look at children's imagination, creativity, and problem-solving and the role memory plays in children's daily lives and in telling the story of who they are.

7 How Do Children Learn Right from Wrong? 105
Describe how children develop fairness, spite, and helping behaviours; understand the role of emotions, punishment, and reputation in moral development; explore cross-cultural differences and similarities in morality.

8 How Do Children Think About Groups? 122
Describe how children think and behave differently in groups; explain the roles of collaboration, self-identity, and categorisation in creating and sustaining groups; understand how group differences can be reduced via intergroup contact, cooperation, and empathy.

9 How Does Imagination Develop? 137
Describe the development of imagination, creativity, and flexible thinking; understand how children express their creativity in their drawings, their imaginary worlds, and in what they are willing to believe; provide examples of how children's imagination is grounded in their everyday experience.

10 How Does Children's Memory Work? 150
Describe different types of memory and how they develop; explain how early experiences are remembered and why they are forgotten; understand why a limited memory can be beneficial for learning.

11 Growing Up Globally: Middle Childhood 166
Consolidate what you learned in Chapters 7–10; revisit the ideas you came across in Chapters 7–10 in a cross-cultural context.

SECTION III ADOLESCENCE

This section explores adolescence, covering the period between 13 and 18 years of age. Thriving in this phase of life is not always easy. Adolescents are trying to figure out who they are and who they want to be, as well as balance the demands of fitting in, standing out, and measuring up. Cognitively, socially, and neurologically, adolescence is not a single snapshot in time but a transitional period. It is marked by increased interest in the self, in relationships, and in finding one's place in society. Just as adolescents are beginning to enjoy more adult-like rights and privileges, they face new responsibilities and obligations. This change occurs at a time when they are pivoting away from the family, and towards a wider peer group, in preparation for becoming independent young adults. Despite these challenges, adolescence can be a period of great personal exploration, innovation, and optimism.

12   Who Do Teenagers Think They Are?   179
Describe key elements of adolescent identity development; evaluate the genetic, social, and cultural influences on identity; understand creativity and cultural change as part of adolescent development.

13   How Do Adolescents Think About Risk and Reward?   194
Describe the social, cognitive, and biological influences on adolescent decision-making; understand the risk and reward systems of the brain and how these can be influenced by different contexts; evaluate the roles of peer groups, executive functions, and sex differences in adolescent behaviour.

14   Are Young People Happy?   213
Describe the mix of emotions and attitudes adolescents have towards themselves and their lives; understand the factors that cause unhappiness, as well as those that promote well-being and buffer against adversity; evaluate the emotional opportunities and risks of adolescence.

15   Growing Up Globally: Adolescence   231
Consolidate what you learned in Chapters 12–14; revisit the ideas you came across in Chapters 12–14 in a cross-cultural context.

16   The Many Paths of Development   239
Describe how children can take different paths in development and reach similar destinations; understand the developmental differences between children as a set of strengths and challenges that are highly sensitive to environmental context; explore how events in children's lives can trigger a cascade of later consequences.

17   Reflections on Child Development   259
Children are alike and different; the value of multiple perspectives; the complexity of child development; the future of the village; last words.

PREFACE

Aims and Scope

Why does love matter? How do children learn language? Are children's memories reliable? How do children tell right from wrong? Can infants understand statistics? Do children confuse fantasy with reality? What is the point of play? Are children mind readers? How do children think about different groups of people? How do children acquire culture? Do children think about fairness in the same way around the world? Who do children trust? How do autistic children experience the world? How do adolescents think about risk and reward? Does the language you speak affect the way you think? Why can't we remember the first years of our lives? Why do adolescent relationships feel like a matter of life and death? How do we learn so much in such a short time? If you are curious about these questions, then this book is for you! *Child Development* nurtures your sense of curiosity into an evidence-based understanding of how children around the world grow, develop, and adapt.

You will learn about the remarkable insights into children's lives that contemporary research is revealing; the technological advances that allow us to follow their experiences in new detail; and the ways in which children around the world are similar and the ways in which they are different. You will be introduced to the people who have changed the way we think about children and childhood; what makes childhood unique for humans compared with other species; the methods researchers use to uncover the secrets of development; and what the current debates are and the big unanswered questions. As part of your learning, you will develop a set of skills that go way beyond child development, empowering you to see the world from different perspectives, to scrutinise the claims people make, and to think for yourself. By exploring child development in a cross-cultural context, you will be better prepared for a world where we are increasingly likely to exchange ideas and meet people from anywhere across the globe. Above all, this book is a celebration of children's lives: what children can do, how they think, and the diversity, complexity, and richness of their experiences.

The descriptions of child development that appear throughout these pages are underpinned by a range of overarching theoretical frameworks, such as evolutionary theory, dynamic systems theory, life-history theory, and the biopsychosocial model of development. But the book also covers theories that focus on particular areas of development, like attachment theory and moral foundations theory, as well as laying out the properties that all good explanations of child development should have.

Each chapter's topic warrants a book on its own, so rather than attempting to offer comprehensive coverage of each one, this book presents fundamental issues of importance to the study of child development and explains why they matter. This approach orientates the reader to the major landmarks of research today and prepares them for other works that assume such previous subject knowledge (of which many excellent ones already exist, and a list of recommended titles and researchers who have heavily influenced this book is contained in the Acknowledgements).

I hope you experience the same sense of discovery in reading this book as I had in writing it, wonder at the scale of what infants and young people achieve, and use this book as an invitation to ask better questions about child development.

The Chapters

The chapters are framed around everyday questions such as 'why does love matter?', 'how do children learn language?', and 'how does imagination develop?'. Organising the book in this way, rather than around the traditional categories of 'social', 'emotional', and 'cognitive' development, aims to better reflect the motivations that brought you here in the first place; they are the kinds of questions you might have already asked yourself and were curious to find out more.

This approach also acknowledges that carving the mind up into neat categories does not reflect the way children develop; they don't work on their memory and attention one day and then their friendships and emotions the next. These capacities interact with one another from day one, and thus they are interwoven throughout this book too. Moreover, some of the most exciting recent findings – those from 'social cognition', for example – cut across traditional topic boundaries. Using the everyday question approach allows us to draw from many different academic areas of knowledge in the same chapter, and that gives us a fuller and more realistic picture of what is going on.

Each of the chapters follows the same format and contains the following elements designed to support your learning and engage your interest:

Title – the main topic of that chapter, expressed as an everyday question such as, 'why does love matter?'.

Learning Outcomes – summarise what you can expect to have achieved by the end of the chapter.

Key Points – bullet points of essential takeaway messages. Think of them this way: 'if you remember nothing else, try to remember this.'

Boxes – contain a brief departure from the main story of the chapter, introducing a sideways look at a topic.

Talking Points – outline what we don't know, a controversy, or an issue that warrants further reflection.

Summary – revisits the key points of the chapter.

References – a list of evidence used to support the claims made in the chapter.

You will also notice these icons appear throughout the book. If you have a smartphone, point the camera at the centre of the icon and follow the link to play a short video that will enrich an idea introduced in the text (for those without smartphones the web addresses are listed at the end of the book). While reading you might find yourself asking '... but how do they know that?'. That is a great question, so as well as videos that bring different ideas to life, each chapter also has an animated 'One-Minute Method' that explains *how* researchers go about their research. By embedding these methods into the core material, it's easier to see a method as a means of answering a particular question about how children develop.

Structure of the Book

We begin by exploring the three perspectives that we will use to understand child development – psychological, anthropological, and evolutionary – and ask some basic questions such as 'what is a child?', 'what develops?', and 'why do we have a childhood at all?'. After this introductory chapter, we follow the journey that children take in roughly chronological order, beginning around birth, through infancy, childhood, and adolescence, and on to becoming young adults. While change is a continuous state of being for all of us, the main part of the book is organised into three separate sections to help structure the story of development. The early years section (Section I) covers 0–5 years of age, the middle childhood section (Section II) spans 6–12 years of age, and the adolescence section (Section III) cover 13–18 years of age. Occasionally, we will look at the lives of children who are older or younger than the focus of that section, where it is useful to make connections across the lifespan and to underline the continuity of development. At the end of every section there is a chapter devoted to re-examining what we have learned previously from a more global perspective. Not only does this provide a space for revision and consolidation, it also challenges us to consider whether our understanding of child development holds up to the diversity of children's experiences around the world. Ultimately, this will lead us to a deeper appreciation of what children have in common, as well as of their differences.

The penultimate chapter retraces our steps to explore the lives of children who have difficulty with language, movement, writing, or regulating their attention, those who are born blind or deaf, and autistic children. Doing so involves celebrating their many strengths, their adaptability, their resilience, as well as acknowledging the challenges they face. Their story warrants its own space, not because their lives represent a different type of development, but because they have much to teach us about development itself. Finally, the book concludes by highlighting some key themes that emerge from considering child development as a whole and by pointing to unresolved issues that are likely to remain significant for years to come.

ACKNOWLEDGEMENTS

This book is built on the hard work, insight, generosity, and integrity of many thousands of scientists and scholars who have, in one way or another, advanced our understanding of child development. I am indebted to them for creating the evidence base on which this book is based and making the ambition of this story possible. There are many excellent existing books on child development that have been particularly influential in writing this book and deserve special mention, including Sarah Hrdy's *Mothers and Others: The Evolutionary Origins of Mutual Understanding*, David Bjorklund's *How Children Invented Humanity: The Role of Development in Human Evolution*, David Bjorkland and Carlos Blasi's *Child and Adolescent Development: An Integrated Approach*, Michael Tomasello's *Becoming Human* and *A Natural History of Human Morality*, Jennifer Lansford, Doran French, and Mary Gauvain's *Child and Adolescent Development in Cultural Context*, Alison Gopnik's *The Gardner and the Carpenter*, Robert Burgess and Kevin MacDonald's *Evolutionary Perspectives on Human Development*, and Catherine Tamis-LeMonda and Jeffrey J. Lockman's *Developmental Cascades*.

Due credit also goes to groundbreaking work on infant learning by Laura Schulz and her team; Katherine McAuliffe and Felix Warneken on cooperation and fairness; Hannes Rakoczy on theory of mind; B. J. Casey, Cat Sebastian, Sarah-Jayne Blakemore, and Laurence Steinbeck on adolescent decision-making, identity, and brain development; Marc Bornstein and Avshalom Caspi on large-scale cross-cultural longitudinal studies of development; Barry Bogin, Bruce Ellis, and Willem Frankenhuis on life-history theory of child and adolescent development; Uta Frith and Francesca Happé on autism; and cross-cultural psychologist Barbara Rogoff and anthropologist Kristen Hawkes. Thank you to those who have offered feedback on parts or all of the manuscript, including Hannah Baker, Sarah Critten, Alyson Davis, Ellesar Elhaggagi, Pamela Gallagher, Naomi Holford, Vessela Howell, Stefan Kucharczyk, Magdalena Muc, Heather Montgomery, Ayomide Oluseye, Dean Petters, Jon Rainford, Gaia Scerif, Kieron Sheehy, Mimi Tatlow-Golden, and several anonymous reviewers; DamnFine Media and Dean Petters for their work on the One-Minute Methods animations; Charles Howell, Emily Watton, and Maggie Jeffers at Cambridge University Press and Assessment; John Stewart Marr for copyediting the volume; and Lara Knight at The Open University.

1 PERSPECTIVES ON CHILD DEVELOPMENT

 Learning Outcomes

After reading this chapter you will be able to:
- Identify different perspectives on child development.
- Describe important features about how children grow, adapt, and change.
- Illustrate what is unique about human childhood.

1.1 Introduction

This book takes three main perspectives on child development: psychological, anthropological, and evolutionary. They each have their strengths and limitations, but by combining perspectives we can gain a richer and more complete view of development (**Figure 1.1**).

 Key Point

- This book takes three main perspectives on child development: psychological, anthropological, and evolutionary.

Let's take a closer look at each perspective in turn.

1.2 Perspective 1: Psychological

Most adults have an opinion about children, not least because every adult was a child once. Personal experience as a child or with other children can have a powerful influence on how we think about children or even what we think childhood should be. A psychological perspective takes a different approach to this in several ways.

First, it goes beyond a collection of anecdotes and personal observations. What do we mean by that? Well, we could try to create 2 billion explanations of child development, one for every child on Earth. That strategy doesn't seem very satisfactory because, despite differences, there

Figure 1.1 Different perspectives illuminate different facets of children's lives. Together, they provide a more complete understanding of child development. Image from Munafò and Smith (2018). Source: David Parkins www-nature-com.libezproxy.open.ac.uk/articles/d41586-018-01023-3.

are some things that are common to all children in the way they grow, adapt, and change, and those general patterns tell us something interesting about the way children develop. At the other extreme, we could try to find one, grand, unifying explanation for the development of all children – past, present, and future – in every aspect of their lives. That doesn't seem very sensible either, because it is hard to imagine one explanation that does justice to the diversity of childhood and the many ways in which children develop: biologically, psychologically, socially, and culturally. So, in practice, psychologists try to find a balance. Most scientists are trying to find the simplest way to explain as many facts as possible. Most psychologists are trying to find the simplest way to explain as much of human behaviour as possible.

The psychological approach describes something more general than what one individual experiences, but it also goes beyond what one individual *could* experience. For example, I have experience of my memories, but I don't experience how they work. This leads us to the second feature of a psychological perspective on child development: it aims to be more than a description of the facts and to offer some causal explanation of why things are this way, rather than some other way they could have been. For example, say you want to compare the effect that reading from an e-book or a paper book has on children's memory. You give some children an e-book with a non-fiction story and give some other children a paper fiction book. You then measure the memory ability of children in the e-book group and paper book group and find a difference in performance. If you are interested in what causes what, there is an issue here: you haven't demonstrated that the difference in memory is *because* of the e-book or the paper book – the thing you are interested in – as you also gave them different types of things to read as well. For whatever reason, non-fiction or fiction might engage children more, and that could explain the difference in memory performance instead.

Now imagine you control for the type of text children read and give them all fiction stories. You then measure memory ability between the e-book and paper book readers and find a difference again. The problem here is that the two groups might have differed in their memory ability *before* you gave them anything to read. Perhaps by chance one group was better at remembering to start with.

Finally, you give all the children the same text and balance the memory ability of the groups before giving them an e-book or paper book by giving them a memory check. Over several months of testing you find that both groups improve equally in their memory. Case closed? Not quite. Children's memory ability improves with age anyway, regardless of whether they read a paper book or e-book. In this case, you need to show that their memory improved more than children who received neither an e-book nor a paper book.

As you can see, cause and effect can be slippery things to pin down. Ultimately, there is no guarantee that the effect we are interested in is because of the cause we think it is due to. Despite the limitations of the scientific method we have developed vaccinations that have saved millions of lives, detected subatomic particles, and discovered the structure of our own DNA. What scientists do is to try to rule out as many plausible alternative explanations as possible. For example, we can change one thing at a time (e.g., e-book or paper book but not fiction or non-fiction as well), compare within- and between-group variation (e.g., balance memory abilities between the groups), and compare one group to a control group (e.g., include a group of children that received neither a paper book nor an e-book). In general, scientists are *obsessed* with arguing over alternative explanations to explain the same set of observations because they care about cause and effect.

Why would a psychologist *want* a better causal understanding of child development? Sometimes their motivation will be to improve the outcomes for children – for instance, an educational psychologist might want to design a better learning environment in schools, or a health psychologist might want to improve the well-being of children. In these situations, having a good understanding of cause and effect saves time and resources by targeting just that thing that brings about the biggest impact. Here's an example: shoe size is associated with reading ability. The larger the shoe size, the higher the reading ability, as both factors are also associated with age. Without a good understanding of cause and effect we might incorrectly predict that giving children bigger shoes will cause them to read better! For other psychologists, their motivation for exploring cause and effect is the simple curiosity of wanting to know how something works, and finding an answer is reward in itself. In both situations, building the best explanation is what matters (see **Box 1.1**).

 Box 1.1 What makes a good explanation?

Think about what makes a good explanation and have these criteria in mind as you read this book. A good explanation does the following:

1. Makes clear predictions that explain a pattern of results beyond the observable – it doesn't just restate the problem or provide another description of the facts.
2. Makes testable predictions that are 'risky' or falsifiable – there is a clear sense of what evidence it would take to prove the idea wrong.
3. Offers a plausible mechanism of causation – the 'nuts and bolts' of how cause gives rise to effect.
4. Agrees with and explains findings from other areas of knowledge – for example, psychological explanations that are consistent with established facts about evolution, biology, and anthropology.

Finally, the psychological approach aims to describe and explain the way things are, not necessarily the way things should be. For example, we might prefer it if children didn't lie, cheat, or harm one another, but they do, and if we want to change things for the better – however we choose to define 'better' – then it helps to first understand the nature of the problem.

This chapter began by introducing some questions like 'why does love matter?' and 'how do children learn right from wrong?', and before we move on it is important not to lose sight of this sense of curiosity. If we already knew the answers to such questions, we wouldn't need to do the science to find them out. Science is not just an accumulation of facts but a systematic way to approach the unknown. The Scientific Revolution of the 1500s was largely an admission of how *little* we understood, and we started to make progress after acknowledging we did not know the answers to some of the most important questions.

In summary, a scientific approach to child development tries to build good explanations (Box 1.1), paying special attention to cause and effect and describing the way things are, not necessarily how they should be.

Key Points

- Child psychology is the scientific study of how the mind, brain, and behaviour change during childhood.
- Child psychologists want to understand how children grow, develop, and adapt at different points in their lives.

The psychological perspective we take in this book typically focuses on a level of explanation between brain and behaviour, although we frequently look 'up' a level towards environmental influences (e.g., physical, social, and cultural) and 'down' a level towards biology (e.g., genes and hormones; **Figure 1.2**).

Because we are interested in how children change, adapt, and grow, we also need to know how these levels relate to one another over time. Mastering any complex skill like walking or talking requires that more basic skills are acquired first. For example, in language development children start out babbling with individual sounds, then they put these together to form

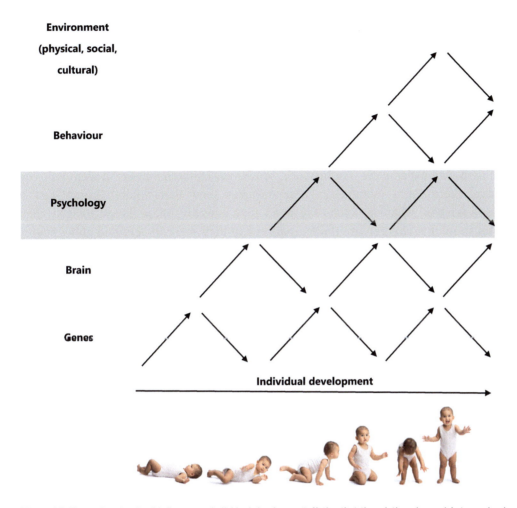

Figure 1.2 The various levels of influence on individual development. Notice that the relations (arrows) between levels go in both directions. Genes influence brains that influence behaviour that influences environment that influences which genes are turned on that influence behaviour and so on. Within these nested relations it is difficult to draw a neat line around what is nature or nurture, emphasising that behaviour emerges from a complex interaction between all levels. Adapted from Gottlieb (1992, p. 186). Source: www.istock....com/.../baby-development-stages-gm527070443-53462348.

first words, and then they join words together to form sentences. They then use sentences to tell stories, hold conversations, and share complex ideas. It's extremely unlikely any child will produce fluent sentences from the start. So, more generally, to fully understand how we use any complex skill that is of significance to us as adults, we need to 'turn back the clock' to when things began. For this reason, the book follows the journey of children as their skills are refined with experience and basic building blocks are assembled into more complex behaviour and thinking.

 Key Point

- Children develop incrementally, with later-acquired skills built on earlier ones.

The final take-home message about the psychological perspective is that development is not something that happens *to* children, as if they were just passive recipients. They are active participants in constructing their own development and in shaping the environment around them. For example, children 'arrive' with different temperaments, which are likely to bring about different responses from their caregivers, which in turn are likely to affect the way children behave in the future, and so on. Adults and children negotiate what parenting looks like in a never-ending cycle of interactions. So, while it's true that children absorb a lot of information, they are not passive sponges. They generate new ideas and go beyond their own experiences. For instance, sometimes children will say 'it went-ed', 'that go-ed over there', or 'I swimmed'. These mistakes show that children cannot just be sponges soaking up whatever adults say as no adult ever says these things. Instead, these examples show that children are finding patterns in their environment and going beyond their experience, trying to figure out the rules adults play by (in this case, 'add -ed' when you talk about things in the past). The more general message is this: children are actively influencing the environment around them, at the same time as the environment is influencing children.

 Key Point

- Children are active participants in their own development.

1.3 Perspective 2: Anthropological

Broadly speaking, the anthropological perspective asks: what makes us human? To answer that very big question, anthropologists study a variety of smaller questions, like how we have changed over thousands of years, how societies are organised today, and what the processes are that transform societies from one generation to the next.

Cultures around the world are different, with different expectations about how members of that culture should think and behave: the language we speak, the clothes we wear, the way we conduct ourselves in public and so on, or what we call **norms**. Children are both the recipients of that diversity – they are born into different cultures – and they are vital in maintaining that diversity – they pass on cultural differences from one generation to the next. The accumulation of this culture over time creates our history, and this is where humankind has unhooked itself from biology. We cannot understand the French Revolution or the Roman Empire by studying our genes – we need to look at culture.

Children around the world are different. This is partly because of the 0.9% of our genetics that makes you, you; partly because of the random events that nudge our lives in different directions; and partly because the environment in which children grow up can be very different. By 'environment' we not only mean the physical space in which children grow up – whether they have access to clean air and water, sanitation, green spaces, and so on – but also their social environment: peers, siblings, parents, society, and culture.

Children around the world are also similar. This is partly because we share 99.1% of our genes with other humans, and that similar blueprint builds similar bodies, brains, and minds that produce similar behaviour. Children are also similar because the environment is similar. Living in three-dimensional space with others creates similar problems that require similar solutions, like walking and talking. We can capture this 'same *and* different' by thinking about common psychological *processes* and variable cultural *content*. For example:

- Children are born with the potential to acquire language – a common psychological process. The content that goes into that process – any one or more of 7,000 different languages – is culturally variable.
- Children are born with the potential to acquire cultural norms. A common psychological process – the content that goes into that process (e.g., rituals, rites, customs) – is culturally variable.
- Children are born with the potential to form emotional attachments. A common psychological process – the content that goes into that process (e.g., whom the child attaches to) is culturally variable.

We seem to have a natural tendency to think dualistically: black or white; true or false; good or evil. The same-and-different perspective encourages us to abandon this way of thinking in favour of something more complex, but more accurate. To appreciate the richness of children's lives we need to acknowledge that children are similar *and* different: they are the product of both universal psychological processes and cultural variation – human nature and nurture (**Figure 1.3**).

Menarche – the first menstrual period of a female – is a good illustration of how a child's life sits at the intersection of biological, environmental, and cultural factors all at the same time. Menarche requires a series of bodily processes to take place, which partly unfold

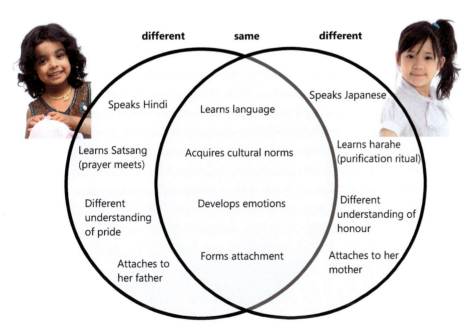

Figure 1.3 An example of taking the anthropological perspective on two children, showing how they are both the same and different. Source: V.S.Anandhakrishna/Shutterstock; ANURAK PONGPATIMET /Shutterstock.

according to a genetically controlled timetable. However, the precise timing of menarche is also affected by stress, disease, nutrition, family environment, and exercise. Furthermore, the same underlying biological event is greeted in different ways around the world: with ceremonies of celebration, rituals of cleansing or purification, rites of strength, or in sex education programmes. The more general message is that for almost all aspects of children's lives we need multiple perspectives – biological, psychological, and cultural – to do justice to the richness of their experience and the complexity of their development.

> **Key Point**
>
> - The anthropological perspective explores how children around the world are similar and different.

Acknowledging the diversity of children's experiences does raise the question of what we mean by 'a child'. This might seem like unnecessary hair-splitting; we all recognise a child when we see one. Nevertheless, it is important to be aware that however carefully we define 'a child', there will be debatable examples at the fuzzy edges, just like with any other category. Let's look at three examples that are relevant to us here.

First, wherever the line is drawn in development between a child and a 'non-child', it is a somewhat arbitrary decision. A child does not go to bed one night and wake up the next morning an adult, even if our legal and social institutions need to assume that they do. The transitions between different stages of life are phased and often take place on imperceptibly gradual timescales. The three sections of this book – early years, middle childhood, and adolescence – are a convenient way to organise a large amount of content, but this doesn't mean children literally experience a neat or sudden transition from one section to another.

Second, the definitions of a child and childhood have changed over time within the same place. An example of this is how one traditional symbol of the child/adult boundary – marriage – has changed over history. Currently, the legal minimum age to enter into a marriage in England and Wales is 18 years; in 1929 it was 16 years with the consent of parents, and before that it was 14 years for males and 12 years for females.

Third, the definitions of a child and childhood are different in different places at the same point in time. To use the previous example, currently the legal marriage age in China is 22 years for men and 20 years for women, in Estonia it is 15 years with court permission, and it is 13 years for females in Iran, or 9 years with a guardian's approval. So, children's development often straddles legal and social definitions, and how childhood is socially constructed can vary according to time and place. This is important to keep in mind when we look at explanations of development throughout this book, especially ones that make strong claims about development according to a strict universal schedule.

Variation in childhood doesn't imply there aren't any important differences between children and adults; if there weren't, this would be a very short book. All cultures distinguish between children and adults. Clearly, the way the average 5-year-old thinks and behaves is different from that of the average 15-year-old, and we are interested why that is and how children develop.

> **Key Point**
>
> - The notions of a child and childhood vary with place and time, but there are important biological, psychological, and cultural differences between children and adults.

Some of the differences between adults and children mean that extra care is needed when conducting research with children, and they need to be treated with dignity, autonomy, and respect.

> **Watch the One-Minute Method.**
>
> Discover the ethical principles researchers need to consider when conducting research with children.

1.4 Perspective 3: Evolutionary

This perspective needs more unpacking than the others because it is the most removed from our everyday experience. Understandably, there is some disagreement over exactly when our own species evolved, but our best current estimates based on DNA and fossil evidence suggest we emerged around 350,000 years ago (Hublin et al., 2017). From when we first walked the planet until today, we have spent almost all of that time living in small, nomadic groups searching for wild food on the African savannah. This way of life used to be called 'hunter-gathering', but now most researchers use the term 'foraging' in recognition that collecting food like tubers and nuts often contributes as many calories, if not more, than hunting meat. The modern world of agriculture, cities, and industry that we recognise around us (at least in the industrialised West) has only been part of the human experience for the past 10,000 year or so. Schools, healthcare, the contraceptive pill, and baby formula are even more recent inventions. If the entire history of *Homo sapiens* was squashed into 1 day, these features of modern life would appear in the last 10 seconds, just before midnight.

Quite why humans went through such a rapid period of change is another story, but the important point is that humans have evolved to 'expect' certain types of environments or have adapted to solve particular challenges relevant to a different time and place from today. That process of adaptation took place in the 97% of our history that revolved around foraging, and not in the most recent 3% (**Figure 1.4A**).

How does a species, like humans, become adapted to its environment? The best answer we have is **evolution** by **natural selection**, a theory published by Charles Darwin over 160 years ago, although Alfred Wallace was homing in on a similar idea at around the same time (Darwin, 1859). Many challenges in life, such as avoiding predators, getting food, finding a partner, fighting infection, or raising children, impact on the chances of survival or reproduction of an individual. Solutions to these challenges are called **adaptations**. We might be familiar with the idea of a biological adaptation like the eye, but the idea of a psychological

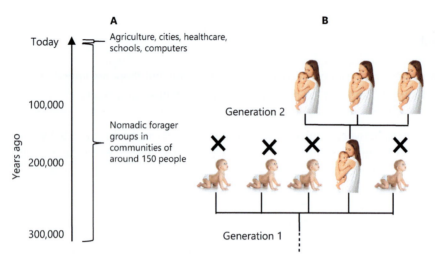

Figure 1.4 **(A)** Approximate timeline of human evolution. **(B)** Two generations of different infant care strategies. Source: Africa Studio/Adobe Stock; Media Home/Shutterstock

adaptation we might be less familiar with. The basic idea is summarised in **Figure 1.4B** with the example of infant care. In this example there is some variation in how mothers of generation 1 care for their infants. Most mothers just abandon their infants, leaving them to it – not an uncommon strategy in the animal world, particularly in insects. However, by chance, one of these human mothers pays special attention to caring for, feeding, and protecting their infant. In this scenario, the mother that provided attentive care nurtures a baby that lives long enough to pass on those nurturing genes to generation 2, because the baby shares 50% of her mother's genes. The infants who didn't receive that kind of care didn't live long enough to pass on the 'leave them to it' parenting strategy. Apply this to a broader range of behaviours that affect reproductive success and repeat over thousands of generations, and thereby species can become adapted to their environment.

> **Key Point**
>
> - The evolutionary perspective explores how the mind is adapted to solve problems that were significant for long periods of human history.

Using this perspective, let's ask ourselves a question that might have occurred to any sleep-deprived parent at three o'clock in the morning: why do we have a childhood?

Because we are so familiar with the idea of childhood, it's easy to forget just how rare it is in the natural world. If we behaved like other mammals of our size, women would give birth every year, to five-pound babies, and the average 6-year-old would already be a grandparent (Pontzer, 2021). Several species of aphid skip the idea of children all together and give birth to offspring who are already pregnant. Some animals mature fast, others slow. Some have thousands of offspring, others few. Some die while giving birth, serving as their offspring's first meal; others die alone, not having seen their offspring in months or years. While the basic facts of life are universal – be born, mature, reproduce, age, then die – there are as many ways to organise these stages of life as there are species (Frankenhuis & Nettle, 2020).

We might not have always had a childhood in the way we recognise it today, and to understand how we got here we need to go back in time. Before our species emerged 350,000 years ago, our distant ancestors had developed many more neurons in an area of the brain called the 'cortex' (Herculano-Houzel, 2019a). Neurons are the basic information-processing units of the brain, and the cortex is the wrinkly outer layer responsible for complex skills like learning, problem-solving, and decision-making. We do not fully understand why this change happened when it did, but a more densely packed cortex would have made us better able to adjust to the harsh and unpredictable environments we found ourselves in at that time (Richerson et al., 2005). When the going is tough, being able to adapt to a changing climate, find an alternative source of food, or learn from others could have meant the difference between life and death.

Whatever the ultimate cause, our supercharged cortex had some rather profound consequences for the way we lived our lives. One outcome was that we started living longer. Across a wide range of species, the more neurons in the cortex an animal has, the longer its lifespan (Herculano-Houzel, 2019b). Why? As well as supporting complex thinking skills, the cortex plays a role in supporting more basic life-support systems too. The core idea is that the more neurons you have, the more you can afford to lose before the vital functions they support start to fail. As a result, all stages of life began to be stretched out for humans, including childhood.

 Key Point

- Humans have a very long period of immaturity compared with other species.

All that extra brainpower created a new problem. Brains are relatively greedy organs to feed, particularly for children: more than 60% of a 4-year-old's calories go to the brain at rest, compared with around 20% for adults (Kuzawa et al., 2014). The brain steals so much energy during the early years of development that it actually slows down growth in the rest of the body (Pontzer, 2021). To find enough food to support our brains, we needed to spend less time asleep and more time foraging for food collaboratively (Engelmann & Tomasello, 2019). What food we did find, we were able to get more calories from with the invention of cooking and food-cutting tools. However, more time spent time fuelling our brains meant less time being able to look after our infants. Unfortunately, this occurred just at the time when infants needed more care than ever. Because of our longer lifespans, infants remained more helpless and hungrier for longer. Mothers needed help, and that help came in the form of pair bond mates, historically known as 'dads'. Humans are among only 5% of mammals in which fathers provide any care to their offspring, and also unlike most mammals we are monogamous (most of the time). More importantly, help also came from of a wider social support network of friends, aunts, uncles, nieces, nephews, grandfathers, and, in particular, grandmothers (Hawkes et al., 1998). A longer lifespan not only led to longer infancy and a longer time to reach sexual maturity, but also a longer post-reproductive period. Along with a few other species of whale, dolphin, and chimpanzee, humans are one of the only species in which females live long after the menopause. So, raising many children through such a long childhood was only possible with the aid of a village, or at least an extended family, with fathers and grandmothers around to help provision and care for the young (Hrdy, 2011).

Of course, the evolution of childhood was not just a neuronal numbers game; it was what children did with those neurons that created the childhood we recognise today. In order to survive and thrive in such a uniquely cooperative childcare environment of our past, children needed some uniquely human social skills, such as mind-reading, language, and cultural learning (Chapters 3, 4, and 5), and they needed to advertise that they were the social partners of the future (Chapter 2). An extended period of immaturity also allowed more time to be spent doing other things we think of as definitively childlike – exploration, play, and learning (Chapter 5).

> **Key Point**
>
> - Humans have evolved some unique social skills that help children survive and thrive in groups.

There is a lot we do not understand fully about this picture, and the casual directions are hard to untangle as they happened so long ago. Whatever happened in our past, we know it has driven us in very different directions from our closest living evolutionary relatives today, the chimpanzees, with which we share 98% of our DNA and are united by a common ancestor from about 6–7 million years ago. Because we are so similar yet so different, studying chimpanzees alongside ourselves can reveal a lot about our childhood (**Table 1.1**).

What do we have in common? **Table 1.1** shows that both humans and chimpanzees go through at least three stages of development: infancy, which extends from birth to weaning; the juvenile period, which follows weaning when young animals must generally fend for themselves, including finding food and shelter; and adulthood, when they become sexually mature. Perhaps these similarities should not surprise us; evolutionarily speaking we are closer to chimpanzees than chimpanzees are to gorillas. But it is the differences that are most revealing. Over the course of our relatively brief separation from chimpanzees, humans have added two new life stages (Bogin, 2001). First is childhood: the time between weaning and the juvenile period, characterised by such developmental milestones as language, imitation, and pretend play. And second is adolescence: a period following menarche in girls, with rapid growth spurts for both boys and girls, characterised by changes in brain organisation, maturation of the body and reproductive system, and psychological and behavioural changes involving increased concern about the self and social awareness. Humans are the only animals that stretch out these teenage years, not having our final growth spurt and delaying reproductive maturity until about 6 years after puberty (Bjorklund, 2020).

So, returning to our sleep-deprived parent: why do we have a childhood? The roots of our childhood are deep, and human childhood started to emerge thousands of generations ago when we were developing smarter brains that stretched out all of the phases of our lives. Infants were helpless and hungrier for longer, but sexual maturity was also delayed, as was

Table 1.1 Some similarities and differences between chimpanzee and human children that are important for understanding childhood.

Life stages	Infancy, juvenile, adulthood	Infancy, childhood, juvenile, adolescence, adulthood
Brain development	50% of their adult size at birth, 90% of their adult size by 2 years of age; about 7 billion cortical neurons (Tomasello, 2020)	20% of adult size at birth and do not reach 90% of adult size until 8 years of age; about 16 billion cortical neurons
Independence	Feeding themselves soon after weaning in infancy, and by 7 years old they are collecting as much food for the group as they consume	Even in forager cultures human children are not self-sufficient until they are at least 15 years old (Hill & Kaplan, 1999)
Reproduction	On average, a female chimp gives birth to one baby every 5.9 years in the wild	In traditional forager societies with no birth control, births are on average 3.4 years apart
Parenting	Entirely from the mother, and youngsters stay in close proximity for some time, often in bodily contact (Tomasello, 2020)	In foraging societies today, parenting not undertaken by the mum or dad typically makes up 40–50% of a child's care, and it is not uncommon for young children to be passed between multiple caregivers many times an hour (Kramer, 2010)

Source: Eric Isselee/Shutterstock; Gelpi/Shutterstock.

the time spent after the menopause. Those greedy brains required a wide social support group around them to keep them alive, and children needed to make themselves attractive to the group that was feeding and protecting them.

For most of our history this picture of childhood has remained relatively stable. But in the latest 3% of our evolutionary history a lot has changed, as cultural revolutions have overtaken the pace of biological evolution. Under these circumstances there can be **evolutionary mismatches**: differences between the expected environment – the majority of our history having been spent in small foraging groups – and the ones that most Western children find themselves in today. For example, an education environment that is passive and sedentary, teacher-led via instruction, and with children separated by age and ability is at odds with the environment of most foraging societies, which are typically more active and exploratory and where adults are largely absent, age groups of children are mixed, and the learning is achieved more by imitation, observation, and apprenticeship (Chaudhary & Swanepoel, 2023).

Mismatches are just as relevant for parents as they are for children. Parents can end up burned out and stressed because they shoulder the responsibility of child-rearing without the large support networks that have been so crucial throughout our evolutionary history (Chaudhary & Swanepoel, 2023). In a survey of 1,904 American grandparents, 43% of them said they live over 200 miles away from their grandchildren (Statista, 2012). There are fewer opportunities for future caregivers to learn about giving birth, which can lessen the anxiety of first-time mothers (hence organisations like the National Childbirth Trust in the UK are attempting to fill this gap), and fewer opportunities to learn about parenting in general (hence parenting books, apps, and gurus together are worth an estimated $372.6 million annually in the US).

To be clear, the point is not that a foraging childhood or parenting style is better or worse than other styles, nor is that way of life to be romanticised. Surveys of small-scale societies suggests that, prior to the advent of agriculture, on average one in two children did not make it past puberty (Volk & Atkinson, 2013). The point is that we can expect some mismatches when children are adapted to solve problems in one environment but find themselves in a radically different environment.

Key Point

- Evolutionary mismatches can occur when there is a large difference between the environment that a trait was adapted for and one that it was not.

The evolutionary perspective is especially useful when we want to understand more than the *what* and *when* of development, but also *why* children develop the way they do. Throughout the book, we will see how our evolutionary past has been a powerful force – but certainly not the only one – in shaping human childhood. For example, children tend to see their in-group as having better qualities than an out-group. This predisposition to think in terms of us versus them may have been helpful in encouraging the cooperation and coherence of small groups in the past. But the dark side of 'groupishness' is that it can motivate intolerance of others. Knowing where something comes from can help us understand it.

Summary

- This book takes three main perspectives on child development: psychological, anthropological, and evolutionary.

- Child psychology is the scientific study of how the mind, brain, and behaviour change during childhood.

- Child psychologists want to understand how children grow, develop, and adapt at different points in their lives.
- Children develop incrementally, with later-acquired skills built on earlier ones.
- Children are active participants in their own development.
- The anthropological perspective explores how children around the world are similar and different.
- The notions of a child and childhood vary with place and time, but there are important biological, psychological, and cultural differences between children and adults.
- The evolutionary perspective explores how the mind is adapted to solve problems that were significant for long periods of human history.
- Humans have a very long period of immaturity compared with other species.
- Humans have evolved some unique social skills that help children survive and thrive in groups.
- Evolutionary mismatches can occur when there is a large difference between the environment that a trait was adapted for and one that it was not.

References

Bjorklund, D. (2020). *How Children Invented Humanity: The Role of Development in Human Evolution*. Oxford University Press.

Bogin, B. (2001). *The Growth of Humanity*. Wiley.

Chaudhary, N. & Swanepoel, A. (2023). Editorial perspective: what can we learn from hunter-gatherers about children's mental health? An evolutionary perspective. *Journal of Child Psychology and Psychiatry*, 64(10), 1522–1525.

Darwin, C. (1859). *On the Origin of Species by Means of Natural Selection*. John Murray.

Engelmann, J. & Tomasello, M. (2019). Children's sense of fairness as equal respect. *Trends in Cognitive Sciences*, 23(6), 454–463.

Frankenhuis, W. & Nettle, D. (2020). Current debates in human life history research. *Evolution and Human Behavior*, 41(6), 469–473.

Gottlieb, G. (1992). *Individual Development and Evolution: The Genesis of Novel Behavior*. Oxford University Press.

Hawkes, K., O'Connell, J. F., Blurton Jones, N. G., Alvarez, H., & Charnov, E. L. (1998). Grandmothering, menopause, and the evolution of human life histories. *Proceedings of the National Academy of Sciences of the United States of America*, 95, 1336–1339.

Herculano-Houzel, S. (2019a). Life history changes accompany increased numbers of cortical neurons: a new framework for understanding human brain evolution. *Progress in Brain Research*, 250, 179–216.

Herculano-Houzel, S. (2019b). Longevity and sexual maturity vary across species with number of cortical neurons, and humans are no exception. *Journal of Comparative Neurology*, 527, 1689–1705.

Hill, K. & Kaplan, H. (1999). Life history traits in humans: theory and empirical studies. *Annual Review of Anthropology*, 28(1), 397–430.

Hrdy, S. (2011). *Mothers and Others: The Evolutionary Origins of Mutual Understanding*. Harvard University Press.

Hublin, J. J., Ben-Ncer, A., Bailey, S., et al. (2017). New fossils from Jebel Irhoud, Morocco and the pan-African origin of *Homo sapiens*. *Nature*, 546, 289–292.

Kramer, K. L. (2010). Cooperative breeding and its significance to the demographic success of humans. *Annual Review of Anthropology*, 39, 417–436.

Kuzawa, C. W., Chugani, H. T., Grossman, L. I., et al. (2014). Metabolic costs of human brain development. *Proceedings of the National Academy of Sciences of the United States of America*, 111, 13010–13015.

Munafò, M. & Smith, G. (2018). Robust research needs many lines of evidence. *Nature*, 553(7686), 399–401.

Pontzer, H. (2021). *Burn: The Misunderstood Science of Metabolism*. Penguin Random House.

Richerson, P. J., Bettinger, R. L., & Boyd, R. (2005). Evolution on a restless planet: were environmental variability and environmental change major drivers of human evolution? In F. M. Wuketits & F. J. Ayala (eds.), *Handbook of Evolution* (pp. 223–242). Wiley.

Statista. (2012). How close do you live to your grandchild? *Statista*. www.statista.com/statistics/241891/distance-between-us-grandparents-and-their-grandchildren

Tomasello, M. (2020). The adaptive origins of uniquely human sociality. *Philosophical Transactions of the Royal Society of London. Series B, Biological Sciences*, 375, 2019049.

Volk, A. A. & Atkinson, J. A. (2013). Infant and child death in the human environment of evolutionary adaptation. *Evolution and Human Behavior*, 34(3), 182–192.

SECTION I

THE EARLY YEARS

This section explores the early years of children's lives, following their development from birth to 5 years old. It is a period that sees huge change in how children behave, think, and learn. We will explore the significance of early experiences, how children begin to read other people's minds and learn language, and the importance of play, imitation, and discovery. We also look at the role that cultural differences and caregivers have on shaping children's experiences, as well as how children begin to shape the world around them.

THE EARLY YEARS

2 WHY DOES LOVE MATTER?

Learning Outcomes

After reading this chapter you will be able to:

- Describe some important features of infant–caregiver relationships.
- Evaluate the role of early life experiences on later development.
- Understand what emotions are for and how they develop.

2.1 Introduction

The previous chapter tackled some big questions and introduced the psychological, anthropological, and evolutionary perspectives on child development. We learned that humans have a very long period of immaturity compared with other species. That period of immaturity starts with absolute dependence on other people for food, warmth, moving about, and protection. It led English paediatrician and psychologist Donald Winnicott to remark 'there is no such thing as an infant', by which he meant that wherever there is an infant, there is someone else to care for them, and without that care there would be no infant (1965, p. 39). This vulnerability is reflected in the fact that the first years of life represent a relatively perilous time for infants. Global infant mortality rates are around 3%, and in some Sub-Saharan Africa countries 10% of children never reach their fifth birthday (Roser et al., 2019). While these rates are thankfully low by historic standards, life does not get this risky again until we are well into our 60s. At the top of the new-born's 'to-do list', then, is to get the care they need to survive. In this chapter we look at some of the first things infants need to do to survive, the kinds of relationships and emotions that support their well-being, and the effects that early experiences can have on their later development.

2.2 The New-Born To-Do List

The journey of development is one of cooperation and competition from the very start. Although mothers share half of their genes with their embryos, they share all their genes with themselves: you can't get more related to yourself than yourself. As a result, the mother's body can reject the embryo as a foreign invader, ending life before it has a chance to begin. Up to one in four pregnancies, it is estimated, end in early pregnancy loss, miscarrying before the mother is aware that she is pregnant (Jurkovic & Kuhan, 2020). To prevent this, the foetus produces a hormone that stops the mother from shedding her uterus lining along with the newly implanted embryo. With the aid of another hormone, the foetus gains control of the main arteries supplying the placenta, altering the balance of insulin in the mother's blood. This ensures the foetus gets the glucose-rich nutrients it needs to grow, but it does so at the risk of the mother developing gestational diabetes or pre-eclampsia (Araujo et al., 2015). While infants are still in womb, they are flooding their mothers with hormones that lower her threshold for responding to the sounds and smells of a warm, wriggling, fluid-covered baby (Hrdy & Burkart, 2020). And it's not just mothers who are impacted: fathers' testosterone levels can crash by up to a third during their partners' pregnancy, a change that is widely understood to help steer fathers from mating towards parenting (Gettler et al., 2011).

Following birth, if the new-born can make it to their mother's nipples, root, suck, and stimulate lactation, further surges in chemicals such as oxytocin, sometimes known as the 'tend and befriend' hormone, enhance her nurturing impulses. In brain scanning studies, women who were given oxytocin to sniff showed more connectivity between the brain's reward centres when they listened to infant laughter – suggesting they enjoyed it more than others. However, when listening to infant crying, oxytocin led these same women to have less activity in a brain region associated with anxiety and more activity in empathy-related brain regions (Riem et al., 2011). Following a sniff of oxytocin, fathers too played with their children in a more stimulating and sensitive way, and their oxytocin levels naturally increase in the first 6 months after their babies are born and during active play with their infants (Abraham et al., 2019; Naber et al., 2013). Given that it takes only seconds after birth before babies cry and around 6 weeks before they smile, the hormonal system can provide an emotional bridge through the first tiring weeks to the social interactions to come.

Becoming a parent is usually a transformative experience, sometimes even a transcendent one, but it almost always is a logistical, emotional, and physical slog. It can take up to 6 years for the sleep of a parent to return to normal following the birth of their baby (Richter et al., 2019), and even in forager cultures children are not self-sufficient until they are at least 15 years of age (Hill & Kaplan, 1999). We are not the only ones for whom parenting is an endurance event. The effort it takes a typical garden bird to raise a clutch of chicks to adulthood is equivalent, in human terms, to cycling the Tour de France (Peterson et al., 1990). So, if parents are going to make a long-term commitment to caring for and nurturing their infants, then nature needs a way to advertise that infants are good bets for survival and worth the investment. Cue cuteness – that means large, round eyes, a head 'too large' for the body, high eyebrows, a small chin, and a plump appearance. Humans are born fatter than almost all other mammals, and our closest relatives, the chimpanzees – who develop independence sooner – are born relatively sleek with 3% fat compared to the 15% lard of the human baby (Hassett, 2022).

Mothers across a range of cultures prefer plump babies who look cute and sound vigorous right from birth, advertising that they are full-term, robust, and likely to survive (Hrdy, 1999; Kuzawa et al., 2014). Both men and women make extra effort to look at cute infant faces

(Hahn et al., 2013) and will prefer to give a toy to or even (hypothetically) adopt a cuter infant (Golle et al., 2015), and infants and children themselves prefer to look at 'cuter' infant faces (Van Duuren et al., 2003). As we learned in Chapter 1, it traditionally took a village to raise a child, so not only is this bias present in mothers, but women who have not given birth and men also find the faces of plump, healthy-looking babies 'cuter' and more rewarding to look at, increasing these babies' chances of being cared for by a wider social network (Glocker et al., 2009).

Cuteness not only increases the chances of receiving immediate care and attention, but by promoting smiling, laughter, and more complex social interactions, it also encourages care in the longer term. Cues like cuteness and the 'biological siren' of crying elicit strong caregiving responses, which have been shown to receive fast-tracked priority in the brain's pathways (Kringelbach et al., 2016). The general assault on the senses that a new-born can generate is a good example of how infants are not passive passengers of their own development. They are actively manipulating – unconsciously or otherwise – the world around them in a way that best ensures their survival (**Figure 2.1**).

It is important to say that 'worth the investment' is defined here by the blind, amoral process of natural selection and does not represent value judgements on children or of parents. Our species emerged around 350,000 years ago, and for almost all of that time we could not rely on the safety nets of medicine or institutionalised social care that have dramatically reduced infant mortality, which – needless to say – is a good thing. Historically in the industrialised West and across traditional societies that still don't have access to such institutions, mothers are known

Figure 2.1 The long journey of development begins with complete dependence on others for food, warmth, and protection.
Source: hadynyah/Getty Images.

to abandon at birth infants they consider unhealthy or unlikely to survive and to adjust their parenting effort in line with their social and environmental circumstances (Hrdy, 1999; Konner, 1972; Scrimshaw, 1984). For example, mothers across many different cultures tend to parent less in circumstances where parenting more would not improve their children's survival, such as during famine or war (Quinlan, 2007).

The reason humans have developed a preference bias for healthy-looking babies is that any animal that invested all its time in offspring that had little or no chance of making it to adulthood wouldn't be around for more than one generation, because such babies would not survive long enough to pass on their genes. This does not mean parents love their children because they 'want to spread their genes'. Most people know little about genetics and care about it even less. Parents love their children not because they want to spread their genes but because they can't get enough of the warm and fuzzy feeling they get from loving them. That feeling comes from having a brain – shaped by natural selection – that tries to put its owner in circumstances like those that caused its ancestors to be successful, such as nurturing, feeding, and protecting one's children (Pinker, 1997).

Infants are not just advertising themselves as good physical investments but also signalling they are the social partners of the future. The long journey towards ingratiating themselves into society begins when they are just hours old. New-borns prefer to look at faces that directly look back at them rather than ones looking away, and they choose to focus in on the eyes and mouths of other people. They can see most clearly at a range of about 25 cm, which corresponds to the distance between an infant's face and that of their mother when nursing. Gazing new-borns engage a wide audience of potential carers, and from just about as early as it is possible to measure infants direct their attention towards voices and faces and make eye contact in a way that suggests they are born expecting a social world (Konner, 2010).

The early social exchanges of infants are often expressed as a back-and-forth exchange of emotional smiles, mirroring of behaviour, synchronised touches, and vocalisations. And by 2–3 months old infants show surprise or distress when their experience differs from such exchanges – an unresponsive face, for example – and try to repair the breakdown by re-engaging the attention of their partner. Child psychologist Colwyn Trevarthen coined the term **proto-conversations** to characterise these types of face-to-face turn-taking episodes between parent and infant, where both participants have a special motivation to share emotions with each other (1979). A special type of emotional bond that develops in this context is called **attachment**, which is explored further in **Box 2.1**.

 Key Points

- In the short term, infants need immediate care from others to survive, and they encourage this with their physical appearance and behaviours.
- In the long term, parenting is a big investment, and over the course of our evolutionary history this has caused infants to advertise their worth and parents to be selective over whom they cared for.

> **Box 2.1** Attachment
>
> Attachment is a special emotional bond that children develop with one or more caregiver(s). That attachment figure gives children a sense of security and stability. The theory of attachment was developed by British psychoanalyst and clinician John Bowlby, who later teamed up with US-Canadian psychologist Mary Salter Ainsworth (Bowlby, 1969; Ainsworth & Bell, 1970). Based on her original work in Uganda, Ainsworth developed an assessment tool, the Strange Situation Procedure, which involved recording the behaviour of infants reunited with their primary caregiver after being left either alone or with a stranger. In this situation she noticed infant behaviour could be generally categorised into several types: *secure* – the baby seeks the attachment figure for reassurance in a stressful situation and uses them as a safe base to explore their environment; *resistant* – the baby explores less and shows intense distress when the mother leaves but resists contact or is in conflict with her when reunited; or *avoidant* – the baby is indifferent to the stranger and is neither upset by the mother's disappearance nor interested by her return. And later on, a fourth category of *disorganised* attachment was added, describing when the child reacts bizarrely by freezing or displaying confusion. Attachment theory proposes that children internalise these types of behaviours and use them as a kind of template for future relationships. The theory also makes some more general claims about how attachment works:
> 1. *Universality* – all children experience some form of attachment.
> 2. *Normativity* – secure attachment is the norm or standard experience.
> 3. *Sensitivity* – sensitive caregiving encourages attachment security.
> 4. *Competence* – secure attachment leads to better outcomes for children.
>
> Bowlby recognised that infant–carer attachment was important for a whole range of species, not just humans. As such, attachment is a biologically rooted system that evolved to protect offspring from danger and to motivate caregivers to care (Del Giudice, 2009). But all development occurs in a context, whether it is biologically rooted or not, and the development of attachment is influenced by cross-cultural differences. In Chapter 6 we re-examine these claims from a global perspective and explore which elements of attachment are sensitive to local circumstances and which are not.

2.3 Early Experiences

Children are born into environments that differ hugely in their geography, languages spoken, parenting practices, social structure, technology, and economic conditions. How are children able to survive and thrive in such diverse circumstances? Even if children knew in advance which environment they were going to be born into, there simply isn't enough space in our genes to instruct where each neuron of the brain should go and how it should wire up. There are about 86 billion neurons in our brain – about 100 trillion connections – but only about 20,000 genes.

Nature has given us a neat solution by over-packing the infant brain with more neurons and connections than it needs, and letting experience dictate which ones are important to hang on to. By about 2 years of age we have the most neurons we will ever have in our lives, after which their density declines as the brain prunes away the unused connections. This process makes childhood one of the greatest periods of **plasticity** in our lifetimes, which at its most basic refers to the ability to change the way we behave, feel, or think as a result of experience or evidence. While it might be depressing to think you will never be as brainy as the 2-year-old you, the trade-off for losing the plasticity of childhood is that we become adults with expertise in what we do focus on.

Plasticity also creates critical or **sensitive periods** in development, when experiences can have an especially significant impact later on in life. For example, researchers have used the idea of a sensitive period to understand the rise in childhood allergy rates and how best to treat them. Over several decades, often following official healthcare advice, some parents have avoided giving young children certain types of food, such as peanuts, eggs, tree nuts, and fish. However, early childhood is a window of opportunity for the immune system to learn about what to expect in the environment. One study showed that introducing peanut products into babies' diets at 6 months of age could reduce peanut allergy by up to 77%, but waiting until they were 1 year old only led to a 33% reduction (Roberts et al., 2023). Anthropologist Elizabeth Cashdan has documented that children's willingness to try new foods often plummets after their third birthday, with early learned preferences often persisting into adulthood (Cashdan, 1994).

Key Point

- A peak in early brain plasticity creates an especially sensitive period early on in development.

What happens if infants experience care that is insensitive, neglectful, or absent in this sensitive period? Unfortunately, recent history provides us with the answer. Orphanages and foundling homes for abandoned children have existed for half a millennium across Europe, Asia, South America, and the United States. To reduce the spread of infectious diseases, mothers and staff in these institutes were often discouraged from close contact with these infants. While their basic needs of food, warmth, and shelter were often met, this social distancing left them psychologically malnourished. Austrian-American psychoanalyst René Spitz was one of the first to notice that, while well intentioned, this policy of isolation undermined the intended effect; it contributed to higher child mortality and emotional wasting (1945). Animal psychologist Harry Harlow demonstrated something similar. Macaque monkeys showed severe emotional distress when separated from their mothers, and they would rather be comforted by physical contact than by food, especially in times of distress. In other words, emotional needs mattered as much or in some circumstances more so than nutritional ones (Harlow et al., 1965). Around this time Konrad Lorenz, an Austrian zoologist, was also documenting how some animals seemed programmed to form a special bond with their caregiver during a sensitive period of early development, regardless of who that caregiver was (1935). Incidentally, Lorenz was a keen advocate of studying animals behaving in their natural context, but needs must, and while a university student he used his parents' apartment to keep a pet capuchin monkey named Gloria. Not coincidentally, Bowlby was influenced by the work of Spitz, Harlow, and Lorenz, and he blended elements of each when forming his theory of attachment (**Box 2.1**).

Today UNICEF estimates that as many as 8 million children are growing up in institutional settings around the world. Thankfully, conditions are not as bad as they were. Infants in institutionalised care at the start of the nineteenth century had a less than 50% chance of making it through their first year. Typically, institutes are still not ideal places to bring up children, with conditions often being described as overcrowded and understaffed and with care that is unresponsive (Bjorkland, 2020). Nathan Fox, a psychologist who studies the impacts of early adverse experiences on children, recounts how he was struck by the silence in the Romanian orphanages he visited: 'The most remarkable thing about the infant room was how quiet it was, probably because the infants had learned that their cries were not responded to' (cited in Weir, 2014).

Researchers have noted that the outcomes for children raised in these environments are very dependent on how long the children spend there. The longer children are in care, the more likely they are to experience difficulty with thinking and planning skills, with understanding others, and with regulating their emotions. Underlining the idea of a sensitive period, the general message of this research is that the earlier children can be rescued from these maladaptive situations, the greater the chance of reversing the ill effects of abuse and neglect. For example, psychologists Emily Merz and Robert McCall looked at 342 children who were adopted from Russian orphanages. They found that children who had been adopted before 18 months of age had similar levels of behaviour problems as the general population, whereas those children who remained in institutionalised care beyond this age showed greater behaviour problems, and these effects persisted into adolescence (2010).

In a separate study, researchers followed 131 children from Romanian orphanages who had been adopted by UK families. If they had been adopted before 6 months of age, they went on to develop IQs in the normal range when they were tested later at 6 years of age. If they were adopted between 6 and 24 months of age they had IQs in the low to normal range, and if they were adopted after 24 months of age they had the lowest IQs of the sample. In this study, the researchers were careful to compare the Romanian children with a separate group of 50 children who had been adopted from *within* the UK so they could be more certain that this pattern was because of the conditions in the orphanage and not just something about the process of adoption in general (Beckett et al., 2006).

Researchers have not just noted different outcomes for these children in terms of their social, emotional, and intellectual functioning, but also in their brain function and physical growth (Gerhardt, 2015). The anthropologist James Tanner documented that children suffering under the direction of a particularly sadistic schoolteacher showed slower physical growth than expected despite receiving adequate food (1978). And post-institutionalised children have been found to have smaller brains on average and to show different patterns of brain electrical activity compared to the general population (Sheridan et al., 2012). However, the institutionalised children who were moved into foster homes recovered some of that brain volume over time, and if the children were moved into foster care before their second birthdays, by age 8 their brains' electrical activity looked no different from that of other children of a similar age.

While the experiences of these children show that there are especially sensitive periods of development, we also now understand that early experiences matter more for some children than others. This idea has been captured through the concepts of so-called dandelion children (who, like the plants, are able to survive and thrive in a wide variety of environments) and those who are more like orchids (who are only able to flourish under a narrower range of environmental conditions). For example, in a study of 338 children aged 5–6 years, researchers identified a group that had lower behaviour problems and did better in school when their home environment was low stress but reacted badly if they grew up in high-stress homes, as reflected by low family income, harsh parenting, and maternal depression (Obradović et al., 2010). These orchid children were highly responsive to their environment, showing greater plasticity, and this made them more susceptible to the effects of both especially positive *and* negative environments. The dandelion children, by contrast, were much less affected by either the harsh or the positive background.

Key Point

- Early experiences matter, but they matter to some children more than others.

There are three subtleties to this big picture that are important for understanding early experiences. First, the categories of dandelions and orchids can be a useful shorthand for talking about sensitivity and resilience to stressful environments, but no one is suggesting that all 2 billion children on Earth can be classified according to only these two types. Most children fall on a continuum between these extremes, and some researchers have taken the flower analogy further, suggesting that 'tulips' are moderately influenced by their experiences. Second, the research shows that some outcomes are *more likely* than others for some groups of children, but this doesn't mean any individual child is deterministically doomed if they experience adverse early experiences (as dandelions show), and, as we will see, adversity can also be a source of strength. Caregivers and children's wider social networks also play a significant role in shaping children's responses to adversity, with the presence of a predictable, stable, and responsive figure helping to buffer some of the more harmful effects of early stress (Gerhardt, 2015; Hostinar et al., 2015). Finally, and perhaps unfortunately, the reverse is also true: if you've had a good start in life, this doesn't mean you've got it made. A bad environment or bad luck later on in life can undo the advantages of a secure and stable childhood (Bjorkland, 2020).

2.4 Can Children Predict the Future?

Megan Gunnar, director of the Institute of Child Development at the University of Minnesota, describes that one of the most common behaviours she sees among post-institutionalised children is indiscriminate friendliness: 'A child who doesn't know you from Adam will run up, put his arms around you and snuggle in like you're his long-lost aunt' (cited in Weir, 2014). In a study of 65 toddlers who had been adopted from institutions, she found the attachment styles of these children were often 'disorganised' (see **Box 2.1**), sometimes approaching the caregiver for comfort and other times showing resistance (Carlson et al.,

2014). Gunnar also thinks that this indiscriminate friendliness was probably an important coping strategy in their socially starved early lives; or, in other words, these infants' attachment style was adjusted to the kind of parenting they received. This suggests that something more general might be going on: early experiences can act as imperfect predictors of things to come and, in turn, shape children's development to help them adapt to that world. Let's look at one example from history in which this has happened.

Towards the end of the Second World War, a portion of the Dutch population was exposed to a severe winter that led to widespread starvation and malnutrition, with many people resorting to eating tulip bulbs and nettles to survive (including a young Audrey Hepburn). While the circumstances of the Dutch famine were tragic, it provided a unique natural experiment to examine the effects of nutrition on subsequent generations. Not surprisingly, women who were pregnant during the famine had babies with lower birthweight. More unexpectedly perhaps, these babies grew up to have a much higher risk of being obese (Lumey et al., 2021). What was going on here? These infants produced higher levels of an appetite-regulating hormone called leptin, which caused them to store greater amounts of fat than children who'd had more nutritious prenatal diets. In this case, the environment signalled to the children – while still in womb – that food was scarce, so they developed a thrifty metabolism that was more likely to hold on to calories for longer. A similar sensitivity was experimentally demonstrated in a study that invited some pregnant women to consume anise-flavoured food while others did not. At birth and 4 days later, only those infants born to the non-anise-consuming mothers displayed an aversion to it (Schaal et al., 2000).

Watch the One-Minute Method.

Discover what natural experiments, like the Dutch famine, and controlled experiments can teach us about child development.

We can extend this idea of predicting the future from physiological responses to psychological ones. For example, children growing up in supportive and predictable environments tend to develop a more future-orientated 'go-slow' strategy, to be less risk prone, and to invest more in their relationships. In contrast, children growing up in harsh and unpredictable environments tend to develop an opportunistic 'go-fast' lifestyle, to engage in risky behaviour, to become sexually active earlier, and to invest relatively little in their relationships (Ellis et al., 2009).

While these latter behaviours might be frowned upon by middle-class society, Dutch developmental psychologist Willem Frankenhuis has argued they are more adaptive for children growing up in harsh and unpredictable conditions than more cautious and culturally approved behaviours: when the future is uncertain, it makes more sense to prefer immediate over delayed rewards and to develop a lifestyle for dealing with threat and rapidly changing conditions (Frankenhuis et al., 2016). That is what researchers found who followed the lives of children, adolescents, and their families from China, Italy, Jordan, Kenya, the Philippines, Sweden, Thailand, and the United States over 6 years (Chang et al., 2019). Those children and adolescents living in unsafe neighbourhoods and with family chaos and fluctuating incomes and experiencing stressful life events during childhood were more likely to adopt a fast strategy, being more aggressive and focused on short-term goals. In contrast, those in more stable environments were more likely to adopt slow strategies, investing in social relationships and focusing on long-term rewards. In Chapter 10, we take a closer look at how early stressful experiences can become encoded in the brain, and how they change our perceptions of risk and reward far into the future.

Key Point

- Some responses to early experiences are adaptive for later life.

Hidden talents.

Children living in adverse conditions are more likely to struggle in school. But what if these children have abilities that are enhanced through adversity – 'hidden talents' that educators can harness to promote their learning?

2.5 Emotions

Because new-borns are unable to feed or protect themselves and keep themselves warm, they are dependent on others to meet their needs. A hungry new-born can get the attention of a carer by crying, but then it is up to the carer to work out whether the infant needs feeding, changing, or cuddling. Later on, when infants gain more independence, they will be able to act on their feelings by getting up and walking to get a bottle of milk themselves. In general, maintaining our well-being – whether it be by influencing others or motivating ourselves – is driven by our emotions.

We experience love, anger, fear, disgust, and pleasure, which regulate the four Fs: feeding, fighting, fleeing, and … sexual behaviour. We also have emotions for dealing with other people: guilt, pride, and honour. As far as we can tell, the emotional vocabulary of children starts simpler, with new-borns distinguishing between generally feeling good – well fed or interested – and generally feeling bad – hungry, irritable, or distressed. Over time, through repeated social interactions, this basic feeling good versus bad starts to separate into subtler shades of emotional meaning. But before some emotions can be experienced or expressed, other psychological milestones need to be achieved first. For example, guilt requires some prior understanding of what the norm or expected behaviour is in order to feel guilty about violating it. Jealously requires some prior understanding of the difference between self and others in order to feel jealous of something else. So, emotions that require more sophisticated understandings of social relationships – pride, jealously, shame, and guilt – tend to emerge later than those emotions that do not – fear, disgust, and pleasure (**Figure 2.2**).

As children get older, they learn to regulate their own emotions with more control: picture the average 3-year-old's explosive tantrum compared with the simmering inner rage of

Figure 2.2 As infants develop, their emotional repertoire expands, as does their ability to recognise emotions in others and, later on, to regulate their own emotions. Source: © Ferli Achirulli Kamaruddin | Dreamstime.

adolescence. What counts as appropriate emotional regulation is influenced by the values of the society that children are born into. For example, researchers studied the reactions of 7–11-year-old children to emotionally charged situations, such as spilling a drink on their homework or being falsely accused of stealing (Cole et al., 2002). American children were more likely to respond with anger and be problem focused and action orientated, consistent with the more American values of self-assertion and personal agency. By contrast, children from Nepal were more likely to respond to the same events with shame than anger and to express more self-control, and they were generally more accepting of the situation, consistent with the values of the Buddhist and Brahman societies these children were raised in.

As well as using emotions to regulate their own well-being, children learn to recognise emotions in others and use them to respond appropriately in different situations. For example, Campos and colleagues (1992) placed 12-month-old infants on a clear table surface under which two levels of flooring produced the appearance of a cliff. To the infants it appeared as if the surface ended abruptly, but if they did crawl farther they would be supported by the clear surface. Some 70% of the infants were willing to cross over the 'cliff edge' towards their mothers *if* they could see that their mothers had a happy expression, but no infants did so if their mothers showed an expression of fear. In this case, being able to read the emotions of others helped to regulate their well-being (i.e., it stopped them falling off a 'cliff'!). In a separate study, a similar age group of infants expressed significantly more fearful signals towards a stranger and avoided them if they had seen their mothers reacting in a fearful way towards the same stranger (de Rosnay et al., 2006). Many studies have shown that from about 10 months of age onwards infants look to their caregivers' emotional expressions to judge how they should behave, particularly when placed in a situation of uncertainty, ambiguity, or novelty. Learning in this way sidesteps risky first-hand trial and error and taps into the experience of others. For example, rats are much more likely to try a new food if they have smelled it on the breath of other rats – a smart strategy to avoid toxic foods (Galef, 1987). So, this kind of learning is not unique to humans, but as we will see in Chapter 5, humans have taken social learning much, much further than any other species.

It is not hard to see how many of our basic emotions are Darwinian adaptations that keep us safe and well. Indeed, it was Darwin himself who provided one of the first recorded case studies of any child, keeping a diary of his infant son's expressions, which he later used in his theory of emotional development in children (1872). A classic example is disgust, which causes a scrunched nose and mouth expression, reducing air intake from potentially harmful substances. Fear causes heavier breathing and a quicker heart rate, which redistributes blood in preparation for rapid movement and puts us on high alert. The widened eyes of individuals with a fearful facial expression have been found to increase the scope of what we can see, allowing individuals to better identify potentially threatening objects in their periphery (Susskind et al., 2008).

Key Points

- Emotions help us set our goals and regulate our well-being.
- Infants start out with a basic repertoire of positive and negative emotions that become more differentiated over time.

So, emotions like disgust, fear, and pleasure can motivate us to take action, and for very young children this often means satisfying a set of biologically rooted needs: feeding, warmth, and protection. But as children develop, emotions soon become imbued with the values, beliefs, and customs of the society they are born into. For example, Röttger-Rössler and colleagues studied the development of shame in a group of toddlers in rural Minangkabau, an ethnic group on the Indonesian island of Sumatra (Röttger-Rössler et al., 2013). They documented that when these young children met a stranger, they often reacted with a mild form of fear that involved hiding behind their mothers, avoiding eye contact, and being both quiet and restrained.

Minangkabau caregivers interpret this behaviour as the first signs of *malu*, a highly esteemed form of shame that is expressed by signals such as avoiding eye contact, hiding the face behind the hands, and a collapsed body posture. Caregivers praise their children for early *malu* displays in front of others, and this reinforces the avoidance behaviour, with the desired long-term effect that children exaggerate this shameful expression as they get older. So, while the initial fear response of children to a stranger is not unique to this culture, the way the adults react is, and this shapes these children's emotional development in a unique way. In Canada, children who are shy or emotionally reserved are more likely to be negatively judged by their peers, whereas these same behaviours are viewed as a sign of emotional maturity in Chinese children, and so they are more often accepted by their peers (Chen, 2012).

As well as differences *between* societies, differences *within* societies in the way caregivers, peers, and siblings respond to emotions also play a key role in shaping children's emotional development. For example, children who have parents who help them explore their feelings and those of others, in what has been called 'emotional coaching', are better able to recognise others' emotions than children in families that discuss their feelings less often (Dunn, 2004).

 Key Point

- Children develop a similar vocabulary of emotions; precisely what those emotions mean is shaped by social interactions and cultural norms.

Talking Point

Love matters, and it matters for children all over the world. In a study that drew together findings from over 31 countries, children's perceptions of their mothers' and fathers' warmth, acceptance, and affection – in short, their love – were associated with greater psychological well-being, whereas feeling rejected predicted children's distress in later life (Khaleque & Ali, 2017). Love goes to the heart of the relationship between parents and children. Being a parent is not about creating a particular kind of child that grows into a particular kind of adult but about experiencing a particular kind of love and providing a protected space for children to grow up in. That structured, stable environment that parents can provide helps children to be variable, unpredictable, and messy (Gopnik, 2016).

Our emotions give us a behavioural compass that regulate interactions with others and the physical world. They point us in the broad direction of what to do (e.g., flee from danger) and when to stop (i.e., feeling safe). Despite what we have learned about the importance of providing nourishing, stimulating, and loving environments, the inner world of children's emotions, by definition, remains hidden. Moreover, the same emotional expression can indicate different experiences. A smile can signal joy, pride, embarrassment, or even contempt. How can we be sure children's experiences of emotions maps onto adults' experiences? More generally, how can we be sure that *anyone* else is experiencing emotions in the same way we do – that the pain of my toothache *feels* like yours? Love, compassion, and empathy might be the closest we will come to feeling someone else's toothache, and in the next chapter we will learn more about how children develop this sense of empathy, imagining what others see, know, and believe.

> **Summary**
>
> - In the short term, infants need immediate care from others to survive, and they encourage this with their physical appearance and behaviours.
> - In the long term, parenting is a big investment, and over the course of our history this has caused infants to advertise their worth and parents to be selective over whom they cared for.
> - A peak in early brain plasticity creates an especially sensitive period early on in development.
> - Early experiences matter, but they matter to some children more than others.
> - Some responses to early experiences are adaptive for later life.
> - Emotions help us set our goals and regulate our well-being.
> - Infants start out with a basic repertoire of positive and negative emotions that become more differentiated over time.
> - Children develop a similar vocabulary of emotions; precisely what those emotions mean is shaped by social interactions and cultural norms.

References

Abraham, E., Hendler, T., Zagoory-Sharon, O., & Feldman, R. (2019). Interoception sensitivity in the parental brain during the first months of parenting modulates children's somatic symptoms six years later: the role of oxytocin. *International Journal of Psychophysiology*, 136, 39–48.

Ainsworth, M. D. & Bell, S. M. (1970). Attachment, exploration, and separation: Illustrated by the behavior of one-year-olds in a strange situation. *Child Development*, 41(1), 49–67.

Araujo, J. R., Keating, E., & Martel, F. (2015). Impact of gestational diabetes mellitus in the maternal-to-fetal transport of nutrients. *Current Diabetes Reports*, 15, 569.

Beckett, C., Maughan, B., Rutter, M., et al. (2006). Do the effects of early severe deprivation on cognition persist into early adolescence? Findings from the English and Romanian Adoptees Study. *Child Development*, 77(3), 696–711.

Bowlby, J. (1969). *Attachment and Loss*. Basic Books.

Campos, J. J., Bertenthal, B. I., & Kermoian, R. (1992). Early experience and emotional development: the emergence of wariness of heights. *Psychological Science*, 3(1), 61–64.

Carlson, E. A., Hostinar, C. E., Mliner, S. B., & Gunnar, M.R. (2014). The emergence of attachment following early social deprivation. *Development and Psychopathology*, 26(2), 479–489.

Cashdan, E. (1994). A sensitive period for learning about food. *Human Nature (Hawthorne, N.Y.)*, 5(3), 279–291.

Chang, L., Lu, H. J., Lansford, J. E., et al. (2019). Environmental harshness and unpredictability, life history, and social and academic behavior of adolescents in nine countries. *Developmental Psychology*, 55(4), 890–903.

Chen, X. (2012). Culture, peer interaction, and socioemotional development. *Child Development Perspectives*, 6, 27–34.

Cole, P. M., Bruschi, C. J., & Tamang, B. L. (2002). Cultural differences in children's emotional reactions to difficult situations. *Child Development*, 73, 983–996.

Darwin, C. (1872). *The Expression of the Emotions in Man and Animals*, 1st edition John Murray: London.

de Rosnay, M., Cooper, P. J., Tsigaras, N., & Murray, L. (2006). Transmission of social anxiety from mother to infant: an experimental study using a social referencing paradigm. *Behaviour research and therapy*, 44(8), 1165–1175.

Del Giudice, M. (2009). Sex, attachment, and the development of reproductive strategies. *Behavioral and Brain Sciences*, 32(1), 1–21.

Dunn, J. (2004). *Children's Friendships: The Beginnings of Intimacy*. Blackwell Publishing.

Ellis, B. J., Figueredo, A. J., Brumbach, B. H., & Schlomer, G. L. (2009). Fundamental dimensions of environmental risk: the impact of harsh versus unpredictable environments on the evolution and development of life history strategies. *Human Nature*, 20, 204–268.

Frankenhuis, W. E., Panchanathan, K., & Nettle, D. (2016). Cognition in harsh and unpredictable environments. *Current Opinion in Psychology*, 7, 76–80.

Galef, B. (1987). Social influences on the identification of toxic foods by Norway rats. *Animal Learning and Behaviour*, 15, 327–332.

Gettler, L. T., McDade, T. W., Feranil, A. B., & Kuzawa, C. W. (2011). Longitudinal evidence that fatherhood decreases testosterone in human males. *Proceedings of the National Academy of Sciences of the United States of America*, 108(39), 16194–16199.

Gerhardt, S. (2015). *Why Love Matters: How Affection Shapes a Baby's Brain*. Routledge.

Glocker, M. L., Langleben, D. D., Ruparel, K., et al. (2009). Baby schema modulates the reward system in nulliparous women. *Proceedings of the National Academy of Sciences of the United States of America*, 106, 9115–9119.

Golle, J., Probst, F., Mast, F. W., & Lobmaier, J. S. (2015). Preference for cute infants does not depend on their ethnicity or species: evidence from hypothetical adoption and donation paradigms. *PLoS ONE*, 10, e0121554.

Gopnik, A. (2016). *The Gardener and the Carpenter*. Vintage Publishing.

Hahn, A. C., Xiao, D., Sprengelmeyer, R., & Perrett, D. I. (2013). Gender differences in the incentive salience of adult and infant faces. *Quarterly Journal of Experimental Psychology*, 66(1), 200–208.

Harlow, H. F., Dodsworth, R. O., & Harlow, M. K. (1965). Total social isolation in monkeys. *Proceedings of the National Academy of Sciences of the United States of America*, 54(1), 90–97.

Hassett, B. (2022). *Growing Up Human: The Evolution of Childhood*. Bloomsbury.

Hill, K. & Kaplan, H. (1999). Life history traits in humans: theory and empirical studies. *Annual Review of Anthropology*, 28(1), 397–430.

Hostinar, C. E., Johnson, A. E., & Gunnar, M. R. (2015). Early social deprivation and the social buffering of cortisol stress responses in late childhood: an experimental study. *Developmental Psychology*, 51(11), 1597–1608.

Hrdy, S. B. (1999). *Mother Nature*. Pantheon.

Hrdy, S. B. & Burkart J. (2020). The emergence of emotionally modern humans: implications for language and learning. *Philosophical Transactions of the Royal Society of London. Series B, Biological Sciences*, 375, 20190499.

Jurkovic, D. & Kuhan, R. (2020). Early pregnancy failure. In P. P. Pandya, D. Oepkes, N. J. Sebire, & R. J. Wapner (eds.), *Fetal Medicine*, 3rd edition (pp. 38–46.e3). Elsevier.

Khaleque, A. & Ali, S. (2017). A systematic review of meta-analyses of research on interpersonal acceptance–rejection theory: constructs and measures. *Journal of Family Theory & Review*, 9(4), 441–458.

Konner, M. (1972). Aspects of the foraging ecology of a foraging people. In N. Blurton-Jones (ed.), *Ethological Studies of Child Behavior* (pp. 285–304). Cambridge University Press.

Konner, M. (2010). *The Evolution of Childhood: Relationships, Emotions, Mind*. Belknap Press.

Kringelbach, M., Stark, E., Alexander, C., Bornstein, M., & Stein, A. (2016). On cuteness: unlocking the parental brain and beyond. *Trends in Cognitive Sciences*, 20(7), 545–558.

Kuzawa, C. W., Chugani, H. T., Grossman, L. I., et al. (2014). Metabolic costs and evolutionary implications of human brain development. *Proceedings of the National Academy of Sciences of the United States of America*, 111, 13010–13015.

Lorenz, K. (1935). Der Kumpan in der Umwelt des Vogels. Der Artgenosse als auslösendes Moment sozialer Verhaltensweisen. *Journal für Ornithologie*, 83, 137–215, 289–413.

Lumey, L. H., Ekamper, P., Bijwaard, G., et al. (2021). Overweight and obesity at age 19 after pre-natal famine exposure. *International Journal of Obesity*, 45, 1668–1676.

Merz, E. C. & McCall, R. B. (2010). Behavior problems in children adopted from psychosocially depriving institutions. *Journal of Abnormal Child Psychology*, 38(4), 459–470.

Naber, F. B., Poslawsky, I. E., van Ijzendoorn, M. H., van Engeland, H., & Bakermans-Kranenburg, M. J. (2013). Brief report: oxytocin enhances paternal sensitivity to a child with autism: a double-blind within-subject experiment with intranasally administered oxytocin. *Journal of Autism and Development Disorders*, 43(1), 224–229.

Obradović, J., Bush, N. R., Stamperdahl, J., Adler, N. E., & Boyce, W. T. (2010). Biological sensitivity to context: the interactive effects of stress reactivity and family adversity on socioemotional behavior and school readiness. *Child Development*, 81(1), 270–289.

Peterson, C., Nagy, K., & Diamond, J. (1990). Sustained metabolic scope. *Proceedings of the National Academy of Sciences of the United States of America*, 87, 2324–2328.

Pinker, S. (1997). *How the Mind Works*. W. W. Norton & Co.

Quinlan, R. J. (2007). Human parental effort and environmental risk. *Proceedings of the Royal Society B*, 274, 121–125.

Richter, D., Krämer, M., Tang, N., Montgomery-Downs, H., & Lemola, S. (2019). Long-term effects of pregnancy and childbirth on sleep satisfaction and duration of first-time and experienced mothers and fathers. *Sleep*, 42(4), zsz015.

Riem, M. M., Bakermans-Kranenburg, M. J., Pieper, S., et al. (2011). Oxytocin modulates amygdala, insula, and inferior frontal gyrus responses to infant crying: a randomized controlled trial. *Biological Psychiatry*, 70(3), 291–297.

Roberts, G., Bahnson, H. T., Du Toit, G., et al. (2023). Defining the window of opportunity and target populations to prevent peanut allergy. *Journal of Allergy and Clinical Immunology*, 151(5), 1329–1336.

Roser, M., Ritchie, H., & Dadonaite, B. (2019). Child and infant mortality. *Our World in Data*. https://ourworldindata.org/child-mortality

Röttger-Rössler, B., Scheidecker, G., Jung, S., & Holodynski, M. (2013). Socializing emotions in childhood: a cross-cultural comparison between the bara in Madagascar and the Minangkabau in Indonesia. *Mind, Culture, and Activity*, 20(3), 260–287.

Schaal, B., Marlier, L., & Soussignan, R. (2000). Human foetuses learn odours from their pregnant mother's diet. *Chemical Senses*, 25(6), 729–737.

Scrimshaw, S. (1984). Infanticide in human populations: social and individual concerns. In G. Hausfater & S. B. Hrdy (eds.), *Infanticide: Comparative and Evolutionary Perspectives* (pp. 419–462). Aldine de Gruyter.

Sheridan, M. A., Fox, N. A., Zeanah, C. H., McLaughlin, K. A., & Nelson, C. A., 3rd (2012). Variation in neural development as a result of exposure to institutionalization early in childhood. *Proceedings of the National Academy of Sciences of the United States of America*, 109(32), 12927–12932.

Susskind, J. M., Lee, D. H., Cusi, A., Feiman, R., Grabski, W., & Anderson, A. K. (2008). Expressing fear enhances sensory acquisition. *Nature Neuroscience*, 11, 843–850.

Spitz, R. A. (1945). Hospitalism – an inquiry into the genesis of psychiatric conditions in early childhood. *Psychoanalytic Study of the Child*, 1, 53–74.

Tanner, J. (1978). *Foetus into Man: Physical Growth from Conception to Maturity*. Open Books.

Trevarthen, C. (1979). Communication and cooperation in early infancy: a description of primary intersubjectivity. In M. Bullowa (ed.), *Before Speech: The Beginning of Interpersonal Communication* (pp. 321–347). Cambridge University Press.

Van Duuren, M., Kendell-Scott, L., & Stark, N. (2003). Early aesthetic choices: infant preferences for attractive premature infant faces. *International Journal of Behavioral Development*, 27(3), 212–219.

Weir, K. (2014). The lasting impact of neglect. *American Psychological Society*, 45(6). www.apa.org/monitor/2014/06/neglect

Winnicott, D. W. (1965). The theory of the parent–infant relationship. In *The Maturational Processes and the Facilitating Environment* (pp. 37–55). International Universities Press.

3 ARE CHILDREN MIND READERS?

 Learning Outcomes

After reading this chapter you will be able to:

- Describe what theory of mind is and how it develops.
- Understand the importance of theory of mind for children's later development.
- Consider the implications of theory of mind for collaboration and human uniqueness.

3.1 Introduction

Imagine you lose your child at the supermarket. Unable to communicate with them, you go back to where you last saw them because you hope they will have the same idea as you. Your child reasons in the same way and you are reunited. Although an everyday example, the ability for two people to read each other's mind in this way has some big consequences for child development and even for the way our species evolved.

Across the tree of life, humans stand out for their extraordinary ability to infer what is going on in the minds of others, and in particular to understand how others have beliefs that may be different from their own. This mind-reading ability gives us an advantage when it comes to cooperating with, competing with, communicating with, and learning from others. It might be one reason why we have such long childhoods and outsized brains compared with other species (Dunbar, 1998). Across 27 different primate species, including humans, anthropologist Tracey Joffe found that the bigger the brain, the larger the social group and the longer the juvenile period tended to be (1997). When it comes to humans, some societies may be technologically more advanced than others, but there are no simple social societies. From the urban dwellers of San Francisco to the foragers of the Kalahari Desert, human relationships are always complex.

In the previous chapter we saw how infants seek out social information from a very early age, directing their attention towards voices and faces, making eye contact, and forming an emotional bond with caregivers. In this chapter we explore this motivation to engage with others in much greater depth. How do children begin to understand the complex inner worlds of other people, and what impact does this have on their later development?

3.2 Theory of Mind

We assume other people might have minds like we do so that we can make sense of their behaviour. Why is that man on his knees looking under a car? He *wants* to find his keys, he *believes* he dropped them there, and he *knows* they will open the car. We imagine what might be motivating other people in order to help us predict how we and other people might act. Without these intuitive theories, human behaviour appears like a random walk, and it would make social interaction a confusing experience. We think about other people's minds all the time, from outwitting someone on the sports field, to understanding the plot of a movie, to negotiating with a toddler that it's time to go to bed (**Figure 3.1**).

The insight that other people have private psychological worlds has a profound effect on development. When infants grasp this, they learn the difference between living things and objects: people feel, perceive, and think; objects don't. They begin to use social cues such as eye contact, body movements, tone of voice, and facial expressions to understand other people's intentions. Eventually, this ability matures into understanding that other people are capable of desires, knowledge, and beliefs that might be different from their own.

Figure 3.1 The ability to see the world from another person's perspective often requires simulating their beliefs, desires, and knowledge. Source: Cartoonstock.

Acquiring intentionality and recognising intentionality in others have all sorts of cognitive, social, and even legal consequences later on in life. For example, although young infants can cause harm to others, we tend not to hold them accountable for it, as aggression requires some intention to cause harm. By eventually sharing intentions, goals, and desires with others, children accomplish ever more complex forms of cooperation: giving and taking objects, rolling a ball back and forth, building a block tower together, putting away toys together, pretend games of eating and drinking, pointing-and-naming games, going for a walk together. The ability to achieve all of this is made possible by a **theory of mind** (ToM).

Key Point

- ToM is the capacity to picture the world from another person's point of view; what they see, know, want, desire, or believe.

ToM is sometimes referred to as a 'meta-cognitive skill' because it essentially involves thinking about thinking. In principle there is no limit to how many times we can nest one of these thoughts inside another: 'I *know* that you *think* that she *believes* ...' and so on. However, for infants learning to get their first foothold within this complex system, things start simpler.

3.3 Basic ToM

Around 9 months of age, infants begin to show basic ToM abilities. They understand that other people might have intentions or goals of their own and that they might have a different perspective on the world than they do. But even before this basic ToM ability develops, infants are busy working out that they have intentions *themselves*. Around 6 months of age, infants start to realise that they can use an object as a means to get another object: 31% of 6-month-olds intentionally use an object to retrieve a toy in comparison with 19% of infants who show no such desire. By 8 months, 69% of infants intentionally use the object, with only 6% showing no interest (Willatts, 1999). By exploring the world in this way, infants are developing their own playbook of goals and the means to achieve them. They begin to understand there are multiple ways to achieve the same goal and several goals corresponding to one means. For example, the exact same pattern of physical movements (means) involved in putting a cup on a piece of paper could achieve the goal of using the glass as a paperweight, putting a tired arm down, giving the glass away, signalling desire for another drink, and so on. They can only be thought of *as* different if we think about the goals and intentions behind the actions.

To test how infants think about *other people's* intentions, developmental psychologist Tanye Behne and her colleagues recorded the reactions of 6–18-month-olds in three different situations (Behne et al., 2005). Sometimes an experimenter handed the infants a toy, and all was well. Other times the experimenter didn't hand over the toy, because they were *unwilling* – for example, they teased the child with it or played with it themselves. On yet other occasions they were *unable* to give it over – for example, they accidentally dropped it. Infants who were 9, 12, or 18 months of age reacted with more impatience (e.g., reaching, looking away) when the adult was unwilling to give them the toy than when they were simply unable to give it. Six-month-olds, in contrast, reacted similarly to both conditions. To appreciate the difference between what was accidental and what wasn't, infants needed some mental model of what the experimenter was trying to do, or their *intentions*. Because the older groups reacted differently on the basis of the adult's intentions but the younger age group didn't, this study – along with others – provides evidence that infants begin to understand others' intentions by around 9 months of age.

 Key Point

- By around 9 months of age, infants show a basic ToM ability, understanding that other people pursue their own goals and can have a different perspective on the world than they do.

3.4 Early Social Interaction

To realise others *have* intentions, infants obviously need regular interaction *with* others, and an important social setting in which these exchanges take place is the dyad, which, with two people in it, is by definition the smallest possible group. In the previous chapter we saw how proto-conversations (i.e., back-and-forth exchanges of emotional smiles, mirroring of behaviour, touches, and vocalisations) and attachment (i.e., a special emotional bond) emerge from this early social context.

A new level of perspective-taking is achieved when infants learn to *share* perceptions and intentions with another person. To do this, both carers and infants must understand each other's role in achieving a common goal and be able to dovetail their actions to achieve this – for example, completing a jigsaw together, building a block tower together, or holding a conversation. This **shared intentionality** is kept on track by monitoring the goal-directed behaviour and perceptions of the partner, with cues such as eye contact, gaze-following, and tone of voice helping infants establish when information is intended for them and when it is not (Grossmann et al., 2006). When children are young, shared intentionality is often played out in highly contextualised, often routinised, mutually understood social situations such as at feeding and changing times, reading a book, taking a walk, or playing a game of peekaboo. With both partners now sharing attention and coordinating their actions to a shared goal, infants have moved from simple dyadic to triadic interaction (**Figure 3.2**).

These early social interactions can act as a training ground for learning about the mental lives of others. For example, the more parents talk to their children about the mental states of others ('she wants …', 'he believes …', 'they know …'), the more proficient children become at ToM, and parents who are more competent at identifying and responding appropriately to the thoughts and feelings of their children ('mind-minded' or sensitive parents in attachment theory) have children with higher ToM proficiency (Aldrich et al., 2021; Meins

Figure 3.2 (A) Dyadic interaction characterised by back-and-forth, face-to-face turn-taking episodes between the caregiver and infant, expressing a sense of shared experience. **(B)** Triadic interaction characterised by the shared attention of both participants on an object or referent of mutual interest in a 'referential triangle'. Source: graytown /iStock/Getty Images Plus (a); Ground Picture / Shutterstock (b).

et al., 2002). It has also been shown that having a brother or sister increases the opportunities to practice the skills of ToM, as siblings try to empathise with, manipulate, compete with, and cooperate with one another. So, you don't have to have a brother or sister to acquire ToM, but it can help accelerate its development (Devine & Hughes, 2018).

It seems like these basic early social interactions are present in all cultures, but the specific structure and frequency of these interactions may be quite different. For example, Andrea Taverna and her colleagues compared how mothers interacted with their 1–2-year-olds in the indigenous Wichi community living in Argentina's Chaco Forest and in Euro-descendant Spanish-speaking families living in Argentina (Taverna et al., 2024). Their study showed the similarity between communities in the proportion of time infants spent alone or in mother–child interaction. What did differ, however, was *how* mothers engaged in these interactions: Wichi mothers spend a greater proportion of their time observing their infants than do Euro-descendant mothers. Moreover, when infants in both groups are alone, their focus in their 'solitary' activities differed: Wichi infants engaged primarily in observation when alone, whereas Euro-descendant infants were more focused on objects. All mother–child pairs engaged in dyadic and triadic interactions, but among Wichi, mothers actively 'watched' infants as they engaged with objects, whereas Euro-descendant mothers actively engaged with their infants in joint attentional episodes.

Compared to some Western societies, many parents in traditional cultures have very little free time to engage in 'non-productive' play and triadic interaction, and so it is the children who are expected to adapt to the adults' world of work, and not the adults who are expected to adapt to the child's world of play. In societies where mothers carry their infants most of the day as they go about their work, face-to-face interaction with infants is less common and is limited to contexts of feeding and cleaning, or else adults will simply give the infant an object or place an object in front of the infant and then go about their business. Through a combination of varying opportunities and motivations for dyadic and triadic interactions, these episodes can look different across cultures. Nevertheless, even young children will naturally experience some spells of joint attention with adults as a result of common kinds of experiences such as offering food, warning about dangerous objects, social games, pointing and naming, and mutual play with objects (Callaghan et al., 2011). We will return to the idea of cross-cultural variability when we look at children's ToM development across the world in Chapter 6.

Key Point

- Dyadic and triadic social interactions are important contexts in which children learn about the minds of others.

3.5 Advanced ToM

We have seen that by around 9 months of age infants typically experience something of a social revolution: they understand that other people can see different things or can pursue different goals from them. At around 4 years of age they are set for another transformation in their understanding. They develop a much more advanced form of ToM that allows them to hold mutually incompatible beliefs and to understand that beliefs can be false. The difference between basic and more advanced ToM abilities is demonstrated by the shift from level 1 perspective-taking to level 2 perspective-taking (**Figure 3.3**).

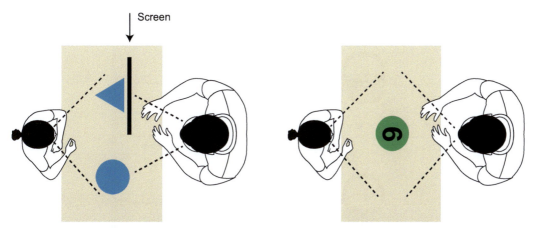

Figure 3.3 In level 1 perspective-taking, the child (left-hand side of the table) knows that the adult can only see the circle, as the triangle is hidden from them by a screen. In level 2 perspective-taking, the child understands that other people can see *the same scene* differently, in this case as a number '6' for the child or a number '9' from the adult's perspective. Adapted from Rakoczy (2022). Source: Adapted from Rakoczy, H. Foundations of theory of mind and its development in early childhood. Nature reviews / Psychology.

Beliefs are the test case for advanced ToM because they require children to coordinate someone's attitude to the facts and the facts themselves. This is complex enough when the facts and reality align, but as we all know, beliefs can be wrong. In these cases, not only do children need to track what they know, they also need to coordinate this with the fact that someone else is wrong about what they know, or has a so-called false belief. Before you read further, see how your ToM performs on the now-classic Sally–Anne test (**Figure 3.4**).

Figure 3.4 The Sally–Anne test (Wimmer & Perner, 1983). Source: Blackwells.

Children who have been able to track what Sally knows and answer *as if they were* Sally will understand that she falsely believes the marble will be in her basket. Children who are unable to dissociate themselves from what they know to be true are more likely to respond as if Sally also believes what they know. The crucial question is: 'where will Sally look for her marble?' Children under the age of 4 systematically answer 'in the box', but at around 4 years of age children begin to be able to put themselves in Sally's position, empathise with what she knows and doesn't know, and answer 'in the basket'. For those who reasonably point out 'Sally doesn't think anything, she's a doll' there is the Smarties Test, which assesses the same mind-reading logic but with non-thinking props. You know that the Smarties in a Smarties tube have been replaced with pencils. What will someone else, who hasn't seen the Smarties being replaced, think is in the tube?

As well as understanding false beliefs, around this time children also start to achieve level 2 perspective-taking (**Figure 3.3**) and to pass appearance–reality tasks (Gopnik & Astington, 1988). In these tasks children are presented with an object that looks different from what it really is, such as a rubber eraser that looks like a walnut. When asked, 'What does the object look like and what is it really?' children younger than 4 years of age tend to answer according to what the object is for, saying, 'It's a rubber eraser and looks like a rubber eraser.' But from around 4 years of age onwards children can acknowledge that appearances aren't the same thing as reality, saying, 'It's a rubber eraser, but it looks like a walnut.' This ability to hold two conflicting views of the world in mind at the same time is a hallmark of more advanced perspective-taking and ToM: 'This is both a walnut and a rubber eraser,' 'This is both a number 6 and a number 9,' 'The marble is in the box for me but in the basket for Sally.' In Chapter 16 we explore how some autistic children[1] have different perspective-taking skills from those demonstrated by non-autistic children in the Sally–Anne task.

Key Point
• By around 4 years of age, infants develop a more advanced ToM ability, being able to hold mutually incompatible ideas about other people's beliefs, their own knowledge, and reality.

Desires and beliefs.
Using two different experiments, psychologist and philosopher Alison Gopnik shows how children of different ages think about the minds of others.

---

[1] The language we use to describe people should respect their dignity and autonomy. Ideally, we should ask the people we are interacting with how they would like to be addressed. Unfortunately, this is not an available option here, so as a substitute I have been guided by a survey of 3,470 members of the UK autism community who preferred the term 'autistic person' over 'person with autism', which is the phrase I have adopted here (Kenny et al., 2016). The same survey also noted that there is no single way of describing autism that is universally accepted and preferred.

3.6 The Effects of ToM on Later Development

Acquiring ToM has far-reaching social consequences: if I understand you as sharing the same psychological vocabulary as me, I have an easier time relating empathetically to you. Having ToM also allows us to share views on the world, talk to one another, and criticise and cooperate with one another. More generally, ToM has been shown to have a significant effect on children's later development in the following ways:

- ToM ability is related to children's peer social skills in early and middle childhood, such as leadership, joining new groups, welcoming new members into groups, and standing up for one's own opinions in exchanges with peers (Peterson et al., 2016).
- Children who are more advanced in their ToM ability have been found to have better communicative competence, specifically tailoring their arguments and persuasive techniques to address their conversation partners' points of view (Peterson et al., 2018).
- Children with more advanced ToM ability tend to be rated as more likeable and popular among their peers (Slaughter et al., 2015).

These relationships are all of the type 'x is associated y', a method explored further in the following One-Minute Method.

Watch the One-Minute Method.

Discover how researchers use relationships between factors to understand child development.

Any powerful tool can be used for good or bad, and ToM is no different. Children can use ToM for **prosocial** ends – that is, behaviour intended for the benefit of others such as sharing, helping, caring, or acts of kindness. Or it can be used for more selfish and manipulative ends – for example, the aggressive behaviour of some playground bullies might depend upon their sophisticated ToM functioning, and advanced ToM reasoning enables children to engage in more sophisticated acts of deception such as lying (Ding et al., 2015; Gasser & Keller, 2009). However, in general, children who are more proficient at ToM tasks tend to act more prosocially, offer more comfort to others, and act more empathetically and cooperatively (Imuta et al., 2016). Currently we don't know why some children put their higher ToM abilities towards more prosocial ends and some put them towards more selfish ones, but this is a question researchers are trying to answer.

 Key Point

- Acquiring ToM has far-reaching social consequences for children's development.

3.7 What Is ToM for?

Clearly ToM is a significant part of the human experience and has important consequences for how children develop. But what is it for? Earlier we raised the idea that ToM gives us an advantage when it comes to cooperating, competing, and communicating with and learning from others. Let's look at cooperation in a little more detail by noting that much of what humans do is **mutualistic**; that is, what is good for you is also good for me. For example, when we trade goods you might benefit from my surplus of wheat while I benefit from your surplus of wine: it's a win–win. These mutualistic relationships involve a kind of alchemy that is more than the sum of its parts: two people can carry a piano up a flight of stairs, but neither of them can carry half a piano on their own. The challenge in these situations is for would-be collaborators to coordinate their actions so that they can achieve their goal together, and ToM plays a key role in this.

Comparative psychologist (someone who studies the psychology of different species) Shona Duguid and her colleagues investigated how children solve a simple coordination problem (Duguid et al., 2020). She tested 40 4-year-olds by sitting them in pairs in front a of puzzle box that had a set of 4 buttons for one child and 4 buttons for the other. When both children pressed the same button (e.g., the endmost one), the puzzle box would release red balls that rolled down a tube into a 'pling machine', producing a pleasant sound. The balls would only be released if both children coordinated their response and pressed the same button. Shona also gave the equivalent test to chimpanzees, although instead of the pling machine the chimps were rewarded with a grape (chimps are highly motivated by grapes). Why also test chimps? Some scientists have argued that the degree to which humans cooperate with each other is unique in the natural world. By studying how our closest living relatives behave in comparison to how we behave we can better understand what we share and what makes us unique (see **Box 3.1**).

In the experiment, both species were able to coordinate their responses to get a grape or make the pling machine play music. However, there were marked differences in the ways they did so. The children were able to coordinate quickly and flexibly, adjusting easily to new collaborative partners, thereby suggesting an understanding of the coordination process. Children were more likely than chimpanzees to communicate with each other about the task with a verbal or gestural reference to a specific choice – for example, saying 'here' while pointing to the button they had or were about to choose.

You might object that this wasn't fair on the chimps, as they don't have language to use as a coordination option. However, it is not the case that chimpanzees cannot coordinate their actions with others. Wild chimpanzees do this regularly: when they are hunting in groups, when patrolling the border of their territory, or when faced with intergroup conflicts. So, while chimpanzees can coordinate with each other in their environment, they seem to have particular difficulty coordinating their decisions with each other – a skill at which humans seem to excel. In the experiment, the few times in which the chimps did communicate, they used general gestural attention-getters but did not refer to which button to press specifically – for example, noisily knocking on the wire mesh between the cages while waiting for their partner to make their decision after having already made their own choice. In general, the chimpanzees took a longer time to converge on a coordinated button choice and did not get any better at coordination across partners. This suggests that their coordination was based only on repeating successful past choices – for example, converging to a single set of buttons rather than flexibly switching between them.

Although the children communicated substantially more often than the chimpanzees, 40% of the child pairs did not use verbal or gestural communication but were still highly successful at coordinating their button presses. In these cases, children often used a leader–follower strategy, in which one partner waits for the other to act first and then follows their lead or possibly uses more subtle cues such as eye gaze.

In summary, this study and others like it suggest children engage with their peers to solve coordination problems together even before making any choices, whereas chimpanzees seem to solve these problems more individualistically. The general point is this: if children have a ToM that allows them to picture the world from another person's point of view – what they see, know, want, desire, and believe – it is going to be easier for them to coordinate their actions with others. Recall that the children in this experiment were 4 years old, an age at which we know more advanced ToM and perspective-taking abilities are kicking in (**Figure 3.3**).

Taking a step back from pling machines and chimpanzees, imagine any complex cooperative endeavour that requires input from multiple people, such as building a bridge. To be successful it requires everyone playing their part at the right time: 'You raise that end of the log while I slide this stone here, then those others can tie that rope there,' and so on. In this context, communication allows people to make their intentions public. When you know what I want and I know what you want, it is a lot easier to coordinate these perspectives towards a common goal than if we keep this information private (Ibbotson et al., 2022). Imagine trying to build a bridge or coordinate any complex activity with a group of people who either couldn't share their intentions or weren't motivated to align their intensions towards a common goal. It would put an upper limit on the ambition of what we could achieve together. The 'meeting of minds' that ToM allows has big consequences when multiplied by the billions of people on the planet today and played out over the thousands of generations humans have existed. It underpins the cultural fabric of our lives, and without it many of our most human of achievements – law, government, trade, education, language – would not be possible.

 Key Point

- ToM helps people coordinate their intensions towards common goals and allows complex cooperation.

 Box 3.1 ToM in the natural world

We have seen how ToM can support collaboration, and that humans are exceptional in the natural world not only in the extent of these collaborations but also in the variety of forms they can take (Rakoczy, 2022). But is ToM uniquely human? Whenever scientists propose something unique about the minds of humans (ToM, culture, language) it usually provokes other scientists to look for fragments of that ability in other species, sometimes revealing that we are not so special after all. Decades of such research on ToM has revealed that other apes and even some birds may have some basic form of ToM, such as appreciating that others have goals, but they tend to lack the advanced ToM of a 4-year-old human child, such as understanding false beliefs (Martin & Santos, 2016). It seems our nearest living evolutionary relatives are essentially stuck at the 9-month-old human stage of ToM. This may be related to what they are using their ToM *for*. Non-human primates tend to use their basic ToM mainly for competing with and manipulating others rather than also for communication or cooperation, as children do. For example, in primates, grooming not only has benefits for the one being groomed; the groomer also benefits from reduced stress, and because such grooming is reciprocated, they benefit from reduced parasites too. When primates console others, they are likely to receive less aggression themselves; and when apes do share food, it tends to be that they have been harassed into doing so or else the food has been begged for by others. Two chimpanzees spontaneously cooperating to carry a log or working together to fashion a tool are very unlikely events (Tomasello et al., 2005). So, it seems humans have both the motivation to see collaborative opportunities where other species might see only competitive ones and the cognitive ability, with ToM, to allow us to put those motivations into practice.

Talking Point

Precisely when ToM emerges in children's development is still widely debated among researchers. This is because estimates of when a capacity emerges in development depend partly on how we measure it. For instance, we can ask children, 'Where do you think Sally will look for her marble?' and then record what they say (e.g., 'in the box'), or where they gesture (e.g., pointing at the box), or even where they look (e.g., their eye gaze focuses on the box longer than the basket) – we will explore this looking time method further in Chapter 6 when we explore false beliefs across cultures. Each one of these methods places different demands on children. For example, looking requires less effort than pointing, which requires less effort than speaking. Not all of this effort is associated with ToM, however; for example, a spoken response might require a child to know something general about the who-did-what-to-whom of grammar. We need to be cautious, therefore, about the timeline of development; it might not just be the development of ToM we are measuring, but also the ability to meet the demands of the test.

In general, the lower the demands of the test, the earlier we have been able to establish the existence of a ToM ability. For example, by carefully recording where infants look and for how long, researchers have found evidence that quite sophisticated aspects of ToM, like false belief understanding, are present from a much earlier age than we traditionally thought (Onishi & Baillargeon, 2005; Southgate et al., 2007). These measures can be controversial though, as the more 'implicit' the test becomes, the more inferences we make about what children know. Do we consider a child looking at the correct answer to be as strong a piece of evidence as them saying the correct answer? Sometimes the same child, in the same test, can give different answers depending on which method we use. To reach a consensus on these kinds of issues, researchers across the world have established large-scale, collaborative ventures like the ManyBabies project (https://manybabies.org). This global consortium of researchers aims to test theories of infant development across a wider range of ages, experiences, languages, and cultural backgrounds than a single team of researchers ever could. By sharing their results and being more transparent about their methods, the researchers want to establish which findings can be consistently replicated across different contexts.

In general, the relative ordering of abilities (e.g., basic ToM before advanced ToM) is less controversial than the absolute time of acquisition (ability x emerges at time point y). Where any particular skill falls on the timeline of development is much more likely to change subject to the methods we use and the technologies we invent to test it. For example, eye gaze trackers represent a comparatively recent innovation, and it's unknown how the next technological advance will alter our understanding of the developmental timeline. It is important to note that this feature of research is not specific to ToM but is of significance to child development more generally.

Key Point

- When a capacity is estimated to emerge in development partly depends on how we measure it.

Summary

- ToM is the capacity to picture the world from another person's point of view; what they see, know, want, desire, or believe.
- By around 9 months of age, infants show a basic ToM ability, understanding that other people pursue their own goals and can have a different perspective on the world than they do.
- Dyadic and triadic social interactions are important contexts in which children learn about the minds of others.
- By around 4 years of age, infants develop a more advanced ToM ability, being able to hold mutually incompatible ideas about other people's beliefs, their own knowledge, and reality.
- Acquiring ToM has far-reaching social consequences for children's development.
- ToM helps people coordinate their intensions towards common goals and allows complex cooperation.
- When a capacity is estimated to emerge in development partly depends on how we measure it.

References

Aldrich, N. J., Chen, J., & Alfieri, L. (2021). Evaluating associations between parental mind-mindedness and children's developmental capacities through meta-analysis. *Developmental Review*, 60, 100946.

Behne, T., Carpenter, M., Call, J., & Tomasello, M. (2005). Unwilling versus unable: infants' understanding of intentional action. *Developmental Psychology*, 41(2), 328–337.

Callaghan, T., Moll, H., Rakoczy, H., Warneken, F., Liszkowski, U., Behne, T., & Tomasello, M. (2011). Early social cognition in three cultural contexts. *Monographs of the Society for Research in Child Development*, 76(2), vii–viii, 1–142.

Devine, R. T. & Hughes, C. (2018). Family correlates of false belief understanding in early childhood: a meta-analysis. *Child Development*, 89, 971–987.

Ding, X. P., Wellman, H. M., Wang, Y., Fu, G., & Lee, K. (2015). Theory-of-mind training causes honest young children to lie. *Psychological Science*, 26, 1812–1821.

Duguid, S., Wyman, E., Grueneisen, S., & Tomasello, M. (2020). The strategies used by chimpanzees (*Pan troglodytes*) and children (*Homo sapiens*) to solve a simple coordination problem. *Journal of Comparative Psychology*, 134(4), 401–411.

Dunbar, R. I. M. (1998). The social brain hypothesis. *Evolutionary Anthropology*, 6, 178–190.

Gasser, L. & Keller, M. (2009). Are the competent the morally good? Perspective taking and moral motivation of children involved in bullying. *Social Development*, 18, 798–816.

Gopnik, A. & Astington, J. W. (1988). Children's understanding of representational change and its relation to the understanding of false belief and the appearance–reality distinction. *Child Development*, 59, 26–37.

Grossmann, T., Striano, T., & Friederic, A. (2006). Crossmodal integration of emotional information from face and voice in the infant brain. *Developmental Science*, 9, 309–315.

Ibbotson, P., Jimenez-Romero, C., & Page, K. M. (2022). Dying to cooperate: the role of environmental harshness in human collaboration. *Behavioural Ecology*, 33(1), 190–201.

Imuta, K., Henry, J. D., Slaughter, V., Selcuk, B., & Ruffman, T. (2016). Theory of mind and prosocial behavior in childhood: a meta-analytic review. *Development Psychology*, 52, 1192–1205.

Joffe, T. H. (1997). Social pressures have selected for an extended juvenile period in primates. *Journal of Human Evolution*, 32, 593–605.

Kenny, L., Hattersley, C., Molins, B., Buckley, C., Povey, C., & Pellicano, E. (2016). Which terms should be used to describe autism? Perspectives from the UK autism community. *Autism*, 20(4), 442–462.

Martin, A. & Santos, L. R. (2016). What cognitive representations support primate theory of mind? *Trends in Cognitive Science*, 20, 375–382.

Meins, E., Fernyhough, C., Wainwright, R., et al. (2002). Maternal mind-mindedness and attachment security as predictors of theory of mind understanding. *Child Development*, 73, 1715–1726.

Onishi, K. H. & Baillargeon, R. (2005). Do 15-month-old infants understand false beliefs? *Science*, 308, 255–258.

Peterson, C., Slaughter, V., Moore, C., & Wellman, H. M. (2016). Peer social skills and theory of mind in children with autism, deafness, or typical development. *Developmental Psychology*, 52, 46–57.

Peterson, C. C., Slaughter, V., & Wellman, H. M. (2018). Nimble negotiators: how theory of mind (ToM) interconnects with persuasion skills in children with and without ToM delay. *Developmental Psychology*, 54, 494–509.

Rakoczy, H. (2022). Foundations of theory of mind and its development in early childhood. *Nature Reviews Psychology*, 1, 223–235.

Slaughter, V., Imuta, K., Peterson, C. C., & Henry, J. D. (2015). Meta-analysis of theory of mind and peer popularity in the preschool and early school years. *Child Development*, 86, 1159–1174.

Southgate, V., Senju, A., & Csibra, G. (2007). Action anticipation through attribution of false belief by 2-year-olds. *Psychological Science*, 18(7), 587–592.

Taverna, A., Padilla, M., & Waxman, S. (2024). How pervasive is joint attention? Mother–child dyads from a Wichi community reveal a different form of 'togetherness'. *Developmental Science*, 27, e13471.

Tomasello, M., Carpenter, M., Call, J., Behne, T., & Moll, H. (2005). Understanding and sharing intentions: the ontogeny and phylogeny of cultural cognition. *Behavioral and Brain Sciences*, 28, 675–735.

Willatts, P. (1999). Development of means–end behavior in young infants: pulling a support to retrieve a distant object. *Developmental Psychology*, 35(3), 651–667.

Wimmer, H. & Perner, J. (1983). Beliefs about beliefs: representation and constraining function of wrong beliefs in young children's understanding of deception. *Cognition*, 13(1), 103–128.

4 HOW DO CHILDREN LEARN LANGUAGE?

 Learning Outcomes

After reading this chapter you will be able to:
- Describe the challenges children face in learning language.
- Understand key features of child language development.
- Explain the strategies children use to learn sounds, words, and grammar.

4.1 Introduction

Despite language being an extraordinarily complex system of sounds, grammar, and meaning, children the world over have mastered many of its intricacies by their fifth birthday. In a few short years, children go from no language to babbling, to producing their first words, to stringing words together into sentences, to holding conversations and telling stories (Ibbotson, 2022). Children learn to use the power of language to form relationships, communicate their most personal thoughts, imagine the future, remember their past, and cooperate with others. The basic nuts and bolts of all these abilities are acquired in under 2,000 days, with a large proportion of that time spent asleep. Language is also the primary channel through which children learn about culture, and it is a powerful cultural tool in its own right.

By calculating back from the average adolescent's vocabulary, we can estimate that children must be learning about one new word every two waking hours from when they begin speaking. Contrast the apparent ease with which children learn language with the effort it takes to learn an additional language as an adult and this raises a question: how do children, who are generally thought to be less skilled and knowledgeable than adults, acquire such a complex system as language at such a young age? This chapter is about how children acquire that incredible aspect of our human nature.

4.2 Early Learning Centre

Language learning certainly begins early. At 35 weeks old, babies can already distinguish between different vowel sounds. That is not 35 weeks after birth, but 35 weeks after conception, while they are still inside the womb. The wall of the mother's abdomen and the amniotic fluid absorb the higher-range frequencies of speech coming from outside, reducing its volume by about a half. For that reason, prenatal infants hear vowels better, which are louder and of a lower pitch than consonants. By week 37 of pregnancy, prenatal babies show a preference not only to listening to their mother's voice but also towards any speaker of their native language (Kisilevsky et al., 2009).

Watch the One-Minute Method.

Discover how the familiarisation procedure, as used by Kisilevsky and colleagues, takes advantage of something young infants are really good at: getting bored.

In one study, shortly after birth babies were fitted with headphones and heard either a story their mothers had read to them twice a day for the last 6 weeks of pregnancy or an unfamiliar one. The babies could change the story they heard by either sucking faster or slower on a dummy in their mouths. Most new-borns sucked the dummy at a rate that caused them to hear the story they had heard in the womb (DeCasper & Spence, 1986). Impressively, this showed that, while only days old, these infants both recognised the story from the womb and were able to change their behaviour (sucking rate) in order to satisfy their preference for the familiar story.

In the first months of life babies are able to tell apart most if not all of the sounds of the world's languages – some 600 consonants and 200 vowels (Tsao et al., 2004). Despite being born equally able to learn any one of 7,000 different languages, infants soon home in on the language(s) they are exposed to, at the expense of those that they are not. Many studies have shown that young infants can distinguish a wider range of sounds than is present in their native language, but they lose this ability somewhere between 6 and 12 months of age (e.g., Werker & Tees, 1984). For example. Japanese-learning infants soon have trouble distinguishing between the English 'l' and 'r' – not an important distinction in Japanese, but it is in English. Likewise, English-learning infants soon have difficulty with Arabic sound ح, which is similar to the English 'h' but with a small puff of air released along with it – an important sound in Arabic, but not in English.

This narrowing of what sounds children respond to is another example of a **sensitive period** in development, first introduced in Chapter 2. It is as if children hedge their bets – that if they haven't heard examples of a particular language in the first 6–12 months, then there is a good chance it isn't a significant part of the culture they are born into, and so it's better to concentrate on learning a language that is. The effects of this early bet-hedging are not limited to language either. For example, Kelly and colleagues (2007) tested 3-, 6-, and 9-month-old infants' ability to distinguish faces within their own ethnic group (white Western) versus three other groups (African, Middle Eastern, and Chinese). The 3-month-olds could distinguish faces in all conditions, but by 6 months old this had narrowed to just white Western and Chinese faces, and by 9 months old successful differentiation was restricted to only their own ethnicity. The more general message is that in the first year of life children are involved in a significant period of sensitisation to their family and cultural surroundings, of which language forms a key part.

 Key Point

- Before birth and after, children are becoming sensitised to the sounds in their native language(s) and insensitive to those that are not.

4.3 Where Are the Words?

We are so familiar with seeing the spaces in written text and hearing a sequence of separate words that it is easy to forget that, in reality, speech is much more like a pulsing stream of sound. Sometimes the pauses in speech line up with the boundaries of words, but often they do not. This becomes apparent if we hear someone talking in a foreign language or if we represent language in a format like a spectrogram that more closely resembles the input to our ears. Have a look at **Figure 4.1** and see if you can figure out where the words are.

Neither the overall volume, the pauses, nor the acoustic frequencies are reliable cues to the word boundaries on their own, so how do children work out where the words are? It was not until relatively recently that we discovered that even very young infants are using sophisticated strategies to track how different cues combine and are distributed across speech in a process called **statistical learning** (Saffran et al., 1996). Consider the phrase 'ha-ppy-dogg-ie'. The basic idea is that infants are able to track how often the individual sounds 'ha' and 'ppy', 'ppy' and 'dogg', and 'dogg' and 'ie' occur together over all the speech they hear. The sounds 'ppy' and 'dogg' have a much lower probability of occurring together than do 'ha' and 'ppy', and so this might signal a boundary between words. Repeat this process over days, months, and years, for all the sounds in the language, and infants begin to understand where the words are. Experimentally, researchers have shown that infants are instinctively using strategies like these right from birth (e.g., Fló et al., 2019), and disruptions to statistical learning processes may underpin neurodiverse pathways of language use, such as developmental language disorder and dyslexia (explored further in Chapter 16; Saffran, 2018).

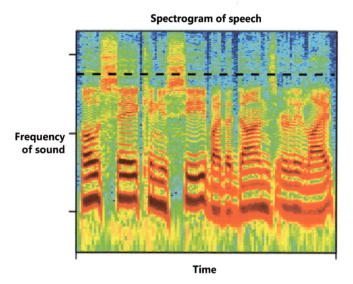

Figure 4.1 This spectrogram is a recording of a male saying, 'Oh say can you see by the dawn's early light.' Source: Monson BB, Hunter EJ, Lotto AJ and Story BH (2014) The perceptual significance of high-frequency energy in the human voice. Front. Psychol. 5:587. doi: 10.3389/fpsyg.2014.00587. This is an open-access article distributed under the terms of the Creative Commons Attribution License (CC BY). https://creativecommons.org/licenses/by/3.0/.

Children are remarkably adept at segmenting speech despite huge variation in the **phonology** of the world's languages – that is, the system of sounds they use. For example, Ubyx, once spoken around Turkey, had as few as two vowels; Rotokas, spoken in Papua New Guinea, has as few as six consonants; while !Xóō, a language with modern-day speakers in Botswana, has around 31 vowels and 77 consonants. Languages also show significant differences in what sounds they will allow to appear together. For example, 'žblnkn' or 'skrbstv' are not acceptable combinations in English, but they are in various Slavic languages – for example, *žblnknutie*, which means 'clunk' or 'flop', and *skrbstvo*, which means 'welfare'.

In one way, it is remarkable that children are born capable of acquiring all this diversity, indicating the incredible **plasticity** of early human development. In another way, it is perhaps less surprising. If the sounds were unlearnable by one generation of children, then they wouldn't be there in the language for the next generation of children to learn them. This flips things around from the way we usually think. Instead of just asking how children learn language, we should also ask how languages evolve to be learnable by children.

Compared with adult-to-adult speech, child-directed speech is much more likely to contain high levels of repetition and more words spoken in isolation, to have a slower rate of speaking, and to use a smaller range of words, all of which also helps children get an early foothold in their language. While this way of speaking to children might help scaffold their language development, it is far from universal, and it interacts with local childcare customs and parental beliefs. For example, Kokwet mothers from Kenya believe that children learn to talk more by listening to other children than their parents, and consequently they talk less to their 2- and 3-year-old children compared with American mothers (Super & Harkness, 1986).

 Key Points

- Children use powerful pattern detection skills to segment speech streams into words.
- Child-directed speech differs in important ways from adult-to-adult speech and has been shown to help language learning.

4.4 First Words

Let us have a look at the first words children produce across three languages. **Table 4.1** shows the common first words spoken by children around their first birthday, when they have between 1 and 10 words in their vocabulary.

As we can see, there are some similarities across languages – 6 of the top 20 words appear across all three languages, with further overlaps between any two of the others – as well as clear differences. Moving beyond the particular words children say, let us look at what *kinds* of words they use in their first utterances, as displayed in **Table 4.2**.

Table 4.1 Rank order of the top 20 words spoken by children who can say 1–10 words and the percentage of children producing them by language (in parentheses). All words have been translated into English equivalents where possible. Words in dark grey are common across all three languages, whereas words in light grey are common across two languages. Data reproduced from Tardif et al. (2008).

English (264 children)	Mandarin Chinese (367 children)	Cantonese Chinese (336 children)
Daddy (54)	Daddy (54)	Mommy (87)
Mommy (50)	Aah (60)	Daddy (85)
BaaBaa (33)	Mommy (57)	Grandma – Paternal (40)
Bye (25)	YumYum (36)	Grandpa – Paternal (17)
Hi (24)	Sister – Older (21)	Hello?/Wei? (14)
UhOh (20)	UhOh (Aiyou) (20)	Hit (12)
Grr (16)	Hit (18)	Uncle – Paternal (11)
Bottle (13)	Hello?/Wei? (13)	Grab/Grasp (9)
YumYum (13)	Milk (13)	Auntie – Maternal (8)
Dog (12)	Naughty (8)	Bye (8)
No (12)	Brother – Older (7)	UhOh (Aiyou) (7)
WoofWoof (11)	Grandma – Maternal (6)	Ya/Wow (7)
Vroom (11)	Grandma – Paternal (6)	Sister – Older (7)
Kitty (10)	Bye (5)	WoofWoof (7)
Ball (10)	Bread (5)	Brother – Older (6)
Baby (7)	Auntie – Maternal (4)	Hug/Hold (6)
Duck (6)	Ball (4)	Light (4)
Cat (5)	Grandpa – Paternal (4)	Grandma – Maternal (3)
Ouch (5)	Car (3)	Egg (3)
Banana (3)	WoofWoof (2)	Vroom (3)

Source: Developmental Psychology.

Table 4.2 Mean percentages of each word type in infants' total vocabulary by language. Data reproduced from Tardif et al. (2008).

Word category	English (264 children)	Mandarin Chinese (367 children)	Cantonese Chinese (336 children)
People	29.9	43.1	77.7
Sounds	29.5	40.6	8.7
Common nouns	19.4	5.7	3.2
Games and routines	15.8	3.4	2.3
Verbs	0.7	4.8	7.0
Adjectives	1.3	2.2	0.7
Function words (e.g., 'and', 'or', 'of', 'this', 'are')	3.3	0.2	0.4

Source: Developmental Psychology.

Here too there is a similar story of similarities and differences. Regardless of the language they are learning, children use their first words to describe people (whether it be in kinship terms or individual names), the sounds of things like animals, and familiar objects that children encounter in their homes. Some of these similarities may be caused not so much because they are *children* learning a language, but rather that they are simply people who don't yet know the language that everyone around them speaks. So, much like an adult who is parachuted into a foreign country might behave, children's first words initiate communication in a conservative way, grounded in the here and now and often tied to fulfilling their immediate needs or commenting on something in shared attention.

The relative ordering of common nouns, verbs, and routines does significantly vary across languages. The English-speaking children in this study produced many more words that fall into the common nouns category, whereas the Cantonese-speaking children produced twice as many verbs as common nouns, and the Mandarin-speaking children produced roughly equal numbers of common nouns and verbs. Overall, there is a combination of psychological, social, cultural, and linguistic factors that interact to make children's first words both somewhat similar and different.

Factors that make children's first words similar	Factors that make children's first words different
• Children around the world share similar motivations to share information about similar things (people, sounds, and common objects) and to request similar resources (food, attention, and care).	• Different languages express the same ideas using different sounds and grammars. • Different parents within a language speak differently to their children (Ibbotson & Browne, 2024).

- Children share a similar set of cognitive and social biases, such as acquiring nouns before verbs (Ibbotson et al., 2018).
- Children share similar vocal tracts, making some sounds easier to articulate than others.
- Child-directed speech shares similar properties across languages.
- Different languages spotlight some meanings more prominently than others – for example, Turkish requires the speaker to state whether a past event was witnessed or not by the speaker.
- There are different cultural expectations about at what age children become conversational partners.

Key Point

- Cross-linguistically the types of first words children use show some similar characteristics and some differences shaped by cognitive, social, and linguistic factors.

The birth of a word.

Just like acquiring any other skill, learning language requires a lot of practice. Listen to how the son of researcher Deb Roy homed in on the pronunciation of 'water' over 6 months.

4.5 Putting Words Together

As children start to string single words together into multi-word utterances, they are presented with a fresh challenge. The difference in meaning between 'dog bites man' and 'man bites dog' does not lie in the words themselves but in their order. Different languages have different word orders that express the same underlying concept, and children are equally prepared to learn any one of them. For example, 'dog (subject) bites (verb) man (object)' in English is equivalent to '*greimíonn*/bites (verb) *madra*/dog (subject) *ar fhear*/man (object)' in Gaelic. That order is part of a wider system of conventions on how to assemble smaller parts of speech into bigger meaningful units, or what we call a **grammar** (Ibbotson, 2022).

Typically, children start to combine words when they are somewhere between 18 and 24 months old. Let us take a look at the kinds of two-word combinations children first use. Developmental psychologist Melissa Bowerman (1975) compared the early multi-word utterances spoken by children learning English, Finnish, Samoan, and Luo (**Table 4.3**).

Even though these languages are very different in their vocabulary, phonology, and grammar, Bowerman found that children's first two-word utterances showed remarkable similarity in the types of combinations they used. For example, the utterances *agent-action* and *action-object* were highly frequent across all languages. Presumably this is because these

Table 4.3 Cross-linguistic examples (all given in English translation) of children's first two-word utterances from Bowerman (1975).

Type	English	Finnish	Samoan	Luo
Agent-action	Mommy push	Man dances	Goes Va	Car runs
Action-object	Bite finger	Drives car	Spank me	Eat medicine
Possessor-possessed	Dolly hat	Aunt car	Ball yours	Head mine
Demonstrator-object-demonstrated	That candy	There cow	Ball there	It clock
Adjective-noun	Big bed	Little fish	Children older	Pepper hot

Source: Academic Press.

Table 4.4 Cross-linguistic examples (all given in English translation) of children's first three-word utterances from Bowerman (1975). No Luo data were available for this developmental period.

Type	English	Finnish	Samoan
Agent-action-object	I ride Horsie	Piggy drives bicycle	Got-rid-of-baby you
Agent-action-location	Tractor go floor	Bunny walk sand	Goes Usu there
Action-object-indirect object	Show me book	Give Rina that	Bring candy baby
Action-object-location	Put truck window	Lifts stone there	Bring baby there

Source: Academic Press.

utterances communicate a scene common to the experience of all children: someone or something intentionally performing an action, and an action having some effect on an object.

This specific example illustrates a broader point. As we have seen with the types of first single words children use, there are different forces at work that make children's language somewhat similar and somewhat different around the world. Children may experience similar basic dynamic events involving people interacting with objects – and share the same motivation to inform and share with others about these – but these are expressed with the unique sounds, vocabulary, and grammar of specific languages. This results in different developmental paths for children learning different languages depending on what aspect of language we choose to look at. Bowerman (1975) also followed the same children as they went on to utter their first three-word utterances (**Table 4.4**).

Interestingly, Bowerman notes how there are virtually no new types of speech in this three-word phase; rather, these utterances are best characterised as combinations of two-word utterances that have been cut and pasted together to express new relationships or concepts. For example, the *agent-action* (e.g., 'I ride') and *action-object* (e.g., 'ride Horsie') types that were separate in the two-word phase have been blended together to form an *agent-action-object* category in the three-word phase ('I ride Horsie').

Between 2 and 3 years of age children express increasingly complex ideas with their use of increasingly complex grammar. They start simple, however, gluing single words together that increase gradually in their complexity. Around 18–24 months, two- and three-word utterances emerge as mini-sentences that contain simple relations.

> **Key Point**
>
> - Children learn grammar incrementally by blending simple grammar that expresses simple ideas like agent-action and action-object into more complex forms like agent-action-object.

4.6 The Meaning of Words

Learning the meaning of words is often framed as a problem of linking the 'word to world' and vice versa. So, upon hearing a piece of new language, say 'gavagai', the infant is confronted with a seemingly endless range of possible things it could mean, or its **semantics**. For example, 'gavagai' could mean that rabbit I see in front of me, the action of hopping, the way it is hopping, the ground it is hopping on, the colour of the rabbit, everything except a rabbit, the direction of the wind at the time, the attitude of the speaker towards rabbits, and so on. How do children know which was the intended meaning? One way in which children start to understand what words mean is through cross-situational learning (**Figure 4.2**).

Adults too obviously play a key role in structuring their interactions with children in a way that can help word learning. For example, when speaking with young children, adults are more likely to use so-called tutorial questions (i.e., asking questions they already know the answer to) and to adopt a child-centred approach (i.e., taking a child's topic as a conversational starting point and expanding thereafter).

The use of intentional-type language by others can also provide a strong cue to meaning. For example, Carpenter and colleagues (1998) had an experimenter say 'There!' or 'Whoops!' after completing an action. Children were much more likely to imitate the action associated with the intentional linguistic description ('There!') than the accidental one ('Whoops!'). Likewise, words such as 'Uh-oh' or 'Oops' reveal that a

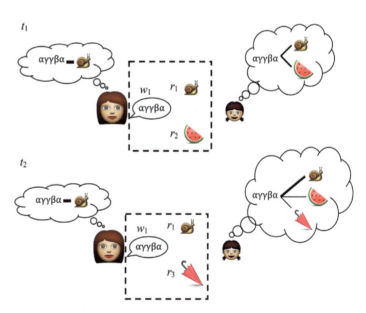

Figure 4.2 An adult chooses a word w_1 associated with idea r_1 that they want to communicate. The first time a child hears that word t_1 the child does not know whether the novel word w_1 refers to r_1 or r_2, and for now the best she can do is remember the associations between the situation and the word. The next time she hears it, at t_2, she hears w_1 with one object r_1 familiar from t_1 and one new object r_3. Cross-situational learning works by building up a history of these associations between language and the context in which it is used. Over time, the idea is that children begin to share the same word–idea associations as adults (Ibbotson, 2013).

speaker has not achieved their goal, and these are used by 2-year-olds to abandon a possible association between a new noun and an object or a new verb and an action. This shows that children are using their **theory of mind** skills to work out what the speaker intended to communicate, and this helps them home in on the meaning of the word.

Adults also seem to have an unspoken understanding that children expect that new nouns will be introduced as so-called basic-level names – such as 'dog' rather than 'mammal' (a bigger category that includes dogs) or 'Spot' (a smaller category of dogs that picks out an individual). It is as if speakers are balancing the needs of being informative (too high level a category is not predictive of an individual) and efficient (too low level a category is predictive of only that individual). When words deviate from this expectation, adults tend to structure their language to mark them in some way – for example, when adults present part names to children, very rarely do they simply point and say, 'Look at the feathers.' Instead, they typically begin by talking about the whole object ('This is a bird …') and then introduce the part name with a possessive construction ('… and these are his feathers'), with similar marking for smaller categories ('A peacock is a type of bird') and bigger categories ('These are animals. Birds and cats are kinds of animals'). And if the meaning isn't clear, then children expect adults to be informative, cooperative speakers. Children as young as 1 year old are able to point and say something like, 'Wha?' 'Tha,' or 'Eh?' and by 2 years old they can ask, 'What's that?' In a classic study of first words, Nelson (1973) found that most of the children she studied had a word that was used in this enquiring/clarificatory way before they learned 50 words, with some of the children acquiring such a word as part of their first 10 words.

So, children don't learn the meaning of words like 'the', 'it', or 'do' by having an adult define them for them – assuming the unlikely situation in which a child could find an adult capable of doing so! They learn the meaning of words and phrases by employing a range of social, linguistic, and statistical strategies.

Key Point

- Through their play, exploration, and social interaction, children use a variety of strategies to understand what words mean.

4.7 Creativity and Conformity

When children are learning language, they are trying to balance creativity with conformity. In so-called **overgeneralisation errors**, children demonstrate they are not passive sponges just repeating back what they hear, as no adult says 'it went-ed', 'that go-ed over there', or 'I swimmed'. Children are finding patterns and being creative with them as they try to figure out for themselves the deeper rules adults play by (in this case, add '-ed' when you talk about things in the past). But children's language needs to also conform to the norms of the language they are learning if they are going to be effective communicators with others who share the same norms.

The first thing to note is that errors are relatively rare in child speech, with estimates ranging from 2% to 5% depending on what areas of language we focus on and what counts as an error. Given the complexity of language, this level of accuracy is incredibly impressive, underscoring what an exquisitely tuned process language acquisition is. Before we consider how children eventually overcome such errors, let us briefly look at the way in which adults respond when they hear children's errors. In theory, this could be one source of evidence children use to gauge whether they have generalised along the right lines. Typically, though, adults do not misunderstand or correct children more often when they speak ungrammatically compared with when they speak grammatically. Look at the following transcript from a real-life father–son interaction as an example:

Father: Where is that big piece of paper I gave you yesterday?
Child: Remember? I writed on it.
Father: Oh that's right don't you have any paper down here buddy?

(MacWhinney & Snow, 1990)

While children receive plenty of *positive evidence* of how their language works, children rarely receive direct *negative evidence* on what is unacceptable in their language – for example, when the child produces an unconventional form and is directly corrected by an adult. Where there are examples of direct feedback in naturalistic discourse, children seem resistant, even wilfully stubborn towards adults' attempts at corrections, as the following transcripts show:

Child: Want other one spoon, Daddy.
Father: You mean, you want the other spoon.
Child: Yes, I want other one spoon, please Daddy.
Father: Can you say 'the other spoon'?
Child: Other ... one ... spoon.
Father: Say 'other'.
Child: Other.
Father: 'Spoon'.
Child: Spoon.
Father: 'Other spoon'.
Child: Other ... spoon. Now give me other one spoon!?

(Braine, 1971)

Child: My teacher holded the baby rabbits and we patted them.
Adult: Did you say your teacher held the baby rabbits?
Child: Yes.
Adult: What did you say she did?
Child: She holded the baby rabbits and we patted them.
Adult: Did you say she held them tightly?
Child: No, she holded them loosely.

(Cazden, 1972)

Interestingly, these overgeneralisation errors can follow a **U-shaped curve** of development – performance starts out as good (few errors), then gets worse (many errors), before getting better again (no errors). During this process children might actually produce both the unconventional form (e.g., 'go-ed') at the same time as the conventional one (e.g., 'went'). U-shaped curves of development are especially interesting to psychologists as they indicate children are restructuring and reorganising what they understand, and they can represent clues that they have switched learning strategies. U-shaped curves are not limited to language learning, however. They are important reminders that development is not always linear. More experience does not always result in better performance.

The problem of how words and phrases like 'writed', 'other one spoon', and 'holded' ever come to be regarded as unacceptable if children are never directly told that they are (i.e., negative evidence) is a key question in the field of language acquisition. There have been a number of ideas put forward to explain how children eventually overcome these errors, including:

- The more often a child hears a verb in a particular grammatical context (e.g., 'I suggested the idea to him'), the less likely they are to use it in a new context they haven't heard it in (e.g., 'I suggested him the idea'; Ambridge et al., 2012).
- If a child repeatedly hears a verb in a particular phrase (e.g., 'I filled the cup with water') that serves the same communicative function as a possible unheard generalisation (e.g., 'I filled water into the cup'), then the child infers that the generalisation is not available (Goldberg, 2007).
- Some combinations of words are associated with particular meanings, and as children refine this knowledge, they will cease to insert verbs that do not bear these meaning elements (e.g., 'The joke giggled him'; Pinker, 1989).
- Evidence from several languages shows that a maturation in cognitive abilities that are independent of language, such as memory and attention, can explain the pattern of individual differences in overgeneralisation errors (Ibbotson, 2020).

 Key Point

- Overgeneralisation errors are powerful illustrations of the creative power of language and the mechanisms children use to learn it.

An excellent example of children's creativity with language use is the case of Nicaraguan Sign Language (**Box 4.1**).

 Box 4.1 Nicaraguan Sign Language – Lenguaje de Señas Nicaragüense

In 1979, the Sandinista National Liberation Front toppled the Nicaragua's de facto ruler, Anastasio Somoza Debayle, whose family had been in power in the country since 1936. The new government brought in sweeping reforms, including a huge literacy campaign, support for special needs in education, and provision for Deaf children. Prior to this, Deaf children were unlikely to meet one another and so had developed their own idiosyncratic gesture systems to communicate with their families at home, known as 'homesign' or '*señas*

caseras'. Under the Sandinista government, children using these homesigns, which varied considerably in their structure and complexity, were brought together for the first time in the context of vocational educational programmes aimed at Deaf children and young adults in Managua, the capital. Interestingly, the children were told not to use gestures and were taught lip-reading and Spanish, the dominant language of Nicaragua. However, by the mid-1980s, the Deaf signers had developed their own sign language, which served as the language input for Deaf children who subsequently entered these programmes. Recall that before these children there wasn't any official sign language in Nicaragua, so the first group of Deaf people to form this community did not learn a sign language from older signers.

Judy Kegl, a linguist then based at the Massachusetts Institute of Technology, began investigating the language in 1986 on the invitation of country's Ministry of Education to observe the children at the schools in Managua and essentially work out the system of communication these children had invented. She made the first systematic video recordings in 1987 and published the first scientific report of Nicaraguan Sign Language (NSL) shortly thereafter. As part of her observations, often with young signers as willing research collaborators, Kegl noted a kind of reversal of the pattern you would expect to see in typical language development. The younger members of the newly emerging NSL community were actually more fluent at the language, building on and going beyond the older speakers' linguistic abilities (**Figure 4.3**).

Since Kegl's work, NSL continues to provide an important source of data for linguists, developmental psychologists, and anthropologists interested in how children learn language and the conditions necessary for language to evolve. It became particularly important in understanding the role of children's own inventiveness in the process of language creation as it happens in front of our eyes. It is also valuable because the political backdrop against which these children's lives played out created a rather unique natural experiment that would be difficult to formally replicate – imagine trying to get approval from a university ethics board for a study that *deprived* children of language in order to examine how children might invent it! NSL shows that, in a relatively short amount of time, a sophisticated language can be developed if that communicative niche is not already served by an existing language, and that this change is often driven by the youngest members of that community (we take a deeper look at sign language in Chapter 16).

Figure 4.3 Today, Nicaraguan Sign Language is a fully fledged language in its own right, with a complex grammar and a broad vocabulary, and it is still evolving. Source: Susan Meiselas.

Talking Point

Despite decades of research, we have only begun to understand how language acquisition works in a minority of the 7,000 languages of the world. For too long the field has been overly reliant on monolingual English speakers, and we don't know whether the developmental processes are significantly different in other languages because researchers simply haven't studied most of them in depth. This situation is made more urgent by the rate at which languages are disappearing. It is estimated over 40% of the world's languages are at risk of extinction. Not only does this represent an enormous loss of cultural identity, values, heritage, wisdom, and accumulated medical, ecological, and technical know-how; from a scientific perspective, it also severely limits our understanding of what language can be and what makes us human. Language diversity manifests itself not just at the global level, but at the level of individual children too. Growing up with two or more languages is the norm for most of the world's children, and this represents another sense in which setting monolingual English acquisition as the default can skew our understanding. If we want to understand how children acquire any language, then we need to take diversity seriously and not treat English as the standard against which other languages are compared. Imagine if we had experimental and experiential data from all 7,000 languages at our fingertips – how much richer would our understanding be of what language is and how we acquire it?

Summary

- Before birth and after, children are becoming sensitised to the sounds in their native language(s) and insensitive to those that are not.
- Children use powerful pattern detection skills to segment speech streams into words.
- Child-directed speech differs in important ways from adult-to-adult speech and has been shown to help language learning.
- Cross-linguistically the types of first words children use show some similar characteristics and some differences shaped by cognitive, social, and linguistic factors.
- Children learn grammar incrementally by blending simple grammar that expresses simple ideas like agent-action and action-object into more complex forms like agent-action-object.
- Through their play, exploration, and social interaction, children use a variety of strategies to understand what words mean.
- Overgeneralisation errors are powerful illustrations of the creative power of language and the mechanisms children use to learn it.

References

Ambridge, B., Pine, J. M., & Rowland, C. F. (2012). Semantics versus statistics in the retreat from locative overgeneralization errors. *Cognition*, 123, 260–279.

Bowerman, M. (1975). Cross-linguistic similarities at two stages of syntactic development. In E. H. Lenneberg & E. Lenneberg (eds.), *Foundations of*

Language Development (pp. 267–282). Academic Press.

Braine. M. D. S. (1971). On two types of models of the internalization of grammars. In D. I. Slobin (ed.), *The Ontogenesis of Grammar* (pp. 153–186). Academic Press.

Carpenter, M., Akhtar, N., & Tomasello, T. (1998). Fourteen- through 18-month-old infants differentially imitate intentional and accidental actions. *Infant Behavior and Development*, 21(2). 315–330.

Cazden, C. B. (1972). *Child Language and Education*. Holt, Rinehart and Winston.

DeCasper, A. J. & Spence, M. J. (1986). Prenatal maternal speech influences newborns' perception of speech sounds. *Infant Behavior and Development*, 9, 133–150.

Fló, A., Brusini, P., Macagno, F., Nespor, M., Mehler, J., & Ferry, A. L. (2019) Newborns are sensitive to multiple cues for word segmentation in continuous speech. *Developmental Science*, 22, e12802.

Goldberg, A. (2007). *Constructions at Work: The Nature of Generalizations in Language*. Oxford University Press.

Ibbotson, P. (2013). The scope of usage-based theory. *Frontiers in Psychology*, 4, 255.

Ibbotson, P. (2020). *What It Takes to Talk: Exploring Developmental Cognitive Linguistics*. DeGruyters Mouton.

Ibbotson, P. (2022). *Language Acquisition: The Basics*. Routledge.

Ibbotson, P. & Browne, W. J. (2014). The effects of family, culture and sex on linguistic development across 20 languages. *Developmental Science*, 27(6), e13547.

Ibbotson, P., Hartman, R. M., & Björkenstam, K. N. (2018). Frequency filter: an open access tool for analysing language development. *Language, Cognition and Neuroscience*, 33(10), 1325–1339.

Kelly, D. J., Quinn, P. C., Slater, A. M., Lee, K., Ge, L., & Pascalis, O. (2007). The other-race effect develops during infancy: evidence of perceptual narrowing. *Psychological Science*, 18, 1084–1089.

Kisilevsky, B. S., Hains, S. M., Brown, C. A., et al. (2009). Fetal sensitivity to properties of maternal speech and language. *Infant Behavioural Development*, 32(1), 59–71.

MacWhinney, B. & Snow, C. (1990). The Child Language Data Exchange System: an update. *Journal of Child Language*, 17, 457–472.

Nelson, K. (1973). Structure and strategy in learning to talk. *Monographs of the Society for Research in Child Development*, 38, 136.

Pinker, S. (1989). *Learnability and Cognition: The Acquisition of Verb-Argument Structure*. MIT Press/Bradford Books.

Saffran, J. R. (2018). Statistical learning as a window into developmental disabilities. *Journal of Neurodevelopmental Disorders*, 10, 35.

Saffran, J. R., Aslin, R. N., & Newport, E. L. (1996). Statistical learning by 8-month-old infants. *Science*, 274(5294), 1926–1928.

Super, C. M. & Harkness, S. (1986). The developmental niche: a conceptualization at the interface of child and culture. *International Journal of Behavioral Development*, 9(4), 545–569.

Tardif, T., Fletcher, P., Liang, W., Zhang, Z., Kaciroti, N., & Marchman, V. A. (2008). Baby's first 10 words. *Developmental Psychology*, 44(4), 929–938.

Tsao, F. M., Liu, H. M., & Kuhl, P. K. (2004). Speech perception in infancy predicts language development in the second year of life: a longitudinal study. *Child Development*, 75(4), 1067–1084.

Werker, J. F. & Tees, R. C. (1984). Cross-language speech perception: evidence for perceptual reorganization during the first year of life. *Infant Behavior & Development*, *7*(1), 49–63.

5. HOW DO CHILDREN LEARN SO MUCH SO QUICKLY?

Learning Outcomes

After reading this chapter you will be able to:
- Understand how children direct their own learning and learn from others.
- Describe the importance of imitation, play, and instruction.
- Explain how children transfer what they know across different contexts.

5.1 Introduction

In previous chapters we explored in some detail *what* children are learning about: relationships, emotions, other minds, language, and much else besides. This chapter unites these topics by looking at *how* children go about learning in general. Young children are noisy, easily distracted, unpredictable, impulsive, messy, and – almost by definition – cannot take care of themselves. Yet they are also highly sophisticated learners, who in a short time acquire an incredible amount of information about themselves, other people, and the world around them. In this chapter we explore this apparent contradiction and discover that some of their supposed limitations actually make them better learners. In particular, their eagerness to play, explore, and be spontaneous turns them into expert information foragers. We focus on two broad types of learning: learning about the world through first-hand exploration; and learning second-hand by imitating and benefitting from what others do, say, and know.

5.2 Exploration

Psychologist Alison Gopnik describes a fundamental tension in learning known as the **explore–exploit dilemma**: stick with what you know and risk missing out on something new, or explore something new and risk not exploiting what you know. She gives the following example: you can choose whether to go to a familiar, reliable restaurant or try a new place that might be better or might be worse. The first option will give you a good meal but no new information. The second option risks a less good meal but will give you more information – and might lead to something even better than your known choice. Which should you do (Gopnik, 2016)?

Children need to solve a general version of this problem all the time in their learning, and it turns out they are experts in balancing when to explore and when to exploit. In a very short time, they learn about objects, people, animals, and plants, so creating their own theories of the physics, biology, and psychology of the world around them. They do this well before they go to school, with no explicit teaching. A long childhood allows for an early protected period devoted to learning and exploration, as seen in young children's love of the new (neophilia) and curiosity, which lead to active exploration and play. Gopnik argues that the whole evolutionary point of childhood is not to get children to do anything in particular; instead, it's to enable them to be creative and to try different solutions in different circumstances. This early exploration phase of development is followed by a later adult period devoted to directed exploitation based on what has been learned earlier, characterised by more focused, skilled action and expertise (Gopnik, 2016).

Key Point

- Children are highly effective, motivated, active, and playful learners, balancing the needs of exploring the world around them and exploiting what they have learned.

Young children are particularly drawn to inconsistent or unexpected outcomes that provide new information about the way the world works. For example, seeing a ball magically hover in mid-air provides new information – it is worthy of attention. Seeing a ball that bounces along the ground, just as expected, adds nothing new – it's boring, so it's better to focus attention somewhere else. Children systematically learn from their exploration, revise their beliefs based on evidence they have gathered, and generate new predictions about the way the world works. In this context 'belief' does not refer to something religious but something more basic – for example, the belief that things exist even though you can't see them; that objects unsupported tend to fall down; or that if someone goes upstairs, their head also tends to go with them.

Key Points

- Children pay particular attention to inconsistent or unexpected outcomes that provide new information about the way the world works.

Surprise!

Aimee Stahl and Lisa Feigenson show how babies not only focus on surprises but learn more from them.

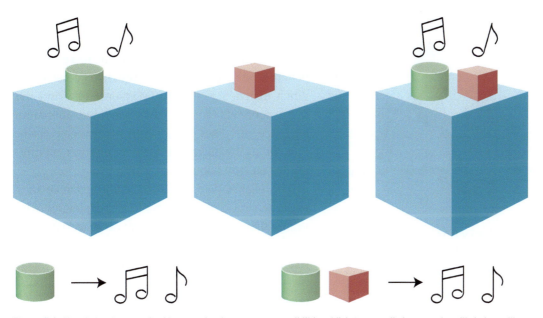

Figure 5.1 The blicket detector. In this example, there are two possibilities: blickets are cylinders or – less likely but still possible – blickets can also be cylinders and cubes when they appear together. There is no evidence that blickets are just cubes.

Let's look at an example of how good young children are at exploratory 'active learning'. The clearest evidence that children are expert information explorers comes from studies that show they actually perform better than adults on precisely the same tasks when those tasks involve broad search or exploration. Alison Gopnik and her team set out to investigate this ability in a series of experiments using a 'blicket detector'. The blicket detector is a box that lights up and plays music when it detects a blicket. Children don't know what a blicket is, and the challenge facing them is to work out what one is by placing shapes on the box and seeing how it responds. In one variation of the blicket experiment, 4- and 5-year-old children were more likely than adults to entertain the improbable but – as it turned out – true possibility that blickets can be pairs of objects (**Figure 5.1**; Gopnik et al., 2015).

As more and more blicket examples were revealed in the experiment, children's broad, exploratory learning style was better than the approach taken by the adults for detecting which objects were blickets. Because adults were convinced they were right – blickets are just cylinders – this caused them to overlook the possibility that blickets could also be pairs of objects as well as single ones. The adults were more susceptible to a **confirmation bias** – a tendency we all have to seek out evidence that confirms our beliefs rather than challenges them. This is the reason why most people read newspapers, watch TV, and surround themselves with friends that reinforce their opinions rather than ones that challenge them (**Figure 5.2**). Children in the experiment, by contrast, were less susceptible to this bias, choosing instead to explore a broader range of possible ideas. They were less influenced by prior assumptions and paid more attention to current evidence.

Adult experience and expertise in this context represent a double-edged sword. We can exploit what we do know, drawing quick and confident conclusions when a problem is

Figure 5.2 Confirmation bias in action. Source: Cartoonstock.

familiar to us. However, a lot of knowledge can be a dangerous thing. These biases can make us less flexible learners, being too reluctant to revise our beliefs when we come across situations outside our direct experience, like a blicket detector. And the more confident we are about an idea, the more evidence it takes to overturn the idea itself. Sometimes the biggest obstacle to the truth is thinking we already know it.

The blicket detector is a specific example of a more general challenge we all face: explaining why things happen the way they do and working out cause and effect. The ability to understand causal relationships and to reason from them is at the heart of many distinctive human abilities, like sophisticated forms of tool use and technological innovation (more on this in Chapter 9). For children, every day the world is full of blicket detectors; they are trying to work out why objects, animals, and people work the way they do. The broader and more complex the possibilities are, the more that exploration will be valuable to them. Children don't have the blessing (or curse) of having strong prior expectations about the complex world of cause and effect because they are busy working out what their first expectations are. When children have an idea about the way the world works, they are more likely than adults to actively explore alternative plausible explanations that would prove themselves wrong, the way a good scientist should. This means they can often home in on the underlying cause and effect of a situation in an optimal way. By 3 years of age, children frequently seek explanations by asking questions, provide explanations for things that happen, and use their causal knowledge to make predictions. Young children not only learn as much or more than adults; they also learn differently. Research suggests younger learners can be better, or at least more open-minded, than older ones.

Finally, children's have-a-go exploratory attitude to learning may require an optimistic view of their own abilities. For example, preschoolers typically think that they can remember more items, communicate more effectively, imitate a model more accurately, and perform better on a range of tasks than they actually can (Lipko et al., 2009). Young children's overly positive opinions of their physical, social, and cognitive abilities could give them the confidence and motivation to attempt things they would not otherwise try.

 Key Point

- Children's exploratory learning is well suited to learning about cause and effect and to using that knowledge to predict how things will behave in the world.

5.3 Generalising from What We Know to What We Don't

As well as being able to learn about what causes what, children are also able to transfer what they have learned in one context to another. This fundamental aspect of learning means we aren't perpetually surprised at every new situation because we have formed expectations of how *categories* of things will behave. For example, if my pet dog needs to eat and sleep, then maybe all dogs need to eat and sleep. If dogs need to eat and sleep, then maybe cats do too – maybe all animals need to. This kind of generalisation can be incredibly powerful because it allows us to go beyond our direct experience and get some information about the world for free. I don't need to have met every dog in the world in order to expect they also need to eat and sleep.

Developmental psychologists Hyowon Gweon, Joshua Tenenbaum, and Laura Schultz were interested in understanding exactly how babies learned to generalise from their experience (Gweon et al., 2010). They tested 130 15-month-olds by placing them in front of an experimenter, who would pull coloured balls out of a box (**Figure 5.3**). The box had a transparent front so the babies could see roughly how many balls of each colour were inside the box. In the first condition infants saw the experimenter draw out three blue balls in a row. The experimenter then squeezed the blue balls, demonstrating they squeaked, and then handed a yellow ball to the infant, saying, 'Now this one's for you to play with. You can go ahead and play.' When the box mostly contained blue balls, the infants would also squeeze their yellow ball and make it squeak. Presumably the infants were reasoning that three blue balls drawn from a box containing mainly blue balls is a plausibly random sample. And if you can reach into a box at random and pull out things that squeak, then maybe everything in the box squeaks.

In the second condition, the experimenter showed the infants a different box containing mainly yellow balls, and again withdrew three blue balls. In this case, it is not a plausibly

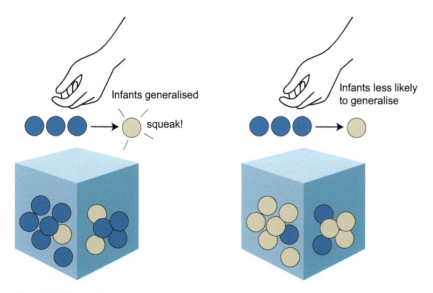

Figure 5.3 The experimental set-up of the study by Gweon and colleagues (2010).

randomly sample; maybe these balls have been deliberately selected and something is special about them – maybe only the blue balls squeak. In this second condition, despite the same invitation to play, infants were significantly less likely to generalise from their experience by squeezing their yellow ball.

Laura Schultz and her team concluded that 15-month-old babies, in this respect, are like scientists. They care whether evidence is randomly sampled or not, and they use statistics to guide their generalisations about the world: what squeaks and what doesn't; what to explore and what to ignore. The implications of this research of course go well beyond learning about which balls squeak. Generalising from what we know to what we don't is something infants do all the time, making inferences about objects, people, and animals and creating their own explanations of the world. The power of generalisation goes a long way to explaining how we can learn so much in such a short time. A wide body of research suggests toddlers and preschoolers explore the world and collect new information in these systematic and evidence-based ways (Ronfard et al., 2018; Schulz, 2012). This is another example of how children are not passive recipients in their learning but able, active participants. As such, parents and caregivers don't have to teach young children so much as they have to let them learn (Gopnik, 2016).

 Key Point

- Children can transfer what they have learned in one context to another, generalising in systematic and evidence-based ways.

 Watch the One-Minute Method.

Like the babies in Laura Schultz's experiments, discover why researchers take care over the generalisations they make.

5.4 Play

There is perhaps no better example of exploratory learning than play. Play is a common behaviour among young animals from a wide range of species, and it provides a safe space to practice many of the skills that will be important later in life. In studies that have deprived rats of opportunities to play early in life, they grow up to be less sensitive and flexible in the way they respond to other rats than rats who were allowed to play (Vanderschuren et al., 2016). The general message from animal studies is that play is important not because it teaches one skill in particular but because it builds general-purpose problem-solving skills, flexibility, and resilience for the future. Or as Marek Špinka, an expert in animal behaviour and welfare put it: play is training for the unexpected (2001). The implications of this research for human development are important. For example, in education, policymakers are under pressure to demonstrate the benefits of scheduling play into a busy curriculum, but the long-term benefits of play for children may only emerge long after they have left the classroom or school, and even then they are difficult to quantify.

Humans have taken play one step further than most other species and engage in pretend play. In its simple form, this begins to emerge by around 12–18 months of age – by pretending a wooden block is a teacup, for example. But it can develop into elaborate, fantastical scenarios played out with the aid of props, language, or gestures. Observe almost any 4-year-old and it won't be long before they are engaging in some kind of pretend play, but the ordinariness of this also raises a question: why would children spend so much of their time and energy engaged in make-believe when it might be better to understand how the real world works? To say that it's fun only pushes the question further back: why is it fun?

Psychologist Daphna Buchsbaum and her colleagues have argued that pretend play has an especially important role in children's ability to reason **counterfactually** (Buchsbaum et al., 2012). Counterfactuals involve a mental simulation of 'what if' – for instance, 'If I had turned up to the job interview without trousers, I would have been embarrassed,' 'If I had revised harder, I would have passed the test,' or, 'If my grandmother had wheels, she'd be a bicycle.' The ability to think counterfactually represents the most advanced stage in children's understanding of cause and effect. At first children merely observe cause and effect in the world (e.g., seeing a toy fall off a table when pushed); then they intervene in the world to cause an effect (e.g., pulling a toy towards them); and finally they imagine what could have been (e.g., 'If I had pulled a different toy towards me, that would have been better'). Counterfactual thinking also underpins moral sentiments like regret, blame, responsibility, and credit, and experimental evidence suggests that children as young as 5 years of age use counterfactual reasoning to make moral and social judgements of others (Gautam et al., 2023; Wong et al., 2023).

Both pretend play and counterfactual reasoning consider events that have not occurred; they separate imagined events from reality and simulate what would be the case if such imagined events had occurred. This skill allows us to imagine past worlds that never were or run simulations of possible futures, an ability that has sometimes been referred to 'mental time travel'. Buchsbaum argues that, just as physical play provides young animals with the opportunity to practice skills that they will need later in life, like how rough-and-tumble prepares animals for fighting, pretend play lets children practice the *cognitive skills* necessary for causal learning, planning, and counterfactual reasoning. To test this idea, she and her colleagues asked 52 children aged 3–4 years to engage in some pretend play with them. They substituted a real machine (similar to the blicket detector we met earlier) for a white wooden box and two coloured blocks. The experimenter explained, 'I thought we could pretend that this box is my machine and that this block [one of the coloured blocks] is a Zando, and that this block [the other coloured block] is not a Zando.' The children then took part in a counterfactual task that involved working out what the machine would do in different scenarios; for example, the experimenter asked the children: 'If this one were not a Zando, what would happen if we put it on top of the machine?' (Buchsbaum et al., 2012).

All the children were able to successfully take part in the pretend play appropriately and answered correctly regarding the counterfactual, but there was some variation in how they did so. The researchers found that the children who were especially good at the pretend play were also the ones who were good at the counterfactual reasoning task. This kind of

Figure 5.4 Children at play in Indonesia (top left), Tajikistan (top right), Ethiopia (bottom left), and India (bottom right). Source: runner of art/Getty Images; Damon Lynch; David Sacks/Getty Images; Mukund Images.

association is what we would predict if pretend play was related to counterfactual thinking, as Buchsbaum suggests. Furthermore, the researchers showed that children transferred their knowledge from the pretend task (e.g., playing with the wooden machine) in order to perform correctly in the counterfactual task (e.g., predicting what a non-Zando would do to the machine). In other words, pretend play helped them in their counterfactual reasoning.

It seems to go against the very nature of play to ask what it might be for. Play, as we usually think about it, isn't designed to achieve anything; if it were, it wouldn't be play, nor would it be so much fun (Gopnik, 2016). Precisely because play isn't designed to achieve anything in the here and now, we need a way to motivate us to engage in it. Making play fun might be one way to make exploration enjoyable for its own sake. The evidence suggests that play – and in particular pretend play – provides a mental training ground for reasoning about and learning from imagined scenarios that can later be applied to real ones, such as learning to regulate aggression and practice conflict resolution in culturally appropriate ways (Pellegrini, 2009).

More generally speaking, play provides the space to imagine how things would behave in imaginary worlds, and this powerful ability allows us to adapt to and anticipate a wide range of alternative possible future environments. Humans, as we know, also have a longer period of childhood than most other species, which means we get more protected time for play and so can benefit from it to a greater extent later in life (**Figure 5.4**).

Key Point

- Play and pretend play help children practice the physical and cognitive skills they will need later in life.

Pretend play shows that children have powerful imaginations, but will they believe anything? Research suggests not (see **Box 5.1**).

Box 5.1 Beyond belief

In both popular and scientific literature young children are often thought to confuse fantasy and reality. However, research suggests they rarely do so, and if they do, they do so for understandable reasons. Children as young as 3 years of age can tell the difference between an imagined object, a picture of an imagined object, and a real object, and if their pretend play is interrupted, they are able to step out of the pretence, engage with reality, and then successfully return to it. By 5 years old, children readily separate pictures of real things from pictures of pretend things and distinguish fantastical events from real ones, and if they do have an imaginary friend, they are quite aware that these friends are not real (Woolley & Ghossainy, 2013).

In fact, the evidence suggests that, far from being uncritical believers, young children are quite sceptical that unusual and unlikely events are real. For example, Shtulman and Carey (2007) created a story containing a set of possible, improbable, and impossible events, with a realistic depiction of each event: a person drinking orange juice, a person drinking onion juice, and a person eating lightning. They read stories of these events to 4- and 8-year-old children as well as to a group of adults, and they asked the participants to decide whether they were possible in reality. As expected, adults spotted the difference between impossible, improbable, and possible events, claiming that only impossible events could not happen in real life. Children, however, showed remarkable resistance to the possibility of improbable events and judged them largely as impossible, presumably because they were not consistent with their experience (e.g., drinking onion juice). Not until 8 years of age did children begin to show a shift towards more adult-like response patterns, allowing for improbable events to also be real and acknowledging the fact that just because you haven't experienced it doesn't mean it's impossible.

Despite this initial scepticism towards the improbable, a variety of factors can pull children towards belief. For example, there is evidence that merely being able to imagine something might make it seem more real. Paul Harris and his colleagues were interested in the persistent fear of imaginary creatures that many children experience, particularly of monsters (Harris et al., 1991). They gave 4- and 6-year-olds three types of item: real items (e.g., a cup), ordinary imagined items (e.g., an image of a cup), and supernatural imagined items (e.g., an image of a monster). Both age groups could tell the difference between the real items and both types of imagined item. However, they found that the children were uncertain that a creature that they have imagined cannot become real. Having imagined a creature inside a box, they showed apprehension or curiosity about what is inside the box, and they often admitted to wondering whether the creature was actually inside. We have already seen how pretend play and counterfactual thinking can help us simulate imaginary worlds. Here, it is as if this imagination is being considered a little too literally. These experiments suggest that children systematically distinguish fantasy from reality, but that they are tempted to believe in the existence of what they have merely imagined.

Children also come to believe in fantasy when everyone else around them is behaving as if the fantasy were true, in particular the testimony and evidence provided by parents that the unreal is real (e.g., the money found under a child's pillow after losing a tooth) and ritual performances (e.g., leaving out cookies and milk for Father Christmas). Children have a powerful motivation to adopt the cultural norms that surround them – explored in much more depth in the next section – and this can override their initial scepticism as to whether impossible or improbable events are real.

 Key Point

- Young children appreciate the difference between fantasy and reality and are often sceptical that unlikely things and events are real. However, they can be encouraged towards supernatural thinking if the belief is shared by others.

5.5 Learning from Others

The previous sections show that children and young infants are prodigious learners, experimenting with ideas and forming expectations about the way the world works. But humans learn information via another channel, which makes a big difference to our individual development and to our species: we learn from others. This **social learning** is a shortcut to the hard-won knowledge of others without needing to go through first-hand, time-consuming trial and error. I don't need to rediscover subtraction to benefit from maths, I don't need to try each type of mushroom to know which are safe to eat, I don't need to reinvent the printing press when I want to read something, I don't need to coin a new word when I want to speak; I can just benefit from some bright spark who worked it out first. This is captured by the

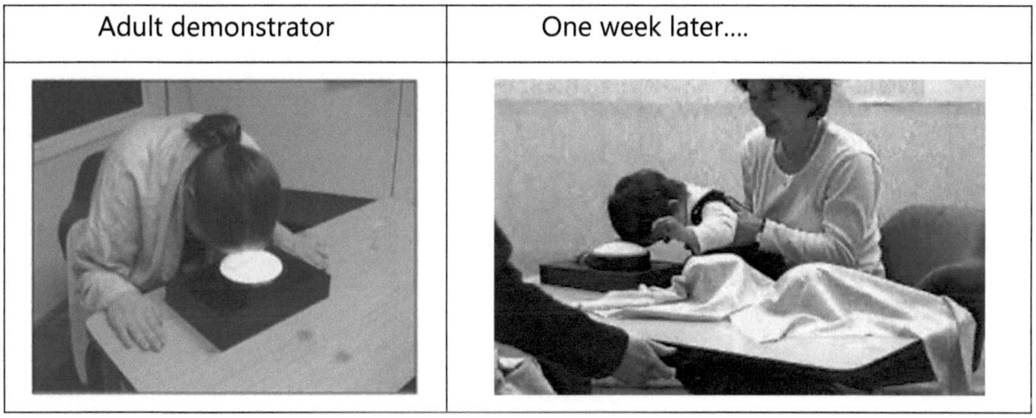

Adult demonstrator	One week later....

Figure 5.5 Infant imitating touching a box with their forehead in a similar set-up to Meltzoff (1988). Source: Gergely, G., Bekkering, H. & Király, I. Rational imitation in preverbal infants. Nature 415, 755 (2002). https://doi.org/10.1038/415755a.

following phrase attributed to Issac Newton: 'If I have seen further, it is by standing on the shoulders of giants.' Indeed, much of human technology is now too complex and sophisticated to be recreated within one individual's lifetime.

A basic form of learning from others is to **imitate** what they do. This typically starts to emerge in the first year of life in some simple forms, such as copying someone sticking their tongue out, and it progresses to more complex behaviours between 1 and 2 years of age. In a classic study by Meltzoff (1988), 14-month-old infants observed adults performing a strange, novel action. The demonstrator leaned forwards from the waist and touched a box with their forehead (**Figure 5.5**). The box had a light bulb hidden in it so that the box was illuminated when the adult made contact with it. When infants were presented with the box on a separate visit a week later with no adult demonstrator present, 67% of the infants imitated the action by leaning forwards and touching the box with their forehead – an action they would not spontaneously perform, as shown by a control condition.

Outside of the lab, observational studies have shown that infants learn an average of one or two new behaviours a day just by watching others, often their siblings (Barr & Hayne, 2003). When researchers looked across different societies from Kenya, India, Japan, Mexico, the Philippines, and the USA, they found that children spent the majority of their waking hours watching others, giving them plenty of opportunity to learn a variety of skills just by observing what other people do (Whiting & Edwards, 1988).

In fact, children are so good at copying others that they have been referred to as 'overimitators'. Compared with our closest living relatives – the chimpanzees – children will imitate the actions of someone else performing an activity, including all the seemingly unnecessary parts of the performance. For example, children will copy someone else acting out an elaborate set of manoeuvres and gestures before they eat a grape. Chimpanzees, by contrast, are more rational, dropping what they see as all the unnecessary bells and whistles and simply eating the grape.

Moreover, children are more likely to imitate the actions of others precisely in those situations where there isn't a clear cause and effect. Researchers think this is because children use the absence of cause and effect as a cue that the other person is acting in a culturally conventional way rather than acting towards a specific goal. For example, an adult lighting a candle could have the practical goal of lighting a dark room or the cultural goal of worshiping a god. Children need to work out which is which, and they use a number of contextual cues (e.g., cause and effect) and social cues (e.g., working out the intentions of others) to do so (see the discussion of theory of mind in Chapter 3).

Let's take a step back and think about social learning in relation to culture. Culture can be defined as any group-typical behaviours shared by members of a community that rely on socially learned and transmitted information. Cultures are also characterised by what they produce: material artefacts, social institutions, beliefs, technological know-how, behavioural traditions, and languages (Legare, 2017). Cultural products such as these are inherited, accumulated, remixed, and refined over generations. In a few thousand generations, humans have moved from hunting with spears to colonising space. As a species, we're not getting any smarter, but our cultural output is; how is that possible? The answer is the **ratchet effect**, whereby we take the discoveries, behaviours, and inventions of previous generations and build on them for future ones – and children play a vital role in this process. To preserve the hard-won insights of previous generations, children must be able to imitate the people around them. Take the example of a wheel: if we were unable to copy how to make a wheel with sufficient accuracy, we would be left hoping that someone will literally reinvent it every generation.

So, humans have this unique capacity for the transmission of social, cultural, and scientific information from one generation to the next. Some of this information is impractical or dangerous to acquire first-hand (e.g., which mushrooms are safe to eat), whereas other information is impossible to learn first-hand because we either weren't there (e.g., something that happened long ago or far away) or it is an arbitrary **convention** (Birch et al., 2020). Language is the classic example of an arbitrary convention. There is no inherent advantage to referring to that four-legged animal over there with the wagging tail as a '*dog*' or '*hund*' or '*chien*', but there is an advantage to using the *same* (arbitrary) sign as everyone else. The advantage is that people understand what you are talking about. There are many other examples of conventions: there is no inherent advantage in driving on the left side of the road or the right, but there is an advantage in driving on the *same* side as everyone else. Sometimes we are so sociocentric we are only made aware that our behaviours *are* conventions when we encounter another way of doing things – for example, using chopsticks instead of knives and forks, or nodding your head to mean 'no' as Bulgarians do rather than to mean 'yes' as almost everyone else does. The point is that the chance of any infant guessing the meaning of any of these arbitrary conventions (i.e., just guessing that the sound 'dog' might mean that animal with the wagging its tail) is practically zero; they must be learned. Children are very adept at this process. We know this because if they weren't so good at it, we wouldn't have seen the cultural, scientific, and technological development we have seen in human history.

Infants imitate in this way because they have a strong emotional motivation to conform, obey, and act in a way that respects the norms of the group (explored further in Chapter 8). No other animal has anything comparable to this ratchet effect. The faithful copying of norms that every generation of children takes part in as well as individual and collaborative inventiveness (as we will see in Chapter 10) form some the key drivers of our cultural evolution.

| | **Key Point** |

- Children's accurate imitation of behaviour allows culture to be passed from one generation to the next.

5.6 Who Do You Trust?

So, a lot of what we know we learn from others. While social learning can be a shortcut to knowledge, standing on the shoulders of giants, it introduces a new challenge: who do you trust? Other people can be misinformed, opinionated, unreliable, or – worse – deliberately misleading. Many studies have shown that young children are highly selective over whom they learn from (Schmid et al., 2024) and thus reduce the chances that they pay attention to unreliable information in the first place:

- Children prefer to learn from those who are accurate – for example, selectively engaging with people who label objects correctly (Birch et al., 2008).
- Children prefer to learn from those who are reliable – for example, selectively engaging with people who behave consistently over time (Zmyj et al., 2010).
- Children prefer to learn from those who are adequately informed – for example, selectively engaging with people who have access to relevant information (Brosseau-Liard & Birch, 2011).
- Children prefer to learn from people who appear confident, but they also keep track of how well the person's confidence has matched with their knowledge and accuracy in the past, and they avoid learning new information from people who have a history of being *over*confident (Birch et al., 2020).
- Children prefer to learn from people who receive more attention from other learners, such as those who are high-status or prestigious, selectively engaging with more skilful peers and avoid attending to less skilful ones (Ronfard et al., 2018).

| | **Key Point** |

- Children are discerning learners, preferring to trust people who are accurate, reliable, skilful, well-informed, prestigious, and appropriately confident.

5.7 Instruction

No other species can learn so much or acquire such a variety of information from others as human children do. But it's also true that no other species goes to such lengths to provide as many opportunities for their children to learn. Every known society makes a huge investment in educating their young about their culture. 'Educating' doesn't just mean the teaching that takes place in formal school environments, which is a relatively recent invention and something that is far from being a universal experience today: worldwide, children's participation in primary schools is around 70% (United Nations, 2018). Here we are talking about something more fundamental and widespread, whereby children, in collaboration with their caregivers and peers, interact in ways that ensure the transmission of cultural practices and beliefs across generations. In this way, teaching works together with imitation to preserve cultural knowledge, increasing the potential for innovation or modifications to accumulate from one generation to the next.

Caregivers have a special motivation to teach children because, along with promoting their health and well-being, most parents want their children to grow into culturally fluent adults: able to speak the language; familiar with the rites, rituals, folklore, religion, dress, jokes, and music of their group; and able to take advantage of the accumulated medical, ecological, and technical know-how of their ancestors.

While the motivation to imitate and instruct might be universal, there is substantial cross-cultural and historical variation in exactly how this takes place (Legare & Harris, 2016). Caregivers in different cultures respond differently to infants' emotional displays and speak or interact with infants differently, variously preferring vocal, visual, or physical means of communication. In one-on-one interactions, caregivers from the USA typically rely heavily on language, asking more questions, encourage planning, and providing high levels of verbal praise, encouragement, and scaffolding – for instance, leaving a jigsaw piece adjacent to its correct location (Clark & Bernicot, 2008).

While this model of caregiver–child interaction is familiar to those in the West, it is arguably a relatively recent development, reflecting the structure of formal educational institutions and the large body of abstract knowledge and skills children are expected to master (e.g., literacy and numeracy). Interestingly, pushback against this kind of highly supervised learning has begun to emerge in these same societies, most notably within the free-range parenting movement, which argues that this approach negatively impacts children's natural tendency for self-directed discovery, exploration, and independence (Skenazy, 2021).

By contrast, in Vanuatu, a South Pacific chain of islands, caregivers use substantially more non-verbal forms of communication, such as gesture and physical touch, and children often learn by close observation of adults as they go about their business without being directly addressed or involved (Little et al., 2016). In nearby Fiji, the kind of direct, active teaching that American parents typically use is also relatively rare compared with less time-intensive and costly forms of teaching, such as teaching by social tolerance or allowing children to be bystanders and to observe behaviours they may need to learn.

The cross-cultural variation we see in different teaching styles is influenced by a range of factors, including parental beliefs about children's ability to teach themselves through observational learning; whether children of a given age have anything interesting to say and therefore whether they are worth addressing; and the presence of formal education and expectations about entering the workforce. For example, children living in communities that rely on labour-intensive agriculture are expected to assist adults from an early age in cooking, planting, harvesting crops, and helping with the childcare of younger siblings (Legare, 2017).

Köster and colleagues observed how 441 parents interacted with their 2-year-olds at mealtimes in five diverse cultural contexts: rural Brazil and Ecuador and urban Argentina,

Germany, and Japan (2022). They found that parents from all backgrounds mainly relied on a set of six teaching behaviours – prompts to do, prompts to stop, communication of knowledge, demonstrations, providing choices, and negative feedback – but that the frequency of each behaviour varied from site to site. In the face of this cross-cultural diversity, the fact that in many – if not most – cases children develop into culturally competent adult members of their communities (e.g., speak the language, internalise the norms, share the beliefs) underlines how incredibly adaptable children are at learning. Humans are some of the most behaviourally flexible of all animals, with this plasticity being greatest in infancy and declining with age, meaning that childhood is a critical period of cultural apprenticeship.

Regardless of cross-cultural variation, all instruction and learning benefits from the kind of mental mind-reading and sharing of intentions that humans the world over seem to excel at. Dyadic and triadic interaction, **shared intentionality**, and a **theory of mind** (Chapter 3) make teaching and learning more efficient. Understanding what a tutor can *see* or grasping what they *want* you to do helps learners work out where they are supposed to direct their attention. Understanding what a learner already *knows* and *believes* helps tutors pitch their instruction at the right level. This effect is not just limited to adult instructors: 3–5-year-old children with higher levels of theory of mind were found to be more effective teachers of *other* children than children whose theory of mind abilities were less developed (Davis-Unger & Carlson, 2008).

Key Point

- While the motivation to imitate and instruct might be universal, there is cross-cultural and historical variation in exactly how such imitation and instruction take place.

So, instruction can be helpful. But can it ever get in the way of children's learning? There is evidence to suggest it can, especially when it undermines children's natural tendency for discovery, creativity, play, and innovation. Psychologist Elizabeth Bonawitz and her colleagues looked at how 4-year-olds learned about a new toy that had four tubes (Bonawitz et al., 2011). For one group of children, the experimenter said, 'I just found this toy!' As she brought out the toy, she pulled the first tube, as if by accident, and it squeaked. She acted surprised ('Huh! Did you see that? Let me try to do that!') and pulled the tube again to make it squeak a second time. With the other group of children, the experimenter acted more like a teacher. She said, 'I'm going to show you how my toy works. Watch this!' She then deliberately made the tube squeak. Then she left both groups of children alone to play with the toy. What the children didn't know was that the other tubes were interesting as well: if you pulled on one tube it squeaked, if you looked inside another tube you found a hidden mirror, and so on. Unsurprisingly, the children in both groups pulled on the first tube and made it squeak. More interestingly, the children in the first group played with the toy for longer and discovered more of its hidden features than the second group. In this case, and in other studies showing similar results, direct instruction from the teacher made the children less curious and less likely to discover new information (Buchsbaum et al., 2011).

> **Key Point**
>
> - Direct instruction is a double-edged sword. It can guide children to a specific answer more quickly, but it can make them less likely to discover new information and to draw unexpected conclusions.

Talking Point

We have looked at different child–parent interaction styles (e.g., contrasting Vanuatu, Fiji, and the USA), and in doing so we touched on a controversial topic: parenting. Putting aside the latest debates in parenting how-to manuals, we can make a more general and less contentious point: across different societies, caregiver–child interaction styles are adapted to the values and norms of the society they are embedded in. In societies where acquiring a large body of abstract knowledge and skills is valued, then it is understandable that caregivers would structure their interactions with this end goal in mind. For example, becoming literate and numerate is a measure of success in most Western societies and requires a lengthy period of direct supervision, relying heavily on language and high levels of feedback and encouragement.

By contrast, in societies where self-reliance is highly valued, caregiver–child interactions will be structured differently, having this end goal in mind. For example, in forager societies autonomy is crucial in an environment where a person needs to look for food each day. Caregivers scaffold this independence by intervening less in children's actions and by giving fewer direct instructions. In the traditional cultures of the Marquesas Islands of French Polynesia, by the time children are 18–24 months old, mothers are often pregnant with another child. Consequently, toddlers are expected to meet more of their own emotional needs, and members of these communities reinforce this by valuing signs of personal autonomy – for example, standing up to adult authority (Martini & Kirkpatrick, 1992).

And, of course, cultures themselves change in what they value over time. Saxe recorded how introducing a market economy into remote villages in Papua New Guinea led to the transition from using a simple numeric system, based on counting body parts (e.g., touching the nose equals 14), to a more abstract system familiar to those in the West (2012). Almost overnight, this changed the everyday experience for a whole generation of children because they were now living in a culture that valued a more abstract number system, and they were also now expected to learn it.

> ## Summary
>
> - Children are highly effective, motivated, active, and playful learners, balancing the needs of exploring the world around them and exploiting what they have learned.
> - Children pay particular attention to inconsistent or unexpected outcomes that provide new information about the way the world works.

- Children's exploratory learning is well suited to learning about cause and effect and to using that knowledge to predict how things will behave in the world.
- Children can transfer what they have learned in one context to another, generalising in systematic and evidence-based ways.
- Play and pretend play help children practice the physical and cognitive skills they will need later in life.
- Young children appreciate the difference between fantasy and reality and are often sceptical that unlikely things and events are real. However, they can be encouraged towards supernatural thinking if the belief is shared by others.
- Children's accurate imitation of behaviour allows culture to be passed from one generation to the next.
- Children are discerning learners, preferring to trust people who are accurate, reliable, skilful, well-informed, prestigious, and appropriately confident.
- While the motivation to imitate and instruct might be universal, there is cross-cultural and historical variation in exactly how such imitation and instruction take place.
- Direct instruction is a double-edged sword. It can guide children to a specific answer more quickly, but it can make them less likely to discover new information and to draw unexpected conclusions.

References

Barr, R. & Hayne, H. (2003). It's not what you know, it's who you know: older siblings facilitate imitation during infancy. *International Journal of Early Years Education*, 11, 7–21.

Birch, S. A., Severson, R., & Baimel, A. (2020). Children's understanding of when a person's confidence and hesitancy is a cue to their credibility. *PLoS ONE*, 15(1), e0227026.

Birch, S. A., Vauthier, S. A., & Bloom, P. (2008). Three-and four-year-olds spontaneously use others' past performance to guide their learning. *Cognition*, 107(3), 1018–1034.

Bonawitz, E., Shafto, P., Gweon, H., Goodman, N. D., Spelke, E., & Schulz, L. (2011). The double-edged sword of pedagogy: construction limits spontaneous exploration and discovery. *Cognition*, 120(3), 322–330.

Brosseau-Liard, P. E. & Birch, S. A. (2011). Epistemic states and traits: preschoolers appreciate the differential informativeness of situation-specific and person-specific cues to knowledge. *Child Development*, 82(6), 1788–1796.

Buchsbaum, D., Bridgers, S., Skolnick-Weisberg, D., & Gopnik, A. (2012). The power of possibility: causal learning, counterfactual reasoning, and pretend play. *Philosophical Transactions of the Royal Society of London. Series B, Biological Sciences*, 367(1599), 2202–2212.

Buchsbaum, D., Gopnik, A., Griffiths, T. L., & Shafto, P. (2011). Children's imitation of causal action sequences is influenced by statistical and pedagogical evidence. *Cognition*, 120(3), 331–340.

Clark, E. V. & Bernicot, J. (2008). Repetition as ratification: how parents and children place information in common ground. *Journal of Child Language*, 35, 349–371.

Davis-Unger, A. C. & Carlson, S. M. (2008). Children's teaching skills: the role of theory of mind and executive function. *Mind, Brain, and Education*, 2, 128–135.

Gautam, S., Owen Hall, R., Suddendorf, T., & Redshaw, J. (2023). Counterfactual choices and moral judgments in children. *Child Development*, 94, e296–e307.

Gopnik, A. (2016). *The Gardener and the Carpenter*. Vintage Publishing.

Gopnik, A., Griffiths, T. L., & Lucas, C. G. (2015). When younger learners can be better (or at least more open-minded) than older ones. *Current Directions in Psychological Science*, 24, 87–92.

Gweon, H., Tenenbaum, J. B., & Schulz, L. E. (2010). Infants consider both the sample and the sampling process in inductive generalization. *Proceedings of the National Academy of Sciences of the United States of America*, 107(20), 9066–9071.

Harris, P. L., Brown, E., Marriott, C., Whittall, S., & Harmer, S. (1991). Monsters, ghosts and witches: testing the limits of the fantasy–reality distinction in young children. *British Journal of Developmental Psychology*, 9, 105–123.

Köster, M., Torréns, M. G., Kärtner, J., Itakura, S., Cavalcante, L., & Kanngiesser, P. (2022). Parental teaching behavior in diverse cultural contexts. *Evolution and Human Behavior*, 43(5), 432–441.

Legare, C. (2017). Cumulative cultural learning: development and diversity. *Proceedings of the National Academy of Sciences of the United States of America*, 114(30), 7877–7883.

Legare, C. & Harris, P. (2016). The ontogeny of cultural learning. *Child Development*, 87, 633–642.

Lipko, A. R., Dunlosky, J., & Merriman, W. E. (2009). Persistent overconfidence despite practice: the role of task experience in preschoolers' recall predictions. *Journal of Experimental Child Psychology*, 103(2), 152–166.

Little, E., Carver, L., & Legare, C. (2016). Cultural variation in triadic infant–caregiver object exploration. *Child Development*, 87, 1130–1145.

Martini, M. & Kirkpatrick, J. (1992). Parenting in Polynesia: a view from the Marquesas. *Annual Advances in Applied Developmental Psychology*, 5, 199–222.

Meltzoff, A. N. (1988). Infant imitation after a 1-week delay: long-term memory for novel acts and multiple stimuli. *Developmental Psychology*, 24, 470–476.

Pellegrini, A. D. (2009). *The Role of Play in Human Development*. Oxford University Press.

Ronfard, S., Bartz, D. T., Cheng, L., Chen, X., & Harris, P. L. (2018). Children's developing ideas about knowledge and its acquisition. *Advances in Child Development and Behavior*, 54, 123–151.

Saxe, G. (2012). *Cultural Development of Mathematical Ideas: Papua New Guinea Studies*. Cambridge University Press.

Schmid, B., Bleijlevens, N., Mani, N., & Behne, T. (2024). The cognitive underpinnings and early development of children's selective trust. *Child Development*, 95, 1315–1332.

Schulz, L. (2012). The origins of inquiry: inductive inference and exploration in early childhood. *Trends in Cognitive Sciences*, 16, 382–389.

Shtulman, A. & Carey, S. A. (2007). Improbable or impossible? How children reason about the possibility of extraordinary events. *Child Development*, 78, 1015–1032.

Skenazy, L. (2021). *Free-Range Kids: How Parents and Teachers Can Let Go and Let Grow*. Jossey Bass.

Špinka, M., Newberry, R. C., & Bekoff, M. (2001). Mammalian play: training for the unexpected. *The Quarterly Review of Biology*, 76(2), 141–168.

United Nations. (2018). *The Sustainable Development Goals Report*. United Nations.

Vanderschuren, L. J., Achterberg, E. J., & Trezza, V. (2016). The neurobiology of social play and its rewarding value in rats. *Neuroscience and Biobehavioral Reviews*, 70, 86–105.

Whiting, B. B. & Edwards, C. P. (1988). *Children of Different Worlds: The Formation of Social Behavior*. Harvard University Press.

Wong, A., Cordes, S., Harris, P. L., & Chernyak, N. (2023). Being nice by choice: the effect of counterfactual reasoning on children's social evaluations. *Developmental Science*, 26, e13394.

Woolley, J. D. & Ghossainy, M. (2013). Revisiting the fantasy–reality distinction: children as naïve skeptics. *Child Development*, 84, 1496–1510.

Zmyj, N., Buttelmann, D., Carpenter, M., & Daum, M. M. (2010). The reliability of a model influences 14-month-olds' imitation. *Journal of Experimental Child Psychology*, 106(4), 208–220.

6 GROWING UP GLOBALLY – THE EARLY YEARS

 Learning Outcomes

After reading this chapter you will be able to:

- Understand why the cross-cultural perspective is important to understanding children's development.
- Consolidate what you learned in Chapters 1–5.
- Revisit the ideas you came across in Chapters 1–5 in a cross-cultural context.

6.1 Introduction

This last chapter of the early years section is structured differently from the others. It is designed to be a breathing space, where we survey the ground we've covered and consolidate what we've understood, and it provides an opportunity for you to revisit areas you haven't fully grasped first time around. And to help you join the dots in the story so far, all the key points from each chapter are repeated here so the essential takeaways are in one place.

The second function of this chapter is to re-examine what we have already discovered from a more global perspective, so every section – The Early Years (Section I), Middle Childhood (Section II), and Adolescence (Section III) – is capped by a 'Growing Up Globally' chapter. For each of the topics we have been looking at, whether that be mindreading, language, or learning, we unpack one claim and explore whether it holds up to the diversity of children's experiences around the world. Why would we want to do that?

In a famous research paper titled 'The WEIRDest people in the world?', evolutionary anthropologist Joseph Henrich and his colleagues pointed out something odd about psychological research: 96% of participants in the studies they looked at were from **WEIRD** societies – or those that were Western, Educated, Industrialised, Rich, and Democratic, despite these societies only representing about 12% of the world's population (2010). Studies that look at child development in particular are also highly biased towards certain populations in the West, usually testing children from white, middle-class, suburban communities. This skewed sample matters if we think that the ways children grow up in the non-WEIRD parts of the world are significantly different from WEIRD ones. There is plenty of evidence to suggest they are, but the main point is that we don't actually know the extent of these differences until we look. If we want to say something about how all children grow up, not just the WEIRD ones, everyone needs to be part of the story. To be clear, children from WEIRD societies represent as good a sample as any other children. But if we want to say something more general about how children grow up in other contexts, we need to be more inclusive.

A big theme of this book is that children around the world are similar *and* different. If we want to understand how they are similar and different, careful cross-cultural work can help us work out which features of our psychology and behaviour are more sensitive to cultural input and flexible, and which are more heritable and stable (Amir & McAuliffe, 2020). For example, take something as basic as learning to walk, which we might think develops in a very similar way for all children. And sure enough, no children learn to run before they can walk. But the precise timing of *when* they walk can be significantly affected by the parenting practices of the culture they are born into. !Kung San infants are born into a society of foragers who live at the western edge of the Kalahari Desert. These infants are encouraged to walk from early on in development, being held upright by their parents, and consequently they learn to walk significantly earlier than American infants (Konner, 2005). By contrast, Ache infants in Amazonian Paraguay, who are actively discouraged from learning to walk due primarily to safety concerns, are delayed up to a year in this area when compared to American infants (Kaplan & Dove, 1987). If the development of something as basic as walking can be affected by culture, then we should expect that many other aspects of child development are too.

 Key Point

- The cross-cultural perspective can help us work out how children are similar and how they are different.

Every effort has been made to address the WEIRD bias in this book by drawing on research from around the world. **Figure 6.1** shows the locations of some of the children that feature in this book. The societies that these children grow up in vary a lot in their culture, community size, geography, way of life, languages spoken, and economic circumstances.

Child development needs greater diversification not only in who it studies but also in who studies it, as researchers themselves tend to be from the same WEIRD societies they study. The cultural values and biases of these societies inevitably seep into the researchers' interpretations of the data and the methodological choices they make. Developmental psychologist Robert Serpell compared how well Zambian and British children could copy a visual display using four different media: pencil and paper, strips of wire, plasticine, and using their hands. The Zambian children did much better at copying than the British children when they were using strips of wire, a common type of material Zambian children might use to make handmade toys. The British children did better with pencil and paper, a common experience

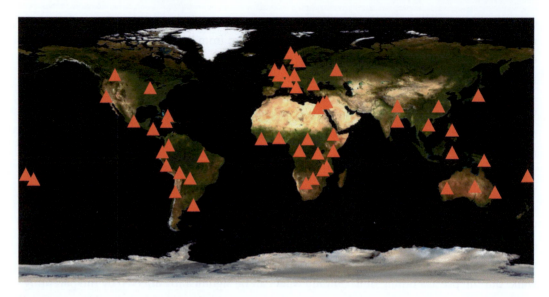

Figure 6.1 Locations of some of the children featured in this book, including Argentina, Australia, Belgium, Bolivia, Botswana, Brazil, Canada, Central African Republic, Chile, China, Columbia, Cuba, Democratic Republic of the Congo, Ecuador, Egypt, Ethiopia, Fiji, Finland, Germany, India, Indonesia, Israel, Italy, Jamaica, Japan, Jordan, Kenya, Liberia, Malawi, Mexico, Namibia, Nepal, Netherlands, Nicaragua, Nigeria, Norway, Papua New Guinea, Paraguay, Peru, the Philippines, Polynesia, Romania, Russia, Rwanda, Samoa, Sweden, Switzerland, Thailand, the UK, the USA, and Zambia. Source: NASA Earth Observatory (NASA Goddard Space Flight Center).

for them as they were all in school, whereas the Zambian children were not. The children performed similarly with the two media that were equally familiar to them: plasticine and using their hands (Serpell, 1979).

So, how researchers ask the question matters, and if a variety of media hadn't been used in this case, we might have drawn some incorrect conclusions about which groups perform better. Hoping to transplant the same test across very different cultures can be naïve or, at worst, a kind of intellectual colonialism (Lansford et al., 2021; **Figure 6.2**). As Serpell's research demonstrated, children are the same (using plasticine and their hands) and different (using strips of wire versus pencil and paper) depending on how the question is framed. The group differences in this case were best explained by different cultural experiences with the materials than by any inherent differences in children's ability to copy.

Watch the One-Minute Method.

Discover why our methods need to be culturally meaningful and sensitive to the experiences of children taking part in research.

6.2 Why Does Love Matter? Recap and Consolidation

- In the short term, infants need immediate care from others to survive, and they encourage this with their physical appearance and behaviours.

"YOU CAN'T BUILD A HUT, YOU DON'T KNOW HOW TO FIND EDIBLE ROOTS AND YOU KNOW NOTHING ABOUT PREDICTING THE WEATHER. IN OTHER WORDS, YOU DO TERRIBLY ON OUR I.Q. TEST."

Figure 6.2 Researchers need to aware of how sensitive their measurements are to context and history. Source: Copyright © 2024 by Sidney Harris www.sciencecartoonsplus.com/.../gallery.php.

- In the long term, parenting is a big investment, and over the course of our history this has caused infants to advertise their worth and parents to be selective over whom they cared for.
- A peak in early brain plasticity creates an especially sensitive period early on in development.
- Early experiences matter, but they matter to some children more than others.
- Some responses to early experiences are adaptive for later life.
- Emotions help us set our goals and regulate our well-being.
- Infants start out with a basic repertoire of positive and negative emotions that become more differentiated over time.

- Children develop a similar vocabulary of emotions; precisely what those emotions mean is shaped by social interactions and cultural norms.

6.3 Attachment in a Cross-Cultural Context

In Chapter 2 we took a brief look at attachment – a special emotional bond that children develop with one or more caregivers, where the attachment figure gives children a sense of security and stability. Let's take a deeper look at attachment and see how well it holds up when we look at children growing up around the world in diverse cultural contexts.

6.3.1 Universality: Attachment Is Universal

There are two aspects of attachment that appear to be common to all children from studies that have looked at patterns of childcare across societies. First, children the world over appear to have a preferential bond with one or more caregivers. In many cultures, children grow up with a network of attachment figures, but the parent or caregiver who takes responsibility for the care of a child during part of the day or the night becomes their favourite source of attachment. For example, across non-Anglo-Saxon and European societies children seek closeness to the attachment figure when they are placed in a stressful situation or feel tense or anxious (van IJzendoorn & Sagi-Schwartz, 2008). Underlining what is at stake here, researchers found that in all 28 of the countries they looked at, the death of the mother – who is typically the primary caregiver in most cultures – was associated with a much higher child mortality rate (Sear & Mace, 2008). Second, different types of attachment – avoidant, secure, insecure, and resistant – have been reliably identified in forager societies with high levels of cooperative parenting (parenting by people other than the mother) and in affluent and deprived urban contexts across Africa, East Asian, and Latin America (Mesman et al., 2016b).

The most straightforward explanation as to why attachment is universal is that infants are born universally helpless, and caregivers are universally predisposed to help. Who children attach to and how they express this attachment are more culturally variable. For example, infants from the Hausa community, a native ethnic group from West and Central Africa, are generally physically restricted in their locomotion by their caregivers and are thus less free to explore the environment by themselves (Marvin et al., 1977). These infants explore their immediate environment in more visual ways and by manipulating objects, but they only do so when in close proximity to an attachment figure, and they cease to explore in this way as soon as caregivers leave. The Hausa infants clearly use adult caregivers as secure bases from which to explore, and they differentiate between attachment figures and strangers, but the way they express attachment is shaped by the local context (Marvin et al., 1977).

 Key Points

- Children the world over appear to have a preferential bond with one or more caregivers.
- Different types of attachment have been reliably classified across very different societies, albeit expressed in culturally specific ways.

6.3.2 Normativity: Secure Attachment Is the Norm

Studies across a range of diverse societies suggest that more children fall into the securely attached category than the other categories of avoidant, insecure, and resistant. The category of 'securely attached' itself emerged from Mary Ainsworth's extensive research in Uganda, and since that early work it has been evidenced in a wide range of cultural contexts.

While securely attached often ranks the most frequent type of attachment, the absolute level depends on local circumstances. For instance, levels of securely attached infants were particularly low in rural, economically poor Mexican samples (Gojman et al., 2012) and in undernourished Chilean populations (Valenzuela, 1997). Not having the economic resources to reliably provide basic care for children in terms of nutrition, healthcare, safe housing, and clothing is likely to be universally stressful for parents, emphasising the importance of socio-economic circumstances in shaping family life and parenting patterns (van IJzendoorn & Sagi-Schwartz, 2008).

 Key Point

- Across diverse societies, more children fall into the securely attached category than other categories, but the absolute numbers are affected by a variety of socio-economic and cultural factors.

6.3.3 Sensitivity: Sensitive Caregiving Encourages Attachment Security

A sensitive caring style involves judging when a response is needed and what a good enough response looks like, as well as adapting the response to the psychological needs of the child in that moment, all of which require the carer to engage with the kind of theory of mind (ToM) reasoning and mind-mindedness we met in Chapter 3.

There is cross-cultural evidence that secure attachment is related to caregiving sensitivity. In a sample of 1,150 Asian families living in the USA, 87% of whom were born in Asia, observations of maternal sensitivity were significantly related to observations of infant attachment security (Huang et al., 2012). Mesman and colleagues (2016a) reported a strong association between maternal beliefs about the ideal mother and attachment theory's description of the sensitive mother across 26 cultural groups from 15 countries.

While the rates of sensitive behaviour by parents are very similar across cultures, what sensitivity and responsiveness look like varies. For example, in some cultures, appropriate responding to infant vocalisation may consist of touching or stroking the infant, whereas in other cultures it may involve imitating the sound that the infant made or smiling at the infant (e.g., Kärtner et al., 2010). Soothing through nursing and feeding is much more common in non-Western than in Western cultures (e.g., True et al., 2001). In societies such as that of Bolivia, infants are typically in sustained physical contact with caregivers throughout most of the day and night, often being carried on the caregiver's back. Consequently, they encounter less direct face-to-face engagement than infants growing up in societies that value vocal and visual interaction, such as that of the USA. These differences in experience change what infants expect sensitive parenting to look like. When US parents stopped engaging with their infants and maintained a still face for a brief period of time, their infants got upset. By contrast, the Bolivian infants were unaffected by a still face, but they became upset when an equivalent task introduced physical unresponsiveness (Broesch et al., 2022).

In cultures where parents are in more continuous close physical contact with infants, caregiving tends to rely less on more distant ways of 'checking in' and sharing attention, such as mutual eye gaze. Overall levels of mutual gaze can be further moderated by social hierarchy – for instance, when there are norms that stipulate low-ranking individuals should not gaze at individuals considered to be higher ranking (Bard & Keller, 2024).

Key Point

- Sensitive caregiving is associated with attachment security across a range of societies, but how that sensitivity is expressed is culturally variable.

6.3.4 Competence: Secure Attachment Leads to Better Outcomes for Children

This aspect of attachment theory has been less cross-culturally documented than universality, normativity, or sensitivity, but there is evidence from Western and non-Western societies that secure attachment is associated with better outcomes for children. For example, Gusii and Chilean infants who were classified as securely attached were better nourished than those with insecure attachments (Kermoian & Leiderman, 1986; Valenzuela, 1997). However, based on these associations alone, we can't say whether secure attachment causes better nutrition, or that healthy infants are more likely to cause more sensitive parenting, especially in situations of economic deprivation when parents are forced to be selective in their investment of time and energy.

Overall, the research suggests that whether children perceive themselves as being loved and accepted is more important for their well-being than the specific behaviours parents use to convey that love. Children use this template of love and affection – or the lack of it – in their future relationships. For example, adults who use aggression in social situations are more likely to have children who behave aggressively (Huesmann & Kirwil, 2007). If the overall parenting style is warm and loving, children are more likely to regard their parents as having legitimate authority to direct their behaviour, are more compliant with their parents' requests, and internalise parents' messages more fully (Darling et al., 2005).

Key Points

- Cross-culturally, there is some evidence for an association between attachment style and developmental outcomes for children, but much more work needs to be done to understand cause and effect in this area.
- Overall, cross-cultural attachment research suggests there are universal trends expressed in culturally specific ways.

6.4 Are Children Mind Readers? Recap and Consolidation

- ToM is the capacity to picture the world from another person's point of view; what they see, know, want, desire, or believe.
- By around 9 months of age, infants show a basic ToM ability, understanding that other people pursue their own goals and can have a different perspective on the world than they do.
- Dyadic and triadic social interactions are important contexts in which children learn about the minds of others.
- By around 4 years of age, infants develop a more advanced ToM ability, being able to hold mutually incompatible ideas about other people's beliefs, their own knowledge, and reality.
- Acquiring ToM has far-reaching social consequences for children's development.
- ToM helps people coordinate their intensions towards common goals and allows complex cooperation.
- When a capacity is estimated to emerge in development partly depends on how we measure it.

6.5 False Beliefs Across the World

As we learned in Chapter 3, compared with other species, humans show an extraordinary ability to infer the beliefs of others, and in particular to recognise that others may hold and act on false beliefs. It has been proposed that this ToM is a universal part of our human nature, giving us an advantage when it comes to cooperating, competing, and communicating with as well as learning from others. If that's true, we might expect to see this skill emerging in a similar way for children across the world.

Biological anthropologist H. Clark Barrett and his colleagues set out to determine whether this is true or not in three diverse, traditional, non-Western cultures: the Salar, who are a Turkic-speaking ethnic minority in rural north-west China and who live in small, traditional settlements; and the Shuar/Colono community, which represents a mix of native Amazonians (Shuar), who were traditionally hunter-horticulturalists, and Ecuadorian immigrants from the Andes (Colono), both of whom now practice small-scale agriculture in the rural Amazon region (Barrett et al., 2013).

They gave 1–4-year-olds from these societies a set of tests that assessed their false belief understanding. For example, in one task, children sat opposite an experimenter (E1) who showed the children two containers: one with a pair of scissors hidden in it and one with nothing in it. E1 took the scissors out of the container and cut up some stickers, put the scissors back in the same container, and then left the room as a second experimenter (E2) arrived. E2 also used the scissors cut up some stickers, but she then put the scissors in her own pocket. E2 then looked thoughtful and said, 'When [E1's name] comes back, she is going to need her scissors again ... where will she think they are?'

If children are tracking E1's false belief, they should expect her to look for her scissors in the container she left them in. If children are tracking their own beliefs, they should expect her to look for her scissors in E2's pocket. As soon as E2 asked the question about where E1 would look, the young children across all societies looked reliably longer at the container, as if the infants were anticipating where E1 would look also, even though they knew E1's belief was false. The researchers also recorded other non-verbal and verbal responses, but the pattern was the same. Early false belief understanding of the non-Western children was comparable with that of Western children, pointing to a remarkable degree of similarity. A different study that involved children from Canada, India, Peru, Samoa, and Thailand found the same degree of similarity in the way false belief understanding emerged in childhood (Callaghan et al., 2005).

 Key Point

- Across diverse cultures, false belief understanding emerges in a similar way.

6.6 How Do Children Learn Language? Recap and Consolidation

- Before birth and after, children are becoming sensitised to the sounds in their native language(s) and insensitive to those that are not.
- Children use powerful pattern detection skills to segment speech streams into words.
- Child-directed speech differs in important ways from adult-to-adult speech and has been shown to help language learning.
- Cross-linguistically the types of first words children use show some similar characteristics and some differences shaped by cognitive, social, and linguistic factors.
- Children learn grammar incrementally by blending simple grammar that expresses simple ideas like agent-action and action-object into more complex forms like agent-action-object.
- Through their play, exploration, and social interaction, children use a variety of strategies to understand what words mean.
- Overgeneralisation errors are powerful illustrations of the creative power of language and the mechanisms children use to learn it.

6.7 Does the Language You Speak Affect the Way You Think?

As we have learned, there are over 7,000 languages in the world, and children appear equally capable of learning any one of them. Recall that, before birth and after, children are becoming sensitised to the sounds of their native language(s) and insensitive to those that are not. But does the language you learn also make you insensitive to some types of *thinking*?

Before we answer that, let's look at the relation between language and thought:
- Very young infants and many other animals are capable of complex thinking, even when they have no language.
- It is possible to translate between languages that have very different words, which would be difficult if words were the same things as what they meant.
- People have ideas that are difficult to put into words; this wouldn't happen if language was thought, as you could just say what you meant.
- If language was thought, people could never invent new words because there would be no way of imagining their meaning.
- Ambiguous phrases, like 'kids make nutritious snacks', wouldn't be ambiguous if language was thought.

So, we can rule out the idea that language is exactly the same thing as thought. If that were true, some languages would make some kinds of thoughts impossible for children to think.

 Key Point

- Language isn't the same thing as thought, and there is no evidence that the language you speak makes some thoughts impossible.

But there is evidence that the language children speak makes some types of thinking *more likely* than others. How we talk about the positions of objects in the world around us is one example.

If I were to describe where my keys are to you, I could say they are in front of the coffee cup (an intrinsic frame of reference), I could say they are on my left (a relative frame of reference), or I could say they are to the east (an absolute frame of reference). All three frames of references are used by humans across cultures, but some cultures – and languages – are more likely to use one system than another. In Dutch (like English), the dominant spatial frames of reference are the intrinsic and relative, whereas in Tzeltal, a Mayan language spoken in Mexico, the absolute frame of reference is more dominant. Linguist Stephen Levinson set out to test how this difference in language affected the way Dutch and Tzeltal speakers thought about the positions of objects (1996). He designed an experiment in which participants were shown objects organised in a row (**Figure 6.3**, left). The participants were then rotated 180° and asked to remake the arrangement of objects (**Figure 6.3**, right).

The Dutch speakers arranged the items according to an egocentric frame of reference (e.g., circle on my left, triangle on my right; **Figure 6.3**), while the Tzeltal speakers appeared to use an absolute frame (e.g., circle south of triangle). To understand why the speakers differed, we need to understand a bit more about Tzeltal speakers' homeland. Tzeltal is spoken in a mountainous area, with many ridges and cross-cutting valleys and with a tendency for the land to decline towards the north. Using the local geography is an efficient way to communicate where something is: downhill comes to mean north, uphill means south, and across can mean either east or west, but to avoid confusion in this latter case, speakers often refer to other landmarks. Obviously, this system relies on a good sense of direction, and Tzeltal speakers can reliably point in a specific direction for down (i.e., north), but they can also point in the same direction when they are out of their territory, or even when they can't see their environment. For Tzeltal speakers, if they wanted to describe where their keys are, the English statements 'The keys are in front of the cup' or 'They are to the left of me' are not possible, but they might say, 'Uphill'; or if you wanted to ask where someone was going, they might say, 'Ascending' (i.e., 'Going south').

These findings and others like them do not mean that people are unable to use frames of reference that their language does not use. The left–right distinction is still *learnable* for Tzeltal speakers. What this research does suggest is that, early on, infants are sensitive to a wide range of spatial distinctions, and over the course of development children develop biases towards certain distinctions, specifically those encoded in their language. So, the

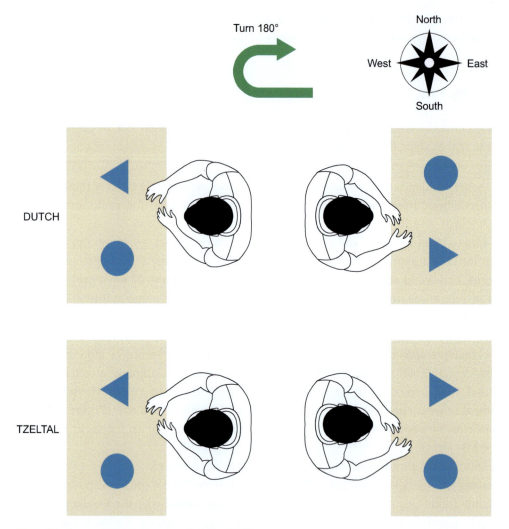

Figure 6.3 The experimental set-up from Levinson (1996).

language we speak can deeply affect the way we think about spatial relations and other aspects of our experience, including colour, number, and motion (Wolff & Holmes, 2011).

Beyond language, children's everyday experiences also affect the ways they think about spatial relationships. For example, Logoli children in Kenya live in communities that routinely explore the local area extensively. Researchers have found that the distance these children regularly travelled from their village predicted their skill in solving more abstract mathematical spatial problems (Munroe & Munroe, 1971). This is a good example of how differences in cultural practices become embedded in children's thinking.

 Key Point

- Long-term use of a particular language causes children to focus on certain aspects of experience to the exclusion of others.

6.8 How Do Children Learn So Much So Quickly? Recap and Consolidation

- Children are highly effective, motivated, active, and playful learners, balancing the needs of exploring the world around them and exploiting what they have learned.
- Children pay particular attention to inconsistent or unexpected outcomes that provide new information about the way the world works.
- Children's exploratory learning is well suited to learning about cause and effect and to using that knowledge to predict how things will behave in the world.
- Children can transfer what they have learned in one context to another, generalising in systematic and evidence-based ways.
- Play and pretend play help children practice the physical and cognitive skills they will need later in life.
- Young children appreciate the difference between fantasy and reality and are often sceptical that unlikely things and events are real. However, they can be encouraged towards supernatural thinking if the belief is shared by others.
- Children's accurate imitation of behaviour allows culture to be passed from one generation to the next.
- Children are discerning learners, preferring to trust people who are accurate, reliable, skilful, well-informed, prestigious, and appropriately confident.
- While the motivation to imitate and instruct might be universal, there is cross-cultural and historical variation in exactly how such imitation and instruction take place.
- Direct instruction is a double-edged sword. It can guide children to a specific answer more quickly, but it can make them less likely to discover new information and to draw unexpected conclusions.

6.9 Play and Social Learning in the Mbendjele BaYaka

As we discussed in Chapter 1, we have spent more than 97% of our time, as a species, living a forager way of life, and so that is the environment we are most adapted to. Even long before modern humans were around, our distant ancestors had been living in a similar way for perhaps as much as 2 million years. The relatively recent advent of agriculture and domestication of animals simply haven't had sufficient time, on an evolutionary timescale, to have a significant effect on our human nature.

This does not mean that that the foraging way of life or the people that live that life today are in any sense less developed or simpler than other societies. The cultural ratchet effect advances in different directions for different societies, and foragers have for many generations accumulated different technologies, tools, know-how, and skills that are exquisitely suited to the demands of their lives. Surviving off the land requires a long apprenticeship with plants, animals, geography, weather, bushcraft, and collaborative foraging techniques. Indeed, the time it takes to learn this complex web of knowledge may have been one of the reasons why humans needed such a long childhood in the first place (Kaplan et al., 2000). Like any society, the foraging way of life is not homogeneous either, with large variation existing between forager societies in how labour is distributed, how resources are gathered,

Figure 6.4 Handprints from a cave in Argentina made by our forager ancestors about 9,000 years ago. Based in part on the sizes and dimensions of the handprints, some researchers believe that much if not most of the art found on ancient cave walls like this was made by adolescents and children (Guthrie, 2005). Source: spatuletail/Shutterstock.

and who occupies which social roles. The long-held trope of 'man as the aggressive hunter' and 'woman as the passive gatherer' has started to break down under closer scrutiny. By considering a broader range of present-day and ancient societies, we now know that women have played and continue to play a substantial role in both hunting and warfare (Anderson et al., 2023; Guliaev, 2003).

Despite the importance of the distant past, we cannot observe how children grew up in forager societies tens of thousands of years ago. We can, however, study how children grow up in forager cultures today, not because these societies are 'primitive' or frozen in time, but because foragers today resemble our past way of life better than urban city-dwellers, with their access to recent inventions of healthcare, supermarkets, birth control, formal education, and so on (**Figure 6.4**).

Anthropologist Deniz Salali and her colleagues were particularly interested in the development of social learning and play in the Mbendjele BaYaka hunter-gatherer children from Congo-Brazzaville. This group spans across the rainforests of the Republic of Congo and Central African Republic, and its members earn a living by hunting, trapping, fishing, gathering forest products such as wild yams and caterpillars, collecting honey, and trading wild products in exchange of farmed food, cigarettes, and alcohol (Salali et al., 2019).

The team of researchers analysed thousands of hours of video recordings of 96 children, ranging in age from early infancy to late adolescence. They created diaries of their activities and recorded how much time they spent foraging, taking part in rituals, resting, cooking, cleaning, collecting firewood and water, manufacturing baskets and mats, making huts, looking after younger children, talking, playing, grooming, trading, singing, and so on. There were three main results that are of relevance to us. First, they found that children mainly learned by observation and imitation when the purpose of the activity was obvious to them in some way, such as foraging, using tools, cooking, preparing food, and grooming. It is not uncommon for even young children in these societies to accompany parents conducting subsistence tasks (e.g., by walking with or being carried by older females in the forest during foraging trips), and in these contexts the children learned by observation, imitation, and play-practicing.

Second, children were more likely to learn via direct instruction from peers and elders when the purpose of the activity was less clear and more of an arbitrary cultural convention, such as the cutting and distribution of meat in accordance with cultural norms around food sharing or rituals. One such ritual involves women singing together and hand-clapping to

Figure 6.5 Mbendjele BaYaka children. The child covered in leaves is mimicking a forest spirit. Initiated men who claim to have captured such a spirit enter the camp dressed in leaves, and this is followed by dancing into the night (reproduced with kind permission of Deniz Salali and Nikhil Chaudary). Source: Dr Gul Deniz Salali; Dr Nikhil Chaudhary.

beckon the forest spirits into the camp while the men prepare for the forest spirits on a secret path, who later arrive in the camp to perform a ritualistic dance (**Figure 6.5**).

Third, the researchers found that the kind of play children were involved in anticipated the division of labour between the sexes in the adults. Specifically, boys engaged more in hunting and climbing trees for honey collection, whereas girls engaged more in food gathering and domestic activities. So, the content of what the boys and girls were playing *about* matched the adult roles of the men and women. Moreover, girls transitioned from play into work sooner than boys did. The BaYaka girls started practicing foraging wild plants with women from early childhood, whereas the boys only started accompanying men on night-time hunting trips during adolescence. This is a specific example of the idea we met in Chapter 5 that pretend play helps children practice the physical and cognitive skills they will need later in life and develop a sense of cultural identity in the here and now.

Exploratory play.

Watch BaYaka infants begin experimenting with machetes soon after they are able to walk. This is a form of exploratory play that prepares them for the skills they will need later on.

When anthropologists and psychologists have looked across a broad range of societies, they have found that some forms of play, social learning, and instruction appear universal to all cultures. Who and what children play with are much more variable and are best explained by the customs, traditions, and values of the society they grow up in. For example, girls in the Okavango Delta of Botswana play house by pounding a stick in the dirt, imitating the way women use a mortar and pestle to crush grain; while Kpelle boys in Liberia practice climbing small coconut trees using a bamboo harness, imitating the way men climb the taller, more dangerous palm oil trees (Bock & Johnson, 2004; Lancy, 1996).

Key Point

- Play, social learning, and teaching appear to be universal aspects of human cultures; the content and timing of these processes during development vary to meet the needs of the culture in which they occur.

References

Amir, D. & McAuliffe, K. (2020). Cross-cultural, developmental psychology: integrating approaches and key insights. *Evolution and Human Behavior*, 41(5), 430–444.

Anderson, A., Chilczuk, S., Nelson, K., Ruther, R., & Wall-Scheffler, C. (2023). The Myth of man the hunter: women's contribution to the hunt across ethnographic contexts. *PLoS ONE*, 18(6), e0287101.

Bard, K. A. & Keller, H. (2024). Increasing inclusivity in developmental research. *Journal of Cognition and Development*, 25(2), 296–302.

Barrett, H., Broesch, T., Scott R., et al. (2013). Early false-belief understanding in traditional non-Western societies. *Proceedings. Biological Sciences*, 280(1755), 20122654.

Bock, J. & Johnson, S. E. (2004). Subsistence ecology and play among the Okavango Delta peoples of Botswana. *Human Nature*, 15(1), 63–81.

Broesch, T., Little, E. E., Carver, L. J., & Legare, C. H. (2022). Still-face redux: infant responses to a classic and modified still-face paradigm in proximal and distal care cultures. *Infant Behavior and Development*, 68, 101732.

Callaghan, T., Rochat, P., Lillard, A., et al. (2005). Synchrony in the onset of mental-state reasoning: evidence from five cultures. *Psychological Science*, 16(5), 378–384.

Darling, N., Cumsille, P., & Peña-Alampay, L. (2005). Rules, legitimacy of parental authority, and obligation to obey in Chile, the Philippines, and the United States. *New Directions for Child and Adolescent Development*, 108, 47–60.

Gojman, S., Millán, S., Carlson, E., et al. (2012). Intergenerational relations of attachment: a research synthesis of urban/rural Mexican samples. *Attachment and Human Development*, 14, 553–566.

Guliaev, V. I. (2003). Amazons in the Scythia: new finds at the Middle Don, southern Russia. *World Archaeology*, 31(1), 112–125.

Guthrie, R. (2005). *The Nature of Paleolithic Art*. University of Chicago Press.

Henrich, J., Heine, S., & Norenzayan, A. (2010). The WEIRDest people in the world? *Behavioral and Brain Sciences*, 33(2–3), 61–83.

Huang, Z. J., Lewin, A., Mitchell, S. J., & Zhang, J. (2012). Variations in the relationship between maternal depression, maternal sensitivity, and child attachment by race/ethnicity and nativity: findings from a nationally representative cohort study. *Maternal and Child Health Journal*, 16, 40–50.

Huesmann, L. R. & Kirwil, L. (2007). Why observing violence increases the risk of violent behavior by the observer. In D. J. Flannery, A. T. Vazsonyi, & I. D. Waldman (eds.), *The Cambridge Handbook of Violent Behavior and Aggression* (pp. 545–570). Cambridge University Press.

Kaplan, H. & Dove, H. (1987). Infant development among the Ache of eastern Paraguay. *Developmental Psychology*, 23(2), 190–198.

Kaplan, H. S., Hill, K., Lancaster, J., & Hurtado, A. M. (2000). A theory of human life history evolution: diet, intelligence, and longevity. *Evolutionary Anthropology*, 9, 156–185.

Kärtner, J., Keller, H., & Yovsi, R. D. (2010). Mother–infant interaction during the first 3 months: the emergence of culture-specific contingency patterns. *Child Development*, 81, 540–554.

Kermoian, R. & Leiderman, P. H. (1986). Infant attachment to mother and child caretaker in an East African community. *International Journal of Behavioral Development*, 9(4), 455–469.

Konner, M. J. (2005). Hunter-gatherer infancy and childhood: the !kung and others. In B. S. Hewlett & M. E. Lamb (eds.), *Hunter-Gatherer Childhoods: Evolutionary, Developmental and Cultural Perspectives* (pp. 19–64). Transaction Publishers.

Lancy, D. (1996). *Playing on the Mother-Ground: Cultural Routines for Children's Development*. Guilford Press.

Lansford, J., French, D., & Gauvain, M. (2021). *Child and Adolescent Development in Cultural Context*. American Psychological Association.

Levinson, S. C. (1996). Frames of reference and Molyneux's question: cross-linguistic evidence. In P. Bloom, M. Peterson, L. Nadel, & M. Garrett (eds.), *Language and Space* (pp. 109–169). MIT Press.

Marvin, R. S., Van Devender, T. L., Iwanaga, M. I., LeVine, S., & LeVine, R. A. (1977). Infant–caregiver attachment among the Hausa of Nigeria. In H. McGurk (ed.), *Ecological Factors in Human Development* (pp. 247–259). North-Holland.

Mesman, J., Van IJzendoorn, M., Behrens, K., et al. (2016a). Is the ideal mother a sensitive mother? Beliefs about early childhood parenting in mothers across the globe. *International Journal of Behavioral Development*, 40(5), 385–397.

Mesman, J., Van IJzendoorn, M. H., & Sagi-Schwartz, A. (2016b). Cross-cultural patterns of attachment: universal and contextual dimensions. In J. Cassidy & P. R. Shaver (eds.), *Handbook of Attachment: Theory, Research, and Clinical Applications*, 3rd edition (pp. 790–815). Guilford.

Munroe, R. L. & Munroe, R. H. (1971). Effect of environmental experience on spatial ability in an East African society. *Journal of Social Psychology*, 83(1), 15–22.

Salali, G. D., Chaudhary, N., Bouer, J., et al. (2019). Development of social learning and play in BaYaka hunter-gatherers of Congo. *Scientific Reports*, 9, 11080.

Sear, R. & Mace, R. (2008). Who keeps children alive? A review of the effects of kin on child survival. *Evolution and Human Behavior*, 29, 1–18.

Serpell, R. (1979). How specific are perceptual skills? A cross-cultural study of pattern reproduction. *British Journal of Psychology*, 70(3), 365–380.

True, M. M., Pisani, L., & Oumar, F. (2001). Infant–mother attachment among the

Dogon of Mali. *Child Development*, 72, 1451–1466.

Valenzuela, M. (1997). Maternal sensitivity in a developing society: the context of urban poverty and infant chronic undernutrition. *Developmental Psychology*, 33(5), 845–855.

van IJzendoorn, M. H. & Sagi-Schwartz, A. (2008). Cross-cultural patterns of attachment: universal and contextual dimensions. In J. Cassidy & P. R. Shaver (eds.), *Handbook of Attachment: Theory, Research, and Clinical Applications*, 2nd edition (pp. 880–905). The Guilford Press.

Wolff, P. & Holmes, K. J. (2011), Linguistic relativity. *WIREs Cognitive Science*, 2, 253–265.

SECTION II

MIDDLE CHILDHOOD

This section explores middle childhood, covering the period between 6 and 12 years of age. During this time, children consolidate and expand upon what they have learned in the early years, building on their understanding of the physical world around them, relationships, play, and language. Middle childhood also sees children develop a new repertoire of increasingly sophisticated social, cognitive, and cultural skills. In this section we explore children's growing sense of right and wrong and the norms that regulate their moral thinking and behaviour, how their sense of self is tied to the group they belong to, and the roles of intergroup contact, cooperation, and empathy in bringing groups together. We will also look at children's imagination, creativity, and problem-solving and the role memory plays in children's daily lives and in telling the story of who they are.

7 HOW DO CHILDREN LEARN RIGHT FROM WRONG?

 Learning Outcomes

After reading this chapter you will be able to:
- Describe how children develop fairness, spite, and helping behaviours.
- Understand the roles of emotions, punishment, and reputation in moral development.
- Explore cross-cultural differences and similarities in morality.

7.1 Introduction

Our sense of right and wrong exerts a powerful influence over us. It can make us feel guilty and ashamed, or proud and righteous. It can motivate us to help and share, or to punish others and act spitefully. It forces us to justify our actions as 'fair', and it creates individual differences in the way we set our moral compass. Throughout middle childhood, moral reasoning, moral identity, and moral behaviour all undergo significant change.

What counts as good might start with a simple act of kindness – for example, picking up accidentally dropped objects or opening doors for an adult whose hands are full. But this develops into a more complex set of intuitions that are sensitive to care/harm, fairness/cheating, loyalty/betrayal, authority/subversion, and sanctity/degradation, all of which can take on culturally specific meanings. As children develop, they show greater skill at weighing one moral principle (e.g., don't lie) against another (e.g., lie if it prevents harm to others). By the time they reach adulthood, matters as diverse as tax evasion, assisted dying, and freedom of speech can take on a moral nature.

Unlike a discussion on particle physics, for example, the entry bar for joining these moral debates is set quite low. We all have an internal moral compass we can consult, and being judgemental comes relatively easily to us. The specifics of the debate may change, but many of the underlying moral principles at stake – justice, fairness, rights – are the same ones philosophers have been arguing about for millennia. Moral debates are here to stay. But where does our moral sense come from, and how does it develop?

7.2 Fairness, Justice, and Spite

Many situations in life create competition for resources. A child might be in competition with their sibling for food, protection, or the attention of a caregiver, for example. This competition can be resolved by fighting, whereby the strongest might win. Or it could be resolved on a first come, first served basis, whereby the quickest might win. Most animals resolve disputes over resources in this way, but there are alternatives. Bonobo chimps will have sex with one another if they discover a new resource like a fruit tree. Apparently, the sex helps to relax them and prevents fighting over who gets the best fruit. Bonobos use sex as a way to diffuse social tension, and they engage in it a lot, as they are seemingly aroused by anything, including cardboard boxes (de Waal, 2016).

Beyond fighting and first come, first served, humans have a third way to resolve such disputes that seems unique to us: a sense of fairness. The advantage of this is that it avoids unnecessary and potentially costly conflict, which is to everyone's benefit. The disadvantage is that we must sometimes experience that all-too-human sting of unfairness when we feel justice has not been served.

Psychologists Peter Blake and Katherine McAuliffe were interested in exactly how this sense of fairness emerges in development (Blake & McAuliffe, 2011). They gave 178 children aged 4–8 years a task in which one child could accept or reject an unequal allocation of sweets. The children, who didn't know each other, were paired up, and one child took the role of the decider. The decider could pull a green handle to accept the offer of sweets, which caused the trays of sweets to tilt towards each child so that the sweets fell into their respective bowls. Or they could reject the offer by pulling a red handle, in which case both trays tilted towards the middle, the sweets dropped into a covered bowl, and nobody got the sweets (**Figure 7.1**). Children who were on the receiving end of the decision could not affect the outcome of the game. Sometimes there were more sweets on the decider's tray, by a ratio of 4:1, and sometimes there were more sweets on the recipient's tray, by a ratio of 1:4.

When 4–7-year-olds played the decider role, they rejected unfair distributions when it was unfair in the favour of their partner (i.e., when their partner got four sweets and they got one), choosing to pull the red handle so that nobody got the sweets. However, when the distribution of sweets was unfair in their favour, they chose to keep the sweets (i.e., they got four sweets and their partner got one). It was only the 8-year-olds who rejected both forms of inequity, as adults do in similar experiments.

So, the 8-year-olds would rather get no sweets than be seen to give one sweet to a stranger and keep four for themselves, hence the title of this paper: 'I had so much it didn't

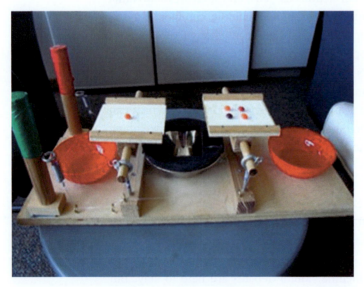

Figure 7.1 The experimental set-up from Blake and McAuliffe (2011). Source: Blake, P. McAuliffe,K. "I had so much it didn't seem fair": Eight-year-olds reject two forms of inequity. Elsevier.

seem fair' (Blake & McAuliffe, 2011). This might seem unremarkable to us, but no other species comes close to this sense of fairness. When an equivalent test has been conducted on chimpanzees, they arguably act more rationally, reasoning that something is better than nothing, and keep the treat no matter the unfairness of the situation. Humans are different, and by middle childhood a strong sense of fairness and an aversion to inequality emerge.

While the previous experiment described how children of different ages responded to fairness, it didn't tell us why the children behaved as they did. To address that question, Katherine McAuliffe, Peter Blake, and Felix Warneken conducted a follow-up study, looking at two plausible possibilities (2014). Children could be rejecting inequality because they are frustrated – they reject their own allocation of sweets because they are annoyed at having received a bad deal relative to others, but they are not particularly motivated to deny others a reward. Or children could be rejecting inequity out of **spite** – that is, a willingness to harm others at a cost to oneself. To find out, the researchers modified their earlier sweet experiment set-up (**Figure 7.1**) such that in one of the trials, the recipient's pay-off was predetermined, so decisions affected only the decider's pay-off. If children were motivated by spite, then they should reject disadvantageous allocations when their rejections deprive their partners of more desirable rewards. By contrast, if children are frustrated at receiving a bad deal relative to others, they should also reject disadvantageous allocations when their partner has already received the more desirable reward.

They found children under the age of 8 were most likely to reject disadvantageous allocations when rejections prevented a peer from receiving a larger amount, which is out of spite, rather being merely frustrated that their partner had already received the more desirable reward. As in the earlier experiment, it was not until the age of 8 that children refused distributions that put them at an advantage relative to others.

 Key Point

- Sensitivity to fair outcomes emerges early in development.

You may have noticed that in the previous experiments the resources (i.e., sweets) were presented to the children as a windfall, as if they had stumbled across an unexpected prize. Developmental psychologist Jan Engelmann, along with others, has argued that this isn't a very good model of human fairness because, from an evolutionary perspective, this type of windfall would have been quite a rare occurrence for our ancestors. He argues that at some point in human evolution the only way we could have survived was by foraging for food collaboratively (Engelmann & Tomasello, 2019). What constitutes 'a fair share' would have been much more likely to be negotiated in these collaborative circumstances, where people had to work together to bring down a large animal, to fish, or to collect honey, for example. If he is right, then we need to test children in the environments that mimic the ones that our moral sense of fairness is adapted to – namely, interdependent collaborative activities. That is precisely the approach that some studies have taken, encouraging children to work together effortfully to get the rewards. In these contexts, people become acutely sensitive to whether they are collaborating with someone who is pulling their weight or whether they are paired with a slacker (Ibbotson et al., 2019).

In one of these experiments, a pair of children had to pull on a rope to receive a sticker each, and if only one pulled on the rope, neither would get the reward. In this context, free-riding on the other person's effort isn't an option: if you want a sticker, you have to work together. As before, the researchers tested inequality in two ways: some children received more of the jointly produced rewards than their partner, while in other cases the partner received more rewards. When children had to work together to gain rewards, even children as young as 3 years of age showed an aversion to both forms of inequity (Hamann et al., 2011). This is strong evidence that collaboration makes a big difference to our sense of fairness (it also reinforces a broader point about methods raised in Chapter 3: when an ability is estimated to emerge in development depends on how we test for it). The evidence here is especially convincing because some of these studies had control groups in which children were confronted with the same unequal distribution upon entering the experimental room (like a windfall) or had to work for the resources but in an independent manner. In these situations the children did not equally distribute the spoils in the same way. This also hints at what our keen sense of fairness is for – namely, to maintain good relationships with other collaborators who we might need to collaborate with in the future. In these collaborative contexts children have an expectation that others are obliged to contribute to the common good.

Children are very strategic over whom they share with, feeling the need to justify their moral reasons as to why they would give some people more than others based on merit, effort, or need. For example, children share more rewards with other children who work more or contribute more to a joint reward (Baumard et al., 2012). Children negatively judge, punish, or choose not to reward or collaborate with other children who are free-riding on the effort of others (Yang et al., 2018), and 6-year-olds will actually pay a cost to themselves (e.g., one of their own sweets) to punish unfair sharing behaviour in others, even when they are not directly affected by the unequal distribution. This shows that by middle childhood children not only have a very strong sense of fairness but are also willing to *police* this fairness in others (McAuliffe et al., 2015). Children also judge poor individuals as more deserving of resources than wealthy individuals, and their wish to support the poor overrules their otherwise very strong desire to share resources equally (Paulus, 2014).

 Key Points

- Collaborative activities heighten children's sense of fairness.
- Children consider merit, effort, and need when allocating a fair share.
- Children are willing to police fairness in others, even when the unfairness does not directly affect them and when doing so incurs personal cost.

In one variation on a fair share study, children decided, together with two puppets, whether to distribute resources in an equal or unequal manner. In all varieties of the test, the puppets ended up distributing resources in an unequal way, thereby disadvantaging the child. What varied was whether children had a 'voice' in the decision-making process. The main result was that children were more likely to be satisfied with the unfair allocation if the puppets had allowed them to participate in the decision-making process (Grocke et al., 2018). Jan Engelmann interprets this as evidence that children are not primarily preoccupied with the material 'stuff' in these sharing games – who gets what exactly – but rather with the social meaning of the act of distribution – that is, whether they and others are being treated with equal respect (Engelmann & Tomasello, 2019).

In Chapter 11 we explore whether this general picture of fairness development in children holds true across the diverse contexts children grow up in around the world.

7.3 Reputation, Guilt, and Shame

Around middle childhood, children are typically starting to make all kinds of moral judgements about others. For example, in one study 4–6-year-old children watched videos of a moral transgression – breaking a doll that belonged to someone else – and then rated how an observer reacted to the behaviour. Either the observer enforced the norm that the transgressor had violated (e.g., she said in a mildly angry tone, 'Hey, you've broken [the victim's] doll! You shouldn't do that. It's not good') or they didn't enforce the violated norm (e.g., she said in a neutral tone, 'Oh, you've broken [the victim's] doll. Oh well, it doesn't matter'). Children judged the observer who enforced the norm as having done the right thing, they rated the non-enforcer as less good, and they also preferred the former individual to the latter (Vaish et al., 2016). Underpinning these social and moral judgements of others appears to be the ability to think **counterfactually**, or to imagine what could have been. In the moral domain, in order to blame or give credit to others for their actions we need to assume they have some choice in the matter, or free will. By around 6 years of age children are able to make inferences about others not only based on how they act but also on how they *could* have acted but chose not to (Gweon & Asaba, 2018; Kushnir et al., 2010)

As well as children judging what is virtuous behaviour in others, they appreciate they themselves are being judged and actively try to control those judgements by managing their own reputation. By around 5 years of age, children are consistently more generous and less likely to steal when they know they are being observed, they are more generous when sharing with someone who might be able to return the good deed later, and they will choose to behave unfairly in a way that is advantageous to them *if they can still appear to others* to be fair. By age 6, children negatively evaluate other children who inflict reputational harm by falsely taking credit for positive actions (e.g., someone else's good idea or helpful behaviour) and, conversely, positively evaluate those who give away credit for their own good ideas and actions. All of this suggests children are relatively skilful reputation managers and are aware of the social implications of their behaviour on others (Silver & Shaw, 2018).

 Key Point

- Children are motivated by the social evaluation of others and, like adults, work hard to present themselves favourably.

By 6 years old, typically children also appreciate that, even if no one else sees you, an action might still be wrong. Thus, if they break a toy that belongs to someone else, many preschoolers show signs of feeling guilty or ashamed, even when no one is looking. Feelings of guilt and shame can be thought of as a kind of self-punishment that functions to prevent individuals from repeating an offence, lessening the chances of actual punishment from others in the future. Guilt, shame, and its opposite, pride, are internalised versions of the kinds of moral judgements that we make of others who violate or follow social norms (Tomasello & Vaish, 2013; Vaish & Tomasello, 2022). In effect, children are learning to sanction themselves before the group does so by saying, 'I'm aware I violated the social norm, I care about it, and I won't do it again.' Displaying guilt to others like this serves an important appeasement function, showing others that they are already suffering, which they hope will evoke concern and forgiveness from the victim and from bystanders, thus reducing the likelihood of punishment (Keltner & Anderson, 2000). It also helps to restore the wrongdoer's reputation among the rest of the group, signalling that they did not mean to cause harm and, more generally, that they are not the kind of person who means harm. By doing so, the wrongdoer hopes to regain their reputation as someone to trust and to avoid being left out of social interactions in the future. By 5 years of age, children show a preference for transgressors who display guilt, and they prefer to distribute more resources to guilt-displaying transgressors than to unremorseful ones (Vaish et al., 2011).

 Key Points

- Guilt, shame, and pride are emotions that help to regulate moral behaviour.
- Children are aware of the social functions of guilt, shame, and pride.

7.4 Empathy, Helping, and Sympathy

Unlike animals that live solitary lives, we are a hyper-social species. We live in complex groups, and we have evolved a keen moral sense to regulate our relationships with others. We have seen how reputation, guilt, and shame can keep these relations on track, but using these emotions effectively also relies on individuals being able to empathise with others using theory of mind (ToM), which we met in Chapter 3. For example, maintaining a reputation as a good individual requires second-order mental reasoning of the kind 'I am thinking about what you are thinking about me'.

Lawrence Kohlberg, an American psychologist who did important work on moral development, found that children who were given the most opportunities for role-taking – putting themselves into another person's shoes and empathising with their point of view – were the most 'morally advanced' for their age (Kohlberg, 1976). We met a related idea in Chapter 3 when we learned that having a brother or sister can help accelerate ToM development, as siblings try to empathise, compete, and cooperate with as well as manipulate one another. Similarly, Kohlberg argued that managing relationships with their peers, collaborating, resolving disputes, and playing provide natural spaces for children to practice empathy because they invite role reversal. Conversely, it is difficult for children to empathise with other roles that they have never had direct experience of; for example, it is difficult for children to see things from a teacher's point of view because children have never been teachers. More generally, Kohlberg saw parents and authority figures who engaged in hierarchical relationships with children as obstacles to their moral development, whereas more egalitarian relationships, which were formed on a peer-to-peer level, helped with moral development.

Key Point
• Sensitive and appropriate moral action requires children to empathise with others.

One of Kohlberg's best-known experiments involved the following story about Heinz:

> Heinz's wife was dying from a particular type of cancer. Doctors said a new drug might save her. The drug had been discovered by a local chemist, and Heinz tried desperately to buy some, but the chemist was charging ten times the money it cost to make the drug, and this was much more than Heinz could afford. Heinz could only raise half the money, even after help from family and friends. He explained to the chemist that his wife was dying and asked if he could have the drug cheaper or pay the rest of the money later. The chemist refused, saying that he had discovered the drug and was going to make money from it. The husband was desperate to save his wife, so later that night he broke into the chemist's and stole the drug. Should Heinz have broken into the laboratory to steal the drug for his wife? Why or why not?
>
> (Kohlberg, 1958)

Kohlberg presented this story to children of different ages and asked them to justify their responses. He noticed younger children tended to respond in a way that avoided punishment, aligned with their self-interest, and used authority as their moral compass. Older children would justify their responses with respect to social obligations, preserving order, and maintaining their reputation as 'a good person'. The eldest children were prepared to argue that laws can be wrong, reputations can be undermined, and norms can be violated if they conflict with more abstract principles of universal rights and justice (Kohlberg, 1958).

Moral judgement of others.
Watch how children of different ages respond to Kohlberg's Heinz dilemma.

Beyond fairness, children show another facet of morality when they show **prosocial** behaviour and act in ways that benefit other people, such as picking up accidentally dropped objects or opening doors for an adult whose hands are full. Children seem to know something about adults' intentions in these situations, as they don't offer help when the adult has deliberately thrown objects down or shows no intention of opening a door for themselves (Warneken & Tomasello, 2006).

The prosocial nature of children's actions is even more clearly demonstrated when they help at some cost to themselves or when they have nothing to directly gain from helping. For example, 12-month-old infants will helpfully point to the location of a lost object, directing an adult's attention to it if they know they are looking for it (Liszkowski et al., 2008). It seems that young children are intrinsically motivated to act in this way rather than conditioned to do so through a system of reward and punishment. For example, the helpfulness behaviour of 20-month-old children actually *decreases* when they are materially rewarded for their behaviour. In contrast, children who are not rewarded at all or who received only verbal praise maintain a high level of helpfulness (Warneken & Tomasello, 2008). In a separate study with older children, trusting them to help others caused them to cheat less. We have known for some time that honesty garners more trust from others, but this study showed that, for 6-year-olds at least, trust can also lead to more honesty (Zhao et al., 2024).

Children show yet another side to moral development when they provide care or comfort to those in emotional distress, such as showing sympathy with another child who is in pain after bumping their knee or who is upset about their damaged teddy bear. Experimental work has also shown that infants have an early preference for characters who are helpful or act sympathetically. For example, Hamlin and colleagues (2007) put on a puppet show for 6–10-month-old infants in which a puppet climber struggled to climb up a hill, and sometimes a second climber came along and helped the first puppet from below. On other occasions a different puppet appeared at the top of the hill and bashed the climber down the hill. A few minutes later the infants saw a second puppet show in which the climber looked back and forth between the helper puppet and the hinderer puppet and then snuggled up to either the helper or the hinderer. The infants stared at the scene longer – indicating surprise – when the climber snuggled up to the hinderer compared to the helper. This suggests that the infants had a stronger expectation that the climber would choose to snuggle up with the helpful puppet.

When the experiment was over, infants were much more likely to reach for the helper puppet than the hinderer puppet when both were placed in front of them. This is important, as it is fairly uncontroversial to claim that nobody likes to be hit. If infants were to be hit directly by the puppet (leaving aside the ethics of such an experiment!), it is pretty certain that they would not want to play with that character. What this experiment shows is a kind of third-party judgement about character: infants saw how these characters were behaving towards each other, and this guided their own personal preferences. These prosocial judgements can translate into prosocial action. For example, by 2 years of age, toddlers are more likely to help those who were helpful to them in previous interactions than those who were not helpful (Dunfield & Kuhlmeier, 2010). And a year later on in development, children reduce their prosocial behaviour towards an individual who caused or intended to cause harm to another individual (Vaish et al., 2010).

 Key Point

- Children show a tendency towards helpfulness, can sympathise with the emotional plight of others, and are selective over who they interact with based on help and harm.

On the basis of how these infants reacted to puppets, researchers have made some bigger claims about how infants understand human prosociality. In such cases, researchers need to ensure that they are measuring what they think they are measuring – its validity – and that they are measuring the same thing consistently – its reliability; see the **One-Minute Method** for more on this matter.

Watch the One-Minute Method.

Discover how researchers ensure that their measurements are both valid and reliable.

7.5 Differences and Similarities

How can we make sense of such different moral traits as fairness, justice, spite, guilt, shame, empathy, helping, and sympathy? One way is to take the cross-cultural approach and ask: to what extent does moral behaviour develop in the same way for children around the world? How does it develop differently? Is there anything that unites children in what they think is immoral? This will help us work out which features of our moral behaviour are more sensitive to cultural input and flexible, and which are more heritable and stable.

Richard Shweder, a psychological anthropologist, was interested in these very questions. He interviewed over 600 Oriyans (residents of Orissa, a state on the east coast of India) and people from Chicago, USA, including 360 children ranging from 5 to 13 years of age. He presented them with 39 short stories in which someone does something that might violate some kind of rule (Shweder et al., 1987). He found differences and similarities in how Oriyans and Americans thought about personality and individuality (**Figure 7.2**).

He found that both societies drew a line between what is acceptable and unacceptable – between what were moral issues and social conventions – but that they sometimes differed on what these issues were. Issues that were mere social conventions to Americans could be matters of moral importance to Indians, and those that were mere conventions to Indians could be of moral significance to Americans. Social conventions are just the way we have agreed to do things while knowing that we could do them differently, whereas moral rules should apply equally to everyone. For example, while it sounds unremarkable to say, 'I don't eat with a knife and fork, but I don't mind if you do,' it sounds odd to say, 'I don't like to murder people, but I don't mind if you do!' Children appear to understand the difference. For example, in a separate study, American 7-year-olds judged issues such as choices about friends, appearance (clothing, hairstyle), and preferences for leisure activities as up to the child to decide (Nucci, 1981). By contrast, moral issues should be universal and unchangeable. Elliot Turiel, a student of Kohlberg (he of the Heinz dilemma presented earlier), argued that children recognise that rules about clothing, food, and many other aspects of life are social conventions, which by their nature are arbitrary and changeable (Turiel, 1983). If you ask children about actions that hurt others – a girl who pushes a boy off a swing because she wants to use it – nearly all of the children say that such actions are wrong. Furthermore, for this situation children say that the girl would be wrong even if her teacher said it was OK and

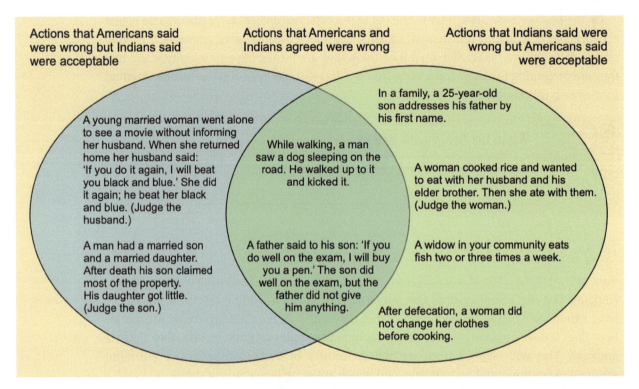

Figure 7.2 Cultural differences and similarities based on some of the 39 short stories used by Shweder and colleagues (1987).

if it happened at another school where there were no rules against this kind of behaviour. Damon (1977) found that young children reject parental commands to engage in acts that violate moral rules, such as instructions to steal or cause harm to another person, and children of 6 years or older judged laws that discriminate against individuals on the basis of age, income, or appearance to be wrong and that breaking them was acceptable (Helwig & Jasiobedzka, 2001).

Turiel defined moral rules as relating to 'justice, rights, and welfare pertaining to how people ought to relate to each other' (1983, p. 3). He argued that the realisation that moral rules are special, unalterable, and universal (i.e., not culturally specific) is the foundation of all moral development. However, Shweder's work in Chicago and Orissa showed that, in reality, the boundary between a moral rule (e.g., preventing harm) and a social convention (e.g., what to wear) is much more culturally variable than had been previously suggested. The scope of what people thought were moral issues in Orissa clearly went well beyond a framework of harm, fairness, and rights, but was there any way to predict what people considered were moral issues and which weren't?

Shweder showed that how the different societies were organised and what they valued predicted some of the individual choices people made about morality. For example, **collectivist societies** place the needs of groups and institutions first and subordinate the needs of individuals. This framework emphasises civic duties, social harmony, obedience to authority, and hierarchy (**Figure 7.3**). In contrast, **individualistic societies** make society the servant of the individual. This framework emphasises individual choice, personal

Figure 7.3 Thousands of students put on a synchronised kung fu display to celebrate China's cultural history. Large public coordinated events highlight group harmony and force individuals to see themselves in relation to something bigger. The larger the display, the smaller the focus on the individual. Source: IMAGO / China Foto Press.

autonomy, and rights. So as cultures differ in how they see individuals and groups, so does the concept of 'self'. What it means to be an individual is dependent on the way the society is organised, and Shweder argued that this led to differences in how individuals thought about morality.

Subsequent experimental work has provided evidence for Shweder's ideas. For example, Chinese 7-, 9-, and 11-year-olds, who grow up in a collectivist culture, are more likely to approve of a lie that benefits the group than a lie that benefits the individual. Canadian children, who are from an individualist culture, are more likely to approve of a lie that benefits the individual than a lie that benefit the group (Fu et al., 2007). All people lie, and all cultures value honesty, but what these children were willing to lie *about* was predicted by how their cultures viewed the self in relation to others (Silver & Shaw, 2018).

In a more recent study with 7–11-year-old Chinese and Canadian children (Fu et al., 2016), the researchers found that both groups were motivated to make a positive impression after performing a good deed in private, but that they deployed different reputational strategies for doing so: Chinese children were more likely to actively conceal their good behaviour, signalling their modesty, while Canadian children were more likely to actively disclose it, advertising their prosociality.

Children are born into a cultural fabric of norms and expectations, and as we have learned from Chapters 3 and 5, they are armed with powerful motivations to imitate and learn from those around them. In Shweder's work, for the children from Chicago, where the society is more individualistic, their moral compass was being orientated towards the protection of individuals and their personal freedom. Even for the 5-year-old Oriyan children, the practices of food, clothing, and gender relations had become moralised in a way that they clearly had not been for the Chicago children.

These cultural differences between independent and interdependent views of the self not only colour what children think of as good, they can affect some very basic aspects of the way they see the world. For example, one study asked 9- and 10-year-olds to sort a set of items, such as a doghouse, dog, and child, into two groups. Chinese children, from a collectivist society, were much more likely to use the relationships between items to form a group (dogs sleep in houses, so doghouse and dog form a group), whereas children from the USA, a more individualistic society, were more likely to form groups around qualities of the items themselves (dogs and children are both living things, so dog and child form a group; Chiu, 1972).

Differences *within* societies (e.g., in the way parents respond to children's behaviour) also shape moral development. For example, when parents explain why children should behave in particular ways during social situations and how their behaviour affects others' feelings, this has much more impact on promoting children's and adolescents' prosocial behaviour than power-assertive forms of discipline, such as corporal punishment and yelling (Mounts & Allen, 2019). Furthermore, those children who experience more power-assertive discipline as children tend to show less empathy to others when they are adults (Lopez et al., 2001).

And, of course, moral norms change. Issues that were once considered amoral can take on a moralised nature – for example, advertising to children, fracking, plastic bags, violence on television, IQ tests, wearing fur, and food additives. At the same time, many behaviours have moved in the opposite direction, switching from moral wrongdoing to a lifestyle choice: divorce, illegitimacy, marijuana use, masturbation, oral sex, and atheism.

National-level descriptions such as 'collectivist' or 'individualistic' have come in for criticism for being too simplistic, with both attitudes being able to coexist within a culture, and such descriptions don't ultimately explain why these attitudes vary in the first place. That said, Shweder's work shone a light on the role of cultural variation in what is considered to be moral. Moreover, he showed that it is possible to predict some of this variation if we look at societal beliefs about individuals and their obligations to society.

 Key Point

- Children's moral sense incorporates the values of the society they are born into.

The fact that the moral domain varies from culture to culture and from family to family does not mean morals vary arbitrarily, nor does it rule out a universal capacity for human-like morality. Haidt and Joseph (2004) suggest some dimensions of morality that are candidates for being universal but are also modified by culture – what they call 'moral foundations theory'. This theory proposes that several psychological systems are the foundations of 'intuitive ethics'. These moral foundations, it is argued, developed in humans because they helped us solve adaptive challenges in our evolutionary past. Each culture then constructs virtues, narratives, and institutions on top of these foundations, creating the variation we see in what is considered moral. The five foundations are:

- *Care/harm:* This foundation is related to our long evolution as mammals with attachment systems and an ability to feel (and dislike) the pain of others. It underlies the virtues of kindness, gentleness, and nurturance.
- *Fairness/cheating:* This foundation is related to the evolutionary process of reciprocal altruism – you scratch my back, I'll scratch yours. It generates ideas of justice, rights, and autonomy.
- *Loyalty/betrayal:* This foundation is related to our long history as tribal creatures able to form shifting coalitions. It underlies the virtues of patriotism and self-sacrifice for the group. It is active any time people feel that it's 'one for all, and all for one'.
- *Authority/subversion:* This foundation is related to our long primate history of hierarchical social interactions. It underlies the virtues of leadership and followership, including deference to legitimate authority and respect for traditions.
- *Sanctity/degradation:* This foundation is related to the psychology of disgust and contamination. It underlies religious notions of striving to live in an elevated, less carnal, more noble way. It also underlies the widespread idea that the body is a temple that can be desecrated by immoral activities and contaminants (an idea not unique to religious traditions).

The main message here is that there seems to be some inbuilt repertoire of moral and emotional sentiments that are shaped by the particular social and cultural context a person finds themselves in (**Box 7.1**). Haidt uses an analogy with taste receptors to illustrate this point (2013). Humans are all born with the same five taste receptors: sweet, sour, salt, bitter, and umami (the savoury taste of foods like meat and mushrooms). Geography and history have meant cultures have evolved incredibly different cuisines, yet they are all variations on the same theme of these five building blocks. Moral foundations theory is an attempt to identify the building blocks of morality. There is now good evidence not only that these moral foundations generalise across cultures, but they also have an important bearing on individuals' political ideology and their stance on debates such as same-sex marriage, abortion, art, and welfare spending (Graham et al., 2009). As Haidt puts it in *The Righteous Mind*: 'We're born to be righteous, but we have to learn what, exactly, people like us should be righteous about' (2013, p. 26). We will explore cultural variation in morality further in Chapter 11.

 Key Point

- Care/harm, fairness/cheating, loyalty/betrayal, authority/subversion, and sanctity/degradation are likely to become significant moral dimensions for children. Precisely what content becomes part of those dimensions can vary according to time and place.

Box 7.1 Moral dumbfounding

Read the following story and decide on whether you think what Julie and Mark did was wrong:

> Julie and Mark are sister and brother. They are travelling together in France on summer vacation from college. One night they are staying alone in a cabin near the beach. They decide it would be interesting and fun if they tried making love. At the very least it would be a new experience for each of them. Julie was already taking birth control pills, but Mark uses a condom too, just to be safe. They both enjoy making love, but they decide not to do it again. They keep the night as a special secret, which makes them feel closer to each other.

Haidt and his colleagues (1993) presented this story, and many more like them, to lots of people and asked them to judge the people in the story. Haidt was less interested in whether people thought what the people in the story did was right or wrong than the reasons people gave to justify their decisions.

Like the majority of their participants, you might have had a gut reaction that what Julie and Mark did was wrong. But after the initial reaction of 'eugh!' you may have struggled to explain why it was wrong. Note that the story has been cleverly crafted to counter the most common objections about why what they did was wrong. For example, the siblings used two forms of contraception so that inbreeding is not a consideration; the story makes it clear that they were not emotionally hurt; it takes place in private so that the act could not offend the community; and Julie and Mark agree never to do it again so that it would not interfere with future relationships. Eventually, participants are left with no rational justification that they can articulate, and so they talk instead of their gut reaction: 'I don't know, I can't explain it. I just know it's wrong.' Haidt calls this kind of reaction 'moral dumbfounding' – we know it is wrong but struggle to explain why. When reading the two further examples at the end of this box, you might think that they are unpleasant, but try to identify who the victim is in these stories. If you think there is no victim, where does the unpleasant feeling arise from? Haidt argues that on some level they tap into deep moral foundations.

> A family's dog was killed by a car in front of their house. They had heard that dog meat was delicious, so they cut up the dog's body, cooked it, and ate it for dinner. Nobody saw them do it.
>
> A man goes to the supermarket once a week and buys a dead chicken. But before cooking the chicken, he has sexual intercourse with it. Then he cooks it and eats it.

Talking Point

Are we born naturally selfish or cooperative? This is an age-old philosophical debate; either human nature is essentially selfish and individualistic unless tamed by culture, or humans are born virtuous and are corrupted by society. We could argue that one idea needs the other – that there is no virtue without the capacity for harm. The reality for children is that they are both competitive and cooperative, but precisely where the balance lies – and what contexts bring out the best or worst of our natures – is still something we are learning much about. In this chapter we have shown that even young children can make choices based on moral principles of fairness and care. Precisely when those moral capacities emerge in development has implications for holding children accountable for their actions. With the development of more moral capacity comes more moral responsibility. There is clearly a difference between the moral competence of a 6-year-old versus a 16-year-old, but where the line of moral responsibility falls needs a conversation that is wider than science, involving philosophers, lawmakers, and not least children themselves. It is also a debate that developmental psychologists can usefully contribute to by providing the evidence of what children are capable of and what they are not, and of how moral development can vary between children.

Summary

- Sensitivity to fair outcomes emerges early in development.
- Collaborative activities heighten children's sense of fairness.
- Children consider merit, effort, and need when allocating a fair share.
- Children are willing to police fairness in others, even when the unfairness does not directly affect them and when doing so incurs personal cost.
- Children are motivated by the social evaluation of others and, like adults, work hard to present themselves favourably.
- Guilt, shame, and pride are emotions that help to regulate moral behaviour.
- Children are aware of the social functions of guilt, shame, and pride.
- Sensitive and appropriate moral action requires children to empathise with others.
- Children show a tendency towards helpfulness, can sympathise with the emotional plight of others, and are selective over who they interact with based on help and harm.
- Children's moral sense incorporates the values of the society they are born into.
- Care/harm, fairness/cheating, loyalty/betrayal, authority/subversion, and sanctity/degradation are likely to become significant moral dimensions for children. Precisely what content becomes part of those dimensions can vary according to time and place.

References

Baumard, N., Mascaro, O., & Chevallier, C. (2012). Preschoolers are able to take merit into account when distributing goods. *Developmental Psychology*, 48(2), 492–498.

Blake, P. & McAuliffe, K. (2011). 'I had so much it didn't seem fair': eight-year-olds reject two forms of inequity. *Cognition*, 120(2), 215–224.

Chiu, L.-H. (1972). A cross-cultural comparison of cognitive styles in Chinese and American children. *International Journal of Psychology*, 7(4), 235–242.

Damon, W. (1977). *The Social World of the Child*. Jossey-Bass.

de Waal, F. (2016). Bonobos Use Sex to Cool Tempers. *Scientific American*, 1 March. www.scientificamerican.com/article/bonobos-use-sex-to-cool-tempers/

Dunfield, K. A. & Kuhlmeier, V. A. (2010). Intention-mediated selective helping in infancy. *Psychological Science*, 21(4), 523–527.

Engelmann, J. & Tomasello, M. (2019). Children's sense of fairness as equal respect. *Trends in Cognitive Sciences*, 23(6), 454–463.

Fu, G., Heyman, G. D., Cameron, C. A., & Lee, K. (2016). Learning to be unsung heroes: development of reputation management in two cultures. *Child Development*, 87, 689–699.

Fu, G., Xu, F., Cameron, C. A., Leyman, G., & Lee, K. (2007). Cross-cultural differences in children's choices, categorizations, and evaluations of truths and lies. *Developmental Psychology*, 43(2), 278–293.

Graham, J., Haidt, J., & Nosek, B. A. (2009). Liberals and conservatives rely on different sets of moral foundations. *Personality Processes and Individual Differences*, 96(5), 1029–1046.

Grocke, P., Rossano, F., & Tomasello, M. (2018). Young children are more willing to accept group decisions in which they have had a voice. *Journal of Experimental Child Psychology*, 166, 67–78.

Gweon, H. & Asaba, M. (2018). Order matters: children's evaluation of underinformative teachers depends on context. *Child Development*, 89(3), e278–e292.

Haidt, J. (2013). *The Righteous Mind*. Penguin Books.

Haidt, J. & Joseph, C. (2004). Intuitive ethics: how innately prepared intuitions generate culturally variable virtues. *Daedalus*, 133(4), 55–66.

Haidt, J., Koller, S. H., & Dias, M. G. (1993). Affect, culture, and morality, or is it wrong to eat your dog? *Journal of Personality and Social Psychology*, 65(4), 613–628.

Hamann, K., Warneken, F., Greenberg, J., et al. (2011). Collaboration encourages equal sharing in children but not in chimpanzees. *Nature*, 476, 328–331.

Hamlin, J. K., Wynn, K., & Bloom, P. (2007). Social evaluation by preverbal infants. *Nature*, 450, 557–560.

Helwig, C. C. & Jasiobedzka, U. (2001). The relation between law and morality: children's reasoning about socially beneficial and unjust laws. *Child Development*, 72(5), 1382–1393.

Ibbotson, P., Hauert, C., & Walker, R. (2019). Effort perception is made more accurate with more effort and when cooperating with slackers. *Scientific Reports*, 9, 17491.

Keltner, D. & Anderson, C. (2000). Saving face for Darwin: the functions and uses of embarrassment. *Current Directions in Psychological Science*, 9(6), 187–192.

Kohlberg, L. (1958). *The Development of Modes of Thinking and Choices in Years 10 to 16*. PhD dissertation. University of Chicago.

Kohlberg, L. (1976). Moral stage and moralization: the cognitive–developmental approach. In T. Lickona (ed.), *Moral Development and Behavior: Theory, Research, and Social Issues* (pp. 84–107). Holt, Rinehart, & Winston.

Kushnir, T., Xu, F., & Wellman, H. M. (2010). Preschoolers use sampling information to infer the preferences of others. *Psychological Science*, 21(4), 1134–1140.

Liszkowski, U., Carpenter, M., & Tomasello, M. (2008). Twelve-month-olds communicate helpfully and appropriately for knowledgeable and ignorant partners. *Cognition*, 108(3), 732–739.

Lopez, N. L., Bonenberger, J. L., & Schneider, H. G. (2001). Parental disciplinary history, current levels of empathy, and moral reasoning in young adults. *North American Journal of Psychology*, 3(2), 193–204.

McAuliffe, K., Blake, P. R., & Warneken, F. (2014). Children reject inequity out of spite. *Biology Letters*, 10(12), 20140743.

McAuliffe, K., Jordan, J., & Warneken, F. (2015). Costly third-party punishment in young children. *Cognition*, 134, 1–10.

Mounts, N. S. & Allen, C. (2019). Parenting styles and practices: traditional approaches and their application to multiple types of moral behavior. In D. J. Laible, G. Carlo, & L. M. Padilla-Walker (eds.), *The Oxford Handbook of Parenting and Moral Development* (pp. 41–56). Oxford University Press.

Nucci, L. (1981). The development of personal concepts: a domain distinct from moral and social concepts. *Child Development*, 52(1), 114–121.

Paulus, M. (2014). The early origins of human charity: developmental changes in preschoolers' sharing with poor and wealthy individuals. *Frontiers in Psychology*, 5, 344.

Shweder, R. A., Mahapatra, M., & Miller, J. (1987). Culture and moral development. In J. Kagan & S. Lamb (eds.), *The Emergence of Morality in Young Children* (pp. 1–83). University of Chicago Press.

Silver, I. M. & Shaw, A. (2018). Pint-sized public relations: the development of reputation management. *Trends in Cognitive Sciences*, 22, 277–279.

Tomasello, M. & Vaish, A. (2013). Origins of human cooperation and morality. *Annual Review of Psychology*, 64(1), 231–255.

Turiel, E. (1983). *The Development of Social Knowledge: Morality and Convention*. Cambridge University Press.

Vaish, A., Carpenter, M., & Tomasello, M. (2010). Young children selectively avoid helping people with harmful intentions. *Child Development*, 81(6), 1661–1669.

Vaish, A., Carpenter, M., & Tomasello, M. (2011). Young children's responses to guilt displays. *Developmental Psychology*, 47(5), 1248–1262.

Vaish, A., Herrmann, E., Markmann, C., & Tomasello, M. (2016). Preschoolers value those who sanction non-cooperators. *Cognition*, 153, 43–51.

Vaish, A. & Tomasello, M. (2022). The early ontogeny of human cooperation and morality. In M. Killen & J. G. Smetana (eds.), *Handbook of Moral Development*, 3rd edition (pp. 200–216). Routledge.

Warneken, F. & Tomasello, M. (2006). Altruistic helping in human infants and young chimpanzees. *Science*, 311, 1301–1303.

Warneken, F. & Tomasello, M. (2008). Extrinsic rewards undermine altruistic tendencies in 20-month-olds. *Developmental Psychology*, 44(6), 1785–1788.

Yang, F., Choi, Y.-J., Misch, A., Yang, X., & Dunham, Y. (2018). In defense of the commons: young children negatively evaluate and sanction free riders. *Psychological Science*, 29(10), 1598–1611.

Zhao, L., Mao, H., Harris, P. L., & Lee, K. (2024). Trusting young children to help causes them to cheat less. *Nature Human Behavior*, 8, 668–678.

8 HOW DO CHILDREN THINK ABOUT GROUPS?

 Learning Outcomes

After reading this chapter you will be able to:

- Describe how children think and behave differently in groups.
- Explain the roles of collaboration, self-identity, and categorisation in creating and sustaining groups.
- Understand how group differences can be reduced via intergroup contact, cooperation, and empathy.

8.1 Introduction

Almost all animals give preferential treatment to a special kind of group called the family. Much of this bias can be explained by how genetically related one individual is to another. The closer two individuals are on the family tree, the more likely they are to share the same genes. Thus, close family members helping one another out are genes helping one another out. This led evolutionary biologist John Haldane, when asked, 'Would you give your life to save a drowning brother'? to quip, 'No, but I would save two brothers or eight cousins' (Connolly & Martlew, 1999, p. 10). Because we share half of our genes on average with brothers and one-eighth with cousins, Haldane was giving the numbers of relatives he would have to save to 'break even'. The link between moral behaviour and kin relations is also captured in the ancient Arab proverb 'I against my brother, my brother and I against our cousin, my brother, my cousins and I against the world' (quoted in Ginitis, 2007, p. 21).

Humans, however, more than any other species, care deeply about all kinds of groups that are both bigger and smaller than the family unit: nations, communes, cults, gangs, clubs, sports teams, political parties, friendship cliques, unions, societies, fellowships, religions, music groups, pressure groups, volunteer groups, the magic circle, the inner circle, the in-group or the out-group, it's us versus them, if you're not with us you're against us. Something more than genetic relatedness is going on here. Groups are all around us, and a major part of growing up is finding your tribe, becoming initiated into it, and caring for it. But where does all this groupishness come from? How do children develop multiple group identities? And is there anything we can do to overcome the dark side of our groupish nature?

8.2 Groupishness

The groupish side of our human nature sits so near the surface that it can be summoned into life almost absurdly easily. In a classic demonstration, Henri Tajfel and his colleague Michael Billig divided people into two groups on the basis of a coin toss: Group A and Group B. Following this, each participant went into a cubicle, where they were told they could award real money to other participants. Group A gave more money to other Group A members and Group B gave more to other Group B members, even though they knew their groups were randomly created (Billig & Tajfel, 1973). The researchers found that just dividing people into groups on an arbitrary basis produced **in-group favouritism** – the tendency to think of and act more positively towards people from our in-groups than we do to people from out-groups.

In the 50 years of research since this initial finding, in-group favouritism has been widely replicated, in a range of cultural contexts, and it is one of the most robust findings in social psychology. It doesn't matter whether people are divided randomly by the colour of their T-shirts, how they perceive dots on a screen, or their art preferences, we know people think and behave radically differently to members of their own group than they do to outsiders: people are more willing to share and cooperate with in-group members relative to out-group members (Gaertner & Dovidio, 2000); they empathise more with the in-group than the out-group (Cikara et al., 2011); in-group members are rated as having more positive characteristics, such as trustworthiness, honesty, loyalty, and attractiveness (Brewer, 1979); people experience pleasure in response to the out-group's failures (*Schadenfreude*) and displeasure in response to their triumphs (*Glückschmerz*; Cikara et al., 2014); and people remember more positive than negative information about in-groups than out-groups, are more critical of the performance of the out-group, and – in a final tragic irony – believe that their own groups are less prejudiced than are out-groups (Shelton & Richeson, 2005). All this judgement from something as random as a coin toss!

The arbitrariness with which this us–them thinking can be generated would be comical were the implications not so tragic. It shows how groups can exist simply because individuals perceive those groups as existing. Even in cases where there is no underlying difference, such as race, we are still prone to perceiving us and them and still demonstrate in-group favouritism. These results offer a sobering view of how even the shallowest of group identities can produce prejudice and discrimination (Jackson et al., 2019). When combined with a dehumanisation of the out-group, groupishness takes on a particularly dark side, motivating xenophobia and out-group hate. And if the in-group is the nation state or an ethnic group, then it could be argued that out-group denigration has been pivotal in justifying some of the darkest episodes of human history, including genocide and war.

Henri Tajfel himself had more than a casual interest in intergroup discrimination. At the outbreak of the Second World War, as a Polish Jew he volunteered to fight in the French

Army, but he was taken as a prisoner of war by the Nazis. On his return home he discovered that none of his immediate family, and few of his friends, had survived the Holocaust. The in-group bias seems universal. In the language of the Dinka people living in the deserts of Sudan, *Dinka* simply means 'people' – the implication being that people who are not Dinka are not people. In the language of the Yupik people spoken by inhabitants of the Siberian tundra, *Yupik* means 'real people' – the implication being that people who are not Yupik are not real people.

Children want to be part of the in-group: they are busy adopting the languages, customs, rites, rituals, and dress of those around them, so it should come as no surprise that they show in-group favouritism from an early age too. For example:

- 10-month-olds would rather play with a toy that has been played with by another in-group member than an out-group member (Kinzler et al., 2012).
- 17-month-olds have an expectation that in-group members will help one another out but not out-group members (Jin & Baillargeon, 2017).
- 4-year-olds express greater liking for in-group than out-group members, expect other in-group members to share their preferences, and trust them more (MacDonald et al., 2013; Richter et al., 2016).
- 4–5-year-olds are more loyal to their in-group, more willing to keep secrets, and more willing to pay a personal cost for the benefit of their in-group (Misch et al., 2016).
- 5-year-olds will stay silent when an in-group member commits an immoral action but are more likely tell someone else when an out-group member does so (Misch et al., 2018).
- 5–6-year-olds report greater liking for national and ethnic in-group members compared to individuals whose national or ethnic identity is different from their own (McLoughlin et al., 2018).
- 3–7-year-olds show greater generosity towards in-group members than out-group members (Fehr et al., 2008).

All of these listed studies took place under controlled experimental conditions, but the same biases have been demonstrated more naturalistically in the field, most famously in the Robbers Cave study conducted by Muzafer Sherif, a Turkish-American social psychologist (1956). In this study, 22 boys aged 11 years were brought to a mock summer camp in Oklahoma and divided into two teams: the Eagles and the Rattlers. The teams were separated, and they only interacted when they were competing in various activities.

Over the time that they were at the camp, the two teams showed increasing hostility towards each other, which eventually escalated into violence. During a cooling-off period, the boys were encouraged to list features of the two groups, which, as you might expect by now, were described in favourable terms regarding their in-group and unfavourable regarding the out-group. Later on, when Sherif encouraged the groups to work towards a common goal, there was some reduced tension and prejudice between the groups (more on this later). There were problems with the original research, including the fact that the boys were exposed to a harsh environment at the camp, which may have made them more competitive, anxious, and aggressive to begin with. That said, Sherif's study offers an important demonstration that conflict can gravitate around group identity (**Figure 8.1**).

Figure 8.1 (Left) Some of the boys from the Robbers Cave study. (Right) One boy holds up the Rattlers' motto: 'Eagles you may win, but we will give you a hell of a fight.' Source: Archives of the History of American Psychology, The University of Akron.

 Key Point

- Children think and behave more positively towards the in-group compared to the out-group.

8.3 Why Are We So Groupish?

Why do children want to be part of the in-group? As with most behaviours, there are two ways of answering this question. Let's take the long-term view first. In the previous chapter, we came across the idea that, at some point in human evolution, the only way we could have survived was by hunting and foraging for food collaboratively, whereby people had to work hard together to bring down a large animal, to fish, or to collect honey, for example (Engelmann & Tomasello, 2019). This, it turned out, had some interesting consequences for how children think about fairness and respect. The basic point is that when our survival became dependent on other people, we became particularly good at reading others' intentions (Chapter 3) and interested in what others think of us – we saw in the previous chapter how children are adept at managing their reputation. We also became choosy over whom we collaborate with, as we don't want to be stuck with someone who doesn't pull their weight or won't return a favour – we also saw in the previous chapter how judgemental and selective children can be in these collaborative contexts.

We do not care about just any other people, though; we care about the same people that we regularly encounter, as those are the ones with the most opportunities to help or harm us. For most of human history we have been living in small groups of 150 or so in which people could cooperate with us through sharing tasks and aiding each other in times of need.

In these smaller groups we could keep track of which people helped us out, which ones we owe a favour to, and which ones are the free-loaders and time-wasters not worth engaging with; in short, we started to value who we can *trust*.

In one study, people who cooperated in a gift-giving game punished non-cooperative in-group members more severely than they punished non-cooperative out-group members (Shinada et al., 2004). The title of the paper sums it up: 'False friends are worse than bitter enemies.' This conclusion makes sense in the context of small groups in which the same people see each other regularly; untrustworthy in-groupers have more opportunities than out-groupers to make our lives a misery – or, at the very least, waste our time – so we should be more wary of them. For similar reasons, 5-year-olds care more about their reputation as a good sharer with in-group members than they do about their reputation with out-group members (Engelmann et al., 2013).

Key Point

- Children are sensitive to groups and group membership because being part of the in-group was key to our species' survival.

If being in the in-group provided us with a variety of benefits, including protection, social support, resource-sharing, and learning from others, then we should expect that being kicked out of the group is really bad news. And it is – so much so that it is sometimes referred to as 'social death'. **Ostracism** from the group can be felt as a loss of belonging and control and an attack on one's self-esteem, and it can even undermine a sense of meaningful existence (Over, 2018). Longer-term exclusion can lead to feelings of insignificance, alienation, worthlessness, high levels of depression, and suicidal ideation, and long-term loneliness has been calculated to be as damaging to your health as smoking 15 cigarettes a day (Holt-Lunstad et al., 2010). Not surprisingly, then, adults and children either directly or indirectly go to great lengths to stay a part of the in-group and avoid being ostracised. One way in which children learn to do this is by adopting the norms of the in-group in a way that publicly shows 'I am one of you'. We have already seen examples of this: the *malu* shame of Sumatran children (Chapter 2); the beckoning of the forest spirits in Mbendjele BaYaka children of Congo-Brazzaville (Chapter 6); and the difference in moral perspectives between the children of Orissa and Chicago (Chapter 7), which are all acquired by a process of imitation and social learning (Chapter 5).

One particularly obvious sign of whether people come from the same group is the language they speak. Both monolingual and bilingual 5-year-old children are more likely to befriend native-accented peers over foreign-accented ones (Souza et al., 2013) and prefer to learn language from native-accented adults compared with foreign-accented ones (Kertesz et al., 2021). In conversation, listeners are quick to identify how their partner compares with their own group on a wide range of membership criteria; for example, adults can detect a foreign accent within 30 milliseconds of speech – basically enough time to say hello – and reliably infer a speaker's sex based on only a single vowel utterance. Those conversational partners who are judged to be part of the native-accent in-crowd are rated more positively in terms of their social status, education, professional success, and credibility than those with a foreign accent. More generally, there is a huge amount of evidence from social psychology that people conform, obey, and act the way they do because they are quite simply not willing to behave differently from others in their group (Williams & Nida, 2011).

 Key Point

- Children adopt the norms of those around them as an important signal of in-group membership.

Obviously, children aren't thinking consciously about their evolutionary history when they are defending their reputation as good collaborators or sticking up for a friend in the playground. Here we need the short-term view of behaviour, and there are two fundamental aspects of our psychology that are relevant.

First, people love to categorise the world around them, pigeonholing objects, actions, places, animals, and so on. These categories help us navigate the physical and social world in the here and now, not in our evolutionary past, and we saw how even young infants are adept at generalising categories from an early age (Chapter 5). This urge to categorise applies to people as much as it does to objects – perhaps more so, because people can categorise you back! People cluster into groups with like-minded others, and mere membership of a group can be a shorthand for predicting how anyone from that group might behave (see **Box 8.1**). We know 5–6-year-old children will form generalised attitudes about a group based on a single encounter with an out-group member (Yu et al., 2022), and groups are also useful for predicting how *we* will behave, because our own identities are partially wrapped up in the social categories we belong to.

 Key Point

- Sorting people into groups is a specific example of our tendency to categorise the world in general.

 Gender groups.

Emily Foster-Hanson talks about her own research (2023) showing how children form stereotypes about gender and how they are related to their parents' political views.

The second relevant aspect of our psychology in this area is that people have a need to feel positive about themselves, demonstrating what has been called a **self-serving bias**.

On most measures, most people see themselves as better than the average person. For example, the majority of drivers, including those who have been hospitalised for car accidents, perceive themselves to be safer drivers than the average driver; most people consider themselves to be more intelligent, more attractive, and less prejudiced than most other people, and if someone else does better them, they consider them a 'genius'; 90% of business managers rate their performance as superior to their peers; most surgeons believe the mortality rate of their patients is lower than average; the majority of adults perceive themselves as giving more support to their ageing parents than their siblings; and most of us tend to believe that we understand others better than they understand us. We also tend to believe that we understand *ourselves* better than other people understand themselves (Myers, 2005). Everyone can't be right, but one way to enhance our own self-image is to rely on stereotypes that demean the out-group and elevate the in-group. Because our identity is so tied up with the group's identity (all for one and one for all), a simple way to boost our own image is to boost the image of the in-group and to do the opposite for the out-group.

These short-term mechanisms provide some answers as to *how* groups are formed and maintained in the here and now; the long-term answer provides a reason *why* we are so sensitive to groups in the first place.

Key Point

- Because self-identity is tied up with the group's identity, in-group favouritism boosts our image and makes us feel better about ourselves.

Box 8.1 Birds of a feather flock together

Researchers examined the friendship networks of 128 children aged 9–11 years in Los Angeles County, USA (Tsai et al., 2016). They asked each child a series of questions about their attitudes towards safe sun behaviours, such as playing in the shade, sunscreen use, and wearing long trousers, and then they also asked them to list their friends. From this information they created a social network (**Figure 8.2**) in which each node represents a child and each link represents a friendship.

As expected, the children showed a tendency to form ties to others within the same classroom and the same sex. More interestingly for the researchers, they found that the children clustered together with friends who have similar safe sun behaviours. In general, whether it is making friends, forming a romantic relationship, or deciding on roommates, people like other people like them – or what is called **homophily**.

The researchers wanted to understand more about the role of popular students, or 'peer leaders' as they referred to them. These children were particularly interesting because they were more interconnected in the network than other children and had more friends. As a result, they had a greater capacity to lead or change the opinion of the group. Advertising companies monetise this group dynamic by targeting the well-connected or 'influencers' of a network, because they can accelerate the diffusion of their product through the market, producing more bang for their buck. These researchers were interested in peer leaders for

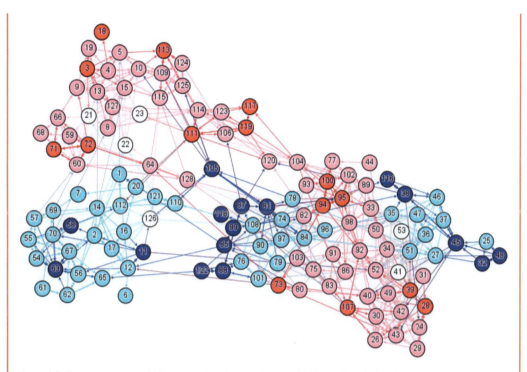

Figure 8.2 The social network of 128 Los Angeles children. Red = girl; blue = boy; darker shades use sunscreen; lighter shades do not use sunscreen. Note how similar colours and shades are clustered close together in the network.
Source: Tsai,J et al. Friendship networks and sun safety behaviour among children. Network Science. (2016). © Cambridge University Press, reproduced with permission. 2016;4(3):314-335. doi:10.1017/nws.2016.6.

similar reasons. We know that social networks, particularly those defined by friendships, influence many childhood and adolescent health behaviours such as the use of alcohol, tobacco, and other drugs, as well as diet and physical activity. In general, the sizes of children's social networks increase with age, and interactions with peers become greater as interactions with family reduce – something we will explore more in Section III (Burke et al., 2022). In a social network, children are competing for resources such as status, reputation, allies, and friends, and the social position achieved in middle childhood can be a springboard for adolescence and adulthood. In the Los Angeles study, peer leaders tended to have better sun safe behaviours and beliefs after the implementation of an intervention designed to educate them. The researchers hoped that these positive behaviours would later spread to the rest of the group, like a contagion.

This effect works especially well when a few people with a large number of connections are in contact with the vast majority of otherwise weakly connected individuals. This kind of network structure is typical of human social networks, and it underpins how the game 'Six Degrees of Kevin Bacon' works. In this game, someone randomly chooses an actor, and then the challenge is to connect them to another actor via a film that both actors have appeared in together, repeating this process to try to find the shortest path that ultimately leads to prolific American actor Kevin Bacon (a Hollywood equivalent of a peer leader). The game was inspired by psychologist Stanley Milgram's work on social networks that showed that people in the USA seemed to be connected, on average, by six degrees of separation.

> **Key Point**
>
> - Children have a strong tendency for homophily, which can emphasise between-group differences.

8.4 Expanding the Moral Circle

We have explored our predisposition to think and behave in terms of us versus them, and we have looked at some of its negative consequences. But the good news about owning a human brain is that it allows you to consider many biases at the same time. This means we are not deterministically doomed to follow one path, whatever evolution might have written into our human nature; instead, we can weigh the cost and benefits of pursuing one instinct against many others. We might have a predisposition for in-group favouritism, but we also have unique capacities for empathy, compassion, and collaboration that appeal to the 'better angels of our nature' in the words of Abraham Lincoln. Groupishness may have motivated some of the darkest moments in human history, but some of our greatest achievements have rested on intergroup cooperation, such as democracy and civil rights. Researchers have begun to uncover which conditions promote the more inclusive side of our nature, and we now understand in some detail the conditions that can expand the moral circle to include the out-group as well as the in-group:

- 5–6-year-olds are more likely to share with the out-group when they are encouraged to talk about the out-group's thoughts, feelings, and actions (McLoughlin & Over, 2019).
- 8–13-year-olds are more willing to alleviate the distress of an out-group member if they have reflected on their distress (Sierksma et al., 2015).
- 5–11-year-olds are more likely to discuss intergroup similarities and differences and report more positivity towards the out-group if they have read stories involving friendships between groups (Cameron et al., 2006).
- 8–13-year-olds are more likely to help the out-group if they have been encouraged to think empathically about them (Sierksma et al., 2015).
- 9–15-year-olds who had higher levels of intergroup contact have more prosocial attitudes towards the out-group than children with lower levels of such contact (Crystal et al., 2008).
- By simply imagining interpersonal contact with an out-group member, 8–10-year-olds had more positive intergroup attitudes and intentions, reducing negative stereotypes of immigrants (Vezzali et al., 2015).
- 4–11-year-olds are more likely to overcome their negative attitude towards an out-group if they anticipate that they are going to have to cooperate with that out-group in the future (Misch et al., 2021).

So, empathising with an out-group member can soften the division between us and them, which is part of our broader ability to picture the world from another person's point of view (i.e., theory of mind; Chapter 3). And the thoughts, desires, and feelings of the out-group become more real to us when we meet them or merely imagine meeting them through stories that promote intergroup conversations and friendships (Aboud et al., 2012). This approach has had most success in reducing prejudice when contact is among groups of equal status, is based on common goals, and is based on cooperation rather than competition (Allport, 1954).

That fact that a new in-group can be defined via cooperation towards a common goal relates to the ideas of fairness and respect that we met in Chapter 7 and to the evolutionary reasons why we are so groupish in the first place. Even 3-year-old children seem to understand the importance of joint commitment in a cooperative task – for example, by continuing to work on it until not only them, but also their partner received their due reward (Hamann et al., 2012). Recall, too, that the Eagles only cooperated with the Rattlers when they were working towards a common goal (Sherif, 1956).

Key Point

- When children in an out-group and in-group make contact, work collaboratively, and empathise with each other, prejudice and discrimination can be reduced.

What happens when a sense of fairness collides with our bias for the in-group? That is the question Laura Elenbaas and her colleagues set out to answer with 185 African-Americans and European-Americans aged 5–6 and 10–11 years olds (2016). These children were shown a story in which school supplies (pens, paper, rubbers) were distributed unequally to children of different racial backgrounds. The children were then asked about the wrongfulness of the inequality, allocated new resources to racial in-group and out-group recipients, evaluated alternative allocation strategies, and reasoned about their decisions. The younger children showed in-group favouritism; however, with age, the children increasingly articulated the importance of equal access to school supplies and correcting past disparities. Older children judged the resource inequality negatively, allocated more resources to the disadvantaged group, and positively evaluated the actions of others who did the same, regardless of whether they had seen their racial in-group or an out-group at a disadvantage. Thus, by middle childhood, children are balancing moral and social group concerns, and in this case they were able to ensure fair access to important resources regardless of racial group membership.

Key Point

- By middle childhood, children can integrate in-group/out-group reasoning with other biases for fairness, equality, and need.

Watch the One-Minute Method.

Discover how researchers compare different age groups of children at the same time, as in the study by Elenbaas and colleagues, or compare how the same children grow up over time.

So, membership of the in-group can change with age and experience, but it is also influenced by wider societal and historical trends. For example, one in seven children born in the USA now have different ethnic-racial backgrounds than their parents (Alba et al., 2018), and multiethnic-racial youth represent the fastest growing demographic in the USA (Csizmadia & Atkin, 2022). Individuals with parents from different ethnic-racial groups identify several benefits of having a diverse heritage, such as pluralistic world views and a stronger sense of self, as well as challenges, such as identity tensions and communal concerns (Soliz et al., 2017). How parents of multiethnic-racial families socialise their children regarding group differences also matters. Children are more likely to access and benefit from two sets of cultural assets when their parents show a willingness to learn about each other's cultures and practices, are reflective about their values and traditions, and protect their children from racial micro-aggressions by advocating for the recognition, inclusion, and appreciation of their children's multiple ethnic-racial heritages (Seider et al., 2023).

Talking Point

Issues of race, gender, sexuality, politics, and religion are issues of group identity; they have been hot-button topics in the past, they are today, and they probably will continue to be in the future (**Figure 8.3**). The first step in understanding why people care about groups so much is to explore where that instinct comes from. From the evidence reviewed in this chapter we know groupthink begins early on, and that it can lead us to prejudice, discrimination, and xenophobia. Yet the research also gives us reason to be optimistic, because we can overcome this bias and appeal to the more egalitarian side of our nature. Where children have been encouraged to make contact with an out-group, empathise, and work collaboratively, in-group favouritism and out-group denigration have been reduced.

The fact that we can change attitudes early on in development is important, as we know biases and stereotypes are difficult to change in adulthood. In the last 20 years, research has shown that we make all manner of social judgements about others that we may not be aware of, creating disparities in hiring practices, student evaluations, law enforcement, and criminal proceedings, and that merely making adults aware of their implicit biases does not usually change their minds (Greenwald & Lai, 2020). Because of children's greater plasticity, they are more open to change. If we can change the attitudes of the young, then they will grow up to be the more inclusive parents of the future, and

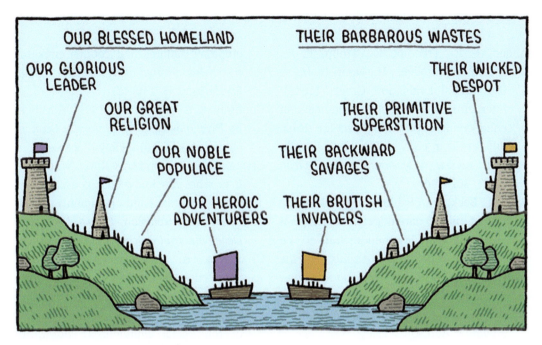

Figure 8.3 The roots of in-group favouritism run deep and can blind us to what we have in common.
Source: © Tom Gauld.

this is important as we know that parents are among the most potent sources of influence on children's intergroup attitudes (Degner & Dalege, 2013).

> ## Summary
>
> - Children think and behave more positively towards the in-group compared to the out-group.
> - Children are sensitive to groups and group membership because being part of the in-group was key to our species' survival.
> - Children adopt the norms of those around them as an important signal of in-group membership.
> - Sorting people into groups is a specific example of our tendency to categorise the world in general.
> - Because self-identity is tied up with the group's identity, in-group favouritism boosts our image and makes us feel better about ourselves.
> - Children have a strong tendency for homophily, which can emphasise between-group differences.
> - When children in an out-group and in-group make contact, work collaboratively, and empathise with each other, prejudice and discrimination can be reduced.
> - By middle childhood, children can integrate in-group/out-group reasoning with other biases for fairness, equality, and need.

References

Aboud, F. E., Tredoux, C., Tropp, L. R., Brown, C. S., Niens, U., Noor, N. M., & Una Global Evaluation Group. (2012). Interventions to reduce prejudice and enhance inclusion and respect for ethnic differences in early childhood: a systematic review. *Developmental Review*, 32(4), 307–336.

Alba, R., Beck, B., & Sahin, D. B. (2018). The rise of mixed parentage: a sociological and demographic phenomenon to be reckoned with. *The Annals of the American Academy of Political and Social Science*, 677(1), 26–38.

Allport, G. W. (1954). *The Nature of Prejudice*. Addison-Wesley.

Billig, M. & Tajfel, H. (1973). Social categorization and similarity in intergroup behaviour. *European Journal of Social Psychology*, 3, 27–52.

Brewer, M. B. (1979). In-group bias in the minimal intergroup situation: a cognitive-motivational analysis. *Psychological Bulletin*, 86(2), 307–324.

Burke, N., Brezack, N., & Woodward, A. (2022). Children's social networks in developmental psychology: a network approach to capture and describe early social environments. *Frontiers in Psychology*, 13, 1009422.

Cameron, L., Rutland, A., Brown, R., & Douch, R. (2006). Changing children's intergroup attitudes toward refugees: testing different models of extended contact. *Child Development*, 77, 1208–1219.

Cikara, M., Bruneau, E., & Saxe, R. (2011). Us and them: intergroup failures of empathy. *Current Directions in Psychological Science*, 20, 149–153.

Cikara, M., Bruneau, E., Van Bavel, J. J., & Saxe, R. (2014). Their pain gives us pleasure: how intergroup dynamics shape empathic failures and counter-empathic responses. *Journal of Experimental Social Psychology*, 55, 110–125.

Connolly, K. & Martlew, M. (1999). Altruism. In *Psychologically Speaking: A Book of Quotations* (p. 10). Wiley-Blackwell.

Crystal, D. S., Killen, M., & Ruck, M. (2008). It is who you know that counts: intergroup contact and judgments about race-based exclusion. *British Journal of Developmental Psychology*, 26(1), 51–70.

Csizmadia, A. & Atkin, A. L. (2022). Supporting children and youth in multiracial families in the United States: racial-ethnic socialization and familial support of multiracial experiences. *Journal of Child and Family Studies*, 31(3), 664–674.

Degner, J. & Dalege, J. (2013). The apple does not fall far from the tree, or does it? A meta-analysis of parent–child similarity in intergroup attitudes. *Psychological Bulletin*, 139(6), 1270–1304.

Elenbaas, L., Rizzo, M. T., Cooley, S., & Killen, M. (2016). Rectifying social inequalities in a resource allocation task. *Cognition*, 155, 176–187.

Engelmann, J. & Tomasello, M. (2019). Children's sense of fairness as equal respect. *Trends in Cognitive Sciences*, 23(6), 454–463.

Engelmann, J. M., Over, H., Herrmann, E., & Tomasello, M. (2013). Young children care more about their reputation with ingroup members and potential reciprocators. *Developmental Science*, 16, 952–958.

Fehr, E., Bernhard, H., & Rockenbach, B. (2008). Egalitarianism in young children. *Nature*, 454, 1079–1083.

Foster-Hanson, E. & Rhodes, M. (2023). Stereotypes as prototypes in children's gender concepts. *Developmental Science*, 26, e13345.

Gaertner, S. L. & Dovidio, J. F. (2000). *Reducing Intergroup Bias: The Common Ingroup Identity Model.* Psychology Press.

Greenwald, A. & Lai, C. (2020). Implicit social cognition. *Annual Review of Psychology*, 71(1), 419–445.

Hamann, K., Warneken, F., & Tomasello, M. (2012). Children's developing commitments to joint goals. *Child Development*, 83(1), 137–145.

Holt-Lunstad, J., Smith, T. B., & Layton, J. B. (2010). Social relationships and mortality risk: a meta-analytic review. *PLoS Medicine*, 7(7), e1000316.

Jackson, C. M., Jackson, J. C., Bilkey, D., Jong, J., & Halberstadt, J. (2019). The dynamic emergence of minimal groups. *Group Processes & Intergroup Relations*, 22(7), 921–929.

Jin, K.-S. & Baillargeon, R. (2017). Infants possess an abstract expectation of ingroup support. *Proceedings of the National Academy of Sciences of the United States of America*, 114, 8199–8204.

Kertesz, A. F., Alvarez, J., Afraymovich, M., & Sullivan, J. (2021). The role of accent and speaker certainty in children's selective trust. *Cognitive Development*, 60, 1–8.

Kinzler, K., Dupoux., E., & Spelke, E. (2012). 'Native' objects and collaborators: infants' object choices and acts of giving reflect favor for native over foreign speakers. *Journal of Cognition and Development*, 13(1), 67–81.

MacDonald, K., Schug, M., Chase, E., & Barth, H. (2013). My people, right or wrong? Minimal group membership disrupts preschoolers' selective trust. *Cognitive Development*, 28(3), 247–259.

McLoughlin, N. & Over, H. (2019). Encouraging children to mentalise about a perceived outgroup increases prosocial behaviour towards outgroup members. *Developmental Science*, 22, e12774.

McLoughlin, N., Tipper, S. P., & Over, H. (2018). Young children perceive less humanness in outgroup faces. *Developmental Science*, 21, e12539.

Misch, A., Over, H., & Carpenter, M. (2016). I won't tell: young children show loyalty to their group by keeping group secrets. *Journal of Experimental Child Psychology*, 142, 96–106.

Misch, A., Over, H., & Carpenter, M. (2018). The whistleblower's dilemma in young children: when loyalty trumps other moral concerns. *Frontiers in Psychology*, 9, 250.

Misch, A., Paulus, M., & Dunham, Y. (2021). Anticipation of future cooperation eliminates minimal ingroup bias in children and adults. *Journal of Expimental Psychology. General*, 150(10), 2036–2056.

Myers, D. (2005). The self in a social world. In *Social Psychology*, 8th edition (pp. 39–81). McGraw-Hill.

Over, H. (2018). The influence of group membership on young children's prosociality. *Current Opinion in Psychology*, 20, 17–20.

Richter, N., Over, H., & Dunham, Y. (2016). The effects of minimal group membership on young preschoolers' social preferences, estimates of similarity, and behavioral attribution. *Collabra*, 2(1), 8.

Seider, S., Huguley, J., McCobb, E., Titchner, D., Ward, K., Xu, H., & Zheng, Y. (2023). How parents in multiethnic-racial families share cultural assets with their children. *Race and Social Problems*, 15(1), 5–18.

Shelton, J. N. & Richeson, J. A. (2005). Intergroup contact and pluralistic ignorance. *Journal of Personality and Social Psychology*, 88(1), 91–107.

Sherif, M. (1956). Experiments in group conflict. *Scientific American*, 195(5), 54–59.

Shinada, M., Yamagishi, T., & Ohmura, Y. (2004). False friends are worse than bitter enemies: 'altruistic' punishment of in-group members. *Evolution and Human Behavior*, 25(6), 379–393.

Sierksma, J., Thijs, J., & Verkuyten, M. (2015). In-group bias in children's intention to help can be overpowered by inducing empathy. *British Journal of Developmental Psychology*, 33(1), 45–56.

Soliz, J., Cronan, S., Bergquist, G., Nuru, A. K., & Rittenour, C. E. (2017). Perceived benefits and challenges of a multiethnic-racial identity: insight from adults with mixed heritage. *Identity*, 17(4), 267–281.

Souza, A., Byers-Heinlein, K., & Poulin-Dubois, D. (2013). Bilingual and monolingual children prefer native-accented speakers. *Frontiers in Psychology*, 4, 953.

Tsai, J., Valante, T., Miller, K., De La Haye, K., Pickering, T., & Cockburn, M. (2016). Friendship networks and sun safety behavior among children. *Network Science*, 4(3), 314–335.

Vezzali, L., Stathi, S., Crisp, R.J., & Capozza, D. (2015). Comparing direct and imagined intergroup contact among children: effects on outgroup stereotypes and helping intentions. *International Journal of Intercultural Relations*, 49, 46–53.

Williams, K. D. & Nida, S. A. (2011). Ostracism: consequences and coping. *Current Directions in Psychological Science*, 20(2), 71–75.

Yu, C., Qian, M., Amemiya, J., Fu, G., Lee, K., & Heyman, G. D. (2022). Young children form generalized attitudes based on a single encounter with an outgroup member. *Developmental Science*, 25, e13191.

9 HOW DOES IMAGINATION DEVELOP?

 Learning Outcomes

After reading this chapter you will be able to:

- Describe the development of imagination, creativity, and flexible thinking.
- Understand how children express their creativity in their drawings, their imaginary worlds, and in what they are willing to believe.
- Provide examples of how children's imagination is grounded in their everyday experience.

9.1 Introduction

Humans are often celebrated – by humans, it has to be said – as the most inventive and creative of species. Chimpanzees can use stones to crush nuts, some crows use sticks to catch grubs, and octopus have been known to use coconut shells to disguise themselves from predators. Impressive as these behaviours are, they do not really compare with the depth and breadth of human innovation: clothes, sanitation, levers, the wheel, the plough, music, paper, writing, architecture, clocks, the compass, currency, refrigeration, vaccines, birth control, gene editing, computers, the internet, and artificial intelligence. Where most other animals adapt to their environment, we adapt the environment to us. We don't wait around to evolve thicker hair; we invent the coat. This adaptability has allowed us to inhabit every continent and make an impact on the Earth's entire ecosystem (not in a positive way). We are good at innovation, and we value it too. Creativity is one of the most desired employability skills, creative industries are major revenue sources for large economies, and highly skilled artists, musicians, dancers, storytellers, and other 'creatives' are among the most idolised members of many societies. The human capacities for technological innovation and creative problem-solving far surpass those of any species and significantly develop during middle childhood. How do children use their imagination? Are children able to innovate new tools, imagine impossible worlds, and suspend reality? How do they make judgements about what is possible? And what can we learn from children's figurative drawing, their pretend play, and their imaginary companions?

9.2 Tool Innovation

One way to measure children's inventiveness is by putting them in situations that demand creative thinking. For example, in one popular problem-solving task children are presented with a transparent tube with a small bucket at the bottom. Inside the bucket is a reward, typically a sticker or a sweet, and alongside the tube is a straightened pipe cleaner. The tube is too long and too narrow for children to simply reach down and grab the reward, so they must find another way to retrieve it. To do so, the children need to bend the pipe cleaner into a hook shape and use that to pull the bucket up out of the tube. When researchers gave this task to children of different ages, they were surprised by just how challenging even the older ones found it. Fewer than 1 in 10 children under 5 years of age made a hook, only about half of 7–8-year-olds were successful in fishing the bucket from the tube, and almost a third of 11-year-olds failed entirely (Beck et al., 2011). However, when Betty the crow was given an equivalent task, she succeeded without a problem (Weir et al., 2002). Crows come from a family of birds called corvids, which are known for their intelligence. Corvids have a much longer period of immaturity compared with birds like chickens, geese, and turkeys. Chickens grow up being good at a few things, like pecking, but corvids grow up to be more adaptable and able to generalise their skills. It is no coincidence that corvids have a relatively long early learning phase of life, play more as juveniles, and have patient adult teachers.

The behaviour of the children we looked at in Section I revealed remarkable sophistication at even young ages in terms of reading other minds (Chapter 3), learning languages (Chapter 4), and inferring cause and effect (Chapter 5), but with tool innovation, they are remarkable for the opposite reason. Despite being prodigious in all these other areas, it's surprising just how difficult children find an apparently straightforward task involving just a bucket and a pipe cleaner; even 11-year-olds are outsmarted by a crow. What is going on here?

First, children's poor performance at this task is not due to difficulty in forming a hook with the pipe cleaner, as they have similar problems in creating a loop to access an out-of-reach platform, pouring water into a tube to bring a toy into reach, or unbending pipe cleaners to push a ball from a horizontal tube. It is also not something particular to **WEIRD** children, as this basic finding has been widely replicated across diverse cultures in over a dozen different countries. For example, Nielsen and colleagues (2014) compared the performance of mostly middle-class 3–5-year-old children from Brisbane with children from five South African San communities, in which children typically lack access to manufactured toys and so make their own. We might expect that experience with regularly making toys would make the San children more likely to innovate a solution to this task. However, only 11% of Brisbane children and no San children formed a hook in this task. And it's not that children lack the physical tool-making abilities to make a hook either. When children watch an adult bend the pipe cleaner into a hook to retrieve the reward, they can copy them without a problem.

Perhaps children lack experience with pipe cleaners or fail to understand that they are free to make whatever they like with them? When children are encouraged to experiment with what pipe cleaners can do – by twisting them around a pen, for example – this doesn't seem

Figure 9.1 Examples of tool use in crows, monkeys, octopuses, and children. In Chapter 1 we mentioned that scientists are obsessed with arguing over alternative explanations to explain the same set of observations because they care about cause and effect. The hook task is a good example of this debate in action, as researchers have explored several plausible explanations for the observed results, ruling each one out in turn. Source: Auscape International Pty Ltd / Alamy Stock Photo; MikeLane45/iStock /Getty Images Plus; Divelvanov /iStock/Getty Images Plus; _jure /iStock/Getty Images Plus.

to put 4–7-year-olds at a significant advantage when later confronted with the hook task (Cutting et al., 2011). And when children are clearly given licence by a puppet to make something new (e.g., 'Heinz says he has some things here you can make something with to get the sticker'), the clear invitation to innovate has little impact on success in the task either (**Figure 9.1**).

There are likely to be a range of factors that make the hook task difficult for children (Rawlings, 2022). While on the surface the solution seems straightforward to us, it places significant demands on children's imagination, memory, planning, and flexible thinking skills. For example, children need to hold the current state of the task in mind (the reward is at the bottom of the tube) while also remembering what they are trying to achieve (get the reward out of the tube) at the same time as visualising a solution (a hook) and planning the sequence of actions to get from the current state to where they want to be. This demands high-level thinking skills that are some of the last to mature in development (we revisit these so-called executive function skills in Section III). In support of the idea that these skills matter, as planning and control abilities develop, children's success on the hook task also gets better.

Another barrier to success is that young children can get fixated on the **conventional** use of a tool and so find it difficult to imagine using it in a way that is different from how it was originally intended. For example, 12–18-month-olds find it difficult to use the handle end of a spoon to illuminate a lightbox, but when a tool is introduced to them that they haven't seen before they show more willingness to use it in different ways (Barrett et al., 2007). Presumably, in their everyday experience, these infants had seen many instances of spoon use before and therefore had a strong expectation about how a spoon *should* be used. We know infants are prodigious imitators of adults' behaviour – recall infants imitating adults touching a light-up box with their head in Chapter 5. Without such faithful imitation, most of our cultural knowledge would be lost from one generation to the next. But in the case of innovation, the preference to copy what has gone before gets in the way of thinking differently, and thinking differently is exactly what is needed in these types of tasks. We will see later in Chapter 12 how teenagers' healthy disregard for tradition ('there must be a better way!') and openness to new experiences can put them at an advantage when it comes to innovating and leading cultural change.

Researchers have had success in boosting young children's performance on the hook task if they are allowed to tinker with their past inventions (Burdett & Ronfard, 2023). Those children who retained tools from earlier failed attempts and who added more novel objects to their tools following failure were more likely to build successful tools later. This is reminiscent of the ratchet effect we met in Chapter 5, whereby we take the discoveries, behaviours, and inventions of previous generations and build on them for future ones. But instead of ratcheting better ideas over generations, children are ratcheting better ideas from their previous selves, tinkering their way to a solution.

Key Points

- Tool innovation emerges relatively late in childhood compared to other complex skills.
- Tool innovation places significant demands on higher-order thinking skills and is hindered by a preference to imitate the conventional use of an object.
- Children show signs of greater inventiveness as they get older and get better at identifying a workable solution among a range of possibilities.

A for effort.

What motivates children more in a problem-solving task: praising their intelligence or their effort?

9.3 The Mental Laboratory

Human inventiveness is marked not just by the inventiveness of what we do or the tools we make, but by the breadth of what we can imagine. A 16-year-old Albert Einstein supposedly imagined chasing after a beam of light in the vacuum of space. He went on to imagine many different worlds, each time analysing what the consequences of his thought experiments would be. Over many years, these musings eventually developed into his special theory of relativity, explaining the fundamental connection between space, time, energy, and matter.

The theory had to wait for another hundred years for experimental evidence to confirm that his initial insights were on the right track (more on a young Einstein later in this chapter). So, thought experiments can permit us to draw new conclusions about the way the world works without direct experience. We have already met this idea when exploring the role of pretend play in counterfactual thinking. Recall that counterfactual thinking is the ability to entertain an idea as if it were true but you know that it isn't. We saw that those children who were especially good at pretend play were also good at counterfactual reasoning (Buchsbaum et al., 2012). The idea is that pretend play provides a mental training ground for reasoning about and learning from imagined scenarios that can later be applied to real ones. If you can imagine the future, you will be better prepared for it.

One of the best predictors of the future is what happened in the past. There is evidence that the more children remember about the past, the more fine-grained are their predictions of the future. For example, Wang and colleagues (2014) asked European-American and Chinese-American children between 7 and 10 years of age to talk about past and future events. The researchers found that the amount of detail that children recalled in describing past events was associated with the amount of detail they generated in imagining future events.

Key Point

- Children capitalise on personal experience when imagining what might happen in the future.

Recall that young children have difficulty understanding the difference between what is hard to imagine and impossible and what is hard to imagine but nonetheless possible (Box 5.1). If children's imaginations are constrained by what they have regularly observed in the past, they are likely to underestimate the wide scope of possible outcomes. As we get older, not only do we get more experience of what is possible in the world, we also get more experience of being wrong about what is impossible. As the old witticism goes: 'predictions are risky, especially about the future'. So, as children develop, they become less confident that they can rule out unlikely events as impossible because they remember that they have been wrong about the impossibility of things before.

Key Point

- As children's experience grows, they get better at acknowledging that improbable events are still possible and that their predictions about what is impossible might be wrong.

9.4 Imaginary Worlds

A common view is that in the imaginary worlds that children create, anything is possible. But is that right? Let's take another look at imaginary play. Research has revealed that, far from being unconstrained fantasy for children, imaginary play adopts many of the rules from real life. For example, when children observe a play partner move an animal that makes the wrong sound (e.g., 'oink' for a duck), children are quick to point out the error (e.g., 'that's not what ducks say' or 'it goes quack'). More generally, a significant amount of research has shown that when children construct imaginary worlds, they assume that those worlds operate by similar rules to reality itself (Harris, 2021). For example, they presume characters are motivated by the same psychological vocabulary as in real life (Cinderella 'desires', 'knows', 'believes', and so on), insist objects behave according to similar constraints as they do in real life (the same teapot can't be in several different places at once), and expect cause and effect to be obeyed (lakes fill with water because it rained, it didn't rain because the lakes filled up).

This is most clearly demonstrated in what children's pretend play is *about*. Most episodes of pretence are not surreal explorations of the impossible but act out stereotypical, familiar scripts and routines drawn from everyday experience: sleeping, eating, going for a ride, packing, going to the store, cooking, having a meal, using the mobile phone, and other domestic scenes. Far from being mundane or showing a lack of imagination, this makes sense when we consider what play is for: a safe place for children to learn the skills they are likely to need later in their lives.

For children born into societies where they are expected to become economically active relatively earlier than their WEIRD peers, these scripts are more likely to be orientated towards work. Children of the Efe community of foragers in the Democratic Republic of the Congo and those of the indigenous Maya of San Pedro, a modernising, agricultural town in Guatemala, pretend to shoot animals with a bow and arrow or make tortillas out of dirt, for example (Morelli et al., 2003). These scripts anticipate the duties and roles they will be expected to perform later on. In many foraging and farming communities, children are further encouraged to engage in work-themed pretence by their parents, who will often provide scaled-down implements such as baskets, bows, or spears to play with. In one study looking at the pretend play of children of the Aka forest foragers and Ngandu subsistence farmers, work-based play (e.g., fetching 'water' with miniature containers; 'cooking' inedible leaves in a sardine can) represented 87% of pretend play among the Aka and 68.5% among the Ngandu (Boyette, 2016). Most episodes of pretend play echoed the everyday lives of work and caregiving, with less than 5% of pretend play involving fantasy.

 Key Point

- The imaginary worlds of young children often reflect the local practices and routines of adults, and their pretend worlds largely reflect the realities of their everyday lives.

9.5 Suspending Belief

There are some contexts in which children are more willing to suspend reality than others. For example, if children are told that all fish live in trees and that a Tot is a fish, they resist drawing the logical conclusion – that a Tot lives in trees – and draw a conclusion based on their experience – a Tot lives in the water, because that's where all fish live. Only when it is made abundantly clear that the context is make-believe (e.g., when the premise is embedded in a story, is described as happening on a faraway planet, or applies only to 'the pictures in their head') are children more willing to entertain the absurd and reason from it. If the set-up is described in more matter-of-fact fashion, with no hint that everyone is in on the make-believe, then younger children mainly draw conclusions about hypotheticals that are based on their experience rather than logic (Harris, 2000).

In a clear demonstration of this, researchers told 2-, 3-, and 4-year-olds stories that all involved suspending belief: for example, 'All sheep ride bicycles' and that 'Bill is a sheep' (Richards & Sanderson, 1999). From this set-up, researchers were interested in whether children could imagine the consequences in a world where these premises were true. Children were directly asked, 'Does Bill walk or ride a bicycle?' Children who were told to just pretend these things were true were more likely to answer 'walk', justifying their answer with 'because I know that sheep walk'. By contrast, children who were given strong cues to use their imagination – either to pretend that they were on another planet where everything was different or to use mental imagery – were more likely to reason logically from the premises and to justify their answer 'ride a bike' by referring back to what the experimenter had said (e.g., 'because the story said that sheep ride bicycles').

Key Points

- When presented with a premise that does not fit within or lies outside their everyday experience, children resist reasoning from it.
- When provided with a make-believe template and given strong cues to use their imagination, children are more willing to suspend belief and reason from false premises.

Box 9.1 explores the lives of those children identified as exceptionally gifted and talented. What can we learn about creativity from those children who show precocious talent – for example, learning to read, write, play piano, or speak multiple languages well before their peers?

Box 9.1 Creative genius

Researchers who have followed child prodigies as they have grown up have found that being a child prodigy is a rather poor predictor of exceptional talent in later life – or, to put it another way, genius kids do not necessarily make genius adults. One study focused on children who had been selected by their schools on the basis that they were the brainiest 0.001% of the population, resulting in a way-above-average IQ for the cohort, scoring 150 on IQ tests (Subotnik et al., 1993). The researchers found that most of these children went on to lead satisfied but no happier than average lives. They were accomplished lawyers, professors, physicians, and orchestral musicians, but there were no Nobel Prize winners, no leaders of nations, and no creative visionaries that led a revolution. In short, there was no evidence of the extreme talent in adulthood for which they were selected as children. Some child prodigies go on to change the course of history, but most do not.

Looking at genius from the other end of life results in a similar story: being an adult genius is no guarantee of an exceptional childhood. Copernicus, Rembrandt, Bach, Newton, Beethoven, Kant, and da Vinci were all notably undistinguished children, giving little hint of the masterminds they were to become. Throughout this book we have seen many examples of the importance of early experiences in predicting later outcomes, so what is going on here?

One possibility is that we are looking at two different sorts of skill in children and adults. In general, child prodigies come to our attention when they have acquired a large body of existing knowledge or show prodigious talent earlier than their peers, like learning calculus or playing grade-8 violin. By contrast, we expect adult geniuses to break new ground, invent something, or force us to look at the world radically differently. This difference has been described as being a 'gifted learner' versus a 'gifted doer' (Gladwell, 2008). Early mastery is not a predictor of later success because prodigies fail to make the transition in early adulthood from being a gifted learner – mimicking what has been done before – to being a gifted doer – making discoveries or creating a style of their own.

What does seem a better predictor of success is an individual's attitude to learning itself. For example, mental grit or perseverance and a passion to see the job through have been shown to be much better predictors of life success and school achievement than early prodigiousness (Duckworth et al., 2007). The poster boy for genius, Albert Einstein, was a famous late bloomer, having failed his school entrance exams on language, zoology, and botany – his mathematics exam was OK, but not exceptional. His biographers do note his exceptional curiosity, doggedness, and perseverance, however. These qualities are arguably less glamorous than the idea of a child prodigy but are perhaps more essential components of genius. And, of course, perseverance is very closely related to practice. By the time 6-year-old Mozart was performing for others, it is estimated he had racked up 3,500 hours of practice after being encouraged by his father, Leopold Mozart, to play for up to 3 hours a day from the age of 3. At least in the field of music, Malcolm Gladwell argues that what we mean when we say someone has natural talent is that they practice a lot, they want to practice a lot, and they like to practice a lot (2008).

To be clear, it is not that just anyone could be a Mozart if they practiced more or that by merely being more persistent you will turn into the next Einstein. The abilities of individuals do matter, but a proportion of what we call 'innate talent' might be a predisposition for grit, extreme stamina, focus, and long-term effort, traits that show a degree of heritability (Rimfeld et al., 2016). What this grit is applied to – playing chess or piano, doing maths, or speaking multiple languages – results from a combination of factors (e.g., having a dad like Mozart's who pushes a child in one direction) and the lottery of experience (e.g., a teacher who, by chance, happens to give a flute to one child to practice and a violin to another).

 Key Point

- Early exceptional talent does not necessarily translate to later genius.

9.6 Drawing, Stories, and Imaginary Beings

Another window into children's imaginations is their drawings. The modern interest in this subject owes much to Georges-Henri Luquet, a French philosopher and ethnographer who studied more than 1,700 drawings produced by his daughter (Luquet, 1927). Based on these drawings, Luquet concluded that children are figurative realists: they try to draw real objects, often including features that they know belong to an object, even those features that cannot actually be seen from a given point of view. For example, children's drawings start out with a loose likeness to reality and progress to drawing human figures as if they were tadpoles with heads and bodies fused together. Children typically then move on to draw scenes from multiple perspectives or an air-view plan, showing objects as if they were folded out or positioned on a table as if they were floating above a rectangular box, not resting on a flat surface (Willats, 1977). Eventually, most children can draw more visually realistic representations with occlusion, suppression of details, and perspective (**Figure 9.2**).

Watch the One-Minute Method.

Discover how case studies, like the one Georges-Henri Luquet conducted on his own daughter's drawings, can give us a rich description of development.

The 'bird' drawing of a 2.5-year-old.

'Tadpole' people of a 3.5-year-old.

A 7-year-old girl's drawing of a man in a boat and a man on a horse.

A 10-year-old's visually realistic drawings.

Figure 9.2 A developmental sequence of children's drawings. Source: Jolley, R. Children and Pictures: Drawing and Understanding. Wiley-Blackwell; Cox,M. 'The Tadpole Figure' (Ch2) in Children's Drawings of the Human Figure. Psychology Press; Jolley, R. Children and Pictures: Drawing and Understanding. Wiley-Blackwell; Jolley, R. Children and Pictures: Drawing and Understanding. Wiley-Blackwell.

It is likely that the change in children's drawing ability reflects a change in their ability to represent three-dimensional objects on a two-dimensional surface rather than a shift in how they fundamentally see reality. As this skill develops, along with development of their attention, memory, and control of their hands, so does the realism of what they draw. Regardless of the accuracy of what children draw, the subjects of their drawings are mainly taken from their everyday experience: human figures, animals, houses, vehicles, and so on (Harris, 2020). As always, development takes place in a context. Like other aspects of children's development, what they draw and when they start drawing are influenced by social and cultural differences. For example, in China, a culture with a long artistic tradition and deference to authority, children receive systematic drawing instruction from an early age and so are relatively more adept at drawing the major themes of Chinese art – goldfish, birds, and flowers – at an earlier age than children not steeped in this tradition (Golomb, 2002).

Key Point

- Children's drawings are typically remixes of reality rather than complete departures from it.

Experimental work supports the idea that children's drawings use the repertoire of the real even when they are encouraged to depict the unreal, adding, subtracting, or changing the position of something already known to them. For example, developmental psychologist Annette Karmiloff-Smith asked 4–6-year-olds and 8–10-year-olds to draw a house, a man, and an animal that did not exist (1990). The older age group invented characters that were made up of real elements, albeit arranged in novel ways – drawing a man with an extra head, a man with a leg growing out of his shoulder, or a man's head and chest fused with the body of an animal, for instance. The 4–6-year-olds had much more difficulty in providing these relatively complex drawings (10% or fewer achieved this goal), and those that did often produced simpler solutions, such as altering the shape of a component part or omitting it altogether.

The fact that children's drawings are resistant to wild departures from reality is perhaps a little unexpected given how much fantasy children are exposed to, at least in WEIRD societies. Children's TV, films, and books frequently start from unrealistic assumptions and are full of characters imbued with magical powers: animals that talk, princes that turn into frogs, and carriages that turn into pumpkins. Even in these cases, when asked to explain what is going on, children ground their explanations in what would make sense in the real world. For example, most children judge owning a unicorn to be impossible, but when pushed to offer an explanation they give non-magical reasons such as, 'Well, they probably got it from the pet store,' or, 'Maybe she won it at the farm in like a different country' (Harris, 2021).

Despite the prevalence of fantasy in media aimed at children, there is some evidence that, when invited to make a choice, children might prefer stories with realistic outcomes over unrealistic ones. For example, when researchers presented 4-year-olds with either a realistic or a fantastical story and asked them to fill in missing parts of the stories, children mostly opted for realistic continuations (Weisberg et al., 2013). Both the realistic and the fantastical stories had the same overall event structure: a boy and his dog got ice cream, went to a petting zoo, and came home for dinner. But, unlike the realistic story, the fantastical story included impossible elements, such as a child who could fly and animals that could talk. Adults, by contrast, when presented with the same set of stories, chose to continue the story in the style they heard, opting for realistic continuations for the realistic story and mostly fantastical continuations for the fantastical story. In Chapter 11, we will look at what children's own stories can teach us about their creativity and how they vary across different societies.

What about the imaginary companions that some children carry around in their own heads? As far as we are able to tell, invisible companions play by similar rules as visible ones. For example, imaginary friends are motivated by the same psychological characteristics of an ordinary person: he or she interacts as a playmate or confidant, expresses thoughts and emotions, eats and sleeps, and is a source of reassurance and sometimes of frustration. This tendency to engage in role-play and to invent an imaginary companion is correlated with the ability to think accurately about other people's mental states (Harris, 2021). The idea here is that role-play and imaginary companions can act as a mental training ground for the kinds of theory of mind skills that children will need later in development.

 Key Points

- Young children have a preference for explaining the supernatural in terms of the natural.
- When children have imaginary companions or impersonate others, they tend to draw on a repertoire of behaviours from real life.

We might think children sometimes wander around in their own reality. But the general message from children's drawings, stories, and imaginary friends is similar to that from tool innovation, pretend play, thinking about the future, and making judgements about possibility: imagination in these areas is not an anything-goes free-for-all. Children do not routinely generate extraordinary possibilities but are instead much more likely to conjure up worlds that obey the rules of everyday life. Far from being a deficit in their creativity, this is better understood as a form of strategic rehearsal for the future. By using their imagination for entertaining unrealised but realistic possibilities, they gain a problem-solving playbook to consult when they encounter analogous situations in the future.

Talking Point

The idea that innovations build on the insights of previous generations is captured by the following phrase: 'If I have seen further, it is by standing on the shoulders of giants.' We first encountered this phrase when we looked at social learning in children (Chapter 5). The quote has been previously attributed to Isaac Newton, but, rather fittingly, variations on the phrase have been around since at least the twelfth century, showing that Newton was just the latest in a long line of people who had tinkered with the same underlying idea in slightly different ways.

Many cultural innovations work this way, as remixes or mashups of history. Innovations are often marked not by how few sources they draw on, but how many – so much so that it becomes difficult to trace the origins of all of them. This does raise the broader question of what we mean by 'imagination', 'creativity', and 'originality'. For any idea, song, poem, or piece of tech that we think of as a true leap of imagination or a radical departure from convention, we can almost always trace its roots back to something that went before, even if the elements are brought together in unique ways. This goes for children's creativity too. As head-mounted cameras, smartphones, and wearable tech are gathering more data on the amount and the variety of children's experiences, we are likely to discover that much of what looks like children's creativity on the surface might be grounded in the roots of their history.

> ### Summary
> - Tool innovation emerges relatively late in childhood compared to other complex skills.
> - Tool innovation places significant demands on higher-order thinking skills and is hindered by a preference to imitate the conventional use of an object.
> - Children show signs of greater inventiveness as they get older and get better at identifying a workable solution among a range of possibilities.
> - Children capitalise on personal experience when imagining what might happen in the future.
> - As children's experience grows, they get better at acknowledging that improbable events are still possible and that their predictions about what is impossible might be wrong.
> - The imaginary worlds of young children often reflect the local practices and routines of adults, and their pretend worlds largely reflect the realities of their everyday lives.
> - When presented with a premise that does not fit within or lies outside their everyday experience, children resist reasoning from it.
> - When provided with a make-believe template and given strong cues to use their imagination, children are more willing to suspend belief and reason from false premises.
> - Early exceptional talent does not necessarily translate to later genius.
> - Children's drawings are typically remixes of reality rather than complete departures from it.
> - Young children have a preference for explaining the supernatural in terms of the natural.
> - When children have imaginary companions or impersonate others, they tend to draw on a repertoire of behaviours from real life.

References

Barrett, T. M., Davis, E. F., & Needham, A. (2007). Learning about tools in infancy. *Developmental Psychology*, 43(2), 352–368.

Beck, S. R., Apperly, I. A., Chappell, J., Guthrie, C., & Cutting, N. (2011). Making tools isn't child's play. *Cognition*, 119(2), 301–306.

Boyette, A. H. (2016). Children's play and culture learning in an egalitarian foraging society. *Child Development*, 87, 759–769.

Buchsbaum, D., Bridgers, S., Skolnick-Weisberg, D., & Gopnik, A. (2012). The power of possibility: causal learning, counterfactual reasoning, and pretend play. *Philosophical Transactions of the Royal Society of London B: Biological Sciences*, 367(1599), 2202–2212.

Burdett, E. R. R. & Ronfard, S. (2023). Tinkering to innovation: how children refine tools over multiple attempts. *Developmental Psychology*, 59(6), 1006–1016.

Cutting, N., Apperly, I. A., & Beck, S. (2011). Why do children lack the flexibility to innovate tools? *Journal of Experimental Child Psychology*, 109, 497–511.

Duckworth, A. L., Peterson, C., Matthews, M. D., & Kelly, D. R. (2007). Grit: perseverance and passion for long-term goals. *Journal of Personality and Social Psychology*, 92, 1087–1101.

Gladwell, M. (2008). *Outliers*. Little, Brown and Company.

Golomb, C. (2002). *Child Art in Context: A Cultural and Comparative Perspective*. American Psychological Association.

Harris, P. L. (2000). *The Work of the Imagination*. Blackwell.

Harris, P. L. (2020). Can young children draw what does not exist? *Empirical Studies in the Arts*, 38, 71–80.

Harris, P. L. (2021). Early constraints on the imagination: the realism of young children. *Child Development*, 92, 466–483.

Karmiloff-Smith, A. (1990). Constraints on representational change: evidence from children's drawings. *Cognition*, 34, 57–83.

Luquet, G.-H. (1927). *Le dessin enfantin*. Librairie Félix Alcan.

Morelli, G. A., Rogoff, B., & Angelillo, C. (2003). Cultural variation in young children's access to work or involvement in specialized child-focused activities. *International Journal of Behavioral Development*, 27, 264–274.

Nielsen, M., Tomaselli, K., Mushin, I., & Whiten, A. (2014). Exploring tool innovation: a comparison of Western and Bushman children. *Journal of Experimental Child Psychology*, 126, 384–394.

Rawlings, B. S. (2022). After a decade of tool innovation, what comes next? *Child Development Perspectives*, 16, 118–124.

Richards, C. A. & Sanderson, J. A. (1999). The role of imagination in facilitating deductive reasoning in 2-, 3- and 4-year olds. *Cognition*, 72(2).

Rimfeld, K., Kovas, Y., Dale, P. S., & Plomin, R. (2016). True grit and genetics: predicting academic achievement from personality. *Journal of Personality and Social Psychology*, 111(5), 780–789.

Subotnik, R. F., Kassan, L., Summers, E., & Wasser, A. (1993). *Genius Revisited: High IQ Children Grown Up*. Ablex.

Wang, Q., Capous, D., Koh, J. B. K., & Hou, Y. (2014). Past and future episodic thinking in middle childhood. *Journal of Cognition and Development*, 15, 625–643.

Weir, A. A. S., Chappell, J., & Kacelnik, A. (2002). Shaping of hooks in New Caledonian crows. *Science*, 297(5583), 981.

Weisberg, D. S., Sobel, D. M., Goodstein, J., & Bloom, P. (2013). Young children are reality-prone when thinking about stories. *Journal of Cognition and Culture*, 13, 383–407.

Willats, J. (1977). How children learn to draw realistic pictures. *The Quarterly Journal of Experimental Psychology*, 29, 367–382.

10 HOW DOES CHILDREN'S MEMORY WORK?

 Learning Outcomes

After reading this chapter you will be able to:
- Describe different types of memory and how they develop.
- Explain how early experiences are remembered and why they are forgotten.
- Understand why a limited memory can be beneficial for learning.

10.1 Introduction

Over the course of this book we have looked at theory of mind, learning, language, morality, groupthink, and creativity. It is hard to imagine how any of these skills could develop without memory; indeed, it is hard to imagine how any adaptive organism could survive without the ability to use past experiences to guide their future behaviour. Even communities of bacteria meet this basic definition of memory.

Decades of human research have revealed that memory is not just one thing, but a set of changing, interrelated systems: memories that tell the story of our lives (e.g., that time I rode my bike on a beach); memories of well-rehearsed actions that are difficult to put into words (e.g., how to ride a bike); memories of facts (e.g., the Tour de France is a bike race); memories that handle multiple things at once (e.g., having a conversation while riding my bike); and memories reminding us to do things in the future (e.g., fix the puncture on my bike). These memory systems develop according to their own schedules, go through significant change during middle childhood, and are influenced by a range of neurological, cognitive, social, and cultural factors. Memory not only supports our daily functioning, but is fundamental to who we are and how we make sense of our lives. In this chapter we take a deeper look at memory and explore how experiences become memories; how forgetting can help learning; and why, if the early years are so important, we cannot remember any of them.

10.2 Practice Makes ... Progress

You may have noticed that a large part of an infant's day is taken up practicing – practicing how to move their arms, how to make sounds, how to eat, how to focus on a face, how to crawl around, how to hold an object, how to get the attention of others, and so on. As they are acquiring these skills, their journey from novice to expert usually occurs in three distinct phases (Fitts & Posner, 1967). First, there is a phase of focused effort and repetition; for example, when infants are learning to produce sounds, they may repeatedly babble the same sound many times over. In this phase, they are on a steep learning curve, and their skills improve directly in line with the amount of practice they do, or what is called **online learning**.

A second phase is reached when the pace of learning levels off, during which infants consolidate what they have previously learned and their skills can improve in the absence of direct engagement or practice, or what is known as **offline learning**. A wide body of evidence supports the role that sleep plays in this consolidation phase of learning, with certain stages of sleep being especially important for making memories stronger and more resilient to forgetting (Stickgold & Walker, 2005).

If children successfully progress through the first two phases of acquisition and consolidation, a third phase is reached during which the skill becomes automatic. This **automatisation** is a basic psychological process that is important for acquiring a wide variety of abilities, including physical (e.g., walking), social (e.g., talking), and cognitive (e.g., numeracy and literacy) skills. This process happens because the brain has a preference to automatise skills wherever possible, freeing our attention to focus on the next challenge. As adults, abilities like walking and talking were automatised so long ago we are no longer aware of *how* we achieve these things. This can be a barrier to appreciating just how complex and remarkable familiar skills are. As a result of automatisation, skills become more fluent and less prone to being forgotten, allowing us to perform them effortlessly in a range of contexts, without awareness of the thoughts or actions that support them, and even when our attention is directed elsewhere.

This shift, from effortful, deliberate practice to automatic performance, is supported by **procedural memory**, and it is important throughout our lives. For example, when first learning to drive, we might find it difficult to imagine how anyone could also listen to the radio or hold a conversation while trying to read road signs and navigate to where they are going. The fact that we eventually have enough mental bandwidth to do this is made possible with the help of procedural memory; processes that were once effortful to learn – controlling the car, monitoring its position on the road, looking out for hazards, and so on – have, without intent or awareness, become automatic.

Walkie Talkie.

Learning any new skill, like walking and talking, requires children to encode, store and retrieve memories effectively. Lots of practice and sleep helps these skills become automatic and effortless.

> **Key Point**
>
> - The shift during skill acquisition from effortful, deliberate practice to automatic performance allows children (and adults) to keep learning new skills.

In Chapter 16 we will explore the idea that a disruption to this normal process of automatisation may underpin problems with learning language, reading, writing, and movement precisely because successful acquisition of these skills involves automating a large amount of information.

10.3 Memory at Work

An especially important kind of memory that sees rapid development in middle childhood is known as **working memory**. This describes the ability to mentally work on multiple sources of information at the same time – for example, remembering the directions of how to get somewhere while also remembering where we want to go. It is often required to solve one-off problems, because an existing solution does not exist in procedural memory. We use working memory every day, but it has limited capacity, and it can be become overwhelmed if there are too many pieces of information that need to be held in mind at once; for example, we might forget the sequence of left and right turns we need to take to a destination if we are interrupted by a conversation.

The number of individual chunks of information that children can hold in mind rapidly expands from 4 to 8 years of age, but working memory is still significantly developing right the way through to adolescence (Ahmed et al., 2022). This ability to mentally manipulate multiple sources of information has been demonstrated to underpin a range of developmental outcomes for children. For example, those children that have relatively strong working memories tend to be relatively strong in reading comprehension, reasoning, arithmetic calculations, and mathematical problem-solving and, not surprisingly, perform better academically in general (Diamond, 2013).

Given its role in so many different outcomes for children, there has been interest in whether working memory can be trained in children, and whether improvements in working memory result in improvements in other areas of children's lives – a phenomenon known as **cognitive transfer**. For example, with a group of 104 children aged 7 years from Cuba, Roque-Gutierrez and Ibbotson demonstrated that when children regularly engaged in tasks that exercised their working memory, not only did their working memory improve (as would be expected), but their language also significantly improved too, even though this was not directly trained (Roque-Gutierrez & Ibbotson, 2022). This kind of cognitive transfer holds special relevance for children whose language can be relatively impaired and for whom directly training language has marginal impact. For example, in a series of studies, Hélène Delage, a psychologist and speech and language therapist, has shown how training the working memory of children who have difficulty with language or who are autistic resulted in indirect improvements in their language ability – improvements that were still present 3 months after the training had finished (Delage et al., 2021a, 2021b). There is widespread interest in whether executive function training in general can improve other areas of cognition, such as early maths skills (Scerif et al., 2023) or attention-regulating difficulties (Klingberg et al., 2005), but we need a better understanding of why results sometimes fail to replicate under some circumstances (e.g., Chacko et al., 2013), as well as better-quality cognitive training research in general (Gobet & Sala, 2023).

Key Points

- Working memory describes the ability to hold some information in mind while working on other information.
- Working memory develops significantly during middle childhood and underpins a wide range of other social and cognitive abilities.

10.4 Where Did the Early Memories Go?

Throughout this book we have seen the importance of early experiences to later life, yet as adults most of us fail to remember *anything* significant that happened in our early years, like learning to walk and talk, and usually we have very sparse recollections of events that occurred to us before the age of 10 (Kihlstrom & Harackiewicz, 1982). How, then, can early experiences have such a significant influence over our lives if we can't remember them?

Let's investigate this paradox by exploring the pathways by which early experiences affect later outcomes. It is important to acknowledge that there is much we do not understand about how these pathways work exactly, and this is an area many researchers are working on, but here is what we do know: when people perceive their environment as threating, challenging, or unexpected, they react with certain behavioural and physical responses. These responses are 'calls to action' and include changes to the hormonal system (e.g., increased cortisol), to the immune system, and to the system that regulates heart rate, blood pressure, respiration, and digestion (Ganzel et al., 2010). In general, these changes cause us to behave in a way that makes the environment less stressful, and so in the long term they can increase our well-being. When the stress is relatively mild or short, like feeling hungry or cold, the response can be adaptive, as it motivates us to find food or warmth. However, if the stress is experienced over a long period or is extreme, uncontrollable, or unpredictable, like neglect, violence, and abuse, it is much harder to adapt to and can have negative outcomes for children.

Why? Long-term stress causes us to experience the stress response over the long term, and this has some profound effects on the structure and functioning of the brain (Smith & Pollak, 2020). Specifically, the stress response has been shown to change the prefrontal cortex (an area associated with planning and decision-making), the hippocampus (associated with learning and memory), and the amygdala (associated with emotion and reward). For example, children who have experienced high levels of stress earlier in life, such as that caused by death, war, illness, conflict, natural disasters, neglect, discrimination, or poverty, tend to have smaller amygdala and hippocampal volumes than children exposed to less intense levels of early life stress (Hanson et al., 2015).

Because infancy and childhood are **sensitive periods** for brain development, stressors experienced during this period can set the long-term expectations for what count as threats and rewards and how to deal with them (Hill et al., 2010). Children who experience physical abuse have higher sensitivity to angry facial expressions compared to non-maltreated children (Shackman & Pollak, 2014), they are more likely to judge emotional situations as angry situations (Pollak et al., 2000), they more readily categorise faces that are morphed between two different emotions as angry (Pollak & Kistler, 2002), and they tend to believe that almost any kind of interpersonal situation can result in an adult becoming angry; by contrast, most non-abused children associate anger with particular social circumstances (Pollak et al., 2009).

So, long-term stress experienced at a critical time for brain development can change how we interact with our environment later on in life. This isn't perhaps what we usually think of as 'memory', and it is certainly not something we are usually consciously aware of. But this is one pathway by which past experiences guide behaviour in the future – a basic definition of memory. This pathway does *not* mean we are deterministically doomed to follow a particular course in life just because we experienced a particular stress. The same stress can be experienced differently by different people (recall orchids and dandelions; see Chapter 2), with events that are perceived as being more under a person's control generally being easier to cope with (Pruessner et al., 2005).

Caregivers and wider social networks also play a significant role in shaping children's responses to adversity, with the presence of a predictable, stable, and responsive figure helping to buffer some of the more harmful effects of stress (Hostinar et al., 2015). A consistent finding is that the quality of family relationships is more important for children's well-being than the structure that family takes; for example, level of parental stress is a better predictor of children's emotional and behavioural problems than whether they come from one-parent, two-parent, divorced, heterosexual, homosexual, or adopted family structures (Golombok et al., 2014).

 Key Point

- Long-term stress experienced during critical periods of early brain development can alter how children perceive future rewards and threats.

Next, let's look at the other part of the paradox: why we aren't aware of what happened in the early years.

We make our first memories before we are born. Recall from Chapter 5 how babies in utero are becoming sensitised to the sound world around them. As soon as they are born, infants can distinguish between novel sounds and sounds familiar to them from in utero, such as their mother's voice (De Casper & Spence, 1986). The fact that new-borns can do this presumably means they have remembered their mother's voice from the womb. So even very young children can remember early experiences, but their memories of the details of the events are extremely fragile and prone to being forgotten, especially if the experiences are not frequently repeated (Bauer, 2015). This means that part of the answer is that, quite simply, young infants are more prone to forgetting, but they get rapidly better at holding onto information for longer over the first months of life. Using the same method we met in Chapter 5 whereby infants learn to touch a light-up box with their head through observing others, researchers have shown that 6-month-old infants are able to imitate an action they saw 24 hours earlier, but by 9-months-old they remember actions they saw up to 5 weeks earlier, and by 10-months-old they remember actions from 3 months earlier (Mullally & Maguire, 2014). This behavioural development is underpinned by a parallel development in the hippocampus, an area of the brain thought to be important for the formation of memories of what, who, where, and when. This area begins to function in the first years of life and reaches full maturity between 3 and 5 years of age, right around the time most adults recall their first memories (Huttenlocher & Dabholkar, 1997).

Research also suggests children start out being relatively good at encoding separate parts of events, such as the objects involved and where it happened, but it takes time to bind these together into a coherent memory of what, who, where, and when. For example, one study tested 4- and 6-year-olds and adults on their ability to recall isolated parts of pictures as well as combinations of these parts (Sluzenski et al., 2006). Children were shown a tiger in a playground and then asked to determine whether they had previously seen the animal (the tiger), the location (the playground), or the animal in the location (the tiger in the playground). Participants' memory scores for the animal and the location in isolation were similar across all three age groups. However, memory scores for the combinations (i.e., animals in locations) increased between 4 and 6 years but not between 6 years and adulthood. The fact that it takes times to develop the ability to bind the elements of an event together into a coherent whole might be another reason why early memories of events are difficult to retrieve.

There are two other ideas as to why our personal history of the first years is difficult to remember. One is that it takes time for a concept of self to emerge in development; that is, memories about things that happened to 'me' require a 'me' for those events to happen to (this is explored more in Section 10.5). We saw in Chapter 3 how young children have to work out that they have intentions before they can work out that others might have beliefs, desires, and so on. These realisations of self and that this self is different from others are likely to place a further lower limit on how far back in time we can remember our personal history (Howe et al., 2003).

Second is the relation between memory and language acquisition. The basic idea here is that it might be difficult to use language to talk about memories if those memories were first formed before language was acquired. In a study designed to directly explore this possibility, adults were asked to estimate when their earliest memories of a range of concepts, such as 'button', 'gorilla', and 'mushroom', stemmed from (Morrison & Conway, 2010). The researchers found that the ages of earliest memory of the concepts 'button', 'gorilla', or 'mushroom' were systematically later, by several months, than the typical ages of acquisition of the words 'button', 'gorilla', or 'mushroom'. This suggests that the word needed to be acquired first in order for the adults to be able to consciously recall memories associated with that word.

However, a range of other mammals also have infantile amnesia, and they don't have human-like language or the same sense of self, so this cannot be the whole story (Howe,

2011). When the same function emerges across a range of species, it sometimes points to a shared evolutionary explanation. One intriguing suggestion is that infant forgetting allows babies to offload some memory-related tasks to caregivers, such as how to navigate or find a reward, freeing up more brainpower to learn about other aspects of the world (Reardon, 2024). However, that strategy only works when you have a cooperative caregiver on hand to pick up the slack, as humans do. When you have to fend for yourself from birth, that isn't an option. In support of this theory, guinea pigs and degus, which are independent from birth, do not experience infantile amnesia as far as we can tell (Akers et al., 2014).

Key Point

- Neurological maturation, reduced forgetting, the ability to bind memories together, and a developing sense of self and language are factors that help explain why adults have difficulty remembering the first years of life.

We started this section by considering a paradox: how can early experiences have such a significant influence over our lives if they are rapidly forgotten? We can resolve the paradox by understanding that not all experiences are treated the same.

Experiences of stressful events can trigger long-term changes in the brain that set expectations at a very general level regarding how to deal with threats and rewards later on in life. Specific experiences of what, who, where, and when take time to develop due to a range of biological, cognitive, and social reasons, rendering it difficult to access memories before these systems have matured.

Given what we have explored about children's memories, can we trust what they say (**Box 10.1**)?

Box 10.1 Can children's testimony be trusted?

The accuracy of children's memories, and the perception of their accuracy by others, becomes especially important when they testify in court. Typically, children are asked to do so when their evidence bears directly on the guilt of the defendant, because either they were the only other witness or they were the victim themselves.

Historically, their testimonies have been routinely discredited, grounded partly in the belief that the line between fantasy and reality is blurred in children. Evidence from Chapter 9 should make us challenge that assumption. Children have also been undermined by the belief that they are more susceptible to false memories and have a poorer recollection of actual events compared with adolescents and adults. Indeed, jurors are often advised of this and encouraged to take this into account when weighing such evidence. As a result, when children's testimony contradicts that of adults, as is common in cases of domestic crimes and child custody disputes, they are less likely to be believed. Decades of detailed research are now helping to overturn these assumptions by showing that, far from being unreliable

Figure 10.1 Under some circumstances children's testimony can be more accurate than that of adults.
Source: FatCamera/ Getty.

witnesses, under certain circumstances young children can be *less* prone to false memories than older children and adults (Brainerd & Reyna, 2012).

The reason for this lies in the way we organise experience into meaningful memories. Throughout development, children encounter familiar situations like eating breakfast, going to school, attending class, going out to a restaurant, shopping at the store, playing at the park, seeing a movie, getting ready for bed, and so on. The sequence of these events tends to play out in rather predictable (albeit culturally specific) ways once they have experienced enough of them. For example, the birthday party script tends to unfold as 'arrive, hand over present, play, sing happy birthday, eat cake, collect party bag, go home'. We store these as templates, playbooks, or scripts in our minds, and they prepare us for the gist of what is going to happen. As children get older, they accumulate more of these scripts through experience. The advantage of automating these scripts is that doing so allows children (and adults) to deal with the less predictable things in life that need our attention in the here and now (see Section 10.2). The disadvantage is that, when it comes to remembering precisely what happened, the gist interferes with remembering the detail, potentially making misremembering events that never happened more likely. Experimental evidence has linked an increase in false memory susceptibility with age to improvements in children's memory for the gist (e.g., Brainerd et al., 2002).

This does not mean we should believe everything young children say or that they can remember everything that has happened in their lives. It does mean that children's ability to recall events accurately has traditionally been underestimated and that their susceptibility to false memories has been overestimated. This is especially true when children directly experience traumatic crimes rather than merely observe them happening to others (Ceci & Friedman, 2000). Gradually, such research is beginning to change how children are treated in court, how cases are tried, and how due credit should be given to their testimony (**Figure 10.1**).

Key Point

- Memory for the gist of a situation can make older children and adults more susceptible to false memories than younger children.

10.5 Memories of Me

Autobiographical memory pulls together memories of past experiences into an overarching life narrative or personal history. At some point memories become not just about what happened, but about what happened to *me*. To achieve that, children must have a more basic psychological building block in place first: a subjective sense of self – the 'I' in 'I remember'. They also need to be able to connect the me *now* who is remembering the event to the same me *then* who first experienced it. This is a complex skill involving a kind of mental time travel, and it takes some time to develop.

Key Point

- Autobiographical memory integrates memories of past experiences into an overarching life narrative or personal history.

Things start off simpler, however, with young children often referring to fragments of events that happened in the immediate past, which sometimes are then restructured and contextualised by adults (Fivush, 2011). For example, a 3-year-old girl might pick up a ball and say, 'Grandad,' and her mother elaborates on this, putting it into a narrative context by saying, 'Yes, you were at the park yesterday playing ball with Granddad.' These examples show young children's cognitive ability to retrieve past events as well their social motivation to want to share them with others. It is by sharing the past with others that children become aware that memories are not necessarily the same as reality and that memories can be remembered differently by different people. It also shows the role caregivers have in scaffolding children's memory, their sense of self, and the consistency of that self over time.

Evidence for the role of caregivers in influencing children's autobiographical memories comes in two forms. First, *within* societies individual differences in the ways in which adults structure their reminiscing with young children are related to individual differences in children's developing autobiographical memories (Bauer & Burch, 2004). For example, some parents show a highly elaborative reminiscing style characterised by long and detailed conversations about the past. These interactions might contain many open-ended questions (e.g., 'What did we buy at the shops today?') that provide a template for an answer at the same time as encouraging children to flesh out the detail (e.g., 'At the shops we bought ...?'). In this style, adults and children weave a bigger narrative about the past together, including the who, what, when, and where of the event (e.g., 'That's right, we went to the shops in town. Who did we meet there?'). Adults might scaffold children's reminiscing with recaps if they lose the thread of the story (e.g., 'So you said, "Can I play with you?" And then what did they say?'), add emotional elements (e.g., 'Was it scary?'), and provide cues to the next sequence in the story (e.g., 'And then you ...'). Interestingly, this particular style seems limited to just the kind of interactions that support autobiographical memory. Mothers who are highly elaborative during reminiscing are not necessarily more talkative in other conversational contexts, such as book reading, free play, and caregiving activities (Lucariello & Nelson, 1987).

Perhaps not too surprisingly, children who have grown up with parents using this rich reminiscing style tend to have richer autobiographical memories themselves and can remember past events more vividly and in greater detail than those with parents using a less elaborate style. For example, those adults using a less elaborate style typically talk less frequently and in less detail about the shared past, use yes/no questions (e.g., 'Did we go to the shops?'), and are more likely to just repeat a question rather than provide more information that would move the story on (Bauer, 2007). Also, children who have grown up with parents who focus more on thoughts and emotions when reminiscing use more mental-state language (e.g., know, feel, think, believe) in their personal narratives (Rudek & Haden, 2005).

We mentioned in Chapter 1 that scientists care about cause and effect, and here is a good example of where researchers have explored a variety of causes that could be responsible for the same effect. It is plausible that some children are good at reminiscing not because their parents talk that way, but because they are different in some other way; for example, their age, language, temperament, attachment style, or concept of self could also affect their memories. Although all these factors predict some of the individual differences in how autobiographical memory develops, maternal reminiscing style still explains most of these differences, even after taking these other factors into account (Fivush et al., 2006). You could reasonably point out that this is still just an association. Maybe children with richer autobiographical memories *cause* more reminiscing in parents? It seems more likely that it is the other way around because when researchers trained parents to use a more elaborative reminiscing style, this caused children who were previously weak on autobiographical memory to get stronger in this area, and the more the parents used that style, the more their children recalled events in detail (**Figure 10.2**; Boland et al., 2003).

 Key Point

- Through their reminiscing style, caregivers can significantly affect how children's autobiographical memories develop.

Another source of evidence for the role of caregivers in influencing children's autobiographical memories is that significant differences *between* societies predict the different ways

Figure 10.2 Reminiscing with others helps children consolidate their autobiographical memories. Source: kali9/Gettyimages; pixelheadphoto digitalskillet/Shutterstock; South_agency/Getty Images; Georgijevic/Getty Images.

in which children construct their autobiographical memories. We explore this source of evidence in more detail in Chapter 11.

10.6 Less Is More

It might be tempting to conclude that infants are merely forgetful adults who get better at learning because they get better at remembering, but this would miss an important point about development. What look like limitations and constraints in children's abilities are sometimes the smartest way to approach learning something complicated (Newport, 1990). For example, linguist Jeffrey Elman ran a computer simulation to understand how children learn grammar (Elman, 1993). One group of children in the simulation were given adult-like memory capacities from the start, while a separate group were given memories that developed much more like real children, starting small but growing larger over time. He trained both groups on some sentences and then asked them to generalise the grammatical patterns they had learned to some new sentences. He found that the children given full adult-like memories from the start made all sorts of grammatical errors that were difficult for the system to unlearn. The children with a limited initial memory capacity took longer overall to learn the patterns but made fewer mistakes, eventually homing in on the right grammar, just as real children do. By constraining memory to begin with, these children only saw a simplified version of what was a bigger and more complicated picture. When their memory capacities eventually grew larger and could take in the whole sentence, they were able to apply what they had learned in the simple cases to more complicated ones, hence the subtitle of his paper: 'the importance of starting small'.

In another computer simulation, Ibbotson and colleagues (2018) took the same basic idea but went further, implementing not just a limited memory capacity but a memory that actively forgets, the way that real children do. They found a 'Goldilocks' zone of forgetting that was neither too strong (forgets everything) nor too weak (remembers everything), but was just right for word learning. In this case the right amount of forgetting was beneficial because it took away some of the incorrect guesses about what a word meant, leaving a stronger memory trace of the correct meanings.

The broader point is that the way children's learning unfolds, with abilities maturing little by little, can be adaptive to the problem they are trying to solve. For example, infants need to learn how to control their arms. There are a vast number of ways in which the joints and muscles of the arm could combine to produce a desired action – say, reaching out to pick up a wooden block. Russian neurophysiologist Nikolai Bernstein worked out that infants solve this problem by gradually releasing the freedom of one joint at a time, allowing them to learn how one element of the system (the shoulder joint) works in isolation before working out how it combines with the next (the shoulder joint plus the elbow joint), and so on. This gives infants a way into the near-intractable challenge of reverse engineering which combinations of muscles, nerves, and tendons are required to produce which action (Bernstein, 1967).

One final example: infants need to learn about objects in their world, but one complication of doing so is that the same-sized object can look bigger when it is close and smaller when it is far away. Turkewitz and Kenny (1982) proposed that infants solve the problem of perceiving size constancy by initially restricting their depth-of-field vision to objects that are very close, allowing them to learn about the size of objects unconfounded by the effects of distance.

Key Point

- Sometimes less is more in development because gradually expanding one's social, cognitive, and physical abilities can be an adaptive problem-solving strategy.

Watch the One-Minute Method.

Discover how researchers build computer simulations to explore how children learn.

Talking Point

Memory is a fundamental part of growing up. It tells the story of who we are, and it is central to the very idea of learning itself. But, of course, memory does not stop being important beyond childhood nor stop changing as we get older. This much is made all too obvious for people living with dementia, who may forget their loved ones' names, important relationships, where they live, and what they did that day. There are many different types of dementia that affect the brain in different ways, but in Alzheimer's disease the hippocampus is one of the first areas of the brain to be damaged. This area is important in converting short-term memories into longer-term ones. This is why the ability to make new memories is one of the first things to be affected, and long-term memories from childhood or young adulthood, before Alzheimer's took hold, are some of the last to fade, captured in the phrase 'first in, last out'.

There is much we do not understand about how memory works in general and dementia in particular. There is a huge effort underway looking for ways to slow the progression of this disease and ultimately offer a cure. Researchers have found that the regions of the brain that encode music-associated memories are some of the last to go in Alzheimer's (Jacobsen et al., 2015). Music seems to be a particularly powerful cue to the past, evoking emotional detail from a time and place when that music was significant: a birthday party, a first kiss, a break-up, a dance at a wedding. This means music therapy can be an opportunity to help people, even those in the later stages of Alzheimer's, to connect with the memories they still have.

There seems a poignancy to the fact that some of the first memories we make as children might be the last ones we ever remember. The impact that memory loss can have on an individual, and perhaps even more so on the people who care for them, reaffirms the central role memory plays throughout our lives.

Summary

- The shift during skill acquisition from effortful, deliberate practice to automatic performance allows children (and adults) to keep learning new skills.
- Working memory describes the ability to hold some information in mind while working on other information.
- Working memory develops significantly during middle childhood and underpins a wide range of other social and cognitive abilities.
- Long-term stress experienced during critical periods of early brain development can alter how children perceive future rewards and threats.
- Neurological maturation, reduced forgetting, the ability to bind memories together, and a developing sense of self and language are factors that help explain why adults have difficulty remembering the first years of life.
- Memory for the gist of a situation can make older children and adults more susceptible to false memories than younger children.
- Autobiographical memory integrates memories of past experiences into an overarching life narrative or personal history.
- Through their reminiscing style, caregivers can significantly affect how children's autobiographical memories develop.
- Sometimes less is more in development because gradually expanding one's social, cognitive, and physical abilities can be an adaptive problem-solving strategy.

References

Ahmed, S. F., Ellis, A., Ward, K. P., Chaku, N., & Davis-Kean, P. E. (2022). Working memory development from early childhood to adolescence using two nationally representative samples. *Developmental Psychology*, 58(10), 1962–1973.

Akers, K. G., Martinez-Canabal, A., Restivo, L., et al. (2014). Hippocampal neurogenesis regulates forgetting during adulthood and infancy. *Science*, 344(6184), 598–602.

Bauer, P. J. (2007). *Remembering the Times of Our Lives: Memory in Infancy and Beyond*. Erlbaum.

Bauer, P. J. (2015). A complementary processes account of the development of childhood amnesia and a personal past. *Psychological Review*, 122(2), 204–231.

Bauer, P. J. & Burch, M.M. (2004). Developments in early memory: multiple mediators of foundational processes. In J. M. Lucariello, J. A. Hudson, R. Fivush, & P. J. Bauer (eds.), *The Development of the Mediated Mind* (pp. 101–125). Erlbaum.

Bernstein, N. (1967). *The Coordination and Regulation of Movements*. Pergamon Press.

Boland, A. M., Haden, C. A., & Ornstein, P. A. (2003). Boosting children's memory by training mothers in the use of an elaborative conversational style as an event unfolds. *Journal of Cognitive Development*, 4, 39–65.

Brainerd, C. J. & Reyna, V. F. (2012). Reliability of children's testimony in the era of developmental reversals. *Developmental Review*, 32(3), 224–267.

Brainerd, C. J., Reyna, V. F., & Forrest, T. J. (2002). Are young children susceptible to the false-memory illusion? *Child Development*, 73, 1363–1377.

Ceci, S. J. & Friedman, R. D. (2000). The suggestibility of children: scientific research and legal implications. *Cornell Law Review*, 86, 34–108.

Chacko, A., Feirsen, N., Bedard, A. C., Marks, D., Uderman, J. Z., & Chimiklis, A. (2013). Cogmed Working Memory Training for youth with ADHD: a closer examination of efficacy utilizing evidence-based criteria. *Journal of Clinical Child and Adolescent Psychology*, 42(6), 769–783.

De Casper, A. J. & Spence, M. J. (1986). Prenatal maternal speech influences newborn's perception of speech sounds. *Infant Behavior and Development*, 9, 133–150.

Delage, H., Eigsti, I. M., Stanford, E., & Durrleman, S. (2021a). A preliminary examination of the impact of working memory training on syntax and processing speed in children with ASD. *Journal of Autism Developmental Disorders*, 52(10), 4233–4251.

Delage, H., Stanford, E., & Durrleman, S. (2021b). Working memory training enhances complex syntax in children with developmental language disorder. *Applied Psycholinguistics*, 42(5), 1341–1375.

Diamond, A. (2013). Executive functions. *Annual Review of Psychology*, 64(1), 135–168.

Elman, J. (1993). Learning and development in neural networks: the importance of starting small. *Cognition*, 48(1), 71–99.

Fitts, P. & Posner, M. I. (1967). *Human Performance*. Brooks/Cole Publishing.

Fivush, R. (2011). The development of autobiographical memory. *Annual Review of Psychology*, 62(1), 559–582.

Fivush, R., Haden, C. A., & Reese, E. (2006). Elaborating on elaborations: the role of maternal reminiscing style on children's cognitive and socioemotional development. *Child Development*, 77, 1568–1588.

Ganzel, B. L., Morris, P. A., & Wethington, E. (2010). Allostasis and the human brain: integrating models of stress from the social and life sciences. *Psychological Review*, 117(1), 134–174.

Gobet, F. & Sala, G. (2023). Cognitive training: a field in search of a phenomenon. *Perspective on Psychological Science*, 18(1), 125–141.

Golombok, S., Mellish, L., Jennings, S., Casey, P., Tasker, F., & Lamb, M. E. (2014). Adoptive gay father families: parent–child relationships and children's psychological adjustment. *Child Development*, 85, 456–468.

Hanson, J. L., Nacewicz, B. M., Sutterer, M. J., et al. (2015). Behavioral problems after early life stress: contributions of the hippocampus and amygdala. *Biological Psychiatry*, 77(4), 314–323.

Hill, J., Inder, T. E., Neil, J., Dierker, D., Harwell, J., & Van Essen, D. (2010). Similar patterns of cortical expansion during human development and evolution. *Proceedings of the National Academy of Sciences of the United States of America*, 107(29), 13135–13140.

Hostinar, C. E., Johnson, A. E., & Gunnar, M. R. (2015). Early social deprivation and the social buffering of cortisol stress responses in late childhood: an experimental study. *Developmental Psychology*, 51(11), 1597–1608.

Howe, M. (2011). Infantile amnesia in human and nonhuman animals. In *The Nature of Early Memory: An Adaptive Theory of the Genesis and Development of Memory* (pp. 47–66). Oxford University Press.

Howe, M. L., Courage, M. L., & Edison, S. C. (2003). When autobiographical memory begins. *Developmental Review*, 23, 471–494.

Huttenlocher, P. R. & Dabholkar, A. S. (1997). Regional differences in synaptogenesis in human cerebral cortex. *Journal of Comparative Neurology*, 387, 167–178.

Ibbotson, P., López, D. G., & McKane, A. J. (2018). Goldilocks forgetting in cross-situational learning. *Frontiers in Psychology*, 9, 1301.

Jacobsen, J. H., Stelzer, J., Fritz, T. H., Chételat, G., La Joie, R., & Turner, R. (2015). Why musical memory can be preserved in advanced Alzheimer's disease. *Brain*, 138(Pt 8), 2438–2450.

Kihlstrom, J. F. & Harackiewicz, J. M. (1982). The earliest recollection: a new survey. *Journal of Personality*, 50, 134–148.

Klingberg, T., Fernell, E., Olesen, P. J., et al. (2005). Computerized training of working memory in children with ADHD – a randomized, controlled trial. *Journal of the American Academy of Child and Adolescent Psychiatry*, 44(2), 177–186.

Lucariello, J. & Nelson, K. (1987). Remembering and planning talk between mothers and children. *Discourse Process*, 10, 219–235.

Morrison, C. M. & Conway, M. A. (2010). First words and first memories. *Cognition*, 116(1), 23–32.

Mullally, S. L. & Maguire, E. A. (2014). Learning to remember: the early ontogeny of episodic memory. *Developmental Cognitive Neuroscience*, 9, 12–29.

Newport, E. (1990). Maturational constraints on language learning. *Cognitive Science*, 14(1), 11–28.

Pollak, S. D., Cicchetti, D., Hornung, K., & Reed, A. (2000). Recognizing emotion in faces: developmental effects of child abuse and neglect. *Developmental Psychology*, 36(5), 679–688.

Pollak, S. D. & Kistler, D. J. (2002). Early experience is associated with the development of categorical representations for facial expressions of emotion. *Proceedings of the National Academy of Sciences of the United States of America*, 99(13), 9072–9076.

Pollak, S. D., Messner, M., Kistler, D. J., & Cohn, J. F. (2009). Development of perceptual expertise in emotion recognition. *Cognition*, 110(2), 242–247.

Pruessner, J. C., Baldwin, M. W., Dedovic, K., et al. (2005). Self-esteem, locus of control, hippocampal volume, and cortisol regulation in young and old adulthood. *Neuroimage*, 28(4), 815–826.

Reardon, S. (2024). The fading memories of youth. *Science*, 383(6688), 1172–1175.

Roque-Gutierrez, E. & Ibbotson, P. (2022). Working memory training improves children's syntax ability but not vice versa: a randomized control trial. *Journal of Experimental Child Psychology*, 227, 105593.

Rudek, D. & Haden, C. A. (2005). Mothers' and preschoolers' mental state language during reminiscing over time. *Merrill-Palmer Quarterly*, 51, 557–583.

Scerif, G., Blakey, E., Gattas, S., et al. (2023). Making the executive 'function' for the foundations of mathematics: the need for explicit theories of change for early interventions. *Educational Psychology Review*, 35(4), 110.

Shackman, J. E. & Pollak, S. D. (2014). Impact of physical maltreatment on the regulation of negative affect and aggression. *Developmental Psychopathology*, 26(4), 1021–1033.

Sluzenski, J., Newcombe, N. S., & Kovacs, S. L. (2006). Binding, relational memory, and recall of naturalistic events: a developmental perspective. *Journal of Experimental Psychology: Learning, Memory, and Cognition*, 32, 89–100.

Smith, K. E. & Pollak, S. D. (2020). Early life stress and development: potential mechanisms for adverse outcomes. *Journal of Neurodevelopmental Disorders*, 12, 34.

Stickgold, R. & Walker, M. P. (2005). Memory consolidation and reconsolidation: what is the role of sleep? *Trends in Neurosciences*, 28, 408–415.

Turkewitz, G. & Kenny, P. (1982). Limitations on input as a basis for neural organization and perceptual development: a preliminary theoretical statement. *Developmental Psychobiology*, 15(4). 357–368.

11 GROWING UP GLOBALLY – MIDDLE CHILDHOOD

 Learning Outcomes

After reading this chapter you will be able to:
- Consolidate what you learned in Chapters 7–10.
- Revisit the ideas you came across in Chapters 7–10 in a cross-cultural context.

11.1 Introduction

This last chapter of Section II is the second 'Growing Up Globally' perspective on child development. To remind you, this end-of-section chapter is designed to be a breathing space, an opportunity for you to revisit areas you haven't fully grasped first time around, where we survey the ground we've covered and consolidate what we know. And to help you join the dots in the story so far, all the key points from each chapter are repeated here so the essential takeaways are in one place.

The second function of this chapter is to re-examine what we have already covered from a more global perspective. Our motivation for doing so should be familiar by now. If we want to say something about how all children grow up, not just the **WEIRD** ones, we need to look at the diverse contexts in which children grow up around the world. The first time we explored this perspective in Chapter 6 we learned that cultural differences matter more in some circumstances and less so in others: it depends on exactly which aspect of child development we are exploring. The important point is that, without looking at development in a global context, we don't know which aspects of our psychology and behaviour are more sensitive to cultural input and flexible, and which are more heritable and stable. In that spirit, we revisit some of the questions we have looked at so far in Section II and explore the commonalties and differences between children in how they develop.

11.2 How Do Children Learn Right from Wrong? Recap and Consolidation

- Sensitivity to fair outcomes emerges early in development.
- Collaborative activities heighten children's sense of fairness.

- Children consider merit, effort, and need when allocating a fair share.
- Children are willing to police fairness in others, even when the unfairness does not directly affect them and when doing so incurs personal cost.
- Children are motivated by the social evaluation of others and, like adults, work hard to present themselves favourably.
- Guilt, shame, and pride are emotions that help to regulate moral behaviour.
- Children are aware of the social functions of guilt, shame, and pride.
- Sensitive and appropriate moral action requires children to empathise with others.
- Children show a tendency towards helpfulness, can sympathise with the emotional plight of others, and are selective over who they interact with based on help and harm.
- Children's moral sense incorporates the values of the society they are born into.
- Care/harm, fairness/cheating, loyalty/betrayal, authority/subversion, and sanctity/degradation are likely to become significant moral dimensions for children. Precisely what content becomes part of those dimensions can vary according to time and place.

11.3 Fair Is Fair?

In Chapter 7 we looked at how children learn right from wrong. As part of that exploration, we learned a lot about what children consider is a fair share. But how well do these ideas of fairness travel? That is, do children reason about fairness in similar ways regardless of the cultural circumstances they are born into?

Cross-cultural psychologist Bailey House and his colleagues were interested in this very question (House et al., 2013). They examined the sharing behaviour of 326 children from 3 to 14 years of age and 120 adults from Aka, American, Fijian, Himba, Martu, and Shuar societies. These societies vary a lot in their culture, geography, and way of life, and they include foragers, herders, horticulturalists, and urban dwellers. The task that the researchers presented to children involved deciding how to share a reward with a peer, in which the reward was a real, visible food item that was immediately edible. In one version of the task, children had a choice between a 1–1 offer, which would deliver one reward to the child and one reward to a peer, or a 1–0 offer, which would deliver one reward to the child and no reward to the peer.

Regardless of cultural differences, older children were much more likely to choose the prosocial 1–1 option over the selfish 1–0 option than the younger children. In a second version of the task, the researchers made the selfish option even more tempting by offering a choice between the same prosocial 1–1 offer and a more advantageous selfish split of 2–0. In the first version of the task, children got one reward no matter what they chose; their only consideration was how much to give their peer. In this second task they had more 'skin in the game' because if they chose to share an equal split with their peer, they would forfeit the extra reward they would have got if they had kept it all to themselves. In this second condition, cultural background did matter. The researchers showed that by middle childhood children's choices began to converge with the choices of adults in their respective societies. The local norms on sharing mattered when the split was costly to children – they had to forgo the one extra reward they could have had by being selfish – but not when being generous was of no personal cost to them – they got one reward regardless. This very much fits with the picture we established in Chapter 6: sometimes cultural differences matter and sometimes they matter less so; it depends on exactly which aspect of child development we are concerned with.

In a similar task known as the dictator game, children are given some commodity (e.g., money, stickers, sweets) to share with a receiver, and the 'dictator' can choose to share any amount, including nothing. Using a technique known as meta-analysis (see **One-Minute Method**), Ibbotson looked at the sharing behaviour of 1601 children aged 3–18 years of age in England, Germany, Brazil, the USA, China, Peru, Fiji, Israel, and Switzerland (2014). Ibbotson showed that across diverse societies young children start from a similar position and share approximately 25% of their resources by age 3. However, beyond that age, the rate at which children developed their sharing behaviour was best predicted by the sharing behaviour of the adults around them. For example, if the adult norm was a higher than average sharing percentage, then the rate at which children developed their sharing behaviour was higher than average. While children started off from similar positions, their developmental pathways diverged as they came to adopt the norms of the society they were born into.

Key Point

- Children have a similar sense of fairness across different societies, albeit expressed in culturally specific ways.

Watch the One-Minute Method.

Discover how meta-analyses can help researchers see the bigger picture that no one study alone can show.

11.4 How Do Children Think About Groups? Recap and Consolidation

- Children think and behave more positively towards the in-group compared to the out-group.
- Children are sensitive to groups and group membership because being part of the in-group was key to our species' survival.
- Children adopt the norms of those around them as an important signal of in-group membership.
- Sorting people into groups is a specific example of our tendency to categorise the world in general.
- Because self-identity is tied up with the group's identity, in-group favouritism boosts our image and makes us feel better about ourselves.
- Children have a strong tendency for homophily, which can emphasise between-group differences.

- When children in the out-group and in-group make contact, work collaboratively, and empathise with each other, prejudice and discrimination can be reduced.
- By middle childhood, children can integrate in-group/out-group reasoning with other biases for fairness, equality, and need.

11.5 Norm Enforcers

In Chapter 8 we explored how children think and behave in groups, paying particular attention to in-group/out-group dynamics. We also learned that children adopt the norms of those around them as an important signal of in-group membership. These norms can be anything from how people speak to how they greet each other, dress, or play certain games. These norms appear to arise universally across societies, but how do children actually enforce these norms when someone else breaks them?

That is the question Patricia Kanngiesser and her colleagues set out to address by playing a game with 376 children aged 5–8 years from eight diverse societies (2021). These included three urban locations on three different continents (South America, Europe, Asia) and five rural locations on two continents (South America, Africa). The sites differed in community sizes, ranging from rural dwellings of a few hundred people to cities with millions of inhabitants. They also varied in the languages spoken and in their economic activities, which included wage labour, agriculture, and foraging.

Children were introduced to a sorting game that involved stacking wooden blocks onto a pin. The rules of the game mimicked many social **conventions** in their arbitrariness; conventions simply dictate 'we do things this way' not because it is the most rational or efficient way, but essentially because that is the way everyone else does it. Half of the children learned a version of the game that required them to stack by the shape of the blocks, as demonstrated to them by an adult. The other half of the children learned that the rules were to stack the blocks by colour. The children were then paired up – one child played the game while the other observed (**Figure 11.1**). The interesting cases were where children were paired up so that their norms were in conflict, with the observer having learned one rule and the game-player another. What would the children do in these cases?

The researchers found that, regardless of the differences in their societies, all children intervened more often to correct a peer who

Figure 11.1 The experimental set-up from Kanngiesser et al. (2021). The game-player following one rule, whereas the observer had learned a different rule. Source: With permission; Kanngiesser, P et al. Children across societies enforce conventional norms but in culturally variable ways. PNAS.

apparently broke the rules than a peer who followed the rules. Children were also similar in how they corrected their peers with physical gestures (e.g., pointing, miming), expressions (e.g., head shakes), and body contact (e.g., holding, pushing); however, verbal protests (e.g., 'This is how you should do it'; 'Don't do it that way') showed more variation between societies. If the observers did intervene, either physically or verbally, to correct the game-player, across all societies the game-player was much more likely to adopt the observer's rule, so that both children were following the same norm.

 Key Point

- Children across societies enforce conventional norms but in culturally variable ways.

11.6 How Does Imagination Develop? Recap and Consolidation

- Tool innovation emerges relatively late in childhood compared to other complex skills.
- Tool innovation places significant demands on higher-order thinking skills and is hindered by a preference to imitate the conventional use of an object.
- Children show signs of greater inventiveness as they get older and get better at identifying a workable solution among the range of possibilities.
- Children capitalise on personal experience when imagining what might happen in the future.
- As children's experience grows, they get better at acknowledging that improbable events are still possible and that their predictions about what is impossible might be wrong.
- The imaginary worlds of young children often reflect the local practices and routines of adults, and their pretend worlds largely reflect the realities of their everyday lives.
- When presented with a premise that does not fit within or lies outside their everyday experience, children resist reasoning from it.
- When provided with a make-believe template and given strong cues to use their imagination, children are more willing to suspend belief and reason from false premises.
- Early exceptional talent does not necessarily translate to later genius.
- Children's drawings are typically remixes of reality rather than complete departures from it.
- Young children have a preference for explaining the supernatural in terms of the natural.
- Whether children have imaginary companions or impersonate others, they tend to draw on a repertoire of behaviours from real life.

11.7 Children's Storytelling

In Chapter 9 we learned about children's imagination – how they innovate new tools, imagine impossible worlds, make judgements about what is possible, and suspend reality. We also looked at stories directed at children. But what about the stories children tell themselves? What can those teach us about their creativity? And how do they vary across different societies?

The first thing to note is the universality of storytelling itself. It occurs in every known society, whether literate or not, and can take many forms – poems, chants, rhymes, fables,

Figure 11.2 Storytelling emerges spontaneously in childhood and exists in all known cultures, and some stories can be traced back for thousands of years. Among a group of Filipino foragers called the Agta, members of which are pictured here, storytelling increases equality, egalitarianism, and cooperation in the group and is more valued than any other skill. The best storytellers also tend to have the most children (Smith et al., 2017). Source: Jacob Maentz/Getty images.

songs, and dances – and can be about almost anything: overcoming a monster, rags to riches, a quest, voyage and return, comedy, tragedy, or rebirth (**Figure 11.2**). Whether these stories are about mythical heroes or a pet dog, what unites them are the ways people organise them, usually as meaningful sequences of events set in a time and place, with some problem or tension that gets resolved.

The way children learn about storytelling reinforces the main message from Chapter 9. We saw how children's imagination, as displayed in their drawings, creative thinking, and pretend play, is rather constrained by reality to begin with, and there is a similar picture with their narrative development too. For example, made-up stories tend to be remixes of reality, so that while the combination of events might be unique, the events have probably been drawn together from past experience. Developmental psychologist Susan Engel has studied thousands of children's stories, and the following example from her own son illustrates the point. He said, 'When Ariel was swimming he saw a huge humongous stingray and it stung him and he had to go to the hospital' (Engel, 1995). Her son had cut and pasted two separate events that did happen to form a sequence of events that never happened. Susan's son knew someone named Ariel who took kayaking trips in Mexico, where there are stingrays, and a different man, related to Ariel, who got stung by something in the water. The story isn't going to win the Nobel Prize for literature, but it does show an appreciation of basic narrative structure: identifying the central character, setting the scene in time and space, things happen to someone, there is emotion, there is an ordered cause and effect, and there is an ending. Note also that Susan's son understands something of the social requirements of the storytelling situation – for example, introducing the main character as 'Ariel' first and only later as 'he' so the audience knows who 'he' refers to.

Psychologist Jerome Bruner has argued that this reminiscing property of storytelling performs several important psychological and social functions, one of which is the effect that stories can have on our self-identity (Bruner, 1986). Reminiscing gives children a sense of the same self across different times and situations. Not only does this build intimacy with others by sharing the inner self, but it can also act as a space to replay events diminished of some their original emotional impact. For example, when recalling upsetting or even traumatic experiences, children can benefit from the distance the retelling gives them, helping them to organise their experiences into a meaningful narrative.

There is another sense in which children lean on experience when telling stories: they structure their stories around familiar templates such as 'knock knock' or 'once upon a time' and imitate different kinds of formats, tropes, and other stylistic aspects of storytelling that adults use. For example, in one study children heard poems and stories written by authors such as Emily Dickinson and Sylvia Plath. When invited to write their own stories in response, many of the children incorporated the rhyming patterns, formats, and metaphoric imagery used by Plath and Dickinson (Engel, 1995).

And, of course, children are not just learning about the style and structure of stories but *what* the stories are about and what is meaningful and valued in that culture. In this respect, storytelling is an important channel through which children become familiar with values, beliefs, and norms. Peggy Miller and her colleague examined the narratives used by European-American and Taiwanese caregivers and their children (2012). While there was overlap in the ways families from both cultures told stories, the Taiwanese families were much more likely to tell stories that emphasised moral and social standards, reflecting cultural values regarding proper conduct, respect for others, and self-control. American stories were much more focused on entertainment and on reinforcing the uniqueness of the child. Recall from Chapter 7 how Richard Shweder and his colleagues' work in Chicago and Orissa showed that the boundary between a moral rule (e.g., preventing harm) and a social convention (e.g., what to wear) is culturally variable (1987). Taken together, this shows how stories play an important role in teaching children about these cultural values, ultimately enabling these values to be passed on to the next generation.

 Key Points

- Whether used for pretence or reminiscence, children's stories are typically based on real events and characters, although sometimes these are organised into new sequences.
- By middle childhood, children are adept at mimicking many of the styles and content of adult narratives.
- Storytelling appears to be universal and is an important channel through which children learn the values, beliefs, and norms of the culture around them.
- Reminiscing provides an important way for children to develop a sense of self and to organise and make sense of experience.

It's a long story.

Watch how aboriginal children create stories about who they are and pass on ancient cultural traditions using the latest digital technology.

11.8 How Does Children's Memory Work? Recap and Consolidation

- The shift during skill acquisition from effortful, deliberate practice to automatic performance allows children (and adults) to keep learning new skills.
- Working memory describes the ability to hold some information in mind while working on other information.
- Working memory develops significantly during middle childhood and underpins a wide range of other social and cognitive abilities.
- Long-term stress experienced during critical periods of early brain development can alter how children perceive future rewards and threats.
- Neurological maturation, reduced forgetting, the ability to bind memories together, and a developing sense of self and language are factors that help explain why adults have difficulty remembering the first years of life.
- Memory for the gist of a situation can make older children and adults more susceptible to false memories than younger children.
- Autobiographical memory integrates memories of past experiences into an overarching life narrative or personal history.
- Through their reminiscing style, caregivers can significantly affect how children's autobiographical memories develop.
- Sometimes less is more in development because gradually expanding one's social, cognitive, and physical abilities can be an adaptive problem-solving strategy.

11.9 The Role of Culture in Shaping Our Personal History

As we have learned, childhood is an intense period of cultural apprenticeship. Children are observing how others behave and they are internalising some of these behaviours as norms. As children reminisce, they become sensitive to the norms that define what is appropriate to remember, how to remember it, and what it means to be a person with a past (Fivush & Haden, 2003).

In **collectivist societies**, the needs of groups and institutions come first, ahead of those of individuals. This framework emphasises civic duties, social harmony, obedience to authority, and hierarchy. In East Asian collectivist cultures such as those of China and Japan, individuals tend to perceive themselves in terms of their roles, responsibilities, and relationships to others, valuing the collective whole. In contrast, **individualistic societies** make society the servant of the individual. Most individuals from cultures like that which predominates in North America tend to value personal autonomy and agency, consider people as inherently distinct from one another, and view themselves in terms of their unique personal attributes and qualities. We first met this idea in Chapter 7 when we looked at how these societal differences predicted some of the individual differences in people's sense of right and wrong. The same basic difference between collectivist and individualistic societies is important for the construction of autobiographical memory too, because this relates to how an individual sees themselves in relation to the rest of society.

Han and colleagues explored this idea with European-American, Chinese, and Korean 3- and 4-year-olds, asking them to recount personal events such as a recent time when they did something special and fun (1998). Compared with the Chinese and Korean children, the European-American children provided more elaborate and detailed accounts, recalled more specific episodes, and more frequently referred to their preferences, feelings, and opinions (e.g., 'I liked the birthday present,' and, 'My mom didn't let me go out but I did anyway'). The Chinese and Korean children were more likely to reminisce about themselves relative to other people, embedding their memories in a network of social relationships and considering their own actions in relation to group norms and needs.

This difference in how children construct their life histories is reflected in how adults remember their pasts. Those adults reminiscing in individualistic societies are more likely to access more distant and more detailed, very-long-term memories such as early childhood experiences, more unique one-time episodes as opposed to generic events, and to focus more on their own roles and characteristics than adults from collectivist societies (Wang, 2006).

Key Point

- Cross-cultural differences shape how children view their personal histories.

References

Bruner, J. (1986). *Actual Minds, Possible Worlds*. Harvard University Press.

Engel, S. (1995). *The Stories Children Tell*. W. H. Freeman.

Fivush, R. & Haden, C. A. (eds.). (2003). *Autobiographical Memory and the Construction of a Narrative Self: Developmental and Cultural Perspectives*. Lawrence Erlbaum Associates Publishers.

Han, J. J., Leichtman, M. D., & Wang, Q. (1998). Autobiographical memory in Korean, Chinese, and American children. *Developmental Psychology*, 34, 701–713.

House, B. R., Silk, J. B., Henrich, J., et al. (2013). Ontogeny of prosocial behavior across diverse societies. *Proceedings of the National Academy of Sciences of the United States of America*, 110(36), 14586–14591.

Ibbotson, P. (2014). Little dictators: a developmental meta-analysis of prosocial behavior. *Current Anthropology*, 55(6), 814–821.

Kanngiesser, P., Schäfer, M., Herrmann, E., Zeidler, H., Haun, D., & Tomasello, M. (2021). Children across societies enforce conventional norms but in culturally variable ways. *Proceedings of the National Academy of Sciences of the United States of America*, 119(1), e2112521118.

Miller, P. J., & Fung, H. (2012). How socialization happens on the ground: narrative practices as alternate socializing pathways in Taiwanese and European-American families. *Monographs of the Society for Research in Child Development*, 77(1), 1–14.

Shweder, R. A., Mahapatra, M., & Miller, J. (1987). Culture and moral development. In J. Kagan & S. Lamb (eds.), *The Emergence of Morality in Young Children* (pp. 1–83). University of Chicago Press.

Smith, D., Schlaepfer, P., Major, K., et al. (2017). Cooperation and the evolution of hunter-gatherer storytelling. *Nature Communications*, 8, 1853.

Wang, Q. (2006). Earliest recollections of self and others in European American and Taiwanese young adults. *Psychological Science*, 17, 708–714.

SECTION III

ADOLESCENCE

This section explores adolescence, covering the period between 13 and 18 years of age. Thriving in this phase of life is not always easy. Adolescents are trying to figure out who they are and who they want to be, as well as balance the demands of fitting in, standing out, and measuring up. Cognitively, socially, and neurologically, adolescence is not a single snapshot in time but a transitional period. It is marked by increased interest in the self, in relationships, and in finding one's place in society. Just as adolescents are beginning to enjoy more adult-like rights and privileges, they face new responsibilities and obligations. This change occurs at a time when they are pivoting away from the family, and towards a wider peer group, in preparation for becoming independent young adults. Despite these challenges, adolescence can be a period of great personal exploration, innovation, and optimism.

12 WHO DO TEENAGERS THINK THEY ARE?

 Learning Outcomes

After reading this chapter you will be able to:
- Describe key elements of adolescent identity development.
- Evaluate the genetic, social, and cultural influences on identity.
- Understand creativity and cultural change as parts of adolescent development.

12.1 Introduction

Adolescence has been summed up as beginning in biology and ending in culture. That is, puberty starts with a cascade of hormonal and neurological changes, and it ends when young people take on adult roles and responsibilities in their society. There are, of course, many significant milestones along the way, a key one of which is identity development: who am I, what do I want to be, who does society want me to be? The answers to these questions are not straightforward, they require experimentation, and they are rarely all resolved by adulthood. Exactly where adolescence begins and ends is a fuzzy boundary that changes over time, place, and with new data. Sarah-Jayne Blakemore has shown how areas of the brain continue to develop throughout adolescence and into adulthood, with regions involved in decision-making, planning, and self-awareness still developing into the 20s and 30s (Blakemore, 2018). Jeffrey Arnett has argued that people aged 18–25 are best defined as 'emerging adults', who have some of the cognitive and social characteristics of more established adults, but who still live at home, are financially dependent, and typically have no children – at least in industrialised societies (Arnett, 2000). However we define it, adolescence can be a challenging transition, but it can also be a time of great personal growth, liberation, and optimism. In this chapter we explore the genetic and social influences on identity development, how adolescents gain greater autonomy over their lives, and how they construct their identities in a network of social relationships. We also celebrate the creative achievements of adolescents and aim to understand teenage rebelliousness as a driver of cultural change.

12.2 Who Am I?

Personal identity is our sense of who we are, the imaginary 'I' hovering above our heads that follows us around – what makes you, you. While this might sound abstract, identity is written through our everyday experience: a consistent sense of self makes the person who had breakfast this morning feel like the same 'me' who took the dog for a walk last Tuesday. Up until this point in development, though, 'who am I?' has generally never seemed like a question that needs an answer; it's rare to find a 5-year-old gripped by the existential angst of an identity crisis. But from early adolescence onwards, adolescents start to question and explore their identities in greater depth, they begin to re-examine who they thought they were, and they imagine who they might like to be in the future.

	Key Point
•	Identity development is an important part of adolescence in which young people work out who they are, what they believe in, and how they will present themselves to others.

Part of who adolescents are – indeed, part of who we all are – we can blame on, or give credit to, the parents. This is because a consistent finding from behavioural genetics is that all psychological traits, including personality, show **heritability** (Plomin et al., 2016). Heritability is a measure of how well differences in people's genes account for differences in their traits, and we inherit half of our genes from each parent.

Personal identity is complex and always changing, but researchers have found that they can predict parts of how our lives will turn out, like which job we will end up doing and overall happiness, by categorising our personality traits into five dimensions: 1. extroversion: *social, gregarious, assertive, active, exciting, cheerful*; 2. agreeableness: *trusting, honest, altruistic, compliant, modest, tender-minded*; 3. conscientiousness: *competent, orderly, dutiful, achievement-orientated, disciplined, plans ahead*; 4. emotional stability (the opposite of neuroticism): *calm, friendly, happy, not self-conscious, future thinking, thick-skinned/not vulnerable*; and 5. openness to experience: *imaginative, artistic, emotionally deep, experimental, curious, diverse* (McCrae & Costa, 2008). To find how people differ on these traits, researchers ask people to place themselves on a continuum based on whether they agree or disagree with different statements (**Figure 12.1**).

In an analysis that combined the results of 134 separate studies on personality traits, representing more than 100,000 people, it was shown that around 50% of individual differences were due to genetic influences, while 50% were due to environmental influences (Vukasović & Bratko, 2015). While genetics might provide a starting point for our personalities, the environment we experience can significantly nudge us in different directions. For example, someone born with a predisposition to score 8 out of 10 on the extroversion scale might be unlikely to ever be as introverted as someone scoring 2 out of 10. However, in some environments this tendency for extroversion can be amplified to be 10 out of 10 or dampened down to 6 out of 10.

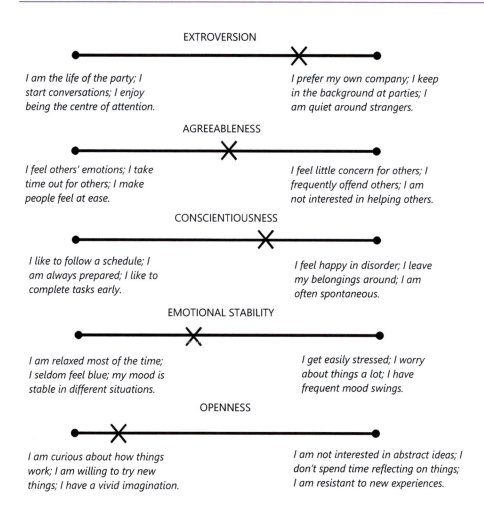

Figure 12.1 The 'big five' personality traits, with statements that exemplify each trait. Note that the actual personality questionnaire researchers use contains many more example statements.

When researchers have looked at other aspects of people's character – intelligence, psychological illness, addiction – there is similarly a 50/50 spilt on average between genetic and environmental influences. So, while it is true that all psychological traits show heritability, it is equally true that no such traits are completely heritable (Plomin et al., 2016).

> **Key Point**
>
> - Genetic and environmental influences are significant factors in explaining the differences between people's personalities.

The easiest way to calculate heritability is to compare identical twins, who share 100% of their genes, with non-identical twins, who share 50%, as do regular siblings. In general, the more genes and environmental context people share, the likelier they are to be similar (**Table 12.1**).

Table 12.1 The relationships between pairs of people regarding intelligence and neuroticism (the opposite of emotional stability; Figure 12.1): 100 means that if we know one individual's score we are able to perfectly predict the other individual's score; 0 means there is no relationship. Data adapted from Knopik et al. (2017, pp. 195, 275).

	Intelligence	Neuroticism
Identical twins reared together	86	46
Identical twins reared apart	78	38
Non-identical twins reared together	60	20
Siblings reared together	47	9
Biological parents and offspring	42	13
Adoptive parents and offspring	19	5
Adopted siblings	32	11

Source: Adapted from Knopik et al., 2017. p195 & 275.

Watch the One-Minute Method.

Learn how twins provide a natural experiment to investigate the relative importance of genes and environment to development.

There are three further details to this big picture that are important for understanding identity development. First, heritability estimates actually *increase* with age, giving some scientific support to the concern you might have that you are turning into your parents. For example, heritability of intelligence is around 20% in infancy, but rises to 60% in adulthood (Haworth et al., 2010).

Second, heritability is caused by many genes, each of which contributes a small effect. This means that it is unlikely – if not impossible – that we will ever find one gene that is solely responsible for something as multifaceted as personality (and for this reason we should be sceptical of newspaper headlines that claim *a single* gene is responsible for any complex behaviour). Heritability estimates can make it sound as if genes directly influence behaviour. They don't. A gene is just a strip of DNA that lines up amino acids, which build proteins, that make cells, some of which might turn into neurons, some which might end up inside brains that make decisions in response to *other* brains and the environment. The many links in this causal chain sum up one reason why the relationship between genes and behaviour is many-to-many and not one-to-one.

Third, environmental influence is itself heritable to some extent. How can this be? Imagine we find that the number of books in a child's home is associated with their academic outcomes: the more books they have on the shelf, the better they do at school. From this we conclude that the home environment is important for academic success. The question is, 'who put the books on the shelf?'. It was probably the parents, who might have been dealt a genetic hand that predisposes *them* to reading – not as a 'gene for reading', but as a more general set of personality traits that make reading an enjoyable thing for them to do. In this scenario the parents pass on a degree of those traits to their children, who also become predisposed to enjoy similar things. We can think of this as nature via nurture (Ridley, 2003). This doesn't mean that reading books is an inevitable thing for these children to do – far from it. We are talking about predispositions – not a law, but a bias to act in one way over another. If there are no books on the shelf in the first place, as was the case for most of human history, then these biases get plugged into different activities that feel similarly rewarding.

The idea that the environment becomes an extension of who we are is perhaps far more familiar to us than we realise. Beavers, for example, modify their environment by building dams, and we can think of dams as an extension of beavers' nature. So, the heritability of dams in the environment is caused by beaver parents and their offspring sharing similar dam-building genes. In a comparable way, the heritability of books on the shelf is caused by parents and their children sharing genes that make reading an enjoyable activity. The important point is that it is hard to find a 'pure' measure of the environment that is not affected by genetics because the environment is not something that is just 'out there' – it has been profoundly affected by humans for hundreds of generations. Humans carry genes, and for that reason we can expect the environment to show some degree of heritability too.

| **Key Points** |

- Estimates of heritability increase through a lifespan.
- Heritability is caused by many genes, each of which contributes a small effect.
- The environment shows some degree of heritability too.

12.3 Who Am I with Others?

Personal identity is not constructed in a vacuum. Becoming you involves feedback from and interaction with others. No study to date has found heritability even close to 100% on *any* psychological trait, let alone something as multifaceted and dynamic as identity. That leaves plenty of room for peers, family, and culture to play a significant role in shaping who we are.

As adolescents talk about their lives, who they are, and what they want to become, how others respond to those conversations can be influential in strengthening, adjusting, or abandoning their developing identity. For example, a supportive network of family and friends can act as a safe space for adolescents to explore who they want to be, and adolescents who have emotionally sensitive and responsive parents tend to explore a wider range of possible identities (Pittman et al., 2012).

One way in which we all make sense of who we are is by integrating our past, present, and future selves into a personal narrative (i.e., **autobiographical memory**). By adolescence there is more personal history to talk about, and young adults are increasingly aware of their distinctiveness and uniqueness from others. Adolescents who have friends who listen more actively and encourage them to connect events in their lives into a personal, meaningful story tend to have a more secure sense of who they are (Ragelienė, 2016). This creates a positive feedback loop, as adolescents who develop a clearer sense of identity are better able to engage in helpful interactions with others and are less likely to abandon their own beliefs (Reiter et al., 2019; Swann et al., 2000).

An important part of creating a personal identity for adolescents is gaining greater control over their own lives, but the shift towards more reciprocal relationships, autonomy, and an equitable balance of power can be a tricky one to negotiate, particularly for parents and friends (Branje et al., 2012). With greater independence comes greater equality in decision-making and more say in how they spend their time and money. The term 'teenager' itself only emerged in the early twentieth century as children began to spend a greater proportion of time together at school, allowing them to develop their own culture away from the watchful eye of the family. Access to technologies such as the car – and, later, mobile phones – gave them even greater independence, and advertisers reinforced the term when they realised 'teenagers' represented a group with enough disposable income to target.

With greater personal autonomy comes more time spent with peers, offering adolescents opportunities to polish their social skills, develop friendships, manage conflict, and work on their identities. The amount of unsupervised time teens have with their peers varies considerably between societies. For example, American high school students reported spending 23.1 hours per week with friends or going on dates compared with 9.7 and 13.5 hours per week, respectively, for students in Taiwan and Japan (Larson & Verma, 1999).

These differences in adolescent behaviour may well be capturing the differences in cultural values we have met before. Namely, adolescents within individualistic cultures, such as European-American ones, might be quicker to adopt independence regarding how they spend their time, as doing so maps onto the values of autonomy and personal choice. By contrast, adolescents from collectivist cultures, such as those of many Asia, Africa, and South America countries, will be relatively slower to adopt these markers of independence, because doing so runs against valuing obligations to others.

Key Point

- Social interaction with friends and family shapes adolescent identity by supporting identity exploration, fostering a sense of personal autonomy, and highlighting uniqueness from others.

The Parenting Across Cultures project is a longitudinal study of parenting and child development in nine countries: China, Columbia, Italy, Jordan, Kenya, the Philippines, Sweden, Thailand, and the USA. Children were recruited at around 8 years old, and family members were interviewed every year for 12 years about parent–child relationships, cultural norms, and children's behavioural, emotional, social, and academic adjustment. One interesting outcome was that adolescents' interpretations of their parents' behaviour predicted how that behaviour affected adolescents. If adolescents perceived their parents' expectations about family obligations were in line with other parents' behaviour in their community, then adolescents were more likely to be socially well-adjusted and to regard their parents' behaviour as legitimate and justified. If their parents' behaviour was an outlier to cultural norms, adolescents were more likely to regard their parents as acting out of hostility or neglect. So, it's not just what parents do that affects adolescents, but also how adolescents perceive what their parents do in relation to everyone else's parents (Lansford et al., 2018).

12.4 Who Does Society Want Me to Be?

As we have seen in the previous section, our identity is constructed through an ongoing conversation between ourselves and others. In that space between self and others, it is inevitable that cultural values come to affect adolescents' emerging identities. The language we speak, the community we belong to, and the values we uphold become parts of who we are. Nowhere is this influence better demonstrated than when looking at the diversity of coming-of-age ceremonies and rites of passage, which have been documented in some form or other in half of the world's societies (**Box 12.1** and **Figure 12.2**; Schlegel & Barry, 1980).

Box 12.1 Coming-of-age

- Jewish communities around the world celebrate Bar Mitzvahs, when boys are 13 years old, and Bat Mitzvahs, when girls are 12 years old. Weeks of preparation and practice lead to a ceremony in front of family, friends, and the broader community involving observing the commandments of the Torah, followed by a large celebration. After the Mitzvah children are responsible for their actions according to Jewish law and can participate in all the same aspects of Jewish community life as adults. Fathers offer thanks to God that they are no longer punishable for their children's sins.
- 13-year-old boys from the indigenous Sateré-Mawé tribe in the Brazilian Amazon wear mitts covered on the inside with bullet ants, so called because their bites cause pain comparable to being shot. The ants' venom typically causes the boy's hands and parts of his arms to become temporarily paralysed, and he may shake uncontrollably for days. If the boys can wear the mitts for 10 minutes or so on many occasions over several months, they emerge as adults, can now marry, have a say in the community, and take on leadership roles. Girls from the same tribe go through a different ritual after their first menstruation. This involves being left alone in a hut for a month, only occasionally seeing their mothers, who bring them food. They also emerge from the ceremony with adult status, ready to marry.
- In the Bashada tribe of Ethiopia's Omo Valley, young boys – known as Ukuli – take part in a multi-day coming-of-age ceremony that includes dancing, singing, and whipping. This climaxes when the young men attempt to leap up onto and run over a several-deep row of cattle repeatedly, without falling. If they are successful, they become respected Maza – men who have just passed the bull-jumping ceremony and who temporarily live apart from the rest of the tribe. Being Maza essentially qualifies men for marriage, raising children, and owning cattle. Note that this transition is only very loosely associated with age, so that a 16-year-old and a 26-year-old could become adults at the same time if they successfully completed the ritual.

Figure 12.2 Left to right, top to bottom: Bar and Bat Mitzvah – Israel; Sateré-Mawé Tucandeira initiation – Brazil; Bashada cow jumping – Ethiopia; sweet 16 – USA; Seijin no Hi – Japan; *quinceañera* – Mexico. Source: ChameleonsEye/Shutterstock; O CONSEHO GERAL DA TRIBO SATERÉ MAWÉ – CGTSM; Eric Lafforgue/Art in All of Us / Contributor / Getty; Zheka-Boss/iStock / Getty Images Plus; Chris Willson/Alamy Stock Photo; Jim West/Alamy Stock Photo.

- Sweet 16 birthday parties in the USA and Canada range from small-scale parties at home with close family to more lavish celebrations with friends, hired DJs, make-up, hair styling, expensive gowns and dresses, and hotel ballrooms. For young Americans, 16 is especially important as it marks the age when they are legally permitted to drive a car, with the personal independence that this allows.
- In Japan, the second Monday of January is an annual public holiday that marks Seijin no Hi or 'Coming of Age Day'. Turning 20 is a significant milestone in Japanese culture, and both men and women celebrate the occasion by attending ceremonies at local civic

venues in traditional dress, where they listen to official speeches and receive gifts, followed by partying with family and friends. After Seijin no Hi, the Japanese recognise the youth as mature citizens, able to vote and drink alcohol, but they also expect them to contribute to society and assume more adult-like responsibilities.

- *Quinceañera* – literally '15 years old' – is celebrated across Mexico and other Spanish-speaking parts of the world. It usually involves a Catholic mass followed by a fiesta, involving coordinated dancing, toasts, and the cutting of cake. The ceremony was originally a sign of a young woman's eligibility for marriage, similar to the upper-class debutante balls of Europe. It marks the transition into adulthood, and it may include the *quinceañera* giving a doll to a younger sister, symbolically showing that the celebrant is giving up her childhood. After the ceremony, *quinceañeras* can enjoy adult privileges but also vow to honour the traditions and values of family and community.

Key Point

- Rituals that mark the passage into adulthood, rites of passage, and coming-of-age ceremonies are common features of many societies.

Coming-of-age ceremonies often require conspicuous amounts of time, effort, and resources, not to mention pain for some of those taking part. Apart from dressing up and having a good time, why do people go to all the trouble?

Despite big differences in how these ceremonies appear on the surface, they share some deeper similarities that suggest a common purpose. Most rites of passage, including adolescent initiations, involve a public expression of values important to that society, or what 'we the people' consider significant. These communal declarations help to reinforce the **social capital** of everyone involved – that is, the network of relationships, values, and resources that allows individuals in a group to work together towards a common purpose. Effective functioning of this network is essential if the knowledge, customs, and traditions of one generation are going to be passed to the next and not be subject to the whims of an individual (van Gennep, 1960). By investing in social capital, everyone stands to benefit from the returns: shared resources (e.g., food, clothes, know-how), childcare, and protection. Synchronised chants, dancing, music, and generally losing yourself in the crowd – common elements of many rituals and religions – also help to create a common purpose, identity, and hive mentality (Haidt et al., 2008).

But what does the adolescent get out of it, especially if they must walk around wearing gloves of stinging ants for days on end? The performance aspect of coming-of-age ceremonies communicates a lot of information to everyone else present. Adolescents take centre stage to advertise that they have internalised and respect the beliefs, know-how, and traditions of their society through speeches, rehearsed dances, and retelling of stories. Their fertility, growth, physical strength, and endurance are also placed in the spotlight – all of which undergo significant changes in adolescence – advertising that they have the physical maturity needed for adulthood – for example, raising children or communal labour. These hard-to-fake signs suggests why it is not enough just to get together, have a party, and declare 'you are an adult now'.

Together, these behavioural and physical displays announce to others that adolescents are ready to take their place in society and to enjoy some of the benefits of adulthood. However, many coming-of-age ceremonies make it very clear that with adult privileges come new obligations, effectively saying something like, 'Yes, you can now have sex, marry, drink, and vote, but you must also take care of others, put food on the table, protect the family, tend to resources, uphold the values of the community, and take personal responsibility for your actions.' Many cultural groups have deeply embedded ideas about honour, respect, gratitude, and loyalty to the family – for example, the concept of *familism* in Latin American countries; *hiya* and *untang na loob* in the Philippines; and *omoluwabi* in the Yoruba people of Nigeria. Across a wide range of cultures, three of the top defining features of adulthood are: 1. accepting responsibility for the consequences of one's actions; 2. deciding on personal beliefs and values independently of parents and other influences, and 3. being financially independent from parents (Arnett & Schwab, 2012).

 Key Point

- Across cultures, key indicators of adulthood are taking personal responsibility for your actions and independence from others.

Many rituals also provide space for adolescents to provide a public statement about who *they* are and what *they* believe. So, as well as internalising the beliefs of the society, these rituals provide another opportunity for adolescents to define their identity. Such public demonstrations also provide evidence that parents need no longer hold themselves responsible – nor be held responsible by other members of the community – for their child in the same way as before.

 Key Point

- Rites of passage and coming-of-age ceremonies signal an adolescent's new status to the community, to the adolescent themselves, and to their parents.

As if the question 'who am I?' wasn't overwhelming enough, there is also the matter of 'who do I want to be?'. And for some adolescents the horizon of possible identities is wider than others. In Chapter 15 we will pick up this idea and examine it more deeply from a cross-cultural perspective.

 More than a label.

Young people talk about how the complexity of their characters defies simple categorisation.

12.5 Creativity Revisited

Many people have noted that, throughout history, adolescents have had a track record of rebelliousness and of leading change in popular culture. In the early nineteenth century young people adopted a sexy, scandalous, and transgressive dance called the waltz and became obsessed with an equally outrageous form of entertainment called the novel. In the twentieth century it was rock 'n' roll, hip-hop, miniskirts, tattoos, and tracksuits (Gopnik, 2016). Teenagers have always been wellsprings of linguistic innovation too, from coining new words to, 'you know, like', different ways of speaking. These trends usually follow a predictable pattern: the previous generation balk at the change and are appalled by the erosion of public standards, the ideas then spread through society and become the new normal as adolescents grow up to become the adults of the next generation, and finally hardly anyone can remember what the moral panic was about.

Adolescents' creativity goes well beyond pop culture, however, and can include startling technical innovation (Rawlings, 2022):

- The 2019 Google Science Fair Introductory Meeting was won by Fionn Ferreira, from Cork, Ireland, who, aged 18, invented a non-harmful method of extracting microplastics from water using vegetable oil and rust powder.
- In 2002, in Masitala village, Malawi, 14-year-old William Kamkwamba built an electricity-generating windmill by using an old bicycle frame with plastic pipes to create a turbine. It powered the family radio and removed the need for kerosene generators, which provide more expensive, lower-quality electricity.
- In Port-au-Prince, Haiti, Wens Dimanche, aged 18, invented an electric-based contactless handwashing system for his local community, powered by a mobile phone battery that can be removed for recharging.
- In Herat, west Afghanistan, a team of adolescent women known as the 'Afghan Dreamers', aged 14–17, built a prototype mechanised ventilator using an engine and battery parts from old cars and a motorcycle chain. Approved by researchers at MIT and Harvard University, the ventilators cost a fraction of the market price of commercially made ones and avoid the need for health workers to manually pump airbags.

Key Point

- Adolescents have been drivers of cultural change and innovation throughout history.

The creativity of these teenagers should not be taken for granted. Given ample time and materials, most of us could not invent a microplastic extractor, electricity-generating windmill, or a mechanised ventilator. What psychological and social factors explain this adolescent appetite for innovation and change?

Let's begin by revisiting why creativity is more limited in younger children. In Chapter 9 we saw how difficult tool innovation was for younger children: even 11-year-olds were outsmarted by Betty the crow on the hook task. Young children's capacity for innovation was constrained by two factors. First, they are prodigious imitators of other people's behaviour. This is our species' superpower, allowing us to pass on a vast body of cultural knowledge, including languages, morals, rites, technologies, and customs, from one generation to the next. But nothing changes if nothing changes, and imitation is the opposite of innovation. A teenage rebellious attitude and disregard for tradition loosen the slavish devotion to norms and create space where new ideas can take hold and disrupt the old order. There is a delicate balance here, though. Too much innovation risks abandoning the accumulated medical, ecological, and technical know-how of previous generations that have served people well. Not enough innovation and societies stagnate – with no inventions to plug into the **ratchet effect**, we wouldn't have any fresh ideas to address new environmental and societal challenges.

In Section 12.2 we saw how people differ on five personality dimensions. As well as individual differences in personality, these dimensions have a greater or lesser influence over us at different points of our lives. Regardless of the differences between people, openness to new experiences is at its highest level during adolescence compared with any other phase of life. Innovation is, by definition, something that relatively few people do to begin with. Therefore, an adolescent peer group that is more likely to adopt a wider variety of unusual behaviours can ensure that the more eccentric inventions get preserved and passed on (we will explore the role of the adolescent peer group in more detail in the next chapter).

The second factor that stops innovation in the young is that they simply haven't had time to build up the repertoire of know-what and know-how required to produce something better than what has gone before. Designing a microplastic extractor, an electricity-generating windmill, or a mechanised ventilator *that works* not only requires a flash of insight but also a vast amount of experience with materials, physical forces, and problem-solving. This kind of knowledge accumulates throughout our lives, so we might expect that the older we get, the more creative we become. However, by late to older adulthood, changes in the openness dimension of our personalities work against this. On average, compared with adolescence, older adulthood is characterised by more resistance to change, lower risk-taking and reward-seeking, and preference for familiarity over the new. This puts teenagers in the Goldilocks zone for creativity: enough life experience to create innovations that can work, and not too much conservatism which would mean they would never try to innovate in the first place.

 Key Point

- Several cognitive and social factors make adolescence a period of creativity.

Today, many adolescents are leading change on one of the most important issues of our time: the environmental degradation of our planet (**Figure 12.3**). This is perhaps both fitting and tragic, as children themselves have often been the first to suffer its negative consequences, including food shortages, economic hardships, and forced migration, with those from low-income families especially vulnerable. Globally it is estimated that 20,000 children are uprooted from their homes every day as the result of climate change, and more than a quarter of all child deaths worldwide are attributable to pollution, with approximately 570,000 children under 5 years of age dying each year as a result (UNICEF, 2023; WHO, 2017). Children are especially at risk from toxins in the environment because of their

Figure 12.3 In 2018, aged 15, Greta Thunberg started spending her Fridays outside the Swedish Parliament, calling for action on climate change and holding up a sign that read '*Skolstrejk för klimatet*' ('School Strike for Climate'). Soon after, millions of students joined in similar protests in cities around the world under the banner 'Fridays for Future'. Later that year, Thunberg delivered an address to the United Nations Climate Change Conference, and she continues to challenge world leaders to mitigate climate change. Source: Daniele COSSU/Shutterstock.

increased brain plasticity, immature immune systems, and rapid growth. One study found that in highly polluted Mexico City, 57% of children had white matter lesions in the prefrontal areas of their brains compared with 8% of children in less polluted Polotitlán; the children from Mexico City also performed more poorly on a variety of cognitive tests (Calderón-Garcidueñas et al., 2011). In the UK, 74% of 11–16-year-olds are worried about the effects of climate change on their future (UNICEF, 2013).

Talking Point

Whether adolescents, or anyone else, can innovate our way out of our current environmental situation remains to be seen. What we do know is that the required monumental shift in public attitude and behaviour has happened before in recent history. At the beginning of the twentieth century, the idea of giving voting rights to women was generally seen in the USA as outrageous; the idea of a female cabinet secretary or supreme court justice was ridiculous; and homosexuality was a taboo subject that could not be openly discussed (Harari, 2015). The fact that these issues have seen such vast change in such a short period of time gives us hope that we will look back on environmentalism in the same way. Another reason to be hopeful is that adolescents have often been some of the most active participants in these changes, a trend that continues today on issues as diverse as civil rights and gun ownership. Adolescents themselves stand to benefit not least because of the world they will inherit, but also because they report that their mental health and identity are positively impacted by the sense of personal control and belonging that environmental activism can bring (Evans et al., 2005).

Teenagers sometimes get a bad reputation as uncommunicative, awkward, and volatile. There is certainly no shortage of reasons to wake up worried – economic crises, climate change, and, recently, a global pandemic. Yet despite these external problems, as well as the internal challenges of identity development, adolescents continuously prove themselves to be innovative, resilient, and optimistic. Young adults sometimes struggle in the course of their transition to adulthood, yet they are also thriving in many ways, and they are remarkably hopeful about how their adult lives will turn out. Their optimism and determination should give us hope too (Arnett & Schwab, 2012).

Summary

- Identity development is an important part of adolescence in which young people work out who they are, what they believe in, and how they will present themselves to others.
- Genetic and environmental influences are significant factors in explaining the differences between people's personalities.
- Estimates of heritability increase through a lifespan.
- Heritability is caused by many genes, each of which contributes a small effect.
- The environment shows some degree of heritability too.
- Social interaction with friends and family shapes adolescent identity by supporting identity exploration, fostering a sense of personal autonomy, and highlighting uniqueness from others.
- Rituals that mark the passage into adulthood, rites of passage, and coming-of-age ceremonies are common features of many societies.
- Across cultures, key indicators of adulthood are taking personal responsibility for your actions and independence from others.
- Rites of passage and coming-of-age ceremonies signal an adolescent's new status to the community, to the adolescent themselves, and to their parents.
- Adolescents have been drivers of cultural change and innovation throughout history.
- Several cognitive and social factors make adolescence a period of creativity.

References

Arnett, J. (2000). Emerging adulthood: a theory of development from the late teens through the twenties. *American Psychologist*, 55(5), 469–480.

Arnett, J. & Schwab, J. (2012). *The Clark University Poll of Emerging Adults: Thriving, Struggling, and Hopeful*. Clark University.

Blakemore, S.-J. (2018). *Inventing Ourselves: The Secret Life of the Teenage Brain*. Public Affairs Books.

Branje, S., Laursen, B., & Collins, W. A. (2012). Parent–child communication during adolescence. In A. L. Vangelisti (ed.), *The Routledge Handbook of Family Communication*, 2nd edition (pp. 271–286). Routledge.

Calderón-Garcidueñas, L., Engle, R., Mora-Tiscareño, A., et al. (2011). Exposure to severe urban air pollution influences cognitive outcomes, brain volume and systemic inflammation in clinically healthy children. *Brain and Cognition*, 77(3) 345–355.

Evans, W. P., Marsh, S. C., & Owens, P. (2005). Environmental factors, locus of control, and adolescent suicide risk. *Child and Adolescent Social Work Journal*, 22, 301–319.

Gopnik, A. (2016). *The Gardener and the Carpenter*. Vintage Publishing.

Haidt, J., Seder, J., & Kesebir, S. (2008). Hive psychology, happiness, and public policy. *Journal of Legal Studies*, 37, S133–S156.

Harari, N. Y. (2015). *Sapiens: A Brief History of Humankind*. Harper.

Haworth, C., Wright, M., Luciano, M., et al. (2010). The heritability of general cognitive ability increases linearly from childhood to young adulthood. *Molecular Psychiatry*, 15, 1112–1120.

Knopik, V. S., Neiderhiser, J. M., DeFries, J. C., & Plomin, R. (2017). *Behavioral Genetics*, 7th edition. Worth Publishers, Macmillan Learning.

Lansford, J., Godwin, J., Al-Hassan, S., et al. (2018). Longitudinal associations between parenting and youth adjustment in twelve cultural groups: cultural normativeness of parenting as a moderator. *Developmental Psychology*, 54(2), 362–377.

Larson, R. W. & Verma, S. (1999). How children and adolescents spend time across the world: work, play, and developmental opportunities. *Psychological Bulletin*, 125(6), 701–736.

McCrae, R. R. & Costa, P. T., Jr. (2008). The five-factor theory of personality. In O. P. John, R. W. Robins, & L. A. Pervin (eds.), *Handbook of Personality: Theory and Research*, 3rd edition (pp. 159–181). The Guilford Press.

Pittman, J. E., Kerpelman, J. B., Soto, F. M., & Adler-Baeder, M. (2012). Identity exploration in the dating domain: the role of attachment dimensions and parenting practices. *Journal of Adolescence*, 35, 1485–1499.

Plomin, R., DeFries, J., Knopik, V., & Neiderhiser, J. (2016). Top 10 replicated findings from behavioral genetics. *Perspectives on Psychological Science*, 11(1), 3–23.

Ragelienė, T. (2016). Links of adolescents identity development and relationship with peers: a systematic literature review. *Journal of the Canadian Academy of Child and Adolescent Psychiatry = Journal de l'Academie canadienne de psychiatrie de l'enfant et de l'adolescent*, 25, 97–105.

Rawlings, B. S. (2022). After a decade of tool innovation, what comes next? *Child Development Perspectives*, 16, 118–124.

Reiter, A., Moutoussis, M., Vanes, L., et al. (2019). Taste uncertainty explains developmental effects on susceptibility to peer influence in adolescence. *Nature Communications*, 12, 3823.

Ridely, M. (2003). *Nature via Nurture: Genes, Experience, and What Makes Us Human*. Harper Collins Publishers.

Schlegel, A. & Barry, H. (1980). The evolutionary significance of adolescent initiation ceremonies. *American Ethnologist*, 7, 696–715.

Swann, W. B., Milton, L. P., & Polzer, J. T. (2000). Should we create a niche or fall in line? Negotiation and small group effectiveness. *Journal of Personality and Social Psychology*, 79, 238–250.

UNICEF. (2013). *Climate Change: Children's Challenge*. UNICEF.

UNICEF. (2023). *Children Uprooted in a Changing Climate*. UNICEF.

van Gennep, A. (1960). *The Rites of Passage*. University of Chicago Press.

Vukasović, T., & Bratko, D. (2015). Heritability of personality: a meta-analysis of behavior genetic studies. *Psychological Bulletin*, 141(4), 769–785.

WHO. (2017). *Inheriting a Sustainable World? Atlas on Children's Health and the Environment*. World Health Organization.

13 HOW DO ADOLESCENTS THINK ABOUT RISK AND REWARD?

 Learning Outcomes

After reading this chapter you will be able to:

- Describe the social, cognitive, and biological influences on adolescent decision-making.
- Understand the risk and reward systems of the brain and how these can be influenced by different contexts.
- Evaluate the roles of peer groups, executive functions, and sex differences in adolescent behaviour.

13.1 Introduction

In this chapter we explore how adolescents think about risk and reward, how they act on these impulses, and what motivates their decisions. Sometimes adults are baffled by the seemingly reckless decisions teenagers make, but as we will discover, adolescence is not a particularly dangerous stage of life, nor are adolescents indiscriminate risk-takers. Risks come with benefits as well as costs. Adolescents take risks and seek rewards under certain circumstances, and they often do so for understandable reasons. Adolescents measurably feel rewards more intensely than at any other point of their lives, they become particularly sensitive about their social status, and their risk-taking is a necessary part of becoming independent. We will dive into the evolutionary, neurological, and social factors that underpin some of this behaviour. By understanding the reasons why adolescents make the decisions they do, we are in a better place to empathise with the demands placed on individuals during this period of transition. How do friends influence risk-taking? How does the teenage brain process rewards? And how do rapidly developing higher-level thinking and planning skills affect decision-making?

13.2 Mishaps and Misadventures

There is a belief that teenagers engage indiscriminately in risky behaviour, making adolescence one of the most dangerous times to be alive, but is this true? One rather stark measure

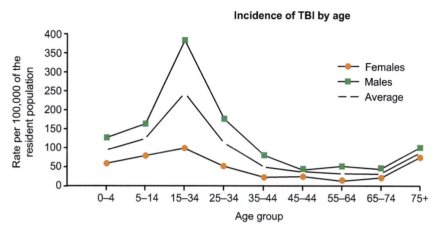

Figure 13.1 Rate of traumatic brain injuries (TBIs) by different age groups for males and females (adapted from Tate et al., 1998). Source: The Brain Injury Rehabilitation Network.

of a risky lifestyle is the likelihood of dying. Concerned parents might be reassured to know that adolescence is actually one of the safest times to be alive, with a lower mortality rate than either young infants or any group older than adolescence (ONS, 2021). What is revealing, though, are the *kinds* of risks that adolescents take. They read like a list of self-inflicted mishaps, misadventures, and tragedies: car crashes and other transport accidents, alcohol and drug overdoses, injuries from fire, weapons, exposure to severe heat and cold, physical confrontations, and extreme sports, and so on (Curtin et al., 2018; Guthold et al., 2019). Among adolescents, accidental injuries are the leading cause of death, claiming more lives than diseases, self-harm, and nutritional or maternal health causes (GBD Adolescent Mortality Collaborators, 2021).

A less binary measure of risky behaviour than death is the chance of receiving a traumatic brain injury (TBI). **Figure 13.1** shows the rate of TBIs by different age groups for males and females based on a sample of 343 Australians from New South Wales (Tate et al., 1998).

While the overall incidence is low (about 0.4%), TBIs among adolescents are relatively higher than among all other age groups, with 15–24-year-olds making up 40% of TBI survivors but only 15% of the population. Also note that across the entire lifespan males have a higher risk of a TBI than females – a sex difference we will return to later. On other measures of risky behaviour, such as unintended pregnancies and sexually transmitted diseases, adolescents are also over-represented, and, in general, adolescents are poorer at judging the long-term consequences of their actions compared with adults (Reyna & Farley, 2006; Santelli et al., 1999).

 Key Point

- Adolescents have a lower mortality rate than those in most other stages of life but are more likely to be accidentally injured and to engage in risky behaviour, and they are poorer at judging the long-term consequences of their actions.

13.3 Moving on and Fitting in

So, what is behind these risky choices? As with other aspects of development, there are two ways of answering this question: the long-term view and the short-term view.

The long-term view starts by noting that we are not the only species where adolescents show a marked change in their behaviour. Across a wide range of mammals, animals on the cusp of adulthood show a significant increase in novelty- and sensation-seeking behaviours (Kelley et al., 2004). This greater interest in new sensations naturally levers individuals away from the safe and familiar environment of the family towards striking out on their own. For most mammals, greater independence means finding food for themselves, establishing their own territory, taking their place in the social hierarchy, finding a mate, and starting a family of their own (Spear, 2000). By their nature, these behaviours involve some degree of risk. Crucially, a social network of similar-aged peers will be more important in helping an individual to achieve many of these milestones than their family, so the relative importance of peers becomes greater through this period too. For most social animals being kicked out of the group is a life-threatening ordeal, and for a range of mammal species an adolescent without a peer group is as good as dead. To guard against this, adolescents busily build alliances with similar-aged peers, whom they are going to need in the future.

Key Point

- Novelty- and sensation-seeking behaviours with greater risk-taking and peer influence are seen in a wide range of species on the cusp of adulthood, suggesting a shared evolutionary explanation.

In humans, adolescence is also a period of increased self- and social awareness. The attachment centre of gravity that children have established with their primary caregivers in the early years (Chapter 2) is beginning to pivot towards their peer group. The upside of this is that teens begin to invest in those relationships that are going to become more significant as they grow up. Close friendships with a small number of trusted peers appear to be predictive of an increased sense of self-worth later on in life and to be protective against anxiety and depressive symptoms (Narr et al., 2019). The downside is that during this period adolescents become hypersensitive to falling out of their peer group or being *ostracised* (Sebastian et al., 2010).

In Chapter 8 we explored how sensitive we are to group membership and how our past survival depended on working collaboratively with others in small groups (Engelmann & Tomasello, 2019). This ancient bias to fit in is played out in less life-threatening modern-day contexts, but it is felt no less intensely. Relative to younger children and adults, adolescents experience social interactions and feedback from others with greater passion, making them sometimes more easily irritated, upset, and moody (Blakemore, 2008). This means that, in a very real and measurable way, adolescent relationships with the peer group – even if it's just one other person – *feel* like matters of life and death. In his book *Brainstorm: The Power and*

Purpose of the Teenage Brain (2014), Daniel Siegel puts it this way: teens sacrifice morality for membership. When the choice is between social ostracism or an ethically iffy decision, teens judge that it might pay to blend in and debate the moral consequences later.

Key Point

- Adolescence is a time of investing in peer relationships, heightened sensitivity to group identity, and emotional intensity.

The long-term view tries to address the broader question of what adolescence is for, but, of course, no adolescent is consciously thinking about their evolutionary past at the moment they decide to run a red light or when they feel the pang of being excluded from the coolest party, so we also need a short-term answer as well.

Although our brains are approximately 90% of their adult size by age 6, the brain continues to undergo significant changes throughout adolescence. When calculating risk and reward from moment to moment, regions of the brain are talking to one another, responding to reward, anticipating reward, inhibiting impulses, and regulating behaviour. Thanks to the work of neuropsychologists like B. J. Casey, Cat Sebastian, and others, we now understand that these systems are more unbalanced in adolescence compared with younger children or older adults (Casey et al., 2011; Sebastian et al., 2008). The systems responsible for reward and motivation mature earlier, are more well connected to other areas of the brain, and shout louder than the systems that suppress inappropriate actions and plan for the future. This is especially true in the heat of passion, in the presence of peers, in the spur of the moment, or in unfamiliar situations (Reyna & Farley, 2006).

There is another factor that helps to amplify this imbalance. A chemical messenger in the brain called dopamine is responsible for making us feel good, rewarding us for certain behaviours like doing something new. Compared to children and adults, the baseline level of dopamine in adolescence is set at a lower level, but when it is released, there is more of it (Steinberg, 2008). Put simply, this means adolescents have a greater motivation to seek out new experiences because they have a lower dopamine baseline, and they get a greater kick out of it when they do because of the higher amount of dopamine released. The downside of this is that when dopamine levels crash, teens get more easily bored and need higher levels of novelty for the same dopamine kick. This drives adolescents to seek change and novelty and to push for the unfamiliar and uncertain, which is what they must do if they are ever going to get out of the house (Siegel, 2014). Indeed, adolescents need informative but non-lethal experiences of risk to prepare them for later life. For instance, risk is part of becoming an astronaut, downhill skier, or business entrepreneur, as well a criminal, drug dealer, or reckless driver.

In summary, adolescents do not underestimate risk and are capable of making rational decisions, but they are more likely to overestimate rewards – or rather, to find rewards more rewarding than adults do. The immediate gratification promised by fast driving, heavy drinking, or unprotected sex is far greater than a measured calculation of their long-term consequences.

> **Key Point**
>
> - The reward systems of the brain mature earlier and are more well connected in adolescents than those that keep impulses in check and that deliberate over alternative choices.

When combined, these long- and short-term views help us better understand adolescent decision-making. In the long term, to reach adult milestones of independence we need the cooperation of a peer group. In the short term, this is motivated by changes in the structure and function of the brain that push us away from the family and pull us towards our friends. As a result, adolescents start to focus on the positive, thrilling aspects of a choice and minimise the negative, dangerous aspects. There are two further important subtleties to this general picture. First, a lot of risk-taking occurs during adolescence, but not all adolescents are risk-takers, and we do not fully understand the reasons for all the individual differences. One possibility is that the neural systems underlying risky behaviour function slightly differently or mature according to different schedules from one teenager to the next. In support of this, researchers have demonstrated that those adolescents who are likely to engage in life-threatening activities in real life also show larger responses to monetary rewards in reward-related neural circuits of the brain (Galvan et al., 2008).

Second, there are some contexts that are much more likely to cause risk-taking than others, a significant one being the presence of other peers, which is explored further in the next section (**Figure 13.2**).

 Wired for life.

Adriana Galván shows how some of the most puzzling teenage behaviours may have some real benefits.

13.4 Peer Influence on Risk-Taking

One of the hallmarks of risk-taking in adolescence, as opposed to risk-taking in any other phase of life, is that it is much more likely to occur in the presence of peers. For example, one of the best predictors if not the single best predictor of whether an adolescent is engaged in substance abuse or crime is whether they have a friend who is also engaged in those activities (Chassin et al., 2009; Zimring, 1998). Jason Chein and his colleagues set out to investigate whether this peer influence extends to driving, an activity that we already know is particularly risky for adolescents. They designed a simulated computer driving game, which was played by 40 adolescents, young adults, and adults (Chein et al., 2011). In each run of the game, participants attempted to reach the end of a straight track as quickly as possible. There were 20 junctions on the track, where participants could either stop the vehicle (STOP) or take a risk and run the traffic light (GO; **Figure 13.3**).

If participants chose to run the light and were fortunate enough not to crash, they could complete the game quicker than if they had stopped. If participants were unlucky and crashed, they would be slower than if they had stopped. Crucially, each of the participants played the

Figure 13.2 Adolescents are on the path to independence, and that means the freedom to make smart and savvy choices as well as unwise and reckless ones. Risks are not risks unless they can turn out badly. Source: Monkey Business Images/Shutterstock.

game under two different conditions: one in which they drove alone and one in which they were being watched by two similar-aged friends they had brought along to the experiment.

Chein and colleagues found no difference between adolescents and older participants in how risky their driving decisions were or how many crashes they had *when they were driving alone*. This is remarkable given that car accidents account for nearly half of all fatalities among American youth (Blum & Nelson-Mmari, 2004). However, when being observed by their friends, the adolescents had significantly more crashes. By contrast, older adults crashed no more nor less when they were being watched by others, and their overall level of risk was the same as if they were driving alone. Chein and colleagues also ran the same experiment while participants played the game inside a functional magnetic resonance imaging (fMRI) scanner, so that the researchers could explore the roles of the reward and inhibition brain systems we met earlier. As predicted, they found that brain regions associated reward and its evaluation showed greater activation for adolescents, but only when they were being watched by their friends, and as before, older adults showed no such differences.

This study and similar others powerfully demonstrate the role that peers play in adolescent risk-taking behaviour. Furthermore, in the Chien et al. study, peers were located in a separate room and were prevented from directly interacting with participants during the driving game. This means adolescents were more likely to take risks when merely *knowing* that they were being watched by friends, and so this behaviour was not due to any direct 'peer pressure'. Similarly, researchers have also shown that adolescents are more likely to be sexually active when they *believe* that their friends are sexually active, whether or not their friends actually are (Babalola, 2004). As we have seen elsewhere in child development, aspects of our

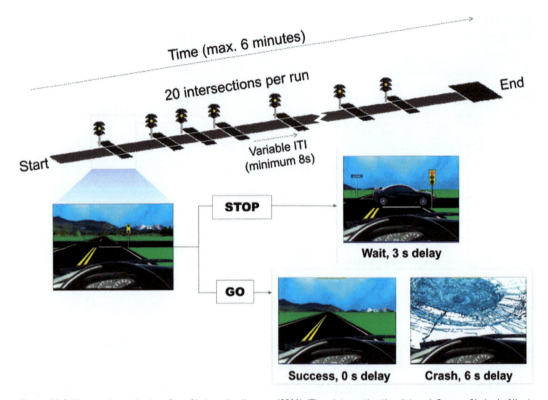

Figure 13.3 The experimental set-up from Chein and colleagues (2011). ITI = intersection time interval. Source: Chein, J., Albert, D., O'Brien, L., Uckert, K. and Steinberg, L. (2011), Peers increase adolescent risk taking by enhancing activity in the brain's reward circuitry. Developmental Science, 14: F1-F10. https://doi-org.libezproxy.open.ac.uk/10.1111/j.1467-7687.2010.01035.x.

psychological make-up, such as risk-taking, are filtered through societal attitudes and beliefs. This means that the same underlying tendency can be expressed differently from society to society. For example, condoms and comprehensive sex education are widely available to Swedish adolescents but not to those in the USA. These population-level attitudes can affect individual-level risk evaluation: teen birth rates are 5.9 per 1,000 in Sweden compared with 41.9 per 1,000 in the USA, and rates of sexually transmitted diseases are between 10 and 300 times higher in the USA (United Nations Statistics Division, 2006).

 Key Point

- Knowing or believing that peers are observing their behaviour significantly increases the risk-taking behaviour of adolescents, even in the absence of any direct peer pressure.

 Watch the One-Minute Method.

Discover how neuroimaging techniques, like those used in the driving simulation study, can reveal much about the relationships between brain, mind, and behaviour.

13.5 In Praise of Peers

In terms of risk and reward, peer influence has come across in a rather bad light so far. However, peers are important sources of **social capital** for one another during adolescence and act as buffers in stressful times, not to mention offering fun and companionship. Recent research has begun to rehabilitate the image of peer influence, exploring the social circumstances in which peers can positively influence one another.

Lucas Molleman and his colleagues designed a set of experimental games to be played by 146 adolescents (2022). The first game tested rule compliance and was very similar to the earlier driving experiment. Participants had to decide whether to follow or break the rule 'wait until the traffic light turns green before moving forward'. The key difference was what happened next. Whatever the adolescents chose, they were then informed that a peer had chosen the opposite. Participants who initially complied with the rule (i.e., moved after the traffic light turned green) were shown three 'bad' examples of peers who moved as soon as possible. Participants who initially broke the rule (i.e., moved before the traffic light turned green) were then shown three 'good examples' of peers who waited until the traffic light turned green. The participants were then asked to play the game again. The crucial question for researchers was: 'how much would adolescents be influenced by the good examples versus the bad examples of their peers?'

The second of their games tested how much adolescents could be swayed by what other peers believed. To test this, the researchers devised a task in which participants looked at an image of 50–60 animals and had to estimate how many there were. They were then shown how many animals other peers had estimated and, as before, encouraged to play the game again. The crucial question was: 'how much would adolescents be influenced by the estimates of their peers?' This task taps into our ability to learn from others (Chapter 5) and our bias to conform with the norms of the group (Chapters 7 and 8).

Finally, the researchers gave adolescents a version of the dictator game we have already met in Section 11.3 (Ibbotson, 2014). Participants received 10 points (worth about €1) to divide between themselves and another person, who had participated in a previous session. After they had played the game once, they were informed how a peer had performed in the same task. Either they were told that the peer had chosen a selfish split (keeping all the points) or that they had split it more equally (sharing the points 50:50). The crucial question was: 'how much would adolescents be influenced by the sharing behaviour of their peers?'

So, what did they find? The title of their paper summed up the results: 'Social influence in adolescence as a double-edged sword.' Adolescents who had seen other peers break the rules were more likely to break the rules, and those who had seen selfish splitting of points were more likely to be selfish. However, those who had seen other peers comply with the rules were more likely to comply with the rules, and those who had seen more generous sharing were more likely to be more generous.

There was an interesting secondary result too. Across all the tasks they used – rule compliance, belief formation, and prosociality – peer influence steadily declined throughout adolescence. The youngest of the participants were around 10 while the oldest were about 20. Those closer to 10 years of age were much more susceptible to the influence of peers, for good and bad, than adolescents closer to 20 years old. This might be because the older adolescents had a stronger identity of who they are, making them less likely to be influenced by peers. In the previous chapter we explored how this openness to new ideas can put teens in the driving seat of social change. In the context of peer groups, younger adolescents, with a more fragile self-identity and less certainty about their personal values, take more of their cues from the group about what is the right thing to do (Reiter et al., 2019).

Key Point

- The behaviour of early adolescents is strongly guided by the social environment, both for positive and negative outcomes.

This study and others like it highlight the potential of peers to spread norms throughout a group. Understanding the relationships between behaviour, social learning, and network formation is key to understanding how peers can promote and consolidate positive behaviour (Paluck & Shepherd, 2012). This can inform the timing and design of interventions that seek to spread positive examples in adolescents' social networks (recall **Box 8.1**).

Much like a reckless attitude to risk, adolescents sometimes get labelled as lazy, spending too long asleep in bed, but is this true (**Box 13.1**)?

Box 13.1 Why do teenagers sleep so much?

Contrary to widespread belief, adolescents sleep no more than expected for their age; in fact, they are some of the most sleep-deprived sections of our society. In a study of the sleep habits of 1.1 million people from the Netherlands, the UK, and the USA, the prevalence of insufficient sleep and sleepiness was much higher in teenagers than in any other age group (Kocevska et al., 2021). What is going on here? Around adolescence, there is a natural drift towards going to bed later, driven by a change in the way hormones respond to the daily cycle of light and dark, specifically a delay in the release of melatonin. Left undisturbed, this shift causes teenagers to sleep in later to maintain a healthy amount of time spent asleep.

However, in many Western societies this natural shift in sleep behaviour is not accommodated by the immovable deadline of getting up and making it to school on time. The timing of the school day has more to do with coordinating bus schedules and (originally) synchronising with industry than it does with optimal learning conditions. Some researchers have referred to this misalignment of social and biological time as 'social jet lag', and it has some serious consequences. We know getting enough quality sleep is important for memory and learning (Chapter 10), and it is also positively associated with emotional regulation, quality of life, and mental and physical health (Short et al., 2019). There are thus strong social, educational, and economic benefits to getting a good night's sleep, and lobby groups have long argued for later school start times on this basis. However, despite numerous studies indicating the benefits of delaying school start times, it has not been widely adopted because the school ecosystem has powerful inertia: a different start time for some pupils would mean different teacher schedules for different pupils, as well as different drop-off and pick-up times for parents, thereby affecting their work, and then there are the impacts on wrap-around care, sports clubs, and so on to consider. Sending teenagers to bed early isn't going to help either because the melatonin shift means they would just lie there awake. Instead, some researchers have focused on providing sleep education to teenagers and utilising light therapy to help combat the problem of sleepy adolescents (Sharman & Illingworth, 2020).

13.6 Sex Differences

Earlier on in the chapter we noted a sex difference on one measure of risk-taking: namely, that across the lifespan males are more likely to experience a Traumatic Brain Injury (TBI) than females. This difference is already apparent by 4 years of age. Is this something peculiar to the sample or to TBIs? In a survey of a broad range of accidental injuries in over 200 countries, adolescent boys are also over-represented compared to girls (GBD 2019 Adolescent Transport and Unintentional Injuries Collaborators, 2019), and interpersonal violence was ranked among the leading causes of death of older adolescent boys in 2019 (World Health Organization, 2020). The sex difference in risk-taking is reflected in the broader picture on longevity: globally one of the best ways to increase life expectancy is to be born female (Rochelle et al., 2015).

Less scientifically, the Darwin Awards are tongue-in-cheek honours given annually to people who die through 'outstanding misapplication of judgement' (https://darwinawards.com). The reference to Darwin implies that the recipients of the award positively contribute to human evolution by selecting themselves out of the gene pool. Previous winners have died while baking bullets in the oven, looking inside a rocket launcher, or having sex while piloting a plane. Honourable mentions go to those who make dumb decisions but who do not die as a result. One notable example is Larry Walters, who, out of curiosity, attached helium-filled weather balloons to his lawn chair to see how high he could float. He eventually reached an altitude of 16,000 ft over Long Beach, California, before being fined for crossing controlled airspace. A paper entitled 'Sex differences in idiotic behaviour' reported that men were nine times more likely to be the recipient of a Darwin Award than women (Lendrem et al., 2014).

Why is this? Do men take relatively more risks because they are trying to live up to some socially reinforced stereotype of masculinity? This seems unlikely to be the complete answer for several reasons. First, if society made a big difference, we would expect the sex differences to be smaller where societies are similar and bigger where societies are more different, but the evidence suggests that this is wrong on both counts: women survive longer than men even when both sexes live in nearly identical societal conditions (Luy, 2003), and where men and women grow up in societies that are different sex differences remain. For example, in the USA adolescent boys are over-represented in car accidents compared to girls, and in foraging societies boys also take more risks than girls and men die earlier than women (Apicella et al., 2017; Berger et al., 2020; Blum & Nelson-Mmari, 2004).

Second, if human societal attitudes around masculinity were responsible for these differences, then we might expect the differences to disappear when there is no human society.

Figure 13.4 Compared to females, males across a range of species are more likely to show high-risk, high-reward behaviours, adopting a live-hard, die-young strategy. Source: DuncanImages/Alamy Stock Photo; AfriPics.com/Alamy Stock Photo; Nature Picture Library/Alamy Stock Photo.

However, males across many different types of animals – frogs, birds, rodents, insects, mammals – engage in more risk-taking than do females (Habig et al., 2017). Presumably, frogs behave the way they do not because they feel under pressure to be macho frogs but because they are just busy being a frog. This greater tendency to take risks can show up in a shorter lifespan. A female's lifespan is on average about 18% longer than that of males across a range of over 100 different mammals – including orca, deer, and squirrels – in the wild (Berger et al., 2020). The fact that males across such a wide variety of species and environments take more risks and die earlier than females points to a set of shared causes (**Figure 13.4**).

 Key Point

- Sex differences in mortality and risk-taking persist within similar societies, between different societies, and across a wide variety of species and environments.

Life-history theory proposes that each stage in a species' development can be seen as an adaptation to the social and ecological challenges that it faces at that time of life. We can apply this idea to risk-taking: a new challenge that presents itself for the first time in adolescence is finding a mate. Across a range of species, including mammals, females typically invest more time, energy, and resources into growing their babies and looking after them than do males. Under these circumstances, it pays females to be more cautious over whom they mate with, because they have more to lose with an unwise choice. This produces competition between males for females because there is more demand than there is supply, and competition is a risky business, with winners and losers. Note that this does not automatically mean that one sex is socially dominant over the other. There are many species of animals, such as elephants and bonobo chimpanzees, in which choosy females and competitive males result in *matriarchal* societies.

This does, however, create a situation in which females should be especially risk-averse regarding their children and in which males should be more willing to take on risk by competing with their male peers (Trivers, 1972). These are exactly the behaviours we see across many species throughout the natural world, and humans show similar behaviours too (Archer, 2019). Adolescence is a time of increased risk-taking, but it is also a time when sex differences are becoming more obvious, groups are becoming less same-sex segregated, and there is increasing curiosity about sex and sexual development. In one study of risk-taking, adolescent girls did not change their levels of risk-taking in the presence of other males or females but showed a strong reduction in risk when paired with babies. By contrast, boys were strongly inclined to take more risks when paired with another male of the same age but showed no change in risk-taking with females of the same age or a child (Fischer & Hills, 2012; see also Salas-Rodríguez et al., 2022).

Key Point

- Life-history theory predicts that boys are more willing to engage in risky behaviour in same-sex competitive contexts.

To be clear, just because a behaviour has a biological basis or is adaptive does not mean that it is acceptable, inevitable, or universal. A behaviour might be 'hardwired' in the brain, but that does not mean experience does not matter. Indeed, our brains are so powerful precisely because they are sensitive to experience. While we share a long history with other animals, meaning we inherit many of the same behavioural biases, we are clearly different in important ways too. One obvious difference is the way we can pass on cultural knowledge from one generation to the next (Chapters 5, 6, 7, and 10). This means societal attitudes and norms around risk-taking can and do change over time and from place to place. Over history there have been radical shifts over *what* risks adolescents are willing to take; witness the marked decline in youth smoking, drinking, and pregnancy in recent years.

Compared with other animals, we also have a more developed area of the brain known as the prefrontal cortex, which deals with complex decision-making, resisting impulses, and planning for the long term. This means that neither men nor women are deterministically doomed to follow one instinct over all others; a brain equipped with the ability to evaluate risk and reward can weigh the relative merits of one decision versus many others. We take a closer look at this ability in the next section.

13.7 Executive Functions

The path from problem to solution is rarely straightforward. Along the way there are time-wasting distractions to resist, dead-end strategies that need to be abandoned in favour of better ones, and unforeseen obstacles that demand a new plan. There is effort associated with this approach, as the easiest option would be to give in to temptation, to repeat what has been done before, and only to consider one thing at a time. However, the benefit of being flexible, controlled, and focused is behaviour that is much more likely to achieve the end goal. The collection of cognitive skills that keep goal-directed behaviour on track are known as **executive functions**, and they offer just-in-time solutions to questions like 'where should I focus my attention next?', 'what actions do I need to inhibit?', and 'what information do I need to update?' (Ibbotson, 2023). At a general level these skills can be organised into three functions:

- **Inhibitory control** allows us block irrelevant actions or thoughts and keep us focused on the goal – for example, resisting eating one marshmallow now for the promise of two later.
- **Working memory** describes the ability to mentally work on multiple sources information at the same time – for example, remembering the directions of how to get somewhere while also remembering the destination.
- **Cognitive flexibility** allows us to suddenly change perspectives or switch task – for example, talking in one language, then talking in a different one, then switching back to the first.

Key Point

- Executive functions represent a collection of skills that enable us to be flexible, controlled, and focused.

Throughout our exploration of childhood we have made many references to executive functions. This is because they underpin such a wide range of developmental outcomes for children, some of which we have already explored in the context of working memory development (Chapter 10). Inhibitory control provides another example. One study found that children who are better at waiting their turn, less easily distracted, more persistent, and less impulsive were more law-abiding and have better educations, higher salaries, and more favourable mental and physical health when they were followed up 30 years later, even after taking into account differences in intelligence, sex, social class, and family circumstances (Moffitt et al., 2011).

The ability to adopt long-term advantageous strategies and resist immediate gratification continues to develop across adolescence. Experimental evidence suggests that the abilities to reason about gains and losses, balance the emotional consequences of reward and punishment, and self-regulate behaviour with others are still developing into early adulthood (Huizenga et al., 2007). More generally, the development of executive functions is influenced by age-related changes in other areas such as emotion regulation and social competence, which interact with each other in non-linear ways (e.g., showing a **U-shaped curve**).

Precisely *what* children and adolescents find difficult to resist is influenced by what their culture values, something that will be explored in greater depth in Chapter 15.

The ability to effectively switch between tasks using cognitive flexibility also takes a long time to develop compared with other cognitive functions like language and memory. For example, children as young as 3 years of age show some degree of cognitive flexibility and have no difficulty sorting objects by either colour or shape (Kirkham et al., 2003). But when they are asked to switch the sorting criteria halfway through the task, from colour to shape or vice versa, they struggle to adopt the new rule and stick with the old one, even though they know what they should do. In this respect, young children perform similarly to adults who have experienced damage to the prefrontal cortex, an area of the brain we know is associated with executive functions (Crone, 2009).

By 4–5 years of age most children have significantly improved on these tasks, but it is not until 7–9 years of age that they can switch flexibly on a trial-by-trial basis, with further age-related improvements in mental flexibility seen in adolescence (Crone et al., 2006; Gupta et al., 2009). Speaking to just how protracted the acquisition of cognitive flexibility is, the cognitive cost of changing tasks persists into adulthood, as indicated by greater response times for switch trials, regardless of whether adults are informed of the upcoming switch or whether there is a gap between trials (Diamond & Kirkham, 2005).

Interestingly, when adolescents fail to perform like adults on tests of executive function, it might not always be that they simply cannot do the task. Rather, their brains' reward systems are set at a higher threshold (e.g., dopamine levels; see Section 13.3), so they might need the stakes to be higher, the tests to be more arousing, and the social consequences to be more real to motivate their executive functions into action (Crone, 2009).

 Key Point

- Executive functions are associated with a wide range of outcomes for children and take a long time to mature.

People from the Marquesas Islands of Polynesia say that someone has reached adulthood when they have outgrown their *taure'are'a*, which means they are now reliable, hardworking, and able to control their impulses. Similarly, the Arabic word *aql* refers to the ability to make rational, informed decisions and to control one's impulses and passions. People who have not obtained *aql* are not adults yet, and in Arabic culture it is believed that females generally develop *aql* at an earlier age. There is some evidence to back this up. While adolescent boys and girls perform similarly on most tests of executive function, there is evidence that inhibitory control matures earlier in girls compared to boys. This is underpinned by the earlier development of brain areas associated with this function, which may relate to sex differences in the timing of puberty (Lenroot et al., 2007). At the behavioural level, this means that boys are likely to be more impulsive than girls of a similar age. Experimentally this has been demonstrated in the ways boys and girls balance speed and accuracy in a task that requires some inhibitory control to succeed: on average, boys are quicker to respond, but girls give more correct responses (Ibbotson & Roque-Gutierrez,

2023). Outside of the lab, inhibitory control is clearly important in the context of risk-taking. Resisting an inappropriate behaviour (e.g., running a red light) requires effortful control, and if girls' inhibitory control matures earlier than boys', then this is another significant factor affecting the risk-taking behaviour of adolescents.

> **Key Point**
>
> - There is some evidence to suggest that inhibitory control emerges earlier for girls than boys, underpinned by earlier maturation of the brain areas that support this function.

Talking Point

What do you do if you are trying to set the insurance premiums for adolescent drivers? Empirically it's true that adolescents, *as a group*, are over-represented in car crashes compared to other groups, especially when they are accompanied by peers. But is it morally right to impose the statistics of a group *on an individual teenager*, who might be the safest driver ever to get behind the wheel?

In December 2012 the European Union introduced controversial new rules insisting that car insurance companies no longer discriminate on the basis of sex. Prior to this, women enjoyed lower premiums as they were known to be safer drivers with lower accident rates. Contrary to expectations, the sex differences in premiums actually increased after the law was introduced. Insurance companies no longer used sex to directly set premiums (which would have been illegal) but instead used a host of other personal data such as occupation, which is closely related to sex; scaffolders are more likely to be men than women while midwives are more likely to be women than men, therefore midwives are more likely to drive fewer miles and have fewer accidents, the accidents they do have are less serious, and the cars they drive are cheaper to repair. Is a similar law in the pipeline for adolescent drivers? And what counts as equality in such cases? Whatever the philosophical and legal outcomes of such debates, the science of adolescence can continue to improve our understanding of why adolescents make the decisions they do.

> ## Summary
>
> - Adolescents have a lower mortality rate than those in most other stages of life but are more likely to be accidentally injured and to engage in risky behaviour, and they are poorer at judging the long-term consequences of their actions.
> - Novelty- and sensation-seeking behaviours with greater risk-taking and peer influence are seen in a wide range of species on the cusp of adulthood, suggesting a shared evolutionary explanation.
> - Adolescence is a time of investing in peer relationships, heightened sensitivity to group identity, and emotional intensity.
> - The reward systems of the brain mature earlier and are more well connected in

- adolescents than those that keep impulses in check and that deliberate over alternative choices.
- Knowing or believing that peers are observing their behaviour significantly increases the risk-taking behaviour of adolescents, even in the absence of any direct peer pressure.
- The behaviour of early adolescents is strongly guided by the social environment, both for positive and negative outcomes.
- Sex differences in mortality and risk-taking persist within similar societies, between different societies, and across a wide variety of species and environments.
- Life-history theory predicts that boys are more willing to engage in risky behaviour in same-sex competitive contexts.
- Executive functions represent a collection of skills that enable us to be flexible, controlled, and focused.
- Executive functions are associated with a wide range of outcomes for children and take a long time to mature.
- There is some evidence to suggest that inhibitory control emerges earlier for girls than boys, underpinned by earlier maturation of the brain areas that support this function.

References

Apicella, C. L., Crittenden, A. N., & Tobolsky, V. A. (2017). Hunter-gatherer males are more risk-seeking than females, even in late childhood. *Evolution and Human Behavior*, 38, 592–603.

Archer, J. (2019). The reality and evolutionary significance of human psychological sex differences. *Biological Reviews of the Cambridge Philosophical Society*, 94, 1381–1415.

Babalola, S. (2004). Perceived peer behavior and the timing of sexual debut in Rwanda: a survival analysis of youth data. *Journal of Youth and Adolescence*, 33, 353–363.

Berger, V., Cohas, A., Colchero, F., et al. (2020). Sex differences in adult lifespan and aging rates of mortality across wild mammals. *Proceedings of the National Academy of Sciences of the United States of America*, 117(15), 8546–8553.

Blakemore, S.-J. (2008). The social brain in adolescence. *Nature Reviews Neuroscience*, 9(4), 267–277.

Blum, R. & Nelson-Mmari, K. (2004). The health of young people in a global context. *Journal of Adolescent Health*, 35, 402–418.

Casey, B., Jones, R. M., & Somerville, L. H. (2011). Braking and accelerating of the adolescent brain. *Journal of Research on Adolescence*, 21(1), 21–33.

Chassin, L., Hussong, A., & Beltran, I. (2009) Adolescent substance use. In R. Lerner & L. Steinberg (eds.), *Handbook of Adolescent Psychology*, vol. 1 (pp. 723–763). Wiley.

Chein, J., Albert, D., O'Brien, L., Uckert, K., & Steinberg, L. (2011). Peers increase adolescent risk taking by enhancing activity in the brain's reward circuitry. *Developmental Science*, 14(2), F1–F10.

Crone, E. A. (2009). Executive functions in adolescence: inferences from brain and behavior. *Developmental Science*, 12, 825–830.

Crone, E. A., Bunge, S. A., Van der Molen, M. W., & Ridderinkhof, K. R. (2006).

Switching between tasks and responses: a developmental study. *Developmental Science*, 9(3), 278–287.

Curtin, S., Heron, M., Miniño, A., & Warner, M. (2018). Recent increases in injury mortality among children and adolescents aged 10–19 years in the United States: 1999–2016. *National Vital Statistics Reports*, 67, 1–16.

Diamond, A. & Kirkham, N. Z. (2005). Not quite as grown-up as we like to think: parallels between cognition in childhood and adulthood. *Psychological Science*, 16(4), 291–297.

Engelmann, J. & Tomasello, M. (2019). Children's sense of fairness as equal respect. *Trends in Cognitive Sciences*, 23(6), 454–463.

Fischer, D. & Hills, T. (2012). The baby effect and young male syndrome: social influences on cooperative risk-taking in women and men. *Evolution and Human Behavior*, 33(5), 530–536.

Galvan, A., Hare, T., Voss, H., Glover, G., & Casey, B.J. (2008). Risk-taking and the adolescent brain: who is at risk? *Developmental Science*, 10(2), F8–F14.

GBD 2019 Adolescent Mortality Collaborators. (2021). Global, regional, and national mortality among young people aged 10–24 years, 1950–2019: a systematic analysis for the Global Burden of Disease Study 2019. *Lancet*, 398, 1593–1618.

GBD 2019 Adolescent Transport and Unintentional Injuries Collaborators. (2019). Adolescent transport and unintentional injuries: a systematic analysis using the Global Burden of Disease Study 2019. *The Lancet Public Health*, 7(8), e657–e669.

Gupta, R., Kar, B. R., & Srinivasan, N. (2009). Development of task switching and post-error-slowing in children. *Behaviour and Brain Function*, 5(1), 38.

Guthold, R., Baltag, V., Katwan, E., Lopez, G., Diaz, T., & Ross, D. A. (2019). The top global causes of adolescent mortality and morbidity by age and sex. *Journal of Adolescent Health*, 69(4), 540.

Habig, B., Chiyo, P. I., & Lahti, D. C. (2017). Male risk-taking is related to number of mates in a polygynous bird. *Behavioral Ecology*, 28(2), 541–548.

Huizenga, H. M., Crone, E. A., & Jansen, B. J. (2007). Decision-making in healthy children, adolescents and adults explained by the use of increasingly complex proportional reasoning rules. *Developmental Science*, 10(6), 814–825.

Ibbotson, P. (2014). Little dictators: a developmental meta-analysis of prosocial behavior. *Current Anthropology*, 55(6), 814–821.

Ibbotson, P. (2023). The development of executive function: mechanisms of change and functional pressures. *Journal of Cognition and Development*, 24(2), 172–190.

Ibbotson, P. & Roque-Gutierrez, E. (2023). The development of working memory: sex differences in accuracy and reaction times. *Journal of Cognition and Development*, 24(4), 581–597.

Kelley, A. E., Schochet, T., & Landry, C. F. (2004). Risk taking and novelty seeking in adolescence: introduction to part I. *Annals of the New York Academy of Sciences*, 1021, 27–32.

Kirkham, N. Z., Cruess, L., & Diamond, A. (2003). Helping children apply their knowledge to their behavior on a dimension-switching task. *Developmental Science*, 6, 449–467.

Kocevska, D., Lysen, T. S., Dotinga, A., et al. (2021). Sleep characteristics across the lifespan in 1.1 million people from the Netherlands, United Kingdom and

United States: a systematic review and meta-analysis. *Nature Human Behavior*, 5, 113–122.

Lendrem, B., Lendrem, D., Gray, A., & Isaacs, J. (2014). The Darwin Awards: sex differences in idiotic behaviour. *BMJ*, 349, g7094.

Lenroot, R. K., Gogtay, N., Greenstein, D. K., et al. (2007). Sexual dimorphism of brain developmental trajectories during childhood and adolescence. *Neuroimage*, 36(4), 1065–1073.

Luy, M. (2003). Causes of male excess mortality: insights from cloistered populations. *Population and Development Review*, 29, 647–676.

Moffitt, T. E., Arsenault, L., Belsky, D., et al. (2011). A gradient of childhood self-control predicts health, wealth, and public safety. *Proceedings of the National Academy of Sciences of the United States of America*, 108(7), 2693–2698.

Molleman, L., Ciranka, S., & van den Bos, W. (2022). Social influence in adolescence as a double-edged sword. *Proceedings of the Royal Society of London: B, Biological Sciences*, 289, 20220045.

Narr, R. K., Allen, J. P., Tan, J. S., & Loeb, E. L. (2019). Close friendship strength and broader peer group desirability as differential predictors of adult mental health. *Child Development*, 90, 298–313.

ONS. (2021). *UK Census, 2021*. Office of National Statistics.

Paluck, E. L. & Shepherd, H. (2012). The salience of social referents: a field experiment on collective norms and harassment behavior in a school social network. *Journal of Personality and Social Psychology*, 103, 899.

Reiter, A., Moutoussis, M., Vanes, L., et al. (2019). Taste uncertainty explains developmental effects on susceptibility to peer influence in adolescence. *Nature Communications*, 12, 3823.

Reyna, V. F. & Farley, F. (2006). Risk and rationality in adolescent decision making: implications for theory, practice, and public policy. *Psychological Science in the Public Interest*, 7(1), 1–44.

Rochelle, T. L., Yeung, D. K., Bond, M. H., & Li, L. M. W. (2015). Predictors of the gender gap in life expectancy across 54 nations. *Psychology, Health & Medicine*, 20, 129–138.

Salas-Rodríguez, J., Gómez-Jacinto, L., Hombrados-Mendieta, I., & Del Pino-Brunet, N. (2022). Applying an evolutionary approach of risk-taking behaviors in adolescents. *Frontiers in Psychology*, 12, 694134.

Santelli, J. S., DiClemente, R. J., Miller, K. S., & Kirby, D. (1999). Sexually transmitted diseases, unintended pregnancy, and adolescent health promotion. *Adolescent Medicine*, 10(1), 87–108.

Sebastian, C., Burnett, S., & Blakemore, S.-J. (2008). Development of the self-concept during adolescence. *Trends in Cognitive Sciences*, 12(11), 441–446.

Sebastian, C., Viding, E., Williams, K., & Blakemore, S.-J. (2010). Social brain development and the affective consequences of ostracism in adolescence, *Brain and Cognition*, 72(1), 134–145.

Sharman, R. & Illingworth, G. (2020). Adolescent sleep and school performance – the problem of sleepy teenagers, *Current Opinion in Physiology*, 15, 23–28.

Short, M., Bartel, K., & Carskadon, M. (2019). Sleep and mental health in children and adolescents. In M. A. Grandner (ed.), *Sleep and Health* (pp. 435–445). Academic Press.

Siegel, D. (2014). *Brainstorm: The Power and Purpose of the Teenage Brain*. Scribe UK.

Spear, L. P. (2000). The adolescent brain and age-related behavioral manifestations. *Neuroscience and Biobehavioral Reviews*, 24(4), 417–463.

Steinberg, L. (2008). A social neuroscience perspective on adolescent risk-taking. *Developmental Review*, 28(1), 78–106.

Tate, R., McDonald, S., & Lulham, J. M. (1998). Incidence of hospital-treated traumatic brain injury in an Australian community. *Australian and New Zealand Journal of Public Health*, 22(4), 419–423.

Trivers, R. L. (1972). Parental investment and sexual selection. In B. Campbell (ed.), *Sexual Selection and the Descent of Man, 1871–1971* (pp. 136–179). Aldine.

United Nations Statistics Division. (2006). *Demographic Yearbook 2006*. United Nations.

World Health Organization. (2020). Global Health Estimates. www.who.int/data/global-health-estimates

Zimring, F. E. (1998). *American Youth Violence*. Oxford University Press.

14 ARE YOUNG PEOPLE HAPPY?

 Learning Outcomes

After reading this chapter you will be able to:

- Describe the mix of emotions and attitudes adolescents have towards themselves and their lives.
- Understand the factors that cause unhappiness as well as those that promote well-being and buffer against adversity.
- Evaluate the emotional opportunities and risks of adolescence.

14.1 Introduction

The United Nations Convention on the Rights of the Child obliges states to protect children from acts that would cause extreme unhappiness, such violence, abuse, neglect, or cruel treatment (UN General Assembly, 1989). If governments assume that their purpose is to maximise happiness, this profoundly changes the way they view their citizens' health (particularly their mental health), the quality of their work lives, their family lives, and their communities (Helliwell et al., 2023). Along with life and liberty, the US Constitution regards the pursuit of happiness as a self-evident truth and an inalienable right of all people. Ask most parents what they want for their children and 'to be happy' is a common reply. But are young people happy, what concerns them, and what factors can promote their well-being?

14.2 The Benefits of Asking and Listening

One obvious way to find out how young people feel is to ask them and listen to what they say. While an obvious idea, it is not always the first option people think of. Too often we – parents, families, researchers, educators, and broader society – assume we already know the answers, and when adolescents do speak, they are either not heard or their feelings are dismissed as unimportant, self-indulgent, or just a passing phase (World Health Organization, 2022). By contrast, Jeffrey Arnett and Joseph Schwab (2012) did ask 1,029

Table 14.1 Adolescent responses in the study by Arnett and Schwab (2012).

How does life feel?	% that somewhat or strongly agreed
This time of my life is fun and exciting	83%
This time of my life is full of changes	83%
Overall, I am satisfied with my life	81%
At this time of my life, I feel I have a great deal of freedom	73%
This time of my life is stressful	72%
This time of my life is full of uncertainty	64%
I often feel anxious	56%
I often feel depressed	32%
I often feel that my life is not going well	30%

Source: Arnett, J. & Schwab, J. (2012). The Clark University poll of emerging adults: Thriving, struggling, and hopeful. Worcester, MA: Clark University.

adolescents how they felt about themselves and their lives and recorded their responses. Adolescents' answers revealed a fascinating combination of emotions (**Table 14.1**).

So, are young people happy? It is a mixed picture. The vast majority felt that they had freedom and were satisfied, and that life was fun, exciting, and full of changes. At the same time, a significant proportion were stressed, anxious, and uncertain, with almost a third feeling depressed and that life was not going well. There were several factors that influenced this overall picture. In general, those who were younger and from poorer economic circumstances were more likely to identify with negative aspects of this time of life. And in line with other studies across the lifespan, females were more likely than males to report that they felt anxious or depressed, a difference that is apparent by age 12 (Hyde & Mezulis, 2020).

 Key Point

- Young people report a complex mixture of emotions and attitudes towards themselves and their lives.

The Arnett and Schwab (2012) study was based on a sample of American young adults, albeit one that was representative of the broader population in terms of sex, ethnicity, economic circumstances, and geographical location. To get a more global perspective on what concerns adolescents, researchers from the World Health Organization (WHO) conducted 71 focus-group sessions with adolescents aged 10–19 in Belgium, Chile, China, the Democratic Republic of the Congo, Egypt, Indonesia, Jamaica, Jordan, Kenya, Malawi, Sweden, Switzerland, and the USA (WHO, 2022). They asked adolescents to talk about their greatest emotional and behavioural challenges and explain how they are shaped – for better and worse – by family, friends, and teachers. The following are some of the key themes that emerged from their responses, along with example quotes from the adolescents that took part in the survey.

Theme 1: While families can be a tremendous source of support, comfort, and understanding, they can pose significant risks to well-being where there is abuse and neglect, pressure and control, and financial instability.

From an older boy in Jamaica:

[It] is a good relationship with their parents that alone can defend them from anything in the outside world because they know that when they come home, they can come home to mom or dad and say, 'This is what happened today, I don't know what to do.' ... Having this strong relationship with their parents ... [they] have the belief in themselves that they are okay, they're safe [and] ... nothing can bother that.

From an older girl in Jamaica:

I believe that we need the support from our parents. We need to have a close ... relationship with our parents to know that they're always there for us, like we can talk to them about anything and not be judged.

From a younger boy in Egypt:

Sometimes fathers force their sons to work with them and if their sons fail to do that work, they shout at them and start to insult them. These kids appear normal from the outside like nothing happened, but from inside they are hurting badly.

From an older girl in Switzerland:

Parents also put pressure .... If there are problems with school or academics, and the parents are always asking for more, and finally the person is more and more stressed, it creates a type of vicious cycle without solutions.

Theme 2: Peers who are understanding, trustworthy, honest, attuned to emotions, easy to talk to, and good at listening without judgement can be powerful buffers against distress and isolation. At the same time, the importance of peer relationships to adolescents makes them especially vulnerable if those relationships go wrong.

From an older girl in Sweden:

If you don't have a good relationship with your parents ... you might turn to friends, or maybe siblings who are of an equal age because they maybe can understand [you] better. Because I think ... that [many adults] don't understand because ... they are adults. Because they are older, they are in a different place in life.

From an older girl in Indonesia:

Not all of us can have that close bond with our family. Not all families are as open and as welcoming. So, if your family is unable to be your protector, then we should find something that can ... make us happy and comfortable .... For example, our friends.

From a younger girl in Malawi:

> Bad friends too can make it hard because when you confide in them, they can also tell other people and it results in the issue being known to everyone .... It is really hard to decide who to confide in, so you just harbour it in your heart.

From an older girl in Switzerland:

> There is a huge pressure. Sometimes, the first parties where there are alcohol and drugs, it is in fashion in a way. If you do not want to use it, you get judged by others ... and you tell yourself, 'Yes, but if I don't do it, I am going to be perceived as not being cool or open minded.' You are kind of stuck.

Theme 3: Despite the many benefits of school, including boosting self-esteem, attending a place that fosters greater awareness of the world, and an environment for spending time with friends, adolescents frequently mention the risks of high academic pressure and unsupportive and abusive teachers.

From a younger girl in Jamaica:

> I think school kinda helps most of us children because sometimes we can get away from the toxic household and we can actually be with friends that make us happy.

From an older boy in Sweden:

> If you feel quite sad, it is good to go to the school counsellor. Because it can be good with someone you do not know, who has a duty of confidentiality.

From an older boy in Jamaica:

> You have teachers that would belittle students ... like tell them, 'Oh, you dunce.' ... The student is not doing well in the class or [will] like just stop learning overall, like shut down completely because of all that emotional abuse.

From an older boy in Kenya:

> If you come from Korogocho ghetto, you know Korogocho does not have a good name. So, when you are in school, and the teachers look at you, they despise you. If he is giving a bad example, he will always be referring to you. That will make you feel very bad.

These experiences show that, much like adolescents' overall happiness, what adolescents are concerned about is also a mixed picture. Many of the conflicting emotions that adolescents express towards other people, groups, and institutions pre-empt the complex social world we recognise as adults: families can be a psychological haven if parents genuinely care about what is going on in teenagers' lives, are able to listen to them without judgement, and help them solve their problems. However, families also have the potential to be a destructive influence through uncaring attitudes, abuse, neglect, controlling behaviours, and financial instability. When friendships are working well, a strong social network can be a source of comfort and act as a protective buffer against stress. When these relationships are unstable, they can expose adolescents to betrayals of trust, bullying, and pressure to engage in risky behaviours. At their best learning environments are sources of support, inspiration, safety, and socialisation, but at their worst they can be sources of abuse and extreme academic pressure.

 Key Point

- Family, peers, and school can both protect and harm adolescents' emotional well-being depending on the individual circumstances.

 Watch the One-Minute Method.

Discover how researchers use interviews and focus groups to get an in-depth understanding of people's experiences.

14.3 What Helps Well-Being

Having listened to the concerns of adolescents, it is natural to want to understand those concerns a little deeper and wonder what can be done to help improve their well-being.

In Chapter 1 we saw that the environment matters for emotional well-being, but that it matters more for some children than others. This is because some children are predisposed to be more sensitive to environmental *differences*, both good and bad. Another way to think about this is that different children in the *same* environment vary in their risk of developing emotional problems. If the environment is the same for children, then the variation in well-being can't be pinned on the conditions that surround them – it must be coming from somewhere else. One likely candidate that explains a proportion of adolescents' well-being is variation in their genetics. It is sometimes said that parents of one child believe in the role of the environment, but parents of two children believe in the role of genetics, based on the observation that parents are often surprised by how different their second child is from their first despite being raised in a similar environment. In Chapter 13 we saw that all psychological traits show heritability, and mental health is no different. For example, depression typically has heritability rates of between 30% and 50% (Kendall et al., 2021). To remind ourselves of what that means: 30–50% of the *differences* between people in terms of depressive traits is explained by *differences* in their genes.

 Key Point

- Adolescent well-being is partially heritable.

But we also know that no traits are completely heritable, and depression is no different either; its heritability doesn't get close to 100%. There are a range of environmental factors that can dampen down or aggravate these predispositions, which is clear to see from the responses adolescents gave to the WHO questionnaire we looked at in the previous section (WHO, 2022).

There will also be individual differences in the events that adolescents experience, such as illness, bereavement, and natural disasters, which make life more or less challenging. While these factors are largely beyond the control of any individual, there are also a number of personal assets that are particularly important in predicting positive adolescent outcomes. The Developmental Assets Profile measures such characteristics of young people, and data from more than 30 countries show that the more of the following assets adolescents identify with, the better their well-being (Scales et al., 2015):

- I feel good about my future (positive identity).
- I think it is important to help other people (positive values).
- I feel safe and secure where I currently live (empowerment).
- I resolve conflicts without anyone getting hurt (social competencies).
- I am actively engaged in learning new things (commitment to learning).
- I am involved in a religious group or activity (constructive use of time).
- I participate in music, dance, art, sports, or other play (constructive use of time).
- I am involved in meaningful tasks (empowerment).
- I am eager to do well in school (commitment to learning).
- I have friends who set good examples for me (boundaries and expectations).
- I have adults who are good role models for me (boundaries and expectations).
- I have support from teachers and adults, other than my parents (support).
- I have family that gives me love and support (support).

While there might be no surprises on this list, it is important to have evidence of precisely what supports well-being and what are the protective buffers against adversity, not least because this information can be used to identify those teenagers most likely to need help (**Figure 14.1**). For example, the Developmental Assets Profile was given to 10–18-year-old Syrian refugees in Iraq, Jordan, and Lebanon and those areas of the Philippines that had been destroyed by Typhoon Haiyan in 2013. How young people responded was a good indicator of how they were coping in the face of adversity, and, in general, the more of these assets children identified with, the better they fared in a humanitarian crisis or a natural disaster (Scales et al., 2015).

 Key Point

- There are a range of personal assets that can support young people's well-being and act as protective buffers against adversity.

There is one final message that comes from adolescents themselves regarding what helps their well-being. Adolescents report frequently masking their mental health struggles, in part because they worry that their feelings and experiences will be invalidated by friends and family. The stigma and taboo around mental health deter adolescents from seeking help for mental health conditions because they feel ashamed or embarrassed. The following are

Figure 14.1 A boy wanders through the destruction caused by Typhoon Haiyan in the Philippines. In general, the more personal assets young people identify with, the better able they are to cope with adversity. Source: Associated Press/Alamy Stock Photo.

some more quotes from the previously discussed WHO survey of adolescents from around the world that illustrate the point (2022).

From an older girl in Chile:

> When I was younger, I did express my feelings much more, but they were not validated.... I could say, 'I have depression' or 'I feel sad,' and they would say, 'No, you don't know what you feel because you are 12 years old.'

From an older girl in Jamaica:

> It's hard for me to open up to my family because they don't make enough time to talk to me or to understand how I feel about certain situations like, they're making choices for me and not giving me the chance to say whether I want this or I want that.

From an older boy in Switzerland:

> I think we have a hard time with mental health as youth because we do not talk enough about it, because people are scared to talk about it. Maybe if we ... [could] express ourselves more without feeling judged or assaulted, maybe we would make some progress.

From an older boy in China:

> If you have psychological counselling [at school], sometimes the conversation may take a long time .... If you go out for a long time, your teacher will wonder: why did you have to

go for so long? Where did you go? Why did you go to the mental room? Do you have a mental problem?

The desire of these adolescents to discuss their feelings without fear of being exposed, free of judgement, and with trustworthy, empathic others aligns well with two other strands of research on mental health. First, we know that one of the most powerful predictors of well-being is having reliable access to a supportive social network of friends and family. Research conducted with 13-year-old boys and girls across 35 countries showed that having **social capital** in the form of dependable and compassionate friends and family was a much better predictor of teenagers' life satisfaction than national income, income equality, or family affluence (Levin et al., 2011). Second, there is evidence to suggest that when people do reach out for help and receive some sort of psychological therapy, the specific type of therapy they receive makes less difference than the presence of a compassionate, judgement-free, confidential therapist and the patient being committed to change – or, in other words, it is the quality of the relationship that matters most (Wampold et al., 2002).

Key Point

- Adults can help adolescents by providing more validation of their experiences, and they can reduce the stigma around reporting mental health difficulties by listening without judgement and in confidence.

One question can change everything.

UNICEF has teamed up with spoken word artist @clickfortaz in support of adolescents living with a mental health condition.

14.4 Goodness of Fit

An important factor in predicting well-being is how well the individual characteristics of children and adolescents align with the demands or expectations of the environment, or what is known as **goodness of fit** (Thomas & Chess, 1977). Take shyness, for example: the same socially reticent and withdrawn child might experience two very different childhoods depending on the circumstances they are born into. On average, people from North America are more likely to evaluate shyness negatively, regarding it as a sign of passivity and low assertiveness and in conflict with the values of being outgoing and friendly. Consequently, a shy child is more likely to receive parenting that steers them towards these desired values, sometimes with negative consequences. For example, some parents in these circumstances respond to shyness by controlling, being overprotective, and micro-managing a child's behaviour – a pattern of parental behaviour that can begin in infancy and extend well into adolescence (Hastings et al., 2010). In contrast to North American parents, Chinese parents tend to evaluate shyness in more positive terms, regarding it as a sign of emotional maturity and aligning with Confucian values of self-restraint and modesty. A shy child in these circumstances is less likely to receive parenting that tries to steer them towards different behaviours because they already fit those values of society. The case of *malu*, a highly esteemed form of shame amongst the Minangkabau caregivers (see Chapter 2), provides another example of how cultural beliefs around child-rearing will influence how much parents are willing to tolerate certain behaviours or want to change them.

We know that the values, customs, and beliefs of cultures evolve over time and vary from place to place. We also know that a proportion of our personality, such as how extroverted or introverted we are, is heritable (Chapter 12). So, through the lottery of history and genetics, if children are born in a time and place where their predispositions are valued, then it might make it easier for them to feel good about themselves. Conversely, if they have the misfortune to live in a time and place where there is a strong mismatch between their temperament and the environment, this is going to potentially make life more difficult. In Chapter 15 we will explore further how the same depressive symptoms are experienced differently depending on what different societies value.

 Key Point

- An important factor in predicting well-being is the goodness of fit between the individual characteristics of children and the demands or expectations of the environment.

Another arena of adolescents' lives where goodness of fit plays out is gender. Much like shyness, gender norms vary from place to place and have changed over the course of history. Today the gendered behaviours, expressions, personalities, and identities of children and adolescents are subjects of intense public debate and scrutiny. But this is just the latest example of a much longer progression in the way we think about gender. Women in ancient Athens could not vote, be a judge, hold government office, or decide for themselves who to marry, and they were legally owned by their fathers or husbands. For modern-day Athenian women, all of these norms have now flipped in the opposite direction, to the benefit of everyone. Today, norms around gender continue to change, but not fast enough for some adolescents. Adolescents report that labouring under entrenched gender norms can create an unhealthy mismatch between what society values and how they feel. Both boys and girls pay the price for this lack of fit, but they do so in different ways. In some societies boys feel the pressure to be tough and never to express their feelings, and some girls are subject to inequitable standards that devalue their lives or curtail their freedoms (WHO, 2022).

From a younger boy in Switzerland:

> Mental health is more dangerous in boys than girls because boys cannot talk about it and ... well, they close themselves off, they never speak of it, and after a while it starts to eat at them.

From an older boy in the USA:

> We all have problems, but guys are supposed to be like robots and people think we can't have feelings.

From an older girl in Egypt:

> I wish to work and have my own independent personality and I don't want to depend on my family in everything or to get married to someone who wants to control me as he wishes .... I wish to live a different way but the society and the whole world is surrounding me with something I don't know, and I feel disabled.

Some adolescents identify with a different gender from the sex they were assigned at birth, or as neither male nor female, or as both, or as a gender identity that is beyond conventional classification all together. More fluid and non-binary identities and presentations have been documented across all recorded history (Feinberg, 1996), although recently gender-diverse identities have become more evident in mainstream awareness. Research has demonstrated that transgender and non-binary adolescents are at greater risk of stigmatisation, victimisation, and bullying (James et al., 2016), with gender-diverse youth having higher rates of anxiety, depression, and self-harm, and they are disproportionately more likely to commit suicide than the heteronormative majority (Newcomb et al., 2020).

Research also suggests that some of the most effective ways to promote well-being in this context are: to create safe and supportive spaces for all youth to give voice to diverse experiences of gender identity and expression; to educate peers, schools, communities, and families (many of whom still have a fundamentally binary notion of gender) about the validity of transgender and non-binary identities; and to provide youth with access to supportive and informed care (Diamond, 2020).

Returning to the concept of goodness of fit: if adolescents have a temperament towards depression but are born in a time and place where these feelings are taboo; if they have a temperament towards independence but are born in a time when and place where they are expected to be subservient to others; or if they have a temperament towards fluid gender identity but are born in a time and place that expects binary conformity – then life can be made more difficult by others who victimise or misunderstand them or deny who they are. In general, the better the fit, the better the chances of psychological well-being and life satisfaction (Chess & Thomas, 1999).

How does social media affect adolescent well-being? This question captures a fast-changing research area, and the long-term consequences of social media use in this group are still unclear, but **Box 14.1** explores some of what we do understand.

 Box 14.1 Social media

Social media has been an integral part of many Western adolescents' lives for decades, with a third of the world's population estimated to have a social media account. As of 2023, social media users were sharing 6.9 billion images on WhatsApp, 1.3 billion images on Instagram, and 350 million images on Facebook every single day (Broz, 2023). Despite the relatively recent rise of social media, research suggests that teenagers' online behaviour is generally a reflection of their offline behaviour (boyd, 2014). For example, if they are popular offline, then they are more likely to be popular online; if they are bullied offline, then they are more likely to be bullied online. Media scholar danah boyd, who has spent thousands of hours observing teenagers' online behaviour, concluded that teenagers use social media to do what they have always done: establish friendships, distance themselves from parents, flirt, gossip, bully, experiment, and rebel (boyd, 2014).

When asked about their own opinions, about two-thirds of adolescents agree that social media helps to maintain or widen their friendship circle, is a source of recreation and relaxation, helps to develop their career prospects, can raise awareness of important social issues, can foster a sense of community and belonging, and protects against loneliness. At the same time, half of adolescents also agreed that social media can be a waste of their time, gets in the way of physical or outdoor activities, and interferes with sleep, eating, and other daily routines (Abraham, 2020). Of particular concern, to parents and researchers at least, is whether social media use increases the likelihood of depression and anxiety. The double-edged nature of social media, reflected in adolescents' attitudes, is also reflected in the research. Some studies have found a negative association between social media use and mental health (Twenge, 2020), some research has found a positive association (Fredrick et al., 2022), and some research has found no association at all (Jensen et al., 2019).

Beyond these associations, a key question is whether using social media in a certain way *causes* poor mental health, such as simply by leaving less time for face-to-face interaction – something we know is a protective buffer against depression (Lee et al., 2019). Or, could it be that poor mental health causes people to use social media in certain ways? For example, adolescents with a tendency towards depression might be more likely to seek out negative feedback from others to confirm their own negative self-concept, reinforcing a downward spiral of mood (Hames et al., 2013).

Using a clever research design, Silje Steinsbekk and her colleagues (2023) were able to tease apart these possibilities by following 800 children in Trondheim, Norway, between the ages of 10 and 16, measuring them every 2 years on anxiety and depression symptoms as well as on their social media use (**Figure 14.2**). By repeatedly testing the same children over time, the researchers were able to determine whether behaviour at an earlier point in development predicted behaviour at a later time.

When they did this over a period of 6 years, they found no evidence supporting either cause-and-effect possibility: the frequency of posting, liking, and commenting was unrelated to future symptoms of anxiety and depression, and the symptoms of anxiety and depression did not impact future social media use. The results were the same for boys and girls. In a separate study that included almost 1 million participants across 72 countries, it was also found that social media use was unrelated to well-being (Matti & Przybylski, 2023).

From this research we cannot conclude that there are no negative aspects of social media use. Previous generations of teenagers did not have to worry about a permanent record of an embarrassing post that might haunt them later on in life. As a consequence, many legislators are considering the 'right to be forgotten'; for example, the European Union proposed that individuals should be allowed to 'determine the development of their life in an autonomous

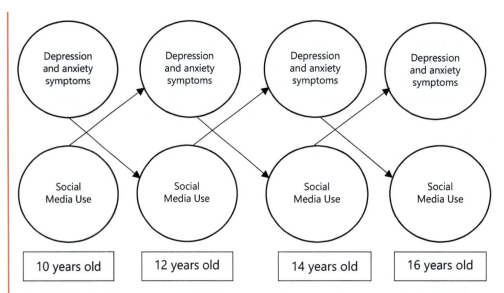

Figure 14.2 A simplified version of Steinsbekk and colleagues' experimental design (2023). Source: Steinsbekk, S et al. Social media behaviors and symptoms of anxiety and depression. A four-wave cohort study from age 10–16 years. This material is available under a Creative Commons-by licence. https://creativecommons.org/licenses/by/4.0/.

way, without being perpetually or periodically stigmatized as a consequence of a specific action performed in the past' (Mantelero, 2013). For many of us it is not hard to think of a 'specific action' from our own adolescence that we are happy to forget.

What we can conclude from this research is that we should change the questions we ask. The question is not 'is social media bad?', but 'who is particularly vulnerable and who benefits from social media, and in what ways?'. For example, although the lack of physical cues and contact may represent disadvantages for some individuals with depression, for other people – with social anxiety, for example – online social interaction may be less distressing than face-to-face interaction, and preferable as a result (Erliksson et al., 2020). Researchers must also consider that the impacts of social media on mental health might not be the same across development, with certain age groups or sexes being especially sensitive to such impacts (**Figure 14.3**; Orben & Blakemore, 2023; Orben et al., 2022).

> **Key Point**
>
> - Adolescents are aware of the risks and benefits of social media use, and research to date does not suggest that social media use strongly causes adolescent depression and anxiety.

14.5 Risks and Opportunities

Psychologist Jeffrey Arnett, who has spent his career studying the lives of young people and the transition to adulthood, has argued that adolescence presents a number of unique challenges, as well as opportunities, for well-being (Arnett, 2000):

Figure 14.3 Many adolescents around the world do not know a world without smartphones, and in the future they may not consider them as technology, in same the way that older generations no longer consider books as technology. Source: Rawpixel.com/Shutterstock.

- Feeling 'in-between' life phases, young people no longer see themselves as children or adolescents, but nor do they see themselves as full adults either, with the financial independence and personal responsibility that adulthood entails. This can create a feeling of camaraderie with other young people, as only they 'get' what it feels like to be this age. But fully identifying neither as an adolescent nor as an adult risks them feeling that they don't really belong anywhere or haven't found their place yet.
- Feeling that adolescence is an age of possibilities, young people can direct their lives in a number of different directions. This can be exciting and liberating, but knowing that decisions might have some big consequences further down the line can be daunting, and too much choice can be overwhelming.
- Feeling self-focused, young people are busy looking inwards, exploring their identities in work, love, and world views. This can be a period of great personal growth and exploration, but too much self-absorption, or not accepting some of the obligations of adulthood, risks them becoming detached or alienated from others.
- Feeling life is unstable, young people can experience this period of life as a period of great change in education, work, residential status, and social relationships. It is a time of firsts: first romantic feelings, first menstrual period, and the first awareness that not all families are the same. Living through so many different transitions, both inside and out, can positively inform who you are; however, it can sometimes be difficult to maintain a stable sense of self.

 Key Point

- The transition into adulthood presents a set of risks and opportunities for well-being.

In a chapter that has explored some of the negative aspects of adolescent mental health, it is important to conclude with a sense of balance on the issue. Recall that the WHO questionnaire asked adolescents to talk about 'their greatest emotional and behavioural challenges', so it's natural that the responses were negatively biased. Most adolescents, however, report that they feel satisfied, free, and that life is fun, exciting, and full of changes. Some 77% agree with the statement that 'my life will be better than my parents' lives have been'; 89% agree that 'I am confident that eventually I will get what I want out of life'; and 83% agree that 'at this time of my life, it still seems like anything is possible' (Arnett & Schwab, 2012).

Although stressful events increase the chances of negative mental health outcomes, most people who experience stressful events do not develop psychological illness as a result. This goes for events that happen to most people, such as losing a valued relationship, and for less common traumatic events, such as experiencing physical abuse (Bonanno et al., 2011; Cohen et al., 2019). The WHO estimates that, globally, 1 in 7 (14%) 10–19-year-olds experience a mental health condition such as depression and anxiety. While a significant minority, this means that most adolescents do not have a mental health condition.

There are two final points that follow from this. First, the reported incidence of mental health problems is likely to underestimate the true rate. As we have heard from adolescents themselves, they generally worry that they would face harsh judgement or ostracism from their friends or family if they disclosed how they truly feel. Also, the stigma and taboo around mental health deter adolescents from seeking help and encourage them to mask their symptoms (WHO, 2022). Second, acknowledging that most adolescents feel satisfied, optimistic, and excited about the future does not invalidate the experiences of those in distress or the attempts to alleviate their suffering.

Adolescents with mental health conditions are particularly vulnerable to social exclusion, discrimination, educational difficulties, risk-taking behaviours, physical ill health, and human rights violations. Because of the stigma or fear of ridicule that prevents adolescents from asking for help, many adolescents are forced to cope on their own, often using maladaptive strategies such as substance abuse. For those who do reach out for professional help, services are often inadequately funded: globally, about 2% of government health budgets are allocated to mental health spending, with some of the poorest countries spending less than 1 USD per person per year (UNICEF, 2021).

As we have seen, adolescents are quite adept at identifying the risks and opportunities they face, and they often have the creativity and optimism to find their own solutions to their problems if they are given the time and space to do so and if they feel their voices are heard.

Talking Point

Throughout the book we have seen how our evolutionary past has been a powerful force in shaping our childhood. When it comes to happiness, however, we can't count on any help from natural selection. It does not care about happiness or misery per se. It works directly on reproduction and survival, and survival matters because it's hard to reproduce when you are dead. From a biological point of view, there is no reason why the arc of history should bend towards greater happiness. Indeed, the opposite may be true: the Agricultural and Industrial

Revolutions might have quite unintentionally, and without any individual to blame, made us all more miserable (Harari, 2015).

Even when there is no mismatch between our lives today and those of our foraging ancestors, there is no guarantee of happiness. To assume so would be a **naturalistic fallacy**, which means just what it says: it is an error to assume that just because something is natural it is good for us. Cancer is 'natural' in this sense, and it has shared a long enough history with humans that we have developed adaptations for responding to it, such as an immune system that removes cancer cells from our bodies on a regular basis. From this no one would conclude that cancer is good for us or that medicines designed to eliminate cancer are bad.

The 'natural' environment that constituted 97% of our prehistory regularly presented children with food scarcity and insecurity, war, disease, infanticide, violence, predation, and cognitive and social deprivation (Frankenhuis & Amir, 2022). Throughout this period, it is estimated that women gave birth to an average of six children over their lifetimes, yet population growth was close to zero for thousands of years (Gurven & Davison, 2019). If women were giving birth to so many children, why did we not see an explosion in our population? There are several possible answers, but one of the most plausible is that most children died young. What we can learn from this is that the expected environment for childhood can at times be an adverse environment too, one that is not guaranteed to make us healthier, happier, or more satisfied.

What about in more recent history? Archaeological evidence suggests that thousands of years ago children were routinely used in religious sacrifices and buried in the walls of buildings to 'strengthen' their foundations (Offit, 2015). The ancient societies of Greece and Rome, who did much to advance ethics, art, philosophy, and science, also saw no problem in selling children as slaves for domestic work or prostitution or in using them as collateral for loans (Forsdyke, 2021). Across much of Europe the killing of an infant who was sick, deformed, one of twins, illegitimate, a girl, or otherwise unwanted was not only common but legal until the Romans outlawed in 374 CE (Obladen, 2016).

By the late eighteenth century children were being used as a cheap and disposable source of labour in mines, factories, and agriculture – ideal employees for industrialists who could pay them less than adults as they were less likely to organise unions (Kirby, 2013). Around this time, some enlightened thinkers like Jean-Jacques Rousseau were beginning to argue that children are important in their own right and not merely as a means to an end (although that didn't stand in the way of him putting all five of his children in foundling homes so that they would not interfere with his work). In case we think that these days are behind us, around 450 million children today – 1 in 6 of all children – live in areas of high conflict (Save the Children, 2022), and the International Labour Organization estimates that 1.2 million children are trafficked each year, with boys mainly used for forced labour and girls for sexual exploitation (International Labour Organization, 2002). So it's hard to find much support for the supposed golden age of childhood, one in which children are universally happy.

Asking the very question 'are young people happy?' might unduly elevate the pursuit of pleasure above other emotions. Centuries of philosophical, religious, and literary wisdom suggest that the direct pursuit of happiness usually backfires, and that it is best approached via the backdoor of self-discovery, enlightenment, and the alleviation of suffering. But the fact that our happiness is not a historical or biological inevitability should give extra reason to cherish it as a precious commodity when it does occur – and because childhood can last a lifetime, the happiness of our children has profound effects on the adults they become.

Summary

- Young people report a complex mixture of emotions and attitudes towards themselves and their lives.
- Family, peers, and school can both protect and harm adolescents' emotional well-being depending on the individual circumstances.
- Adolescent well-being is partially heritable.
- There are a range of personal assets that can support young people's well-being and act as protective buffers against adversity.
- Adults can help adolescents by providing more validation of their experiences, and they can reduce the stigma around reporting mental health difficulties by listening without judgement and in confidence.
- An important factor in predicting well-being is the goodness of fit between the individual characteristics of children and the demands or expectations of the environment.
- Adolescents are aware of the risks and benefits of social media use, and research to date does not suggest that social media use strongly causes adolescent depression and anxiety.
- The transition into adulthood presents a set of risks and opportunities for well-being.

References

Abraham, B. (2020). Attitude of adolescents towards use of social media. *International Journal of Advanced Research*, 8(2), 443–453.

Arnett, J. (2000). Emerging adulthood: a theory of development from the late teens through the twenties. *American Psychologist*, 55(5), 469–480.

Arnett, J. & Schwab, J. (2012). *The Clark University Poll of Emerging Adults: Thriving, Struggling, and Hopeful*. Clark University.

Bonanno, G. A., Westphal, M., & Mancini, A. D. (2011). Resilience to loss and potential trauma. *Annual Review of Clinical Psychology*, 7, 511–535.

boyd, d. (2014). *It's Complicated: The Social Lives of Networked Teens*. Yale University Press.

Broz, M. (2023). Photo Statistics: How Many Photos are Taken Every Day? https://photutorial.com/photos-statistics

Chess, S. & Thomas, A. (1999). *Goodness of Fit: Clinical Applications, From Infancy through Adult Life*. Routledge.

Cohen, S., Murphy, M. L. M., & Prather, A. A. (2019). Ten surprising facts about stressful life events and disease risk. *Annual Review of Psychology*, 70, 577–597.

Diamond, L. M. (2020). Gender fluidity and nonbinary gender identities among children and adolescents. *Child Development Perspectives*, 14, 110–115.

Erliksson, O., Lindner, P., & Mortberg, E. (2020). Measuring associations between social anxiety and use of different types of social media using the Swedish Social Anxiety Scale for Social Media Users: a psychometric evaluation and cross-sectional study. *Scandinavian Journal of Psychology*, 61(6), 819–826.

Feinberg, L. (1996). *Transgender Warriors: Making History from Joan of Arc to Dennis Rodman*. Beacon Press.

Forsdyke, S. (2021). *Slaves and Slavery in Ancient Greece*. Key Themes in Ancient History. Cambridge University Press.

Frankenhuis, W. & Amir, D. (2022). What is the expected human childhood? Insights from evolutionary anthropology. *Development and Psychopathology*, 34(2), 473–497.

Fredrick, S., Nickerson, A., & Livingston, J. (2022). Adolescent social media use: Pitfalls and promises in relation to cyber-victimization, friend support, and depressive symptoms. *Journal of Youth and Adolescence*, 51(2), 361–376.

Gurven, M. D. & Davison, R. J. (2019). Periodic catastrophes over human evolutionary history are necessary to explain the forager population paradox. *Proceedings of the National Academy of Sciences of the United States of America*, 116, 12758–12766.

Hames, J. L., Hagan, C. R., & Joiner, T. E. (2013). Interpersonal processes in depression. *Annual Review of Clinical Psychology*, 9, 355–377.

Harari, N. Y. (2015). *Sapiens: A Brief History of Humankind*. Harper.

Hastings, P. D., Nuselovici, J. N., Rubin, K. H., & Cheah, C. S. L. (2010). Shyness, parenting, and parent–child relationships. In K. H. Rubin & R. J. Coplan (eds.), *The Development of Shyness and Social Withdrawal* (pp. 107–130). The Guilford Press.

Helliwell, J. F., Layard, R., Sachs, J. D., Aknin, L. B., De Neve, J.-E., & Wang, S. (eds.). (2023). *World Happiness Report 2023*, 11th edition. Sustainable Development Solutions Network.

Hyde, J. S. & Mezulis, A. H. (2020). Gender differences in depression: biological, affective, cognitive, and sociocultural factors. *Harvard Review of Psychiatry*, 28(1), 4–13.

International Labour Organization. (2002). *Every Child Counts: New Global Estimates on Child Labour*. ILO.

James, S. E., Herman, J. L., Rankin, S., Keisling, M., Mottet, L., & Anafi, M. (2016). The report of the 2015 U.S. transgender survey. www.transequality.org/sites/default/files/docs/USTS-Full-Report-FINAL.PDF

Jensen, M., George, M., Russell, M., & Odgers, C. (2019). Young adolescents' digital technology use and mental health symptoms: Little evidence of longitudinal or daily linkages. *Clinical Psychological Science*, 7(6), 1416–1433.

Kendall, K., Van Assche, E., Andlauer, T., Choi, K., Luykx, J., Schulte, E., & Lu, Y. (2021). The genetic basis of major depression. *Psychological Medicine*, 51(13), 2217–2230.

Kirby, P. (2013). *Child Workers and Industrial Health in Britain*. Boydell & Brewer Ltd.

Lee, M., Murphy, K., & Andrews, G. (2019). Using media while interacting face-to-face is associated with psychosocial well-being and personality traits. *Psychological Reports*, 122(3), 944–967.

Levin, K. A., Torsheim, T., Vollebergh, W., et al. (2011). National income and income inequality, family affluence and life satisfaction among 13 year old boys and girls: a multilevel study in 35 countries. *Social Indicators Research*, 104(2), 179–194.

Mantelero, A. (2013). The EU Proposal for a General Data Protection Regulation and the roots of the 'right to be forgotten'. *Computer Law & Security Review*, 29(3), 229–235.

Matti, V. & Przybylski, A. (2023). Estimating the association between Facebook adoption and well-being in 72 countries. *Royal Society Open Science*, 10(8), 221451.

Newcomb, M. E., Hill, R., Buehler, K., Ryan, D. T., Whitton, S. W., & Mustanski, B. (2020). High burden of mental health problems, substance use, violence, and related psychosocial factors, in transgender, non-binary, and gender diverse youth and young adult. *Archives of Sexual Behavior*, 49, 645–659.

Obladen, M. (2016). From right to sin: laws on infanticide in antiquity. *Neonatology*, 109(1), 56–61.

Offit, P. (2015). *Bad Faith: When Religious Belief Undermines Modern Medicine*. Basic Books.

Orben, A. & Blakemore, S. J. (2023). How social media affects teen mental health: a missing link. *Nature*, 614(7948), 410–412.

Orben, A., Przybylski, A. K., Blakemore, S. J., & Kievit, R. A. (2022). Windows of developmental sensitivity to social media. *Nature Communications*, 13(1), 1649.

Save the Children. (2022). *Stop the War on Children: The Forgotten Ones*. Save the Children.

Scales, P.C., Roehlkepartain, E.C., Wallace, T., Inselman, A., Stephenson, P., & Rodriguez, M. (2015). Brief report: assessing youth well-being in global emergency settings: early results from the Emergency Developmental Assets Profile. *Journal of Adolescence*, 45, 98–102.

Steinsbekk, S., Nesi, J., & Wichstrøm, L. (2023). Social media behaviors and symptoms of anxiety and depression. A four-wave cohort study from age 10–16 years. *Computers in Human Behavior*, 147, 202.

Thomas, A. & Chess, S. (1977). *Temperament and Development*. Brunner/Mazel.

Twenge, J. (2020). Why increases in adolescent depression may be linked to the technological environment. *Current Opinion in Psychology*, 32, 89–94.

UN General Assembly. (1989). *Convention on the Rights of the Child*, 20 November 1989, United Nations, Treaty Series, vol. 1577, p. 3.

UNICEF. (2021). *The State of the World's Children 2021*. World Health Organisation.

Wampold, B. E., Minami, T., Baskin, T. W., & Callen Tierney, S. (2002). A meta-(re)analysis of the effects of cognitive therapy versus 'other therapies' for depression. *Journal of Affective Disorders*, 68(2–3), 159–165.

World Health Organization. (2022). *On My Mind: How Adolescents Experience and Perceive Mental Health Around the World*. A companion report to The State of the World's Children 2021. World Health Organization.

15 GROWING UP GLOBALLY – ADOLESCENCE

 Learning Outcomes

After reading this chapter you will be able to:
- Consolidate what you learned in Chapters 12–14.
- Revisit the ideas you came across in Chapters 12–14 in a cross-cultural context.

15.1 Introduction

This last chapter of Section III is the final 'Growing Up Globally' perspective on child development. As before, all the key points from each chapter are repeated here so the essential takeaways are in one place, and we re-examine what we have already covered from a more global perspective.

15.2 Who Do Teenagers Think They Are? Recap and Consolidation

- Identity development is an important part of adolescence in which young people work out who they are, what they believe in, and how they will present themselves to others.
- Genetic and environmental influences are significant factors in explaining the differences between people's personalities.
- Estimates of heritability increase through a lifespan.
- Heritability is caused by many genes, each of which contributes a small effect.
- The environment shows some degree of heritability too.
- Social interaction with friends and family shapes adolescent identity by supporting identity exploration, fostering a sense of personal autonomy, and highlighting uniqueness from others.
- Rituals that mark the passage into adulthood, rites of passage, and coming-of-age ceremonies are common features of many societies.
- Across cultures, key indicators of adulthood are taking personal responsibility for your actions and independence from others.

- Rites of passage and coming-of-age ceremonies signal an adolescent's new status to the community, to adolescents themselves, and to their parents.
- Adolescents have been drivers of cultural change and innovation throughout history.
- Several cognitive and social factors make adolescence a period of creativity.

15.3 Who Do You Want to Be? I Want to Be Aka, of Course

The Aka are a diverse set of forager groups living in small, intimate camps of 25–35 individuals in the tropical forests of the Congo Basin. We first learned about this society when we looked at imitation and pretend play in the Mbendjele, a subgroup of Aka, in Chapter 6. The daily life of Aka children is characterised by physical and emotional intimacy, self-motivated and directed learning, personal autonomy, extensive sharing and giving, trust of others, and frequent play, as well as socialising and resting in mixed-age groups. By 10 years of age, Aka have acquired most of the skills necessary for life in the forest: they know how to net fish, hunt, gather plants, honey, nuts, and mushrooms, prepare food, take care of babies, build huts and baskets, and make medicines for illnesses. This lived experience is important for understanding how Aka children become Aka adolescents.

When anthropologist Bonnie Hewlett asked one young Aka boy, 'What do you want to be or do when you are older?', the boy simply replied, 'I am Aka' (Hewlett, 2012). The question of 'who do you want to be?' is not really a question that needs answering when from a very young age children in this society have been apprentices in the skills and roles they are expected to assume as adults, encouraged by a community that values exploration and interdependence (**Figure 15.1**).

Compare this with the career options laid out before the average American high school student, not to mention the possible gender, music, dress, online, and mental health identity options available to them. As a student I once filled out an online career questionnaire and, based on my responses, the algorithm suggested I was best suited to being a lumberjack *or* an accountant. In many Western societies an extended period of higher education may mean delaying professional identity until well into mid-adulthood. But for most of human history children started their apprenticeship at 7 years old, not 27 (Gopnik, 2016).

To understand how we got here, we need to go back to the late nineteenth and early twentieth centuries, when many societies shifted from a rural and agricultural way of life to one that was urban and industrial. Around the same time, formal schooling started to appear for children while their parents, for the first time in human history, were far away at work. This led to some profound changes in the everyday lives of children, including in the ways they learn. Whereas before children spent most of their days with a family member and got involved in everyday activities of the home and community, now children spent most of their days in school being trained for the workforce. There was a big reduction in play that was generated by children and an increase in play that was created and monitored by adults. There was also a big reduction in mixed-age groups, because it was more efficient to teach same-age groups, but this also meant fewer opportunities for children to learn from older children and practice caring for younger ones (Lansford et al., 2021). High-stakes testing in formal schooling, where a lot is riding on the outcome of a particular test (for both student and teacher), has been associated with a number of negative outcomes for children,

Figure 15.1 Members of the Aka society. Apprenticeships start early and gradually prepare adolescents for their adult roles, responsibilities, and privileges. Source: Veronique DURRUTY/Contributor/Getty images.

including higher dropout rates, high levels of test anxiety, and lower academic self-confidence if students do not do as well as they expected (Segool et al., 2013).

Compare this with learning through participation, in which children get involved in practical activities alongside older children or adults involved in the daily activities of life, which is especially important in cultural contexts where explicit instruction is uncommon (Lancy et al., 2010). In these contexts, children receive a practical introduction to the roles and responsibilities they will face later on in life – for example, learning to weave or fish. Adults support this process through guided participation, structuring interactions and giving tasks appropriate to the child's needs and ability.

Apprentice-style, on-the-job learning potentially also makes for a smoother transition between childhood, adolescence, and young adulthood, as children gradually take on increasing power, responsibility, and autonomy. Because of this, Aka adolescence does not appear to be a time of marked turmoil or rebelliousness, indicating that increasing independence does not need to be gained at the expense of family closeness. Aka adolescents are granted a high degree of autonomy, there is a lack of parental interference, and they are acknowledged as unique individuals by others. In such circumstances, what is there to rebel against?

 Key Point

- Cross-cultural differences in the daily lives of children significantly affect how they think about their identity and the transition to adulthood.

Watch the One-Minute Method.

Discover how researchers live within the societies they are studying, sometimes for many years, to gain an insider's perspective and to share similar experiences.

15.4 How Do Adolescents Think About Risk and Reward? Recap and Consolidation

- Adolescents have a lower mortality rate than those in most other stages of life but are more likely to be accidentally injured and to engage in risky behaviour, and they are poorer at judging the long-term consequences of their actions.
- Novelty- and sensation-seeking behaviours with greater risk-taking and peer influence are seen in a wide range of species on the cusp of adulthood, suggesting a shared evolutionary explanation.
- Adolescence is a time of investing in peer relationships, heightened sensitivity to group identity, and emotional intensity.
- The reward systems of the brain mature earlier and are more well connected in adolescents than those that keep impulses in check and that deliberate over alternative choices.
- Knowing or believing that peers are observing their behaviour significantly increases the risk-taking behaviour of adolescents, even in the absence of any direct peer pressure.
- The behaviour of early adolescents is strongly guided by the social environment, both for positive and negative outcomes.
- Sex differences in mortality and risk-taking persist within similar societies, between different societies, and across a wide variety of species and environments.
- Life-history theory predicts that boys are more willing to engage in risky behaviour in same-sex competitive contexts.
- Executive functions represent a collection of skills that enable us to be flexible, controlled, and focused.
- Executive functions are associated with a wide range of outcomes for children and take a long time to mature.
- There is some evidence to suggest that inhibitory control emerges earlier for girls than boys, underpinned by earlier maturation of the brain areas that support this function.

15.5 I Can Resist Anything but Temptation

Part of growing up involves learning to regulate behaviour in culturally appropriate ways. To do so, we use our **executive functions**: the collection of skills that include working memory, cognitive flexibility, and inhibitory control. Executive functions are still undergoing significant change during adolescence and do not reach full maturity until early adulthood.

Figure 15.2 Japanese children in preschool have frequent opportunities to practice customs and rituals around waiting for food, while children in the USA have frequent opportunities to practice customs around waiting for gifts. Source: SOURCENEXT/Alamy Stock Photo; Kzenon/Alamy Stock Photo.

A classic measure of inhibitory control is the marshmallow test. Children are left alone in a room with a marshmallow and told that they can eat one marshmallow now or wait some time and eat two marshmallows later. The basic idea is that a tempting response (eat the marshmallow now) needs to be resisted or inhibited in order to achieve a different goal (eat two marshmallows later). Yanaoka and his colleagues suspected that what children were being asked to inhibit would affect how good they were at inhibiting it and, furthermore, that these differences would be related to customs around waiting in different cultures (2022). They found that Japanese children delayed gratification longer for food than for gifts, whereas American children delayed gratification longer for gifts than for food. This suggests culturally specific habits support delaying gratification: waiting to eat is emphasised more in Japan than America, whereas waiting to open gifts is emphasised more in America than Japan (**Figure 15.2**).

Lamm and colleagues (2018) used a similar marshmallow test with children from rural Cameroon Nso families and middle-class German families. The Cameroonian Nso children were better at delaying gratification than were the German children, and the researchers argued that this was because children were picking up on what their mothers valued, which in turn were reflections of wider cultural beliefs. As revealed by a questionnaire, Nso mothers tended to value social harmony and respect for authority and older people, whereas the German mothers valued teaching their children to express personal preferences and ideas. This made the German children more likely to follow their immediate impulses in expressing their agency and eating the marshmallow now, whereas the Nso children, who had more experience of inhibiting their impulses to maintain social harmony and show obedience, were more likely to be able to wait and so eat two marshmallows later. These studies, along with others, show how cultural values, embodied by the behaviours that parents encourage or discourage, have a significant effect on the development of executive functions.

The economic background children grow up in also seems to matter. In one study, a group of highly disadvantaged children outperformed children of middle and high socio-economic backgrounds on some tests of executive function (Howard et al., 2020). It might be that to survive and thrive in such disadvantaged circumstances children need extra vigilance, autonomy, and adaptability – skills that would require regular and efficient use of their executive functions. The authors make it clear that these results do not mean that we should disadvantage children to improve their executive functions. Rather, they do suggest that highly disadvantaged backgrounds do not automatically translate into negative cognitive outcomes and can even be sources of strength if the risks are mild.

Key Point

- Executive functions are present in children around the world; what those executive functions work on is more culturally variable.

15.6 Are Young People Happy? Recap and Consolidation

- Young people report a complex mixture of emotions and attitudes towards themselves and their lives.
- Family, peers, and school can both protect and harm adolescents' emotional well-being depending on the individual circumstances.
- Adolescent well-being is partially heritable.
- There are a range of personal assets that can support young people's well-being and act as protective buffers against adversity.
- Adults can help adolescents by providing more validation of their experiences, and they can reduce the stigma around reporting mental health difficulties by listening without judgement and in confidence.
- An important factor in predicting well-being is the goodness of fit between the individual characteristics of children and the demands or expectations of the environment.
- Adolescents are aware of the risks and benefits of social media use, and research to date does not suggest that social media use strongly causes adolescent depression and anxiety.
- The transition into adulthood presents a set of risks and opportunities for well-being.

15.7 The Blue Planet

Imagine two adolescent girls: Himari from Japan and Olivia from the USA. Both have the same set of mental and physical signs of depression: lack of pleasure, loneliness, hopelessness, loss of appetite, fatigue, and insomnia. However, as we know, different cultures have different norms around what is acceptable or unacceptable, valued or not valued, normal or abnormal, providing people with a framework to interpret personal experience in relation to what others think and do. This means that despite having the same set of symptoms, some feelings are brought to the surface or experienced more vividly than others. For Olivia, the lack of personal agency and pleasure might be felt more acutely because these undercut the American values common to **individualistic societies**. For Himari, the social withdrawal and failure to maintain social obligations brought about by depression might be more significant because these are at odds with Japanese **collectivist society** (Chentsova-Dutton et al., 2014). If cultures differ on the extent to which they stigmatise depression, this is also going to affect the ways teens try to regulate their symptoms and whether they reach out for help.

> **Key Point**
>
> - While depression appears to exist across all cultures, how adolescents give meaning to the distress associated with depression is shaped by their cultural context.

The World Happiness Report annually ranks countries based on asking a nationally representative sample of youth and adults aged 15 and older how satisfied they are with their lives (Helliwell et al., 2023). For the period 2020–2022, the top-ranked countries were Finland, Denmark, Iceland, Israel, and the Netherlands, while the least happy were Afghanistan, Lebanon, Sierra Leone, Zimbabwe, and the Democratic Republic of the Congo.

Behaviours and conditions that were associated with happiness included acting prosocially (e.g., helping strangers, donating money, giving blood, volunteering), good mental and physical health, being ruled by an effective government (e.g., able to raise money, deliver services, maintain the rule of law), having someone to count on, a sense of personal freedom to make key life decisions, and prosperity. The last item on that list shows that wealth *is* part of what makes us happy, but only up to a point. Once income satisfies basic needs, like food, sanitation, and shelter, money gives a diminishing return on happiness. If you are on the breadline, then a 50% increase in your income means not having to worry about where the next meal will come from, taking away a significant source of stress. If you are a millionaire, a 50% increase in wealth means you can buy your next yacht, but it is unlikely to significantly nudge your happiness dial in the long term. Notably, the Nordic countries have the highest well-being, though they are not wealthier than many other countries. They do, however, have higher levels of trust and of mutual respect and support. Factors that subtract from overall happiness include war, political turmoil, poverty, corruption, and a large inequality in happiness – or, in other words, a big gap between the happiest and the least happy in society.

 Our tomorrows.

Teenagers around the world share their fears and dreams.

References

Chentsova-Dutton, Y. E., Ryder, A. G., & Tsai, J. L. (2014). Understanding depression across cultural contexts. In I. H. Gotlib & C. L. Hammen (eds.), *Handbook of Depression* (pp. 337–352). Guilford.

Gopnik, A. (2016). *The Gardener and the Carpenter*. Vintage Publishing.

Helliwell, J. F., Layard, R., Sachs, J. D., Aknin, L. B., De Neve, J.-E., & Wang, S. (eds.). (2023). *World Happiness Report 2023*, 11th edition. Sustainable Development Solutions Network.

Hewlett, B. (ed.). (2012). *Adolescent Identity: Evolutionary, Cultural and Developmental Perspectives*. Routledge.

Howard, S. J., Cook, C. J., Everts, L., et al. (2020). Challenging socioeconomic status: a cross-cultural comparison of early executive function. *Developmental Science*, 23(1), e12854.

Lamm, B., Keller, H., Teiser, J., et al. (2018). Waiting for the second treat: developing culture-specific modes of self-regulation. *Child Development*, 89, e261–e277.

Lancy, D., Bock, J., & Gaskins, S. (2010). *The Anthropology of Learning in Childhood*. Altamira Press.

Lansford, J., French, D., & Gauvain, M. (2021). *Child and Adolescent Development in Cultural Context*. American Psychological Association.

Segool, N. K., Carlson, J. S., Goforth, A. N., von der Embse, N., & Barterian, J. A. (2013). Heightened test anxiety among young children: elementary school students' anxious responses to high-stakes testing. *Psychology in the Schools*, 50, 489–499.

Yanaoka, K., Michaelson, L. E., Guild, R. M., Dostart, G., Yonehiro, J., Saito, S., & Munakata, Y. (2022). Cultures crossing: the power of habit in delaying gratification. *Psychological Science*, 33(7), 1172–1181.

16 THE MANY PATHS OF DEVELOPMENT

Learning Outcomes

After reading this chapter you will be able to:

- Describe how children can take different paths in development and reach similar destinations.
- Understand the developmental differences between children as a set of strengths and challenges highly sensitive to environmental context.
- Explore how events in children's lives can trigger a cascade of later consequences.

16.1 Introduction

Throughout the book we have been exploring the reasons why children grow up differently and why they are alike. These reasons include identity, morality, group behaviour, well-being, language, family environment, brain maturation, heritability, play, memory, sex, culture, and the historical, economic, political, and geographical circumstances of the time and place children are born (**Figure 16.1**).

In this chapter we continue that exploration of individual differences by considering the perspectives of children who have difficulty with language, movement, writing, or regulating their attention, those who are born blind or deaf, and autistic children.[1] We retrace our steps from birth to adolescence and ask whether some of the processes of development we have already encountered apply to their experience. Their story deserves its own space not because it represents a different type of development, but because the diversity of their experiences has much to teach us about development itself.

---

1 The same point was mentioned earlier in the book, but it is worth repeating here: the language we use to describe people should respect their dignity and autonomy. Ideally, we should ask the people we are interacting with how they would like to be addressed. Unfortunately, this is not an available option here, so as a substitute I have been guided by a survey of 3,470 members of the UK autism community who preferred the term 'autistic person' over 'person with autism', which is the phrase I have adopted here (Kenny et al., 2016). The same survey also noted that there is no single way of describing autism that is universally accepted and preferred.

16 THE MANY PATHS OF DEVELOPMENT

Figure 16.1 The author at 3 years of age. Everyone's development is a one-off story, and, paradoxically, that is what we have in common. As the expression goes: you are unique, just like everybody else.

Can children take different paths in development and reach similar destinations? To what extent are children's strengths and difficulties defined by the world around them? How do we change the world to play to children's individual strengths and reduce the day-to-day challenges they face? How do significant events in a child's life trigger a cascade of later consequences?

16.2 Different Paths, Similar Destination

Children can follow different developmental paths and reach a similar outcome, technically known as *equifinality*. For instance, en route to walking, infants vary tremendously in how they get there: crawling, cruising, supported walking, or even bum-shuffling (Schneider & Iverson, 2023). Children who are born with no hearing at all are able to learn any one of the 2–300 signed languages as effortlessly as hearing children can learn anyone of the 6–7,000 spoken languages, provided they receive signed language early enough and with enough opportunities for high-quality communicative interactions. Thus children can take very different paths – acquiring spoken or signed language – and end up at the same destination – using language fluently. As well as being yet another example of children's remarkable adaptability, this also says something important about our species. Within all of us is the capacity to acquire language by two drastically different media – sound and vision – and this suggests that both media have been important for a significant proportion of human history (Tomasello, 2010).

Because of this long, shared history, there are many similarities between signed and spoken languages, as well as differences. Some of these similarities cause children to follow similar paths of development, and some differences nudge them in different directions (**Table 16.1**). Regardless of how they get there, children have the potential to arrive at the same destination in both cases.

So, whether by sound or vision or both (bimodal bilingualism), children show adaptability in acquiring language. Another example of this adaptability comes from children who are born blind and acquire shared attention. In Chapter 3 we took a closer look at early social interactions and the role of shared attention. Around their first birthday infants start to

Table 16.1 Some notable similarities and differences between spoken and signed languages.

Similarities	Differences
Like words, most signs are cultural **conventions** and are not pantomimed actions. Because of this, children can't guess what signs mean any more than they can guess what words mean; they need to learn them, and they do so using many of the same learning mechanisms as for spoken language (e.g., reading others' intentions, Chapter 3; statistical and cross-situational learning, Chapter 4; exploration and generalising, Chapter 5).	Try as you might, you can't really say more than one word at a time. Signed language is different in that it can convey many meanings simultaneously using the direction and speed of the sign, the expressivity and emotion on the signer's face, and body posture. While this might not make a difference in terms of *what* is learned – sign languages possess grammars and vocabularies as sophisticated as any spoken language – it might affect the route Deaf children take towards mastering language.
Signed languages, like spoken languages, are mostly unintelligible to non-native speakers. For example, American Sign Language (ASL) and British Sign Language (BSL) are as different as Hawaiian and Dutch are from one another, and they also bear no relation to their spoken 'counterparts'. ASL grammar has more in common with spoken Japanese than it does with the speech of Americans.	Most hearing children have hearing parents. But most Deaf children do not have Deaf parents and are therefore unlikely to be parented by native signers. This makes Deaf children relatively more at risk of not receiving the early rich linguistic experience necessary for language development. This in turn jeopardises the development of other outcomes that are related to language, such as social-emotional skills, school-readiness, and academic success. Currently, only 1–2% of Deaf children worldwide receive an education with a sign language as their language of instruction (Haualand & Allen, 2009).
Both signing and speaking children go through a similar *sequence* of language development. For example, hearing-impaired infants are babbling with their hands by 8 months of age; by 12 months of age sign language learners are typically producing their first signs; by 18–24 months of age they are putting together two or more signs to form simple sentences; and by 30 months they have command of the basic word order of the language, including how to use this flexibly in certain communicative contexts (Lillo-Martin & Henner, 2021; Petitto & Marentette, 1991).	Signed language requires mentally rotating the signs as they appear from the signer's perspective to those as they appear from the recipient's perspective and vice versa. Relatedly, autistic children learning sign language can have particular difficulty with this change of perspective, similar to the difficulty some autistic children have with perspective-taking in spoken language: 'I' means 'me' when I say it, but it means 'you' when you say it.
Signed languages, like spoken languages, also combine smaller units of language into bigger units of meaningful language. For example,	Because signing typically involves the coordination of two hands, children must learn to inhibit the movement of the dominant hand for

Table 16.1 (*cont.*)

Similarities	Differences
signed languages combine handshape, hand orientation, location in the signing space, movement, and facial expression into larger meaningful combinations, in a similar way to how spoken languages combine sounds into syllables, into words, into phrases, into sentences, into dialogue, and so on.	some signs – a challenge that does not come into play in spoken language in the same way.

coordinate their attention between a partner and an object of mutual interest. In sighted infants, this shared attention is largely negotiated face to face by monitoring cues such as eye gaze, facial expression, and body posture. For example, an infant and an adult might be playing with a toy together and the infant looks from the toy to the adult's face and back to the toy. In this space, not only do infants learn a lot about the solid physical world of objects and actions, but they also learn a large amount of social and cultural information too, including language. Infants can use shared attention to work out when information is intended for them versus when it is not; they can use the eye gaze of adults to locate interesting objects by following where they are looking; and they can direct the attention of others to get what they want – for example, by pointing (Butterworth & Jarrett, 1991; Grossmann et al., 2006) But how does this shared attention work if you can't see what the other person can see?

Developmental psychologist Anne Bigelow set out to answer this question by studying the behaviour of two 1-year-old infants who were born totally blind (Bigelow, 2003). She discovered several examples of joint attention between infants and parents, which typically took place during play:

- When the mother of one infant was playing with a toy, the blind infant found the mother's arm by reaching out; they then worked their way down the arm and felt the toy that the adult was holding in their hand so that they shared attention on the same object. This shows that the infant was using the parent as a social tool to find objects, in a similar way to how a sighted child might follow the eye gaze of a parent towards an object of interest.
- During a guessing game, the mother of one infant would shake a toy that jingled and place it in front of the infant. The infant would then reach out to find the toy, shake it to make it jingle, and place it down. The mother would then place the toy in a different location and repeat the game.
- On one occasion, an infant and his mother played together with a toy that produced a sound when a string was pulled. The infant pulled the string while the mother pulled back the toy. After a few repetitions the mother stopped playing her part in the game, which caused the infant to react by swinging the toy at the mother several times before beginning to fuss; he only became re-engaged with the toy when the mum resumed her role. This shows that the infant was aware of the mother's role in achieving the shared goal, something that could be described as **shared intentionality**.

So, just as hearing is not necessary to develop language, this study and others like it show that vision is not necessary to develop joint attention. That is not to say that acquiring joint attention in this way is without its challenges. In comparison to sighted children, blind children need to work harder to know exactly where they are in the physical environment, to know where objects are in relation to each other and themselves, and to track how these relationships change over time. Judging the emotional reactions of others to objects of mutual interest is made relatively more difficult too, because blind children cannot directly rely on seeing other people's facial expressions. To overcome this, blind infants use a broader, subtler, and more indirect range of non-visual cues such as touch, body movement, sound changes, air currents, and echolocation, and they rely more heavily on language (Millar, 1988). Notably, Deaf children of hearing parents, exposed to basically no conventional language during their first year of life (either spoken or signed), still begin to use the pointing gesture to direct attention in the same way as hearing children and at around the same age (Lederberg & Everhart, 1998).

Despite the adaptability and workarounds to joint attention that blind infants show, they can still be at risk of falling behind their peers in the development of joint attention because of the challenges they face (Dale & Salt, 2007). This risk can be offset, however, by caregivers who are sensitive to the difficulties they face and who structure social interactions that play to their strengths: for example, using the child's body as a reference point to share attention to an object (e.g., 'it's beside *you*', 'down by *your* toes'); using speech that refers to things that are already in their attentional focus, such as a toy they are holding or recently held; and using a child-centred conversation style, in which adult's take the child's topic as the starting point and follow their lead (Bigelow, 2003). Thus, caregivers can play a significant role in scaffolding the development of joint attention in a way that is appropriate to the needs of the child. This is true of sighted infants, but it is especially so of those who are born blind.

 Key Point

- Children can take very different paths to reach similar developmental milestones, as demonstrated by the sign-language of Deaf children and shared attention of blind children.

16.3 Strengths and Difficulties

We all have a set of strengths and difficulties that are unique to us. Here we apply this idea to autistic children or children who find regulating their attention challenging. Sometimes, people with these behavioural and cognitive characteristics have been given the label 'autistic spectrum disorder' or 'attention deficit hyperactivity disorder' (ADHD). The terms 'deficit', 'disorder', and 'dysfunction' are avoided here because they do not reflect the many ways these characteristics can be strengths as well as difficulties, nor do they indicate how sensitive these characteristics can be to the environment.

Let's examine what we mean by that by taking a sidestep away from psychological characteristics and considering a physical one. We could label a man who is 6'6" tall as having 'excessive tallness disorder' or 'appropriate height deficit', and, indeed, life might be challenging for someone who is this tall trying to navigate a world largely built by and for the average 5'8" man. He could find legroom on aeroplanes a problem, and bending down to walk through doorways might become tiresome, as would being the subject of predictable jokes about being tall. However, the same trait turns from a difficulty into a strength when we change the environment to a basketball court: 6'6" is the average height of players in the National Basketball Association, a professional basketball league in North America, where the typical player in the 2022–2023 season earned USD 9,662,447.

Likewise, being autistic, for example, might be challenging, especially in a world largely built by and for non-autistic people. Some autistic people need extra time to process information or experience anxiety in social situations or when things change unexpectedly, and some find noises, smells, and bright lights painful and distressing (National Autistic Society, 2015). However, in some circumstances, the same underlying traits can be expressed as strengths – for example, being able to appreciate detail, see complex patterns, and make more rational decisions (**Table 16.2**).

With regards to autism, it is important to note that there are huge individual differences in how autism is expressed, ranging from children who can talk fluently to those who cannot talk at all, from those who happily maintain many relationships to those who happily have none, and from those who display repetitive behaviours like hand-flapping, rocking, and repeating words (or 'stimming') to those who do not. Stephen Shore, autism advocate and autistic professor of special education, captures the diversity of experiences in the following phrase: 'If you've met one individual with autism, you've met one individual with autism.' Likewise, there is huge individual difference between children in how their

Table 16.2 The relative strengths and challenges of autism and attention-regulating differences.

	Relative strength	**Relative challenge**
Autism	The ability to appreciate detail and see complex patterns that others overlook; make more logical and rational decisions; develop deep expertise on a specific topic (De Martino et al., 2008; Happé & Frith, 2006)	Intolerance of uncertainty; difficulties with communication and social interaction; hypersensitivity to sensory information (Fletcher-Watson & Happé, 2019; Frith, 2003; Jenkinson et al., 2020)
Attention-regulating differences	Enhanced creativity; higher verbal ability and emotional intelligence; greater energy; adventurousness; hyperfocus; willingness to try new things and take risks (Climie et al., 2019; Ek et al., 2007; Hoogman et al., 2020)	Difficulty engaging with or disengaging from a task; impulsivity and restlessness; difficulty setting and remaining committed to long-term goals (Kohn & Griffiths, 2023; Mueller et al., 2017; Winstanley et al., 2006)

attention is expressed. This is partly because attention itself is not one single thing but comes in many varieties: it can be directed, switched, divided, sustained, or inhibited – and all children have a slightly different profile of strengths and difficulties across these varieties (Steele et al., 2012).

Key Point

- Despite similarities, there are large differences in how autism and attention-regulating difficulties are expressed in children.

It is also important to note that we are often describing extreme examples of normal developmental processes and abilities. For example, a *degree* of distractibility and impulsivity is adaptive – it helps us notice important changes in the environment and enables us to react quickly to them. A *degree* of preference for predictability is adaptive – surviving in the environment involves being able to forecast what is going to happen in our surroundings. So, many of these traits are rooted in adaptive behaviour and only come to our attention when taken to the extreme or if they are significantly mismatched with the demands of the environment.

Having the capacity to picture the world from another person's point of view – what others see, know, want, desire, or believe – can help us in communication, social interaction, and collaborative activities. If there are significant differences in how this **theory of mind** ability works, as can be the case for some autistic children, then these activities become relatively more difficult (Baron-Cohen et al., 1985)

Having the skill to be flexible, controlled, and focused allows us to achieve long-term goals. If there are significant differences in how this **executive function** ability works, particularly regarding inhibitory control and working memory, then these activities become relatively more difficult, which is the experience of some children with attention-regulating difficulties (Schreiber et al., 2014).

Key Point

- Difficulties are often expressed as extreme examples of normal developmental processes and abilities rooted in adaptive behaviours.

If autism and attention-regulating difficulty are extreme examples of normal variation, then this suggests that many of these individual traits will be shared by others. And, indeed, this is largely true. For example, the basic three-part structure of executive function – working memory, inhibitory control, and cognitive flexibility – is shared by adolescents with special educational needs and those not requiring any additional support (Messer et al., 2022). Likewise, many people in the general population show autistic-like traits, with autistic individuals being at the extreme end of this distribution (Constantino & Todd, 2003). As public awareness of autism has grown in recent years, it has become increasingly common to hear people say that they are 'on the spectrum'. On the one hand, it is positive that there is widespread recognition that autistic people are not a separate category of person and instead have a constellation of experiences that many of us share to a greater or lesser extent. On the other hand, the notion that we are 'all a little bit autistic' risks diminishing the experiences of some autistic people, for whom life is extremely challenging; for example children who have no verbal communication, are profoundly constrained by their intolerance of uncertainty and are persistently uncomfortable due to their sensory sensitivity.

16.4 The World Around the Child

Notice that the same underlying trait can appear in either the 'strength' or 'difficulty' column in **Table 16.2** depending on the circumstances. Take logical reasoning as an example: it has been shown that, in general, people are more likely to consent to an operation when a surgeon frames the odds in terms of what they have to gain (e.g., 'there is an 80% chance of surviving an operation') than if the surgeon frames the odds in terms of what they have to lose (e.g., 'there is a 20% chance of dying'; Tversky & Kahneman, 1981). Individuals with autism are more likely than non-autists to correctly see that the odds of surviving the operation are the same in both cases because their judgement is less likely to be swayed by their gut reactions or social-emotional considerations (De Martino et al., 2008).

However, in some circumstances, like the quick-fire back-and-forth of conversations, gut reactions are exactly what is needed because there is not enough time to crank through all the logical possibilities of what other people mean, and there is no guarantee of finding the 'right answer' even if that were possible. This often makes understanding what is *not* said in conversation but is inferred by the social and emotional context relatively more challenging for autistic people (Fletcher-Watson & Happé, 2019).

 Key Point

- The same underlying characteristic can often be expressed as a strength or difficulty depending on the circumstances.

Another example of the importance of circumstances comes from children who experience difficulty regulating their attention, or who are impulsive and easily distracted. This can mean these children have both 'slippery' attention – finding it hard to stay engaged with an activity – *and* 'sticky' attention – finding it difficult to disengage from a task once they have started. However, this way of thinking turns into a strength in circumstances that reward spontaneous leaps of imagination, thinking outside of the box, and making unexpected connections between ideas – in other words, exactly the kinds of skills that are valued in creativity (Ek et al., 2007; Zabelina et al., 2016). Perhaps not unrelatedly, Mozart was described by people who knew him as 'impatient, impulsive, distractible, energetic, emotionally needy, creative, innovative, irreverent, and a maverick', a profile shared by other creative visionaries such as Albert Einstein, Edgar Allan Poe, Salvador Dalí, and Henry Ford (Hallowell & Ratey, 1994). The ability to reach unexpected conclusions from a shared premise also underpins a lot of humour, another trait associated with attention-regulating differences (Sedgwick et al., 2019).

Unfortunately, perhaps, for some children born into many Western educational systems, impulsivity and distractibility are the exact opposite skills to what most schools value, where sitting still and staying task-focused for long periods of time are rewarded because learning to read and write requires sustained periods of focused attention. In this case, the mismatch between the demands of the school environment and children's characteristics can lead to frequent experience of negative feedback, frustration, and failure (Jensen et al., 1997).

Schools can increase **goodness of fit** by beginning with children's strengths and gifts, recognising what is working well, identifying potential, and building from that starting point (Climie & Mastoras, 2015; Seligman & Csikszentmihalyi, 2000). For example, children who have difficulty regulating their attention or who are impulsive and easily distracted are often excellent brainstormers, have natural energy, are able to carry out many tasks with enthusiasm, are eager to please, and are creative (Sherman et al., 2006). Sherman and colleagues suggest that a learning environment that plays to these strengths and minimises difficulties can be created by:

- Providing opportunities to demonstrate skills and understanding in media other than writing, such as verbally, through physical activity (sports, dance), or via nature, crafts, or music;
- Offering incentives to stay on task and plan for the future, including rewards for being prepared and organised, and tools such as graphic day-planners, as well as visual checklists that break down larger tasks into smaller sub-tasks;
- Creating hands-on lessons and giving opportunities to solve problems or summarise stories by using paints, modelling clay, or dramatic skits;
- Building on a gift for exploration with mini-experiments and maintaining engagement by calling on students frequently, giving immediate feedback, and switching media (SMART Boards, iPads, presentations, charts, videos);
- Arranging classrooms to limit distraction and increase teacher availability.

Just as a rising tide lifts all boats, so most teaching strategies found to be useful for children with attention difficulties have also been found to be beneficial for the entire classroom because they are based on sound principles of teaching and learning (Rief, 2000). Goodness of fit also has implications for how we measure cognitive skills, like executive function. If we measure a child's performance in a poorly fitting situation, when they are stressed, hyper-aroused, or unmotivated, it is likely that we will capture the lower limit of their abilities and not the full range of what they are capable of in better-fitting environments (Hendry & Scerif, 2023).

Building on strengths.

How can we understand and support children with attention regulating difficulty (and those without)?

To be clear, autism and attention-regulating differences can be challenging and disadvantaging. By only focusing on strengths, we risk a kind of reverse discrimination that holds neurominorities to a higher standard or places them on a pedestal. It could be argued that the test of real acceptance is when minorities of any kind are allowed to be as flawed and complex as the dominant majority without being stereotyped for it, and that means being frank about their frustrations and challenges. However, by highlighting strengths as well as difficulties, we can offer a more balanced view than the labels of 'disorder' and 'deficit' would imply. In any case, many of the disadvantages children face come not from their differences directly but from the circumstances they find themselves in (**Box 16.1**), which can be made harsher or more humane depending on the attitudes and understanding of others.

Key Point

- Recognising children's unique strengths as well as the challenges they face is important for helping children reach their social, emotional, and academic potential.

Box 16.1 The distractable forager

To fully appreciate the role of context in defining children's strengths and difficulties it is often insightful to consider what the same behaviour would look like in a different time and place. In *ADHD: A Hunter in a Farmer's World*, Thom Hartmann asks us to imagine how distractibility, impulsivity, and risk-taking might be adaptive in a foraging environment compared to a school-based one (2019).

School environment	Foraging environment
Rewards sustained attention on one task, and focusing on it until completion	Rewards constantly scanning the environment, high vigilance, being ready to change strategies, and reacting instantly to new sights or sounds
Rewards patience and being purposefully organised	Rewards quick and intuitive decision-making, especially in highly stimulating, stressful, or risky situations
Rewards repetitively engaging with the same tasks, skills, and activities	Rewards novelty-seeking behaviours and exploration
Rewards individual achievement	Rewards loyalty and cooperation with the group
Rewards sitting still and mental stamina	Rewards moving around and physical stamina

The idea is that normal behavioural strategies that were once adaptive for a foraging lifestyle have become an **evolutionary mismatch** with formal school environments, which appeared in the last 0.5% of human history. What is the evidence for this speculation?

First, twin studies have consistently shown high **heritability** rates of around 75% for attention-regulating difficulty (Faraone et al., 2005). This shows that there is mechanism for passing on this behaviour from one generation to the next, and we also understand this pathway from genetic predisposition to behavioural profile in some detail (Scerif & Baker, 2015).

Second, by looking at different populations today it is possible to reconstruct how these genes have changed over time. Using this method with 20,000 people diagnosed with ADHD and 35,000 controls, researchers found that genes associated with ADHD were more frequent in the past, suggesting that these behaviours were more adaptive in environments where foraging was a more dominant lifestyle than it is today (Esteller-Cucala et al., 2020). Third, populations who have experienced much higher levels of migration compared to more sedentary populations have a higher proportion of a gene variant that has been linked to novelty-seeking and hyperactive behaviour (Chen et al., 1999). Migration is usually harsh, full of new challenges, and frequently changing; therefore, the idea is that exploratory behaviours might be adaptive during migration because they allow people to better exploit resources in these challenging conditions.

However, perhaps the strongest evidence for the *Hunter in a Farmer's World* idea comes from modern-day hunter-gatherers themselves. Evolutionary anthropologist Dan Eisenberg and his colleagues looked at a society of traditional cattle-herders called the Ariaal, who live in northern Kenya (2008). Some of the men in this society still live a nomadic way of life, but recently some have begun to settle in one place to grow crops and live a farming way of life. Dan and his team found that a particular gene was associated with being *better* nourished in the men living the nomadic way of life but *less* well-nourished in the settled population. The same gene has been associated with greater food and drug cravings, novelty-seeking, and ADHD symptoms in industrialised Western societies. This is the first evidence to show how this gene could be adaptive in a different environment – one that was closer to our foraging past.

16.5 Cascades of Development

One of the first key points we established in Chapter 1 was that children develop incrementally, with later-acquired skills being built on earlier ones. We saw how language, emotion, and theory of mind start out simple and develop towards greater complexity. While this is a basic fact of development, it can be a very useful framework when thinking about why we grow up differently and why we are alike.

The presence *or absence* of some event in a child's life can trigger a cascade of later consequences, some of which are predictable, some more unexpected. These cascades start *early*. For example, genetically identical twins in the womb do not share identical environments. Slight differences in the way they receive nutrients from the placenta can cause a cascade of effects, which, in rare cases, can mean identical twins can be born with different eye colours; even though they share the same genes, the way those genes are *used* is different because of the environment (Cohen, 1999).

Because development is both progressive (changes over time) and hierarchical (has many levels), this means that if basic skills aren't in place first, it can be more difficult to acquire

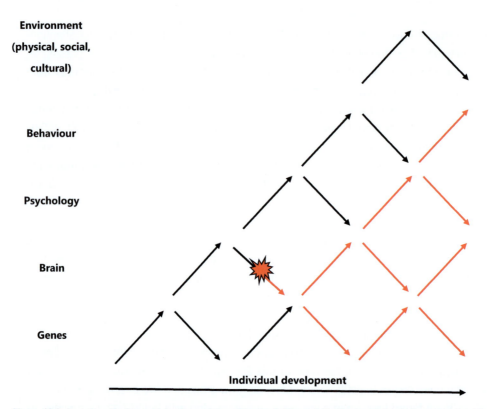

Figure 16.2 Revisiting the figure of development from Chapter 1 (Figure 1.2). Development is both progressive (changes over time) and hierarchal (has many levels). At any point in development, a significant event (the red star in the figure) can have consequences (red lines) that cascade through children's lives, affecting all levels. The event in this figure is shown as originating in the brain, but such events can occur at any level, and at more than one level at a time. Source: Adapted from Gottlieb (1992, p. 186); Adapted from Individual Development and Evolution: The Genesis of Novel Behavior, by Gilbert Gottlieb, 1992, New York: Oxford University Press.

complex ones later on. The ability to use language, think creatively, and reason about other people's minds are higher-order skills at the pinnacle of a very broad pyramid built upon increasingly more basic skills. The more secure the foundations, the more secure the top of the pyramid. As well as using this framework to understand how development typically unfolds for most children, we can use it to understand how development can be disrupted too (**Figure 16.2**).

> **Key Point**
>
> - The presence *or absence* of some significant event in a child's life can trigger a cascade of later consequences, some of which are predictable, some more unexpected.

Let's look at a concrete example of this developmental cascade in action. Some children have trouble reading, writing, with movement, or with language. If children are significantly affected by these difficulties and have been assessed by a professional, they may have received a diagnosis of dyslexia, dysgraphia, developmental coordination disorder, or developmental language disorder. At first glance these difficulties might appear unrelated, but there is evidence to suggest that under the surface they share a common cause (Nicolson & Fawcett, 2011).

To get good at reading, writing, moving, and speaking, these skills not only require a lot of practice but also need to become automatic, quick, and effortless if we are to use them effectively in everyday life. Recall from Chapter 10 that **automatisation** is a phase of learning during which skills become fluent, flexible, and performed without awareness, whereas before these skills were effortful, hesitant, and deliberate. So, automatisation is a normal part of learning, but the basic idea is that for some children this process is disrupted and, consequently, skills that require automatisation become relatively harder to acquire.

What is the evidence for this idea? Children with these difficulties are often challenged by just those tasks that require automatisation, like tying shoelaces, balancing, or catching a ball, but have less difficulty or no difficulty at all on tasks that do not require automatisation. The fact that these difficulties are quite *task-specific* points to a cause that is quite *cognitively specific* – namely, these children's difficulties are limited to just that part of the learning system that deals with automatisation. Memory for learning facts, meanings, and other consciously accessible information can be similar or better than their peers, but memory for skills, habits, and other not consciously accessible procedures are relatively impaired.

More evidence comes from the fact that children who struggle to automatise in one activity frequently struggle on another activity that requires automatisation. For example, over half of all children with dyslexia have diagnosed difficulties with fine movement (e.g., tying shoelaces) and vice versa (Crawford et al., 2006). A substantial overlap of this kind is sometimes a clue that they have a common underlying cause, albeit expressed in different ways. Finally, an area of the brain that we know is associated with movement, language, and coordination – the cerebellum – also is associated with tasks that require automatisation (Doyon et al., 2009; Ito, 2008). Neuroimaging studies have shown that children with extreme difficulties in reading, writing, movement, and language sometimes have a cerebellum that is structured and functions differently compared with similar-aged children who do not have such difficulties (e.g., Bo & Lee, 2013).

To recap: differences in the way areas of the brain work – differences that are perhaps present at birth or before – cause disruptions to the normal way in which learning certain skills becomes automatic. These neurological and cognitive differences can have a cascading effect on behaviour, making learning to talk, move, read, and write relatively more challenging. Precisely which one of these activities is made most challenging will be influenced by a range of factors, including the random events that nudge some children's lives in one direction rather than another; whether they receive the cushioning effect of sensitive parenting and teaching; and the extent to which children compensate by relying on other strengths, meaning that they catch up with their peers later on or find a different developmental route to the same destination. The extent to which they are difficulties at all, as we have already seen, often depends on their environmental circumstances. For example, having trouble reading and writing is not a problem – much less a disorder – when a society doesn't value reading and writing or in which they haven't been invented yet, as was the case for almost all human history.

There are two important caveats to this story. First, we don't know for sure whether differences in automatisation are the ultimate causes of these difficulties or whether automatisation is the result of some other cause further up that chain of cascades. Reading and writing, for instance, are such complex skills that a problem almost anywhere in the brain might result in failure to acquire these skills fluently. Second, even if these difficulties can be pinpointed to automatisation at a neurological level, any disruption to typical functioning has a cascading effect on the broader cognitive, physical, social, and cultural aspects of children's lives. So, understanding how children *experience* these difficulties needs a multi-level approach.

Key Point

- Multi-level cascades of cause and effect can help us understand how development typically unfolds for most children as well as how it can be disrupted.

If the automatisation idea is on the right lines, then how can we help the lives of affected children? Having a good model of cause and effect can help us target our resources to bring about the greatest good. For instance, if one child has good memories for *what*, *where*, *when*, and *who* but relatively poor memory for *how*, the appropriate support for that child will look quite different from that for a child with the opposite strengths and weaknesses. Indeed, there is evidence that children with these differences can learn to perform better at automatisation tasks through targeted training, although this requires substantially more effort from the child and results in relatively more fragile memories than those of their peers (Biotteau et al., 2015).

Training studies such as these show that whatever the causes of these cascades, their effects do not have to be a life sentence and can be cushioned by other factors. Although heritability estimates are often high for these types of differences (e.g., 50–70% of children with developmental language disorder have at least one family member who also has the disorder), this still leaves substantial room for environmental effects. Genes run in families, but so do social inequalities related to health, education, and employment, which can make underlying disadvantages worse (Calder, 2016). And unlike genes, we can change environmental sources of inequality in such a way that makes children's lives better through better public understanding and public health policies.

Talking Point

In this chapter we touched on a controversial topic: diagnosis. How people react to receiving a diagnosis can vary greatly from one individual to another. For some, a diagnosis comes as a relief after years of worry that they were the only ones who felt a certain way, giving them validation of their experience. When healthcare systems mainly respond to medical vocabulary, a diagnosis is often the quickest way to open doors and receive the support that some individuals and their families need, including therapy and medication. It can also introduce individuals to a community – more often online nowadays – of like-minded individuals who have also received the same diagnosis, offering support, advice, and a common identity. Diagnoses can also be useful shorthand for others to understand the rough ballpark of an individual's day-to-day lived experience without having to give a one-hour life history each time they meet someone new.

For others a diagnosis can be a disempowering experience – 'that confirms what I thought, there is something wrong with *me* and I can't do anything about it' – and it opens people up to stigmatisation, misunderstanding, and victimisation. It is also not always made obvious to the people using diagnostic labels – both clinicians and patients – how specific they can be to a particular time and place, and how the same underlying trait can be a source of strength as well as one that causes challenges. For that reason, there has been a shift by some clinicians away from diagnosing what is wrong (deficit-focused) to understanding what happened (cause-focused), which requires actively listening to the full experience of people's lives rather than searching to box-tick certain criteria.

As we have seen throughout this chapter, many of the challenges faced by autistic children and children with attention-regulating difficulties are often not created by the traits themselves but by the mismatch between the traits and the environment. And in fairness to the diagnostic process, it is sensitive to this to some extent. For example, individuals cannot receive a diagnosis of autism without it causing 'significant impairment in social, occupational or other important areas of current functioning', and to receive a diagnosis of ADHD it needs to 'cause impairments in living' (American Psychiatric Association, 2013; World Health Organisation, 2018) – criteria that would presumably exclude the nomadic Ariaal people.

What this misses, however, is that the environmental context is not just a source of conflict but sometimes the problem itself. For example, is the deficit with the minority of autists who struggle to see the world from the perspective of non-autists or with the majority of non-autists who struggle to read the minds of autistic people (or both – the so-called double empathy problem; Damian, 2012)? Is the deficit with children who have difficulty regulating their attention in school or with a school system that is not flexible enough to accommodate natural variation in attention regulation?

The framing of such questions matters because it changes how we address them. In the case of ADHD, there is certainly more financial incentive to treat it as a problem of the individual – with a pill for every ill – than as a problem with the way intuitions are organised, which are slower and more difficult to change and less easy to monetise. Among all children aged 2–17 years with ADHD in the USA, 6 out of 10 take medication for their ADHD; that represents 1 in every 20 of *all* US children being on some form of ADHD drug (Danielson et al., 2018). The effect of context is powerfully demonstrated by one study that showed that in states where high-stakes testing was introduced, the rate of ADHD diagnoses increased dramatically soon after, particularly for poor children in public schools (Hinshaw & Scheffler, 2014).

The framing also matters for people's everyday experience of living differently. Just 16% of autistic people and their families feel that the public understands what it means to be autistic, and around 75% feel socially isolated *because* of this lack of understanding (National Autistic Society, 2015). So, in a society with greater understanding, *being* autistic, blind, or deaf becomes less of a challenge, in the same way as an environment with ramps instead of

Figure 16.3 Left to right, top to bottom: Simone Biles, the most decorated gymnast in history, has difficulty regulating her attention. Sir Richard Branson, multi-billionaire entrepreneur, has dyslexia. Daniel Radcliffe, star of *Harry Potter*, has difficulty with controlling his movement. Hannah Gadsby, award-winning comedian, actress, and writer, has autism. These people credit their differences as sources of strength as well as challenges, and as reasons why they have been successful in their chosen fields. Source: Salty View/Shutterstock; Kathy Hutchins/Shutterstock; Fred Duval/Shutterstock; Associated Press /Alamy Stock Photo

stairs is less disabling for those in wheelchairs. Sometimes this deeper understanding can come relatively cheaply. For example, researchers have found that merely increasing intergroup contact (Chapter 8) between able-bodied and disabled children increased positivity towards disabled children and reduced discrimination (Cameron & Rutland, 2006).

Giving an accurate account of children's experience not only acknowledges the day-to-day challenges they face, but also recognises their individual strengths, their adaptability, and their resilience (**Figure 16.3**).

Summary

- Children can take very different paths to reach similar developmental milestones, as demonstrated by the sign language of Deaf children and shared attention of blind children.
- Despite similarities, there are large differences in how autism and attention-regulating difficulties are expressed in children.
- Difficulties are often expressed as extreme examples of normal developmental processes and abilities rooted in adaptive behaviours.

- The same underlying characteristic can often be expressed as a strength or difficulty depending on the circumstances.
- Recognising children's unique strengths as well as the challenges they face is important for helping children reach their social, emotional, and academic potential.
- The presence *or absence* of some significant event in a child's life can trigger a cascade of later consequences, some of which are predictable, some more unexpected.
- Multi-level cascades of cause and effect can help us understand how development typically unfolds for most children as well as how it can be disrupted.

References

American Psychiatric Association. (2013) *Diagnostic and Statistical Manual of Mental Disorders*, 5th edition. American Psychiatric Association.

Baron-Cohen, S., Leslie, A., & Frith, U. (1985). Does the autistic child have a 'theory of mind'?, *Cognition*, 21(1), 37–46.

Bigelow, A. (2003). The development of joint attention in blind infants. *Development and Psychopathology*, 15(2), 259–275.

Biotteau, M., Chaix, Y., & Albaret, J.-M. (2015). Procedural learning and automatization process in children with developmental coordination disorder and/or developmental dyslexia, *Human Movement Science*, 43, 78–89.

Bo, J. & Lee, C.-M. (2013). Motor skill learning in children with developmental coordination disorder. *Research in Developmental Disabilities*, 34(6), 2047–2055.

Butterworth, G. & Jarrett, N. (1991). What minds have in common is space: spatial mechanisms serving joint visual attention in infancy. *British Journal of Developmental Psychology*, 9(1), 55–72.

Calder, G. (2016). *How Inequality Runs in Families: Unfair Advantage and the Limits of Social Mobility*. Policy Press Shorts Insights.

Cameron, L. & Rutland, A. (2006). Extended contact through story reading in school: reducing children's prejudice toward the disabled. *Journal of Social Issues*, 62, 469-488.

Chen, C. S., Burton, M., Greenberger, E., & Dmitrieva, J. (1999). Population migration and the variation of dopamine D4 receptor (*DRD4*) allele frequencies around the globe. *Evolution and Human Behavior*, 20(5), 309–324.

Climie, E. A. & Mastoras, S. M. (2015). ADHD in schools: adopting a strengths-based perspective. *Canadian Psychology/Psychologie canadienne*, 56(3), 295–300.

Climie, E. A., Saklofske, D. H., Mastoras, S. M., & Schwean, V. L. (2019). Trait and ability emotional intelligence in children with ADHD. *Journal of Attention Disorders*, 23(13), 1667–1674.

Cohen, D. (1999). *Stranger in the Nest: Do Parents Really Shape Their Child's Personality, Intelligence, or Character?* John Wiley.

Constantino, J. & Todd, R. (2003). Autistic traits in the general population: a twin study. *Archives of General Psychiatry*, 60, 524–530.

Crawford, S. G., Kaplan, B. J., & Dewey, D. (2006). Effects of coexisting disorders on cognition and behavior in children with ADHD. *Journal of Attention Disorders*, 10(2), 192–199.

Dale, N. & Salt, A. (2007). Early support developmental journal for children with visual impairment: the case for a new developmental framework for early intervention. *Child: Care, Health and Development*, 33(6), 684–690.

Damian, M. (2012). On the ontological status of autism: the 'double empathy problem'. *Disability & Society*, 27(6), 883–887.

Danielson, M. L., Bitsko, R. H., Ghandour, R. M., Holbrook, J. R., Kogan, M. D., & Blumberg, S. J. (2018). Prevalence of parent-reported ADHD diagnosis and associated treatment among U.S. children and adolescents, 2016. *Journal of Clinical Child & Adolescent Psychology*, 47(2), 199–212.

De Martino, B., Harrison, N. A., Knafo, S., Bird, G., & Dolan, R. J. (2008). Explaining enhanced logical consistency during decision making in autism. *The Journal of Neuroscience*, 28, 10746–10750.

Doyon, J., Bellec, P., Amsel, R., et al. (2009). Contributions of the basal ganglia and functionally related brain structures to motor learning, *Behavioural Brain Research*, 199(1), 61–75.

Eisenberg, D. T., Campbell, B., Gray, P. B., et al. (2008). Dopamine receptor genetic polymorphisms and body composition in undernourished pastoralists: an exploration of nutrition indices among nomadic and recently settled Ariaal men of northern Kenya. *BMC Evolutionary Biology*, 8, 173.

Ek, U., Fernell, E., Westerlund, J., Holmberg, K., Olsson, P. P., & Gillberg, C. (2007). Cognitive strengths and deficits in schoolchildren with ADHD. *Acta Paediatrica*, 96(5), 756–761.

Esteller-Cucala, P., Maceda, I., Børglum, A. D., Demontis, D., Faraone, S. V., Cormand, B., & Lao, O. (2020). Genomic analysis of the natural history of attention-deficit/hyperactivity disorder using Neanderthal and ancient *Homo sapiens* samples. *Scientific Reports*, 10(1), 8622.

Faraone, S. V., Perlis, R. H., Doyle, A. E., et al. (2005). Molecular genetics of attention-deficit/hyperactivity disorder. *Biological Psychiatry*, 57, 1313–1323.

Fletcher-Watson, S. & Happé, F. (2019). *Autism: A New Introduction to Psychological Theory and Current Debate*. Routledge/Taylor & Francis Group.

Frith, U. (2003). *Autism: Explaining the Enigma*, 2nd edition. Blackwell Publishing.

Gottlieb, G. (1992). *Individual Development and Evolution: The Genesis of Novel Behavior*. Oxford University Press.

Grossmann, T., Striano, T., & Friederici, A. D. (2006). Crossmodal integration of emotional information from face and voice in the infant brain. *Developmental Science*, 9(3), 309–315.

Hallowell, E. & Ratey, J. (1994). *Driven to Distraction*. Simon & Schuster.

Happé, F. & Frith, U. (2006). The weak coherence account: detail-focused cognitive style in autism spectrum disorders. *Journal of Autism and Developmental Disorders*, 36, 5–25.

Hartmann, T. (2019). *ADHD: A Hunter in a Farmer's World*. Healing Arts Press.

Haualand, H. & Allen, C. (2009). Deaf people and human rights. World Federation of the Deaf and Swedish National Association of the Deaf. https://inee.org/resources/deaf-people-and-human-rights

Hendry, A. & Scerif, G. (2023). Moulding environmental contexts to optimise neurodiverse executive function performance and development: a goodness-of-fit account. *Infant and Child Development*, 32(5), e2448.

Hinshaw, S. P. & Scheffler, R. M. (2014). *The ADHD Explosion: Myths, Medications, Money, and Today's Push for Performance*. Oxford University Press.

Hoogman, M., Stolte, M., Baas, M., & Kroesbergen, E. (2020). Creativity and ADHD: a review of behavioral studies, the effect of psychostimulants and neural underpinnings, *Neuroscience & Biobehavioral Reviews*, 119, 66–85.

Ito, M. (2008). Control of mental activities by internal models in the cerebellum. *Nature Reviews Neuroscience*, 9, 304–313.

Jenkinson, R., Milne, E., & Thompson, A. (2020). The relationship between intolerance of uncertainty and anxiety in autism: a systematic literature review and meta-analysis. *Autism*, 24(8), 1933–1944.

Jensen, P. S., Mrazek, D., Knapp, P., Steinberg, L., Pfeffer, C., Schowalter, J., & Shapiro, T. (1997). Evolution and revolution in child psychiatry: ADHD as a disorder of adaptation. *Journal of the American Academy if Child & Adolescent Psychiatry*, 36, 1672–1681.

Kenny, L., Hattersley, C., Molins, B., Buckley, C., Povey, C., & Pellicano, E. (2016). Which terms should be used to describe autism? Perspectives from the UK autism community. *Autism*, 20(4), 442–462.

Kohn, M. & Griffiths, K. (2023). Attention deficit hyperactivity disorder (ADHD), In B. Halpern-Felsher (ed.), *Encyclopedia of Child and Adolescent Health*, 1st edition (pp. 1021–1033). Academic Press.

Lederberg, A. R. & Everhart, V. S. (1998). Communication between deaf children and their hearing mothers: the role of language, gesture, and vocalizations. *Journal of Speech, Language, and Hearing Research*, 41(4), 887–899.

Lillo-Martin, D. & Henner, J. (2021). Acquisition of sign languages. *Annual Review of Linguistics*, 7, 395–419.

Messer, D., Kearvell-White, J., Danielsson, H., Faulkner, D., Henry, L., & Ibbotson, P. (2022). The structure of executive functioning in 11 to 14 year olds with and without special educational needs. *British Journal of Developmental Psychology*, 40(3), 453–470.

Millar, S. (1988). Models of sensory deprivation: the nature/nurture dichotomy and spatial representation in the blind. *International Journal of Behavioral Development*, 11, 69–87.

Mueller, A., Hong, D. S., Shepard, S., & Moore, T. (2017). Linking ADHD to the neural circuitry of attention. *Trends in Cognitive Science*, 21(6), 474–488.

National Autistic Society. (2015). *Too Much Information*. National Autistic Society.

Nicolson, R. & Fawcett, A. (2011). Dyslexia, dysgraphia, procedural learning and the cerebellum. *Cortex*, 47, 117–127.

Petitto, L. A. & Marentette, P. F. (1991). Babbling in the manual mode: evidence for the ontogeny of language. *Science*, 251, 1493–1496.

Rief, S. (2000). ADHD: common academic difficulties and strategies that help. *Attention!*, September/October, 47–51.

Scerif, G. & Baker, K. (2015). Annual research review: rare genotypes and childhood psychopathology – uncovering diverse developmental mechanisms of ADHD risk. *Journal of Child Psychology and Psychiatry and Allied Disciplines*, 56, 251–273.

Schneider, J. L. & Iverson, J. M. (2023). Equifinality in infancy: the many paths to walking. *Developmental Psychobiology*, 65(2), e22370.

Schreiber, J. E., Possin, K. L., Girard, J. M., Rey-Casserly, C. (2014). Executive function in children with attention deficit/hyperactivity disorder: the NIH EXAMINER battery. *Journal of the International Neuropsychological Society*, 20(1), 41–51.

Sedgwick, J. A., Merwood, A., & Asherson, P. (2019). The positive aspects of attention deficit hyperactivity disorder: a qualitative investigation of successful adults with ADHD. *ADHD Attention Deficit and Hyperactivity Disorders*, 11(3), 241–253.

Seligman, M. & Csikszentmihalyi, M. (2000). Positive psychology: an introduction. *American Psychologist*, 55(1), 5–14.

Sherman, J., Rasmussen, C., & Baydala, L. (2006). Thinking positively: how some characteristics of ADHD can be adaptive and accepted in the classroom. *Childhood Education*, 82(4), 196–200.

Steele, A., Karmiloff-Smith, A., Cornish, K., & Scerif, G. (2012). The multiple sub-functions of attention: differential developmental gateways to literacy and numeracy. *Child Development*, 83(6), 2028–2041.

Tomasello, M. (2010). *Origins of Communication*. MIT Press.

Tversky, A. & Kahneman, D. (1981). The framing of decisions and the psychology of choice. *Science*, 211, 453–458.

Winstanley, C. A., Eagle, D. M., & Robbins, T. W. (2006). Behavioral models of impulsivity in relation to ADHD: translation between clinical and preclinical studies. *Clinical Psychological Review*, 26(4), 379–395.

World Health Organization. (2018) *International Statistical Classification of Diseases and Related Health Problems*, 11th revision. WHO Press.

Zabelina, D., Saporta, A., & Beeman, M. (2016). Flexible or leaky attention in creative people? Distinct patterns of attention for different types of creative thinking. *Memory & Cognition*, 44(3), 488–498.

17 REFLECTIONS ON CHILD DEVELOPMENT

We have followed the journey of child development – a journey that begins when a single sperm enters an egg the size of this full stop. From those beginnings we undergo numerous physical, cognitive, and social revolutions. Eventually we begin to adopt the roles, responsibilities, and privileges of adulthood. It is a journey full of paradoxes. Infants seem so helpless, vulnerable, and distractible, yet we have discovered that they are sophisticated learners and experts at eliciting the care they need. As Alison Gopnik notes in *The Gardener and The Carpenter* (2016), children start out life dependent on their parents for their very survival, and yet by the time they are grown up, parents can consider themselves lucky to receive the occasional text from them in a distant city. What's really strange is that this shift from extreme clinginess to vaguely interested is considered some measure of success. Children need parents so that they can learn to stand on their own feet, and in that regard, successful parenting involves parenting yourself out of a job.

We have attempted to understand this remarkable transformation from dependence to independence by exploring the processes of development. What we have learned is that it is not age itself that drives development. Development is driven by a cascade of events, experiences, and children themselves. Children change not because of the passing of time but through what changes as time passes (Skinner, 1971).

We have considered everything from peanut allergies and marshmallows to fake walnuts and eating pet dogs; from using pling machines, blicket detectors, and zandos to a cast of chimpanzees, beavers, macho frogs, and Betty the crow. To reveal the hidden inner world of infants we needed to employ the latest high-tech brain scanners and eye trackers, and to understand the range of children's behaviour and experiences sometimes we simply needed to listen to what they say and do. Doing this kind of research can involve multinational projects needing the combined effort of hundreds of researchers following children as they grow up over many decades. On other occasions it relies on the in-depth study of a single child playing at home.

Studying child development from a global perspective involves taking a look at the familiar – play, learning, language – in the context of the less familiar: the sign language inventors of Nicaragua, the machete-wielding children of Congo, and the cattle-jumping young men of Ethiopia's Omo Valley. Doing so has revealed a mosaic of landscapes, parenting practices, peer relationships, attitudes towards children, beliefs about childhood, and ways of living. The fact that children not only survive these diverse environments and cultures but thrive in them too is testament to their adaptability and is a feat few adults would be able to achieve.

The sheer scale of child development can seem overwhelming, but there are some common threads that tie the story together. Here are some final reflections on child development based on the themes that have re-occurred throughout the book.

17.1 Children Are Alike and Different

An alien hovering above Earth might conclude that all human life plays out in pretty much the same way. From that vantage point, little human-shaped dots appear, they organise their daily business along largely similar lines – eating, drinking, talking, moving, and sleeping – and after a number of years they disappear with unremarkable regularity. Zoom in to the level of individuals, however, and our imaginary alien might conclude that two randomly chosen humans are not even from the same species: they might speak a different language, eat different food, look and behave radically differently from one another, possess different technologies, succumb to different diseases, and lead very different lives.

Throughout the book we have been putting human beings under the microscope, sometimes zooming in to study interesting differences and sometimes zooming out to see what we have in common. What we can conclude from this is that whether we choose to focus on what divides us or what unities us is largely a matter of magnification. Children interpret their experiences through a complex prism of cultural customs, attitudes, and beliefs. But even after taking account of cultural differences, humans still have more in common with one another than they do with other species, even our closest evolutionary relatives – not least the ability to create culture in the first place.

So, children – and the societies they grow up in – can be vastly different from one another, but they are not *infinitely* different. Every society we know of has children who take a long time to grow up (relative to our nearest evolutionary relatives) and parents prepared to invest in such lengthy childhoods. The people in these societies experience fear, trust, violence, cooperation, jealousy, competition, and love. Our familiarity with these human traits hides the fact that it does not have to be this way, and it is not this way for most other species on Earth. That uniqueness deserves an explanation, in the way that other species' adaptations, like the echolocation of the bat and the metamorphosis of the butterfly, also deserve explanations. We are unique, but we are not unique in our uniqueness.

17.2 The Value of Multiple Perspectives

One clear message from the approach taken in this book is the value of integrating multiple perspectives on human childhood. Take fairness as an example. Using experimental psychology, we have been able to isolate what factors influence children's sense of fairness. Using anthropology, we have been able to document the diverse ways in which children use fairness in their everyday lives. Using evolution, we have been able to offer explanations about why we have a sense of fairness in the first place (and why other species do not).

No single perspective should be relied on too heavily or for too long without cross-referencing and triangulating with the others. Just because a behaviour might be the product of natural selection does not mean that it can occur without experience, without development, or without environmental influence. To understand human development, and to best support children as they grow, we need to study the full range of global contexts in which humans develop.

Where data from psychology, anthropology, and evolution all point to similar conclusions, this should give us more confidence that we are on the right lines. Even better is when those facts also align with a bigger story that includes history, archaeology, primatology, and neuroscience. In many cases we have a very good understanding of how development works on any given level (analysis). The challenge for those interested in a more interdisciplinary understanding of child development is bringing these levels together (synthesis).

17.3 The Complexity of Child Development

Synthesising knowledge between levels is itself a challenge because development is complex. If it were not, this would have been a much shorter book. There are also significant methodological obstacles to gaining a deeper understanding of development in the first place. For example, infants can't tell us what they know, which is part of what makes them so fascinating to study, but it also means we need to indirectly measure what they understand. The more indirect the method, the more inferences the researcher makes on behalf of the infant.

Despite the advances made towards de-**WEIRD**-ing psychology, researchers are always limited by money, time, and resources, which place practical constraints on the diversity of children they can study. For example, most research labs offer parents a very modest amount of money (if any) for bringing along their infants and children to take part in research. As a result, the parents (and their offspring) who are attracted to take part in research tend to be the ones who can afford to do so and for their own curiosity because they are relatively well-off and well-educated. The challenge of recruiting enough participants means most lab managers are happy to get who they can through the door, yet we know that social economic status is a significant moderator of child and adolescent behaviour.

The fact that cultures themselves are not monolithic and do not stand still adds to the challenge. Cultures are not uniform: they contain great variation within them, such as social classes and castes, which significantly alter the life outcomes of children and adolescents. Cultures also change over time. For example, since the introduction of a market structure into various economic sectors of Chinese society in the 1980s, cultural norms have been moving away from traditional collectivist values and towards those of independence and individual assertiveness, with children being encouraged via educational reforms to express more personal opinions and acquire greater self-confidence (Lansford et al., 2021). As a result, some of the long-standing cultural norms that influence child development, such as the value placed on shyness, have also begun to change.

Children are also moving between cultures like never before. The International Organization for Migration estimates that 258 million people (3.4% of the world's population) live in a different country from the one they were born in, with 14% of immigrants being younger than 20 years old (2018). While these transnational childhoods add to the richness of studying child development, they also add to the complexity. Perhaps the first rule of child development should be 'it depends'.

But we should value the complexity that diversity causes while it lasts. The Industrial Revolution that began in Great Britain during the mid-eighteenth and early nineteenth centuries has been responsible for exporting two institutions around the world: the school and the factory. The more widespread these institutions have become, the more the lives of children have been shaped by similar forces. From the mid-twentieth century onwards, the Information Age has made the world smaller still: multinational media, corporate capitalism, and the globalisation of a small number of languages mean that children are more likely than ever before to watch the same programmes, listen to the same music, consume the same products, and speak the same language.

17.4 The Future of the Village

For 97% of human history we have lived in small, nomadic foraging groups in communities of around 150 people, and raising a child was only possible with a village or at least an extended family, with fathers and grandmothers around to help provision and care for the young (Hrdy, 2011). From the cradle to the grave, the village now looks very different for many WEIRD families, and policymakers are waking up to some of the consequences of this. For example, putting older adults into nursing homes decreases their life expectancy by 3.4 years on average when compared with being cared for at home, even after controlling for pre-existing health conditions (Brent, 2022). This result might seem counterintuitive at first: the skilled nursing and access to medicine that justify the very existence of nursing homes have a worse impact than unskilled family care or even no care at all. But it makes more sense when we consider the value of family and a wider supportive social network for providing a protective buffer against some of the effects of ageing – something that a medical model of ageing has not always costed in. To nudge people back to village-based family life, even in sprawling cities of millions of people, some governments are now providing incentives. In Singapore, if you are buying a resale flat to live with or near your parents or children, you can apply for a Proximity Housing Grant that offers 30,000 Singapore dollars (SGD) to live with your parents or children or SGD 20,000 to live within 4 km of them. The Singapore government has calculated that the cost of running the scheme is a fraction of the cost it would take to care for older adults in institutionalised care. The loss-of-life-years from nursing home care is estimated to be around USD 1.87 trillion in the USA alone (Brent, 2022).

The disjoint between village life and the modern world is an example of an **evolutionary mismatch**. Throughout the book we have met examples of evolutionary mismatches, and it has always been important to stress that what is expected or natural does not automatically equal good or bad. Mismatches need to be considered on their own terms. A metabolism adapted for foraging should reward gorging on sugar, fat, and salt whenever we can get it because as opportunistic foragers we can never be sure where the next meal is coming from. What is natural serves us poorly when we are in an environment of abundant processed food and convenience. On the other hand, women could expect that many if not most of their infants would not survive childhood until relatively recently in history. No one is bemoaning the good old days of high infant mortality, a phenomenon equally as natural as our metabolism, and the reduction in infant mortality is rightly considered one of the greatest achievements of modern healthcare.

17.5 Last Words

The roots and reasons why children develop differently are multifaceted and individual. Given the complex network of cause and effect in which child development is situated, it is remarkable that we understand as much as we do, and we understand a considerable amount when compared with only a few decades ago. Yet the breadth and depth of child development make it feel like we have only scratched the surface of what there is to uncover. There are still many basic features of childhood that we do not have a full explanation for, such as why we forget our earliest memories and how children learn language. Nor will we ever fully know what it is like to be a child, or an earlier version of ourselves.

For almost all human history children were thought of as not being able to provide much insight into the big philosophical puzzles, like where our knowledge of the world comes from. It turns out that children had the answers to many of these riddles all along in the way they naturally approach learning; we just needed to look harder and ask smarter questions. Because children are the most powerful learners on the planet, big tech companies like Google, Meta, and Apple, wanting to design more intelligent systems, are very interested in how children learn so much in such a short time. Their current systems produce impressive results by compiling massive datasets from the internet, but they perform less well when going out into the world and doing something with that knowledge. One of the best ways to teach a robot to walk is by letting them make and learn from their own mistakes, just as children do.

Advances in our understanding of the natural world occur more often as the result of a surprise 'hmm, that's odd a result, I didn't expect that' than a 'Eureka!' moment. In years to come children will no doubt keep providing us with surprises, revealing more secrets of development, as well as many opportunities for us to learn from them and with them.

References

Brent, R. (2022). Life expectancy in nursing homes. *Applied Economics*, 54(16), 1877–1888.

Gopnik, A. (2016). *The Gardener and the Carpenter*. Vintage Publishing.

Hrdy, S. B. (2011). *Mothers and Others: The Evolutionary Origins of Mutual Understanding*. Harvard University Press.

International Organization for Migration. (2018). *Global Migration Indicators*. International Organization for Migration.

Lansford, J., French, D., & Gauvain, M. (2021). *Child and Adolescent Development in Cultural Context*. American Psychological Association.

Skinner, B. F. (1971). *Beyond Freedom and Dignity*. Hackett.

GLOSSARY

Adaptation a heritable trait that impacts on the survival or reproduction of an individual.

Attachment a special type of emotional bond that children can develop with one or more caregivers.

Autobiographical memory integrates past experiences into an overarching life narrative or personal history.

Automatisation a phase of learning in which skills are performed fluently, flexibly, and without awareness, whereas before they were effortful, hesitant, and deliberate.

Cognitive flexibility the ability to suddenly change perspectives or switch tasks.

Cognitive transfer when training one area of children's cognition, like memory, causes improved performance in another untrained area, like attention.

Collectivist societies societies that value family duty, social harmony, obedience to authority, and hierarchy and that consider individuals the servants of society; in contrast to **individualistic societies**.

Confirmation bias the tendency to seek out information that validates our beliefs rather than that which does not.

Conventions a mutually agreed way of doing things that could be done differently, like driving on the left instead of the right, or using a knife and fork rather than chopsticks.

Counterfactual imagining the consequences of something being true but knowing that it is false – for example, 'If I had four legs, then I would be able to run faster.'

Evolution the change in the heritable traits of a population over generations.

Evolutionary mismatch the difference between the environment a trait was adapted for and one that it was not.

Executive functions a collection of skills that enable us to be flexible, controlled, and focused; see **working memory**, **inhibitory control**, and **cognitive flexibility**.

Explore–exploit dilemma evaluating the costs and benefits of exploring new information and exploiting old information.

Goodness of fit the alignment between a person's temperament and the expectations or demands of the environment.

Grammar the norms that regulate how smaller chunks of language are arranged into bigger, meaningful units.

Heritability a measure of how well differences in people's genes account for differences in their traits.

Homophily a bias for people to associate with similar people.

Imitation copying the behaviour of others.

In-group favouritism a bias to view the group you are a member of as more favourable than the group you are not.

Individualistic societies societies that value personal choice, autonomy, and individual uniqueness and that consider society the servant of the individual; in contrast to **collectivist societies**.

Inhibitory control the ability to resist or supress a tempting thought or behaviour.

Life-history theory explains some stages of development as **adaptations**.

Mutualism what is good for you is good for me, and vice versa.

Natural selection the process by which species can become better suited to their environment over many generations.

Naturalistic fallacy wrongly assuming that what is natural is good for us.

Norms obligations about how group members should think or behave.

Offline learning a stage of learning in which performance can improve in the absence of direct engagement or practice, typically occurring after **online learning** and before **automatisation**.

Online learning a stage of learning characterised by focused effort and repetition, in which performance improves as a result of practice.

Ostracism exclusion from a group or relationship.

Overgeneralisation errors unconventional language use based on a conventional pattern, such as 'holded', 'swimmed', or 'the joke giggled him' in English.

Phonology the norms that regulate the use of sounds or signs in a language.

Plasticity the ability to change the way we behave, feel, or think as a result of experience or evidence.

Procedural memory long-term unconscious memory of how to perform actions and skills, like riding a bike.

Prosocial behaviour intended for the benefit of others, such as sharing, helping, caring, or acts of kindness.

Proto-conversations early social exchanges between infants and caregivers, often expressed as vocalisations, touches, smiles, and mirroring of behaviour.

Ratchet effect the process by which cultural innovations accumulate from one generation to the next.

Self-serving bias the tendency to see oneself in a favourable light or as above average.

Semantics the meaning of words, signs, and phrases in a language.

Sensitive periods times of life that have an especially influential effect on later development.

Shared intentionality the ability of people to hold each other's intentions in mind and to use them to collaborate towards a common goal.

Social capital the network of relationships, values, and resources available to an individual.

Social learning learning by observing, imitating, and modelling what others do.

Spite a motivation to disadvantage others even at a cost to oneself.

Statistical learning recognising patterns and forming categories based on the distribution and frequency of things in the environment.

Theory of mind (ToM) the capacity to picture the world from another person's point of view; what they see, know, want, desire, or believe.

U-shaped curve describes performance that improves, gets worse, and then gets better again.

WEIRD societies that are Western, Educated, Industrialised, Rich, and Democratic.

Working memory the ability to mentally work on multiple sources of information at the same time.

ONE-MINUTE METHODS

Chapter 1

Watch the One-Minute Method.

Discover the ethical principles researchers need to consider when conducting research with children. www.open.edu/openlearn/one-minute-methods-ethics

'Conducting ethical research is an important part of understanding child development. Ethical research involves respecting the dignity, rights, autonomy, and welfare of people taking part in research. This is especially important when conducting research with vulnerable groups, such as children and young people. Children are at risk of carrying out requests that they are not actually comfortable with or do not fully understand. Special care must be taken to explain research to children in a way they understand and to look out for signs they might want to stop participating, such as becoming withdrawn or behaving anxiously. Researchers use ethical frameworks that try to minimise harm and maximise good in their research. How we define "harm" and "good" needs a debate from a wide range of people in society, not least children themselves.'

Chapter 2

Watch the One-Minute Method.

Discover what natural experiments, like the Dutch famine, and controlled experiments can teach us about child development. www.open.edu/openlearn/one-minute-methods-experiments

'At its most basic, an experiment is a way to discover something new or test an idea. In this sense, children themselves are avid experimenters, constantly investigating the world around them and updating their theories of how it works. Scientific experiments usually involve changing something, keeping other things the same, and then measuring the effect. We can use the results of experiments to come up with a better understanding of how things work or to reject an idea as false. Sometimes controlled experiments are difficult, impossible, unethical, or illegal. In such cases we might take advantage of naturally occurring situations to test an idea. For example, to understand the effects of nature and nurture, it might be questionable to create human genetic clones, but we don't need to. We can observe identical twins, who have been separated at birth, and raised in different environments. In general, the more often an experiment is repeated with similar outcomes the more confidence we have in the results.'

Chapter 3

Watch the One-Minute Method.

Discover how researchers use relationships between factors to understand child development. www.open.edu/openlearn/one-minute-methods-correlations

'When studying child development, researchers often want to know how one thing is related to another. For example, how the number of words a child knows is related to their age. To find out how things are co-related or correlated, researchers need to know how things *differ* between children. Sometimes there is no relationship at all between factors, but sometimes the relationship is positive – the more of one thing the more of another; sometimes the relationship is negative – the more of one thing the less of another; or sometimes the relationship is more complicated, like a U-shape. U-shaped relationships in child development are especially interesting. They can indicate when children's learning stops or even goes into reverse for a period, before progress resumes. Along with experiments and observations, correlations are an essential part of the child researcher's toolkit.'

Chapter 4

Watch the One-Minute Method.

Discover how the familiarisation procedure, as used by Kisilevsky and colleagues, takes advantage of something young infants are really good at: getting bored. www.open.edu/openlearn/one-minute-methods-familiarisation

'Babies tend to get bored by familiar faces, objects, and repeated sounds and actions. They then react differently when things change. Sometimes they look longer, their pupils dilate, they start to sweat and suck more, they might turn their heads, show a spike in brain activation, or their heart rate quickens. By carefully measuring infants' reactions, we can tell whether they notice a change from the old to the new, and we can use that to make a best guess about what they thinking. For example, if a baby does not react to a change from triangles to circles, then perhaps for this infant, they *are* the same shape. An older infant might react differently when the shapes change. Maybe for this infant, they think the shapes are different kinds of things. This technique is especially useful for young infants as getting bored is something they are really good at. We can use this simple fact of development to study how children are carving the world into categories that are meaningful to them.'

Chapter 5

Watch the One-Minute Method.

Like the babies in Laura Schultz's experiments, discover why researchers take care over the generalisations they make. www.open.edu/openlearn/one-minute-methods-sampling

'Researchers study how children think, behave, change, and adapt. Often they are looking for the simplest way to explain as much of child development as possible and to describe something that is true for as many children as possible. However, researchers are not able to study all children, just some of them. That means they sometimes make generalisations from smaller groups to bigger groups. This wouldn't be a problem if all children were the same. If they were the same, then something true of one child would be true of all children. But there are of course big individual differences between children in their age, family circumstances, abilities, and culture, which means generalisations need to be made with care. On the characteristics they think are important, researchers try to make sure the group they study is representative of the group they are making generalisations about.'

Chapter 6

Watch the One-Minute Method.

Discover why methods need to be culturally meaningful and sensitive to the experiences of the children taking part in research. www.open.edu/openlearn/one-minute-methods-cultural-sensitivity

'Child development does not take place independent of cultural context, and neither does our research. How we go about research with children can be deeply affected by our own cultural experiences, values, and traditions. This means researchers need to think very carefully how well their methods will travel. Are we measuring the same thing across different cultures? What have we assumed children value? Methods designed in one cultural context can be interpreted entirely different in a different context. This matters for the conclusions we draw about children from different cultures: differences between children might not be caused by their underlying abilities or character but because they interpret *the methods* differently. When we are aware of what assumptions our research makes, we can decide if it is important to the questions we are asking, and, where appropriate, take steps to make it more meaningful and sensitive to children's experiences.'

Chapter 7

Watch the One-Minute Method.

Discover how researchers ensure that their measurements are both valid and reliable. www.open.edu/openlearn/one-minute-methods-validity-reliability

'The quality of our research depends on whether we are measuring what we think we are measuring – its validity – and whether we are measuring the same thing consistently – its reliability. Measures tend to have more validity when they agree with other well-established measures that test similar things or they make successful predictions about what they intend to measure. Researchers have more confidence in the reliability of their measures when they reproduce the same results under the same circumstances, even when the measurements are made by different people, or at different times and places. Researchers are aiming for measurements with good validity and reliability and avoid those with poor validity or poor reliability.'

Chapter 8

Watch the One-Minute Method.

Discover how researchers compare different age groups of children at the same time, as in the study by Elenbaas and colleagues, or compare how the same children grow up over time. www.open.edu/openlearn/one-minute-methods-cross-sectional

'To understand how children adapt, change, and grow, we need to compare children at different ages. To make those comparisons, researchers tend to rely on two main ways of structuring their research. In so-called cross-sectional designs, researchers observe different children at different ages and make comparisons between the age groups. For example, a researcher might measure the attitudes of 4-year-olds, 6-year-olds, and 8-year-olds to their friends. This provides a snapshot of how different children think at different ages. In so-called longitudinal designs, researchers repeatedly measure the same children as they grow up. For example, a researcher might measure the attitudes of a group of

4-year-olds, and then 2 years later test the same children again, and then again 2 years after that. Comparing different children at the same time, or the same children at different times, tells us subtly different things about development, and researchers need to choose the design that best fits their research questions.'

Chapter 9

Watch the One-Minute Method.

Discover how case studies, like the one Georges-Henri Luquet conducted on his own daughter's drawings, can give us a rich description of development. www.open.edu/openlearn/one-minute-methods-case-studies

'Case studies can provide us with rich long-term biographical information about children's lives. They have been used to explore the influence of rare historical events, unusual talents, or uncommon conditions on child development. Even though case studies usually focus on a single child, their results can sometimes challenge whole theories. For example, if a single child has functioning short-term memory but has no long-term memory, it undermines the idea that memory is just one thing. Darwin and Piaget both studied their own children's development over many years. The insights they gained helped them generate new theories of development, that others later tested with larger groups of children. If we want to explore something that is rare, or we want a detailed portrait of children's lives, then a case study offers a good approach.'

Chapter 10

Watch the One-Minute Method.

Discover how researchers build computer simulations to explore how children learn. www.open.edu/openlearn/one-minute-methods-computer-simulations

'For decades scientists have used computers to model how the world works; everything from predicting the weather, financial systems, and the spread of disease. Likewise, those interested in how children change and learn are using computer simulations to study the complex process of child development. To get a handle on complex systems, like language and memory, researchers often create a simplified version, or a model, of what they want to understand more about. Computational models can be a good way of understanding how parts of a system interact to produce more complex behaviour. They force us to be precise about what we mean, and the results can often generate fresh insights and predictions that can be later tested with children. Along with experimental and observational methods they have become an essential tool in child development research.'

Chapter 11

Watch the One-Minute Method.

Discover how meta-analyses can help researchers see the bigger picture that no one study alone can show. www.open.edu/openlearn/one-minute-methods-meta-analysis

'A meta-analysis combines multiple studies and uses statistical techniques to integrate their results. We can think of it as a study of studies. Meta-analyses can help us establish whether there is a reliable effect of some cause and how big that effect is. Sometimes there are patterns and trends in the data that only become clear when we pool together lots of results. Combining research in this way can also help us settle long-standing controversies that arise when individual studies have conflicting results. When drawing on lots of different studies, we need to be careful that we are comparing like with like, not oversimplifying the big picture, or overlooking important details. When done correctly, meta-analyses are a useful method for making sense of a large amount of data, summarizing what we know, and what we don't.'

Chapter 12

Watch the One-Minute Method.

Learn how twins provide a natural experiment to investigate the relative importance of genes and environment to development. www.open.edu/openlearn/one-minute-methods-twin-studies

'Twin studies provide a unique opportunity to explore the origins of our individual differences. Identical twins share all their genes with one another, because they have developed from a single egg and sperm. Non-identical twins share half their genes, like regular siblings, because they developed from two separate eggs and sperm. Twins also share many aspects of their environment, like their family, as well as experiencing events that are unique to just one of them, such as accidents. By using mathematical tools researchers are able estimate the relative influence of genetics, shared experience, and unique experience on development. For example, identical twins raised together tend to be more similar than those raised apart. Non-identical twins raised together are more similar that siblings raised together. And biological parents and offspring are more similar than adoptive parents and offspring.'

Chapter 13

Watch the One-Minute Method.

Discover how neuroimaging techniques, like those used in the driving simulation study, can reveal much about the relationships between brain, mind, and behaviour. www.open.edu/openlearn/one-minute-methods-neuroimaging

'It has been said that the mind is what the brain does. Neuroimaging techniques allow us to look inside children's brains and make inferences about how their minds work. These techniques are safe and non-invasive and can be used with children of different ages. In neuroimaging experiments children are asked to perform an action, or look at an image, or think about a particular idea. Researchers then measure which parts of their brain are working harder than others and how they are communicating with one another. Changes in the brain's electrical activity, its magnetic fields, or blood flow give us an indirect measure of how the brain is processing information. When the same part of the brain is activated by the same stimulus we can build a map of the brain's functions. Child development researchers are particularly interested in when these functions emerge in development and how they change as children grow up.'

Chapter 14

Watch the One Minute Method.

Discover how researchers use interviews and focus groups to get an in-depth understanding of people's experiences. www.open.edu/openlearn/one-minute-methods-interviews-focus-groups

'Interviews and focus groups are a flexible form of data collection used by researchers across the social sciences. They are a great way to explore people's beliefs, opinions, and attitudes towards different topics such as gender, inequality, nationalism, and ethnicity. They reveal how people make sense of their lives grounded in the context of their individual experience. Interviews can be conducted face to face, by telephone or online, involve asking the same questions in the same order, or follow a more conversational style guided by the participants' responses. Sessions are usually recorded, transcribed, and analysed later when researchers have had a chance to familiarise themselves with the data, categorise responses, and identify similarities and differences between people's answers. The data that emerges from interviews is the product of a social interaction, so researchers need to be aware of how they are creating meaning together with participants and be transparent about their role in the research.'

Chapter 15

Watch the One-Minute Method.

Discover how researchers live within the societies they are studying, sometimes for many years, to gain an insider's perspective and to share similar experiences. www.open.edu/openlearn/one-minute-methods-participate-observer-research

'Whether it's hanging out with inner-city gangs of New York or spending all day foraging with the Hadza, some researchers fully immerse themselves in the communities they want to understand more about; eating, sleeping, working, and playing alongside them. Researchers observe, take notes, and ask questions as they participate in day-to-day activities, cultural practices, and customs. As far as it is possible, this allows researchers to experience life as if they were an insider or local and explore the way the group organise their lives around different social, moral, and political frameworks. This type of long-term fieldwork usually results in a written account of a group, place, or institution based on the experience of the researcher, interviews with people, or analysis of the group's documents and artefacts. Participant–observer research with different groups around the world has led to a deeper understanding of the diversity of human cultures as well as our shared ways of life.'

VIDEO SUMMARY

Chapter 2

Hidden talents.

Children living in adverse conditions are more likely to struggle in school. But what if these children have abilities that are enhanced through adversity – 'hidden talents' that educators can harness to promote their learning? www.open.edu/openlearn/hidden-talents

Chapter 3

Desires and beliefs.

Using two different experiments, psychologist and philosopher Alison Gopnik shows how children of different ages think about the minds of others. www.open.edu/openlearn/desires-beliefs

Chapter 4

The birth of a word.

Just like acquiring any other skill, learning language requires a lot of practice. Listen to how the son of researcher Deb Roy homed in on the pronunciation of 'water' over 6 months. www.open.edu/openlearn/birth-of-a-word

Chapter 5

Surprise!

Aimee Stahl and Lisa Feigenson show how babies not only focus on surprises but learn more from them. www.open.edu/openlearn/surprise

Chapter 6

Exploratory play.

Watch BaYaka infants begin experimenting with machetes soon after they are able to walk. This is a form of exploratory play that prepares them for the skills they will need later on. www.open.edu/openlearn/exploratory-play

Chapter 7

Moral judgement of others.

Watch how children of different ages respond to Kohlberg's Heinz dilemma. www.open.edu/openlearn/moral-judgement

Chapter 8

Gender groups.

Emily Foster-Hanson talks about her own research (2023) showing how children form stereotypes about gender and how they are related to their parents' political views. www.open.edu/openlearn/gender-groups

Chapter 9

A for effort.

What motivates children more in a problem-solving task: praising their intelligence or their effort? www.open.edu/openlearn/a-for-effort

Chapter 10

Walkie Talkie.

Learning any new skill, like walking and talking, requires children to encode, store and retrieve memories effectively. Lots of practice and sleep helps these skills become automatic and effortless. https://www.open.edu/openlearn/walkie-talkie

Chapter 11

It's a long story.

Watch how aboriginal children create stories about who they are and pass on ancient cultural traditions using the latest digital technology. www.open.edu/openlearn/long-story

Chapter 12

More than a label.

Young people talk about how the complexity of their characters defies simple categorisation. www.open.edu/openlearn/more-than-a-label

Chapter 13

Wired for life.

Adriana Galván shows how some of the most puzzling teenage behaviours may have some real benefits. www.open.edu/openlearn/wired-for-life

VIDEO SUMMARY

Chapter 14

One question can change everything.

UNICEF has teamed up with spoken word artist @clickfortaz in support of adolescents living with a mental health condition. www.open.edu/openlearn/one-question-can-change-everything

Chapter 15

Our tomorrows.

Teenagers around the world share their fears and dreams. www.open.edu/openlearn/our-tomorrows

Chapter 16

Building on strengths.

How can we understand and support children with attention regulating difficulty (and those without)? https://www.open.edu/openlearn/building-on-strengths

INDEX

abuse, 25, 153–154, 215–217, 226
adaptation, 9–10, 30, 227, 260, **264**
adoption, 21, 25–26, 154, *182*, 272
anxiety, 14, 21, 196, 222–224, 226, 233, 244
appearance–reality, 43
apprenticeship, 14, 81, 97, 173, 232–237
archaeology, 227, 261
attachment, 7, 23, 26, 39, 90–92, 117, 159, 196, **264**
attention, 22, 68, 81, 151, 206
    difficulty regulating, 243–249
    shared, 39–41, *40*, 56, 92, 240–254
authority, 82, 92, 111, 114, 117, 146, 235
autism, 152, *241*, 243–246, 252–254
automatisation, 151, 251–252, **264**

bilingualism, 64, 126, 240
blindness, 240–254
brain, *5*, 12, *13*, 20, 25, 36, 153–155, 197, 199, 205, 250–252, 272
    cortex, 11
    hippocampus, 153, 155, 162
    injury, 195, *195*
    metabolism, 11
    neurons, 11, 23
    prefrontal, 153, 191, 205

cause and effect, 3, 70, 73, 77, 171, 252
chimpanzees, 12, *13*, 20, 44–46, 77, 107, 137, 205
cognitive flexibility, 206–207, 234, 245, **264**
cognitive training, 152, 252
cognitive transfer, 152, **264**
collectivist societies, 114–116, 173, 184, 236, 261, **264**
coming of age, 185–188
confirmation bias, 69, **264**
conventions, 57, 61, 78, 98, 113, 139, 169, *241*, **264**
cooperation, 12, 38, 44–46, 90, 118, 126, 131, 260
counterfactual, 73–74, 109, 141, **264**
creativity, 147, 170, 189, *244*
cross-situational learning, *59*, 59, *241*
crows, 138, *139*
cuteness, 20

deafness, 62, *241*, 243
dementia, 162
dependence, *13*, 19, 23, 90
depression, 26, 126, 217, 222–223, 226, 236
determinism, 26, 130, 154, 205
developmental coordination disorder, 152, 250
developmental language disorder, 152, 251–252
diagnosis, 252
dopamine, 197
drawing, 145–146
dyadic interaction, 39–40, *40*, 81, 91
dysgraphia, 250
dyslexia, 250–252, *254*

emotions, 7, 22, 153, 180, *182*, 183, 246
    emotional well-being, 217–220
    function of, 28–31
    moral, 109–113
empathy, 20, 43–44, 110, 116, 123, 136, 253
evolution, 9–14, 20–22, 68, 97, 107, 117, 125, 127, 130, 196, 226, 249, 260, **264**
    mismatch, 13, 227, 245, 248, 262, **264**
    natural selection, 9, 21, **264**
executive functions, 139, 153, 206–208, 234, 245, **264**
explore–exploit dilemma, 67, **264**
eye gaze, 22, 30, 37, 39, 46–47, 92, 242

fairness, 106–109, 117, 125, 131, 167–168, 260
false beliefs, 41, *42*, 47, 93–94
fantasy, 73, 75, 141–142, 156
foraging, 9, 11, 13, *13*, 20, 90, 97–98, *98*, 107, 125, 142, 203, 227, 248
fun, 73–74, 201, 214

gender, 116, 132, 221–222, 275
generalisation, 71–72, 268
genetics, *5*, 6, 10, 19, 22–23, 122, 180–183, 217, 249, 252, 271
gestures, 38, 41, 47, 62, 73, 77, 80, 170, 242–243

giftedness, 143
gist, 157
globalisation, 262
goodness of fit, 220–222, 247, **264**
grammar, 57–59, 160, *241*, **264**
grandparents, 10–11, 14, 262
guilt, 28, 109–110, 113

helping, 44, 90, 110–113, 122, 126, 237
heritability, 87, 144, 180–183, 217, 221, 249, 252, **264**
homophily, 128, **264**
hormones, 19–20, 27, 153, 179, 202

identity, 64, 99, 124, 128, 172, 180–189, 202, 218, 221–222, 232–233, 239, 253
imaginary friends, 147
imagination, 73–76, 130, 140–142, 146–147, 170–172, 246
imitation, 12, 14, 59, 77–79, 91, 98, 140, 155, 172, 189
in-group, 14, 123–128, 130–131, **264**
independence, *13*, 20, 28, 80, 82, 156, 184, 196, 225, 233, 259
individualistic societies, 114, 173, 184, 236, **264**
Industrial Revolution, 9, 21, 227, 232, 262
inhibitory control, 197, 199, 206, 234–236, 245, **264**
institutionalised care, 21, 24–27, 262
instruction, 14, 79–82, 98

justice, 106–109, 111, 114, 117

less is more, 160–161
life-history theory, 10, 204, **264**
love, 22, 28, 31, 92, 218, 225, 260
lying, 4, 105, 115

memory, 139, 146, 150, 202, 251–252
    autobiographical, 158–160, 173–174, 183, **264**
    forgetting, 161–162
    infant amnesia, 153–156
    procedural, 151–152, **264**
    reminiscense, 158–160, *160*, 172–173
    working, 151–152, 206, 245, **265**, 276

menarche, 7, 12
menopause, 12–13
mental health and well-being, 31, 92, 153, 191, 213–228, 236–237, 277
metabolism, 27, 262
migration, 130, 190, 249, 261
morality, 105–119, 172, 189, 197
    expanding the moral circle, 130–131
    moral dumbfounding, 118
mortality, 19, 21, 24, 90, 195, 203, 227, 262
mutualism, 44–46, **264**

naturalistic fallacy, 14, 227, **264**
neglect, 24–25, 153, 185, 213, 215–216
norm, 109
norms, 7, 28, 30, 60, 78, 82, 98, 110, 115–116, 126, 167, 169, 173, 190, 202, 205, 221, 236, 261, **264**
number, 96, 153

offline learning, 151, **264**
online learning, 151, **264**
ostracism, 126, 196, 226, **264**
overgeneralisation errors, **264**
oxytocin, 20

peers, 31, 44, 79, 110, 128, 183, 196, 198–202, 215
phonology, 54, 57, **264**
plasticity, 24, 26, 54, 81, 132, 191, **264**
play, 12, 40, 67, 72–75, 81, 97–99, 124, 159, 232, 242, 275
    pretend, 141–142

policy, 72, 208, 262
pollution, 190
pre-natal development, 20, 27, 51, 249
prosocial, 44, 111–112, 115, 130, 167, 201, 237, **264**
proto-conversations, 22, 39, **265**

ratchet effect, 78, 97, 140, 190, **265**
rebelliousness, 189–190, 223, 233
reputation, 109, 115, 125, 129, 191
resilience, 26, 72, 144, 192
responsibility, 14, 90, 119, 173, 179, 188, 225, 233, *233*
reward, 20–21, 27, 107, 112, 153, 167, 190, 197, *204*, 248
risk, 19, 27, 67, 190, 194–200, 204, 215, 217, 222, 224, *241*, *244*, 248

school, 9, 26, 73, 79, 88, 144, 184, 202, 232, 247–248, 262, 274
self-serving bias, 127, **265**
semantics, 59–60, **265**
sensitive period, 52
sensitive periods, 24, 26, 154, **265**
sensitivity, 20, 23, 39, 91, 183, 196, 217, 246
sex differences, 203–205, 207
shame, 28, 30, 110
shared intentionality, 39, 81, 242, **265**
sharing, 44, 98, 107–109, 123, 126, 167, 201, 232
shyness, 31, 220, 261
siblings, 31, 40, 77, 80, 110, *182*, 271

sign language, 62, 240, *241*
sleep, 11, 20, 151, 202, 223
social capital, 187, 201, 220, **265**
social learning, 29, 76–81, 97–99, **265**
social media, 222
spite, 107, **265**
statistical learning, 53, *59*, 71, *241*, **265**
status, 79, 126, 129, 131, 185, 194
storytelling, 130, 137, 146, 170–172, *171*, 187, 276
stress, 14, 23, 26–27, 90–91, 153–154, 201, *214*, 216, 226
substance abuse, 198, 226
sympathy, 111

testimony
    of adults, 76, 79
    of children, 156
theory of mind, 36–39, 41–48, 60, 81, 93, 110, 131, 147, 245, **265**
tool use, 11, 70, 138 140
triadic interaction, 39–40, *40*, 81
trust, 79, 110, 112, 124–125, 216, 237
twins, *182*, 227, 249, 271

U-shaped curve, 62, 206, **265**, 267

validation, 218, 220, 252

weaning, 12, *13*
WEIRD, 86, 138, 142, 146, 166, 261–262, **265**
work, 80, 97, 99, 187, 227, 232